Center for the Fine Arts, Photograph by Steven Brooke

In Quest of Excellence

Civic Pride, Patronage, Connoisseurship

Jan van der Marck

With contributions by:
J. Carter Brown
Sherman E. Lee
Agnes Mongan
Philippe de Montebello

Center for the Fine Arts
Miami, Florida, January 14—April 22, 1984

This exhibition was made possible by a generous
grant from the American Express Foundation.

Additional support for the exhibition has been
provided by the Dade County Council of Arts
and Sciences and the Florida Arts Council.

The catalogue has been partially funded by
a grant from The Knight Foundation

Library of Congress Catalog Card Number:83-073138

In Quest of Excellence embodies three important principles on which great public collections were built and thrive: civic pride, patronage and connoisseurship.

It pays tribute to individuals whose civic pride has enhanced their communities' quality of life. Through these individuals' patronage, museums have been able to realize their dreams of building fine collections and of making them widely accessible to the public. This patronage has fostered connoisseurship that is responsible for the scholarship and high quality of art now found in public institutions throughout the country.

As an active presence in hundreds of communities across the United States, American Express is proud to join the citizens of Miami in celebrating these great American principles of civic pride, patronage and connoisseurship through our support of *In Quest of Excellence*. For American Express, this exhibition reinforces our continuing commitment to support the arts and to broaden cultural perspectives worldwide.

James D. Robinson III
Trustee, American Express Foundation,
Chairman and Chief Executive Officer,
American Express Company

Foreword and Acknowledgments

To the memory of Joshua C. Taylor, who witnessed its beginning, I dedicate the completion of this enterprise.

J.v.d.M.

In Quest of Excellence, the Center's inaugural exhibition, focuses attention on the uniquely American virtues that have brought museums into being and endowed them with treasure for the benefit of every man, woman and child in the land. Besides that high purpose, it demonstrates an equally high level of quality which museums aimed at and attained in forming collections by accepting gifts and bequests and by selectively acquiring the best offerings in the market. As such, this exhibition is a tribute to the foresight, genius and generosity of those who founded, enriched and led our art museums from the early nineteenth century, in some cases, to the present day. With a spectacular range of more than 200 works of art, of all periods and in all media, borrowed from 60 institutions in 50 cities, it illustrates the civic pride which inspired, the patronage which endowed, and the connoisseurship which articulated our ranking public collections.

There may be some irony in the fact that the Center for the Fine Arts, a self-professed museum without a collection—and one which by charter is prohibited from forming a collection any time soon—should undertake, as its opening statement, to organize a panegyric devoted to that noble but prohibited activity. Yet, how is a community to know the standards that apply to, the quality that can be achieved by, and the sights that can be raised through the institution it has newly brought into being, unless an example of the highest attainable type is set? This community owes a debt of gratitude to communities across the country, through whose effort and sacrifice the miracles we see before us have been wrought.

In presenting the "success story" of American museums at the Center for the Fine Arts in Miami, a city without strong cultural traditions in which a large part of the population was born elsewhere, we hope to enlighten residents about the concepts of civic pride and philanthropy in the arts, making them aware of their importance to the health of communities and planting the seeds for future support. Or, as Hsun-Tzu so aptly advised: "If you are looking toward next year, plant a crop. If you are looking toward ten years from now, plant a tree. If you are looking toward the next one hundred years, educate the people." South Florida, by many accounts the most energetic, thriving and expanding metropolitan area in the country, should be proud to live up to the high standards implicit in the Center's inaugural presentation—in less time than the third century Chinese philosopher allowed.

In Quest of Excellence incorporates an ambition I have nurtured ever since an academic endeavor, more than twenty-five years ago, exposed me to the riches of American art museums. On a Rockefeller Foundation grant, I put sociology to work in seeking a better understanding of the way in which museums view and are perceived to exercise their public mandate. The art was enjoyed serendipitously and it begged the question whether I had not given myself an unnecessarily restrictive focus. In retrospect, a study of the art our taste-makers privately collect for eventual transferral, in a uniquely American manner, to public custody would have been the better choice. My recollections of the period confirm that the experience of art and people in the arts, not academic findings left the greater imprint.

I recall being overwhelmed, from one city to the next, by the visual feast invariably awaiting behind those predictably columned facades of institutions that, until then, had been names on my itinerary. I gratefully remember the readiness with which directors and curators, educators and business managers, patrons and trustees gave me insights, disabused me of cliché notions, conveyed their enthusiasms, and invited me to their homes.

Of that period of seeing and learning about museums, intensely experienced moments leap to mind: being introduced, on my first day in New York, to the Metropolitan Museum of Art by Dick Randall and Leo Steinberg; sitting spellbound in Meyer Schapiro's class on Cézanne; seeking the advice of Erwin Panofsky to find myself chastized for impugning the biblical origin of Salome's dance and putting too much faith in Freud; agonizing over an impromptu invitation from James Rorimer to celebrate Thanksgiving with his family because, the day before, I had accepted somebody else's to visit the new Clark Institute in the Berkshires; being entertained, in the Modern's cafeteria, by both René d'Harnoncourt and Alfred Barr.

There were other encounters: with Lincoln Kirstein, who warned me that the National Gallery looked like the oversized bathroom of a fashionable English club; with the gracious Edgar Schenck, who took me to see the Robert Lehman collection; with Hans van Weeren-Griek, who cut the fine figure of a rear admiral and held a record for home-sitting rudderless museums; with Thomas Munro, who impressed on me that I study John Dewey: with three of that era's most impressive women in the arts, Grace Morley, Adelyn Breeskin and Nancy Hanks; with Frank Lloyd Wright as he stood, majestically, on the top ramp of a yet unfinished Guggenheim Museum; with Edward Hopper, that tall prince of art, to whom I was introduced, at a Knoedler benefit, by David Rockefeller, prince of the adjoining realm of finance.

On tour, in Boston, Perry Rathbone showed me a recently acquired van Gogh, and Tom Messer invited me to the preview of a Mondrian exhibition—both mistook me for a scholar of Dutch art; snowbound in Buffalo, I attended a Christmas party for the Albright Art Gallery staff; at the Toledo Club, my eyes were riveted on Blakemore Godwin's red suspenders as he lectured me on how his museum had acquired its treasures; in Minneapolis, Harvey Arnason and Carl Weinhardt mixed professional courtesy with midwestern

hospitality; in Oberlin, Charles Parkhurst whom I first met at the University of Utrecht, welcomed me to a "typical" campus museum and in Merion, Pa., Violette de Mazia screened me before I was admitted to see Dr. Barnes' heavily guarded legacy.

After many years, I fondly remember a sleeping bag and campfire weekend spent in the Sonoma Valley with those gentle museum educators, Myriam and Charles Lindstrom; the Western informality of that trip in which Jim Foster in Santa Barbara, Pat Malone in La Jolla, Forest Hinkhouse in Phoenix and Fred Bartlett in Colorado Springs took time to familiarize me with their institutions; Jermayne McAgy's prefab Contemporary Arts Museum in Houston, famous for the originality of its exhibitions; Bill Eisendrath's personal tour of St. Louis, matched only by Henry McIlhenny's personal tour of his house; the fantasy land appearance of the John and Mable Ringling Museum of Art—the Getty, in Malibu, had not yet been built.

Before seeing Seurat's *La Grande Jatte* at the Art Institute of Chicago, I joined a wake for its presumed demise by fire in a glum and tearful crowd that had gathered on New York's 53rd Street. The segregation of cultural facilities was still fresh in everybody's minds when, on a Columbia University team, I interviewed patrons of the Virginia Museum of Fine Arts in Richmond. Roaming those parts on a motor scooter, in search of the American past, somewhere between Williamsburg and Jamestown, I came close to losing my own future when a driving rainstorm forced me off the road.

These were the impressions and experiences prompting my return to this country in pursuit of a career. If I may voice one regret, it is having focused on educational rather than on aesthetic issues, thus handicapping, by a few years, my progress from knowing how museums deal with the public to enjoying what they have in store. Yet, in doing so, I learned how community dynamics affect, enlightened patronage enables, and professional stewardship determines the quality for which our institutions are justly famous.

Such conditioning factors strike a person with background, training and biases different from those of colleagues born and bred here, as unique to the American ethos, expressive of this country's free enterprise and indicative of world-wide future trends. European museums trace their origins, by and large, to one-time royal hoards, imperial conquests and state appropriations. They do not derive from collective efforts of civic-minded individuals concerned with community enlightenment through art. Nor have they grown, as a result of endowments and bequests from loyal supporters, into monuments to the spirit of philanthropy. A third factor accounting for the American museum's ascendancy, is the active encouragement directors and curators receive from their boards to go out into the marketplace and compete for the best that money and brains can buy. Their European counterparts, mostly civil servants appointed by the government, or recognized scholars in their fields, tend to be custodians rather than acquisitors and operate within more restrictive mandates.

It is obvious that these comparisons are painted with a broad brush, and as a long time observer of those differences, I have noticed a growth of individual and corporate partronage in Europe, greater mobility and flexibility within their systems, more awareness of museums' public responsibilities, and expanding acquisition budgets that now allow Europeans to outbid Americans in the international market. Our colleagues in Europe are just as keenly aware that museums and first rate exhibitions contribute to the quality of life and economic welfare—their institutions just developed in different ways.

In 1966, Sherman E. Lee wrote of the Cleveland Museum that it had had a fortunate history of generous endowments, wise collecting, and creative education accomplished by "the concatenation of trustees, donors, staff, and sympathetic public support." As the term *concatenation* struck me as possibly a key to the success of our institutions, I visited this respected colleague and solicited his thoughts on what has made American art museums so unique and different from their European counterparts. Several others—those who agreed to write essays for this catalogue prominently among them—helped me conceptualize the theme of the exhibition. The momentum they provided and their sustained interest proved singularly important to the genesis of *In Quest of Excellence* and the choice of its subtitle, *Civic Pride, Patronage, Connoisseurship.*

This exhibition was not organized from memory or by long distance. Yet memory helped, and long distance became a subsequent tool. From the fall of 1980, I visited and revisited museums, region by region, as often as my other duties allowed, making a point of identifying the founding spirit, the collecting bias and the unique quality of each institution. Typically, I would start by reading about its history, take notes on works displayed, explain my purpose to the director, seek advice or concurrence from curators, propose an ideal choice, accept some inevitable compromises, reflect on how three or four newly selected works would complement prior selections or would make new demands of their own, and then initiate the long process of obtaining the desired loans. In the final analysis, better than two-thirds of all works in the exhibition represent first choices, which reflects the cooperation I was fortunate to receive.

A perfect geographic spread and a balanced representation of the different types of museums was aimed at though, admittedly, not fully achieved. Institutions with a long history, multiple donors and encyclopedic collections were favored

9

in the organization of this exhibition over those of recent date, with single patronage or specialized collections. A lack of response, in some instances, and the generously offered participation by institutions not on the original working list, may have nudged the exhibition's claim of being representative but has not impeded its quality or scope. The press of time and a lack of space led to the decision to omit, however regretfully, a few institutions on our working list, thus leaving some facets of public art's kaleidoscope unexposed. While never the express object of *In Quest of Excellence*, the creation of a "dream museum" for 100 days became its organizer's attendant ambition.

Of course, there have been setbacks and frustrations. Working in several capacities, I could not always keep the momentum going. As the representative of a not yet existent and therefore untested enterprise, I met with understandable caution, scepticism and, in some instances, outright refusal. *Civic Pride, Patronage, Connoisseurship*, the theme of our exhibition, drew greater approbation from directors than from their protective curators. As favors are done for favors received or anticipated, how can a fledgling art center without a collection return the compliment? What guarantees can it give of professional handling, from shipping and insurance to catalogue and installation, without a full staff and a completed building?

As of the fall of 1982, the Center's staff grew rapidly from its two-and-a-half year skeletal base. The building was another matter altogether. Construction delays, all too familiar on projects where quality cannot be compromised, moved the original opening date from the winter of 1982 to the spring of 1983. Then, a fully unanticipated non-compliance of the building's smoke evacuation system with the City of Miami's exacting fire code threw off all bets. The scrapping of the original non-functional system necessitated redesign,

deconstruction, reinforcements, equipment replacement and a twice revised schedule of completion. While all those directly involved with the project had to bear the brunt of this turn of events, lenders were inconvenienced and loans needed to be renegotiated as the exhibition's opening date was pushed farther into the future. As of this writing, the worst is behind us and the best is yet to come. For their forbearance, Governors, Trustees, County colleagues and co-workers all deserve my heartfelt thanks.

Understanding a beginning institution's need and generously responding to it, trustees, directors, curators and conservators of the museums featured in this exhibition, have liberally interpreted their restrictive policies and mandates. Without their understanding, there would have been no show. On behalf of the Governors and Trustees of the Center for the Fine Arts as well as on behalf of the Commissioners of Metropolitan Dade County and thus all citizens of this community, I wish to thank those mentioned below through whose decisive effort and administrative follow-through we obtained the loans for *In Quest of Excellence*:

The Baltimore Museum of Art: Arnold Lehman, Brenda Richardson, Melanie F. Harwood, Anita Gilden. *The Walters Art Gallery, Baltimore:* Robert P. Bergman, Richard H. Randall, Jr., William R. Johnston, Lilian M. C. Randall, Jeanny Vorys Canby, Leopoldine H. Arz. *University Art Museum, University of California, Berkeley:* James Elliott, Mark Rosenthal, Barney Bailey, Susan J. Stearns. *Museum of Fine Arts, Boston:* Jan Fontein, Cornelius Vermeule, John Walsh, Jr., Theodore E. Stebbins, Jr., John Moors Cabot, Florence Wolsky, Helen Hall, Linda Thomas, Suzanne Koppelman. *The Brooklyn Museum:* Michael Botwinick, Linda S. Ferber, Diana Fane, Sarah Faunce, Annette Blaugrund, Amy Poster, Susan Edwards, Glenda S. Galt. *Bowdoin College Museum of Art, Brunswick:* Katharine J. Watson, John Coffey, Brenda Pelletier. *Albright-Knox*

Art Gallery, Buffalo, New York: Robert T. Buck, Jr., Douglas G. Schultz, Sarah Ulen. *Fogg Art Museum, Harvard University, Cambridge:* John M. Rosenfield, Agnes Mongan, Priscilla S. England, William Robinson, Steven D. Owyoung, Jane Montgomery, Ada Bortoluzzi, Miriam Stewart, Phoebe Peebles, Martha Heintz. *The Art Institute of Chicago:* James N. Wood, Harold Joachim, Esther Sparks, A. James Speyer, Anne Rorimer, Richard R. Bretell, Susan Wise, Richard Townsend, Joanne Berens, David Travis, Wallace D. Bradway. *Cincinnati Art Museum:* Millard F. Rogers, Jr., Laurie H. Pepe, Beth DeWall. *The Cleveland Museum of Art:* Sherman E. Lee, Evan H. Turner, Edward B. Henning, Patrick M. de Winter, Michael R. Cunningham, Elinor Pearlstein, Stephen Fliegel, Delbert R. Gutridge, Renate D. Marshall. *Columbus Museum of Art, Ohio:* Budd Harris Bishop, Steven W. Rosen, Catherine Glasgow, Susan R. Visser, Martha Morford. *Lowe Art Museum, University of Miami, Coral Gables:* Ira Licht, Brian Dursum, John Haletsky. *Dallas Museum of Art:* Harry S. Parker, Steven A. Nash, John Lunsford, Deborah Richards. *The Dayton Art Institute:* Bruce H. Evans, Kent Sobotik, Dominique H. Vasseur, Lucy Callihan. *The Denver Art Museum:* Thomas N. Maytham, Lewis W. Story, Dianne P. Vanderlip, Richard Conn, Tony Wright, Mary Ann Igna. *Des Moines Art Center:* James T. Demetrion, Peggy Patrick, Euphemia Conner. *The Detroit Institute of Arts:* Frederick J. Cummings, Alan P. Darr, Patricia K. Lawrence, Agnes J. Derbin, Michele Peplin. *Hood Museum of Art, Dartmouth College, Hanover:* Richard Stuart Teitz, Hazel A. Burrows. *Wadsworth Atheneum, Hartford:* Tracy Atkinson, Gregory Hedberg, David M. Parrish, Patrice Spillane, Wilfred Stebbins. *The Museum of Fine Arts, Houston:* Peter C. Marzio, David B. Warren, Anne Tucker, Judith McCandless, Edward B. Mayo, Charles Carroll. *Indianapolis Museum of Art:* Robert A. Yassin, Anthony F. Janson, A. Ian Fraser, Delores Wilson, Janet Feemster. *The Nelson-Atkins Museum of Art, Kansas City:* Marc F. Wilson, Ross E. Taggart, Martha S. Stout, Cynthia Draney. *Los Angeles County Museum of Art:* Earl A. Powell III, Alla T. Hall, Pratapaditya Pal, Maurice Tuchman, Renee Montgomery, Christine E. Vigiletti, Karen Sirus. *The Currier Gallery of Art, Manchester:* Robert M. Doty, Richard Ayer, Sharon Callahan. *Milwaukee Art Museum:* Gerald Nordland, Rosalie Goldstein, Thomas Beckman. *The Minneapolis Institute of Arts:* Samuel Sachs II, Carroll T. Hartwell, Karen Duncan, Melissa M. Moore, Christian A. Peterson, Catherine Parker, Rosamond Hurrell, Molly Harris. *Walker Art Center, Minneapolis:* Martin Friedman, Graham W. J. Beal, Carolyn Clark DeCato, Jane E. Falk. *The Newark Museum:* Samuel C. Miller, Ulysses G. Dietz, Gary A. Reynolds, Audrey Koenig, Robert Carlucci. *Yale University Art Gallery, New Haven:* Alan Shestack, Michael Komanecky, Rosalie Reed, Sarah Cash. *New Orleans Museum of Art:* E. John Bullard, William A. Fagaly, Valerie Loupe Olsen, Nancy Barrett, Daniel Piersol. *The Solomon R. Guggenheim Museum, New York:* Thomas M. Messer, Diane Waldman, Lisa Dennison, Jane Rubin. *The Metropolitan Museum of Art, New York:* Philippe de Montebello, Carol Moon Cardon, Sir John Pope-Hennessy, Charles F. Moffett, Katherine Baetjer, Helmut Nickel, George Szabo, Sarah Bertalan, Carmen Gómez-Moreno, Douglas Newton, Prudence O. Harper, Holly Pittman, Barbara A. Porter, Dietrich von Bothmer, Maxwell Anderson, Clare Vincent, Weston J. Naef, Colta Ives, John Buchanan, Marceline McKee, Frederick John Gordon, Mary Doherty. *The Museum of Modern Art, New York:* Richard E. Oldenburg, William Rubin, John Szarkowski, Riva Castleman, J. Stewart Johnson, Cora Rosevear, Carolyn Lanchner, Ethel Shein, Susan Kismaric, Deborah Wye, Aileen K. Chuk, Thomas D. Grischkowsky. *The Pierpont Morgan Library, New York:* Charles A. Ryskamp, William M. Voelkle, Cara Dufour Denison, David W. Wright, Priscilla C. Barker, Nancy Davis. *Whitney Museum of American Art, New York:* Thomas

11

N. Armstrong III, Patterson Sims, Elizabeth Carpenter, Sandra Seldin. *Smith College Museum of Art, Northampton:* Charles Chetham, Betsy B. Jones, Michael Goodison, Louise A. Laplante. *Allen Memorial Art Gallery, Oberlin College:* Richard E. Spear, William Olander, Chloe Young, Ellen Johnson, Christine A. Dyer, Marianne Richter. *Joslyn Art Museum, Omaha:* Henry Flood Robert, Jr., Hollister Sturges, Holliday T. Day, Edward R. Quick, Bermeal V. Anderson, Charmain Schuh. *Philadelphia Museum of Art:* Anne d'Harnoncourt, Joseph J. Rishel, Darrel L. Sewell, Irene Taurins, Julia Addison, Ann C. Bixler. *The Phoenix Art Museum:* James K. Ballinger, Claudia Brown, Rosemary O'Neill, Susan Gordon. *Museum of Art, Carnegie Institute, Pittsburgh:* John R. Lane, Henry Adams, Gail Stavitsky, Ellie Vuilleumier, Beverly Specht. *Portland Art Museum, Oregon:* Donald Jenkins, Polly Eyerly, Kathryn B. Gates, Rachel Lafo, Gwen Putnam. *The Art Museum, Princeton University:* Allen Rosenbaum, Frances Follin Jones. *Museum of Art, Rhode Island School of Design, Providence:* Franklin W. Robinson, Thomas Lentz, Robert Workman, Patricia Loiko, Laura Stevens. *Memorial Art Gallery of the University of Rochester:* Bret Waller, Donald A. Rosenthal, Patricia Anderson, Sandra Markham, Janet Otis. *The Saint Louis Art Museum:* Emily R. Pulitzer, James D. Burke, Jack Cowart, John Nunley, Marie-Louise Kane, Mary-Edgar Patton, Helene Rundell, Mary Ann Steiner. *Washington University Gallery of Art, St. Louis:* Gerald D. Bolas, Joseph D. Ketner II, Natalie Mondschein. *The Fine Arts Museums of San Francisco:* Ian McKibbin White, Thomas P. Lee, Margaretta Lovell, Kathleen Berrin, Therese Chen. *San Francisco Museum of Modern Art:* Henry T. Hopkins, F. Van Deren Coke, Katherine C. Holland, Garner Muller, Pamela Pack. *The Santa Barbara Museum of Art:* Paul C. Mills, Richard V. West, Robert Henning, Jr., Barry M. Heisler, Elaine Dietsch, Merrily Peebles. *The John and Mable Ringling Museum of Art, Sarasota:* Richard S. Carroll, Michael Auping, Elizabeth S. Telford, Lynell Morr, Roma Morgan. *Seattle Art Museum:* Arnold Jolles, Henry Trubner, Pamela McClusky, Michael Knight, Gail E. Joice, Suzanne Kotz, Dale Rollins, Paula Thurman. *The Toledo Museum of Art:* Roger Mandle, Patricia J. Whitesides. *National Gallery of Art, Washington, D.C.:* J. Carter Brown, Charles P. Parkhurst, John Wilmerding, Carroll J. Cavanagh, Dodge Thompson, Andrew Robison, Carlotta J. Owens, Ann Bigley, Stephanie Belt, Rita Cacas. *National Museum of American Art, Smithsonian Institution:* Charles C. Eldredge, Virginia Mecklenburg, Ralph T. Coe, William H. Truettner, Melissa Kroning, Susanne Owens, Margy P. Sharpe, Peggy Gilges, Maggie Rahe. *The Phillips Collection, Washington, D.C.:* Laughlin Phillips, Willem de Looper, Joseph Holbach, Janet P. Dorman. *Norton Gallery and School of Art, West Palm Beach:* Richard A. Madigan, Bruce Weber, Pamela S. Parry, Michelle Shields. *Sterling and Francine Clark Art Institute, Williamstown:* David S. Brooke, Rafael A. Fernandez, Martha Asher, Jennifer A. Gordon. *Worcester Art Museum:* Tom L. Freudenheim, James A. Welu, Timothy A. Riggs, Stephen B. Jareckie, Sally R. Freitag.

Key enabling support for this exhibition came from the State of Florida. House and Senate passed, in June 1981, the Florida Arts Indemnification Act, a first among States in the Union, offering qualifying museums a shelter from part of the cost of insuring important art borrowed from institutions and individuals outside Florida but within the United States. For their insurance and legal advice I am grateful to Paul C. Mills, Huntington T. Block, Alice Whelihan and Vance Salter; for their endorsement and implementation of this legislation, the Center for the Fine Arts recognizes former Representative William Sadowski, former Senator Dick Anderson, Governor Bob Graham, Secretary of State George Firestone, Director of Cultural Affairs Chris Doolin, Director of Risk Management James Bearden, and Chief of Property Risk Retention J. David Rabon. In addition to benefiting from Florida Arts Indemnity, *In Quest of Excellence* was awarded a grant for organizational support by the Florida Arts Council.

Recognizing its potential to attract visitors and promote the cultural welfare of South Florida, the Metropolitan Dade County Tourist Development Council, through the Council of Arts and Sciences, subsidized *In Quest of Excellence*. For initiating and executing this essential funding agreement, Frank Cooper, former, and Kenneth Kahn, present Council Director, deserve the Center's gratitude as do 1981-83 Tourist Development Council and Council of Arts and Sciences members.

Through a Visiting Specialist grant from the National Endowment for the Arts' Museum Program, matched by Metropolitan Dade County, we were able to secure graphic and interior advice from Vignelli Associates, New York. To Massimo and Lella Vignelli, aided by Michele Kolb, and to Peter Laundi, who designed this catalogue, as well as to the National Endowment for the Arts, a Federal Agency, goes our appreciation for having helped the Center strive for quality in these important areas.

The Knight Foundation, having been convinced of its educational intent and communicative purpose, generously aided the production and distribution of this catalogue. As John L. Knight, Lee Hills and C. C. Gibson were helpful in this, they earned the Center for the Fine Arts Association's particular gratitude.

The Junior League of Miami in cooperation with the Dade County School Board and the Miami Dade Public Library, has undertaken an ambitious and innovative 5th grade art education project, called *Art Path* which is geared to address 20,000 students. These organizations for their initiative, McDonald's for its sponsorship, the County Commission for waiving admission fees and Margarita Cano, Sue Cesarano, Betty Fleming, Jackie Hinchey, Betty Huck, Laura Pegues and Richard Russey deserve the community's appreciation.

The Center for the Fine Arts gains international prestige, and *In Quest of Excellence* draws financial comfort from its association with American Express. On behalf of Metropolitan Dade County and the Center for the Fine Arts Association, I gratefully recognize the American Express Foundation for its generous support, and James D. Robinson III, Chairman of the Board, Susan B. Bloom, Director of Cultural Affairs, and Dee Topol, Manager of Shearson Contributions, for their valued participation.

A number of individuals have contributed to this exhibition and the catalogue accompanying it. In addition to the names already mentioned, I wish to acknowledge, for varying but specific instances of advice and support, Joseph Z. Fleming, Rosalind Jacobs, Pamela B. Johnson, Philip Johnson, Connie B. Jones, Donald Kahn, Francisco Mestre, Sr., Barbara Novak, Brian O'Doherty, Ana Reville, Richard Shack, SKF Industries' A. H. Kohnle and Ralph C. Palmer, Roger Sonnabend, Allen Wardwell and Carl J. Weinhardt, Jr.

Finally, my colleagues on the Center's staff, with perseverance, humor, sacrifice of personal time, and a talent for improvising, have saved the day. For contributions in areas of their expertise to catalogue and exhibition, I recognize Priscilla Sargent, Brenda Williamson, Arlene B. Dellis, Dorothy Downs, Daniel Pike, Nancy Williams, Marian Sutton and Esther Byrd. Caroline Otto (Smith'85) volunteered research assistance in the summer of 1983. Ann W. Heymann was our valued freelance catalogue editor.

My wife, Ingeborg, stood behind this effort and, for her patience and inspiration, deserves singular recognition.

Jan van der Marck
Director
Center for the Fine Arts

The Flowering of Art Museums

Agnes Mongan

Although rarely noted, one of the most remarkable developments of the twentieth century has been the astonishing flowering of art museums. When The Museum of Modern Art opened in New York in the Fall of 1929 and was followed, in a few years time, in that same city by the Guggenheim and Whitney Museums, and, in 1941, by the National Gallery in Washington, no one even imagined that well before the end of this century every one of those institutions would have to have a substantial addition to its original building. At one point in the mid '60s, it was estimated that as many as 48 new art museums were opening every year in the United States.

Their coming into being naturally posed questions: What would they show? For what audience did they exist? Who was to be responsible for the choice of exhibitions? How were they to be financed? And finally: What would be the links, if any, to local educational institutions? Undeniably, the problems they presented were difficult, varied and continuous. Yet, by and large, the newly founded institutions have not only become a valid part of their local scenes, they have also, when well conceived and imaginatively managed, as the majority were, played a not inconsiderable role in the lives of their communities, touching the young as well as the elderly, those with few worldly goods, as well as the affluent.

Many of the questions raised today have already been faced by some of the older, larger and more distinguished institutions. The Metropolitan in New York and the Museum of Fine Arts in Boston both celebrated their centennials a little more than a decade ago. This year the art museum in Indianapolis held its centennial celebration. One is apt to think that such prestigious institutions only have come into existence when a rich and powerful collector was willing to give not only a notable collection but also the funds to house and maintain it. True, that pattern has been the origin of many

art museums in many cases. Yet Indianapolis shows that there can be another route. In 1883 a group of citizens, led by Mary Wright Sewall, the principal of a local girls' school, formed an art association in Indianapolis. According to its constitution, the purpose of the organization was "the cultivation and advancement of art..." The volunteers of that early group brought together nearly three hundred objects. In 1895, the bequest of John Herron, who was not a collector, gave them the means to build an art gallery. Today that museum houses more than eighty thousand works of art!

Somewhat similar patterns have initiated museums in Minnesota, Texas and California, to name only three of the many states which could offer comparable patterns of growth. Even more surprising in this ever-expanding field is the number of cities in each of which there now is a separate and very lively museum dedicated solely to contemporary art. Again to name only three: Houston, Chicago and Cincinnati. In these contemporary museums one can find constantly changing exhibitions of extraordinary diversity, each planned with the aim of illuminating, through visual means, some aspect of contemporary art.

An interesting example was afforded us when the American Association of Museums, an organization of national scope, held its annual meeting in the early Fall of 1982 in Chicago. The Art Institute of Chicago and the Museum of Contemporary Art planned a complimentary program. The resurgence of interest in the quality of paint and the actual use of that medium was discussed by a noted painter committed to the present movement. More extraordinary was the appearance of a contemporary composer who spoke of his own work and then performed it. The announced goal of the meeting was "to stimulate creative thinking in an environment conducive to sharing ideas."

A few years ago the sharply defined boundaries between the arts would have made such a mixture of creative talents unlikely. Now music, both popular and classical, the dance, in even more varied categories, and photography are more often than not given equal time and exposure, sharing the stage with sculpture, painting, the graphic arts and architecture. With the broadening of the fields, the problems, of course, multiply. The questions of to whom and how the limited funds will be allocated are constant and complex. With new limitations about to be imposed on the National Endowment for the Arts and the National Endowment for the Humanities, new formulae are being considered nation-wide and new solutions are being sought.

Obviously it is a time of dramatic and inescapable change. Innovations and inventions have altered both our ways of looking and of learning. The speed and ease of transport has had an enormous effect. Who would have thought, even a decade ago, that the historically unique collection of early armour from the Tower of London would be flown this year to Cincinnati or that the treasures of the Vatican will be shown in New York, San Francisco and Chicago?

Collections of such quality, which can, of course, be compared to the "King Tut" exhibition, do not raise questions about their excellence, but one may seriously wonder if the majority of viewers have the knowledge or taste or perception to realize the historic importance of what they are seeing or its relevance to their daily lives. That is exactly where the present day museum of contemporary art can step in to play a fundamental role.

Artists have always questioned the nature of the universe. That is, in essence, their function. Today's problems, problems even of daily life, may be new and unique, but they are not inhuman. Art has always dealt with such problems even if only obliquely: the poor, the violent, the unhappy, the dislocated, as well as the powerful, the possessive, and the patriarchal. There has been a never-ending

dialogue between the content and its relation to humanity even if that dialogue is not always interpreted in depth until the epoch has passed.

A problem presented visually may only slowly evoke a response, but if it is presented with sympathy and understanding, it may result in surprising clarification, interpretation and eventual solution. Just as our judgments of the past alter with the changing generations, a provocative and unusual presentation may stir our sensibilities to a reconsideration or even a new interpretation. Just as our judgments of the past alter with the changing generations, a provocative and unusual presentation may stir our sensibilities to a reconsideration or even a new interpretation. The essential is, of course, that the quality of the presentation be valid, perceptive and profound, not leading into alluring but useless bypaths and not misleading in the use of fashionable but ephemeral artifices.

Twenty years ago, the worldwide effect of some of the recent exhibitions of Urban Planning would not have been expected. Harvard and M.I.T. advanced studies under the patronage of the Aga Khan are dealing with city living in the Islamic world. Their aim is to propose communities balanced in every sense that will bear witness to the local Islamic heritage from Ankara to Malaysia.

Florida is in an extraordinary position for a similar kind of orientation. Miami can, not only because of its position and its several universities but also because of its problems, become a key area in which to consider some of the difficulties of contemporary life. In a community which has grown in population nearly 50 percent in a little over a decade, it is not easy to discover a clear civic spirit or all possible sources of potential patronage and support. Yet in our present world there are few institutions as capable of defining and dramatically presenting both the problems and their possible solutions as an art museum centered on contemporary interests and manned by a dedicated, knowledgeable, well-trained and highly imaginative staff.

Speaking to a small but distinguished group which had assembled this past summer in the remote, and quiet McDowell Colony in New Hampshire to celebrate that retreat's 75th birthday, Brendan Gill, the *New Yorker's* drama critic said: "We Americans of the late 20th century live daily in the midst of a masquerade of euphemisms in which nothing bears its honest name...we are expected to deny the existence of suffering, of ugliness, of failure...who is to stand up and shout the simple, awful truths by which we ought to live?...it is the artists and composers and practitioners of the performing arts who have the responsibility for doing so." Then he added that "year after year a small group of people have gathered here in quiet, unheralded pursuit of excellence in their fields." It is, as he sees it, the duty of those who can recognize and appraise these carefully nurtured talents to make them known and appreciated by a far wider world.

Miami is now one of the notable crossroads of the world. The civilizations of this hemisphere's past lie only a few hours away, those of Europe and those of Asia only slightly more distant. Recent phenomenal inventions and experiments have their place of origin almost within this city's limits. Surely these new scientific aids can play their role in helping to understand today's plight and show some new path toward sympathetic solutions inspired by the linkage of art and humanity. This handsome, carefully planned and beautifully constructed Center for the Fine Arts can surely help make real that possibility.

The Sins and Virtues of Collecting

Sherman E. Lee

I had thought of beginning with a paraphrase or rather, parody, of Cole Porter: "Squirrels do it; jackdaws do it; even Bob and Ethel Scull did it..." I refer, of course, to collecting—whether nuts, twigs, bright gew-gaws, or the current *avant-garde*. Since my words are few, I cannot examine here the collecting of anything and everything but must consider only the serious problems involved in collecting works of art. Works of art are the most positive and pleasurable representatives of the collecting instinct and process; but, how are we to examine these factors so that we may be enlightened and led to collect, or at least to understand the nature of art collecting?

My second thought was to produce a rational and prosaic account of the collecting process—beginning with motivation, continuing with process, and ending with an evaluation of results. So, we could follow Max Friedlander's excellent, if laconic, advice given in 1930 in his *Genuine and Counterfeit* (pp. 20, 21):

1. Trust your own eyes, study pictures carefully yourselves...2. Go to the dealers, look at what they have, do not wait for offers...3. Do not overestimate the significance of the artist's name. There are some excellent pictures whose creators are unknown. 4. The opinions regarding artists rest upon more or less certain guesswork...5. Many pictures are badly preserved...The value of a painting is to a great degree, dependent upon its condition. 6. Seek intercourse with connoisseurs...In this way you can (destroy) that mutually protective relation between dealers and scholars.

But this paled for me and so, I was convinced, it would for my readers. Prescriptions, even couched in Latin, make boring reading. Clearly another gambit was required.

And so we begin with a personified collector—a serious man. Prowling among the once fruitful little shops on the Left Bank of the Seine, he looks at a portfolio of prints or drawings. But even as he searches, his glance moves to a red chalk drawing on the wall. Even as he searches, he is uneasy, afraid of missing the great opportunity. The collector is not to be confused with the generality—the visitors to the Salon of 1852. These art lovers are but spectators, puzzled, their only direct concern the derriere of a sculpture of the female form divine. At a later Salon of 1865, Daumier comments upon more serious types—the connoisseurs named in the title of the lithograph—wielding the magnifying glass of true connoisseurs or critics. They inhabit the threshold of the collectors' realm, short of the crucial credential of possession.

The true collector is epitomized by a British representation, executed by that astute recorder Johann Zoffany, of *Charles Townley Esq. and Friends in the Townley Gallery*, (Fig. 1). The acquisitive instincts of the early collector are expressed by the visual jumble of ancient works. The collector's circle is engaged in friendly discourse, supported by books, opened or closed, strewn about the floor, scarcely distinguishable from the reclining dog obligatory in any gentleman's establishment.

Such groups of amateurs were not uncommon in late 18th century London—the Antiquarians and the Cognoscenti were but two of numerous such circles. What moves us in Zoffany's canvas is the idea of a collector's world, of an intimate association of friends bound by the challenge of a newly discovered antiquity.

Still another conversation piece by Zoffany, the *Tribuna of the Uffizi* (Fig. 2), reveals yet more of the collector's world. While the collectors are in a "public" museum, they have made it private by their very presence. They discuss the various works—by Carracci, Raphael, Correggio—as if they were their own. Their richness is mirrored by the riches about them, a visual refutation of the Miesian paradox, "less is more."

But within this embarrassment of riches there are

certain details revealing some of the baser, more fundamental elements of the collector's profession—accoutrements of the trade: a packing box, paper padding, pliers for nail-pulling. In this Zoffany was most prescient, for collecting embraces the delights of Christmas everyday, of unpacking, of revealing the unknown or the anticipated—delights annotated a hundred years later by Freud, though arguably not applicable to English gentlemen.

Still, from both of these pictures, the *Townley Gallery* and the *Tribuna*, we learn that these collectors do not collect just anything. They are not possessors or admirers of all products of man and nature like the Renaissance masters of the Wunderkammer with its paintings, sculptures, stuffed animals, coral, and other strange manifestations of nature; they collect works of Classical Antiquity or they admire the Classic masters of Italy. What is collected has become important and is still the most critical element in any evaluation of the collecting syndrome. Or is it, as has often been said, a disease?

This heady thought tempts us to further speculation. Titian painted the portrait of a *marchand-amateur* (what New York calls a private dealer) in 1568, one Jacopo Strada. Strada is accompanied by the representation of the elements of pleasure, and yet his countenance is troubling—he is neither happy nor open. A degree of indecisive calculation emanates from his image. Or consider Lorenzo Lotto's portrait of a real collector, Andrea Odoni, who puts his hand upon his chest and observes the beholder. But what are we to take as his expression? Pride? Anxiety? Envy? It is impossible to say for certain, but like Strada, who evokes uneasy feelings, Odoni confronts us with a troubling image. I thought of Pride and Envy and these immediately recalled *The Seven Deadly Sins* (Fig. 3). Suddenly I was intrigued by the possibility of revealing the connections between the mores of collecting and the ancient personifications of sin.

Before we go further, let us understand what follows to be a "caprice". The collecting of art is really not a social disease. I would hope that no one would believe me to be equating collecting with *The Seven Deadly Sins*. Rather, as we so sophisticated moderns know, these sins are simply very true and perceptive recognitions of elements of human character which, when developed to excess, can indeed become sinful. These basic drives can be controlled by reason and measure to become productive and beneficial. If pride is carried too far it becomes superbia—pride as a sin. To have a sense of identity and worth is no sin. Lust can be considered as a form of love carried to distorted excess. Prudence could be mistaken for sloth, deliberation frozen into inaction. When does appreciation of good food become gluttony? Or thrift become avarice? What I propose is to examine collecting within the framework of the seven sins considered as embodiments of human nature—a metaphoric exercise designed to stimulate thoughts and feelings about collecting.

The Seven Deadly Sins are perhaps most successfully and succinctly rendered in visual form on the table top in the Prado painted by Hieronymous Bosch. They occupy the central circle of the panel while the corners display representations of the Four Last Things: Death, Last Judgment, Paradise, and Hell. The infernal scene shows the punishment for the sins depicted on the central disc, supervised by the all-seeing Eye of God. The sins we shall consider are Pride, Lust, Sloth, Anger, Gluttony, Avarice, and Envy.

Pride or Superbia is represented by a lady admiring her mirror image, surrounded by the aids to and accoutrements of beauty. She collects what enhances her, what is needed now to accommodate the current fashion. Vanitas imagines herself to be up-to-date and consequently beautiful. In this she mirrors those collectors who constantly worry about being in the swim, being at what is sometimes called "the cutting edge of the *avant-garde*." Some museum charters forbid the acquisition of works by living artists, or even by those who have not been dead for at least fifty years.

Such apparently antediluvian ideas are not quite so foolish as they appear, for it is indeed difficult to distinguish between fashion and true style, between the momentary surge and the steady, long pull. Many famous and presumably clairvoyant collectors, upon closer examination, prove to have been prudent by contemporary standards. Thus the great collection of early Picassos at The Museum of Modern Art was formed some 25 years after the fact, while John Quinn's Cézannes were acquired around 1920. The recent desire to be at the cutting edge can have only one logical conclusion: one must collect the works of an artist before his birth, a conceptual mode that must surely be now in process somewhere. That one should be interested in what is produced in one's own time goes without saying but that one can wisely form a balanced collection in this area is highly unlikely. The only true path to the role of seer is to buy the total art production of, say 1973, and then show in 1983 only those things considered a decade later to have merit. Where are the basements and storerooms of the clairvoyants? Or were their dogs anonymously flogged at auction, to use an apt British expression for works discarded to the market place. Pride warns the collector to distinguish between style and fashion, to be deliberate, if not slothful, in his activities. This first sin is also a warning to the collector not to substitute his ego for that of the artist. Art and property can have adversary positions. The ownership, surely transient, of a Braque—"my Braque"—in no way changes the nature of the work, whether of the first or a far lower order.

For Bosch, Lust (Luxuria) is embodied by a lady and gentleman seated, drinking in a tent while yet another couple in the background are engaged in

Fig. 1

Fig. 2

intimations of immorality. Surely the collector must possess a degree of lust as well as of pride. One must really desire, want to have what one collects. To acquire for reasons of investment or of social station involves still other sins, inappropriate in the context of this one. Perhaps one of the most striking historical descriptions of the motivation rooted in lust is Cardinal Mazarin's note about Queen Christina of Sweden. In a letter to the caretaker of his country mansion he writes, "This mad woman must be kept away from my cabinets, because otherwise some of my miniatures might be taken."

Sloth (Accidia) is personified as a man dozing in his chair before a fire. A dog is curled up nearby. A book is unopened—not even its metal clasps have been unfastened. Nothing happens. Nothing is done. To excess, this sin is a cautionary one for the collector. The slothful collector achieves nothing. Research is too tiring, time consuming, boring. The lazy collector ignores knowledge at his peril for he will probably be both a collector and a participant in a law-suit. Research does not involve only reading books; it involves looking—intelligent looking—what the French call goût-de-comparaison. Constant looking and direct comparison are the best means to provide both a rational and intuitive basis for taste. Until one is familiar with an extensive series of works by the same artist, or of objects of the same type, one cannot place any one work within the hierarchies of importance, rarity, or quality. Lazy collectors are also the bane of scholars and curators. How depressing to visit the collection unknown to its owner! In this context works of art become either possessions or decorations rather than visual embodiments of thought and feeling.

Anger (Ira) is an almost emblematic depiction of two drunken peasants fighting. The female figure restraining one of them can be considered either an attempt at saintly repression or as the cause of it all. For a dedicated collector, it is not far-fetched to associate anger with thoughtless or willful damage to works of art. The collector must be aware of the ever-present danger of destruction and deterioration of art objects and the corollary need for thoughtful and sensitive conservation. Every collector buys more than the work of art he adds to his hoard. He also acquires the responsibility to protect it, care for it, and hand it on to posterity—whether in the form of his descendants, other collectors, or a museum.

Historically more things have been destroyed through neglect than anger, but that sin was responsible for the wanton destruction of some of Cardinal Mazarin's precious collection after his death. His executor, the Duc de Meilleraye, had servants destroy that part of his group of antique marbles inherited by Hortense Mancini because the sculptures' nudity aroused the wrath of Mazarin's prudish successors.

Gluttony (Gula) is easily recognizable—a gentleman stuffing himself, encouraging the incipient gluttony of the child at his knee. Here we have the archetype of the pack-rat or series collector—one who buys every item he can lay his hands on within a given category. One remembers with pain the seemingly endless evenings spent looking at hundreds of netsuke or marrow spoons.

Such series have their scientific uses—the natural history museum requires such efforts. But the fine art collection could be said to be a grouping of sorts, of the unusual and dissimilar reconciled in terms of quality. The large collection of average works withers interest; the small collection of truly excellent quality encourages one to explore still further. I remember the marvelous collection of Japanese prints formed many years ago by Louis Ledoux, two hundred in all. And it always stayed at two hundred! If Ledoux wished to acquire another print, he forced himself to give up one of the sheets he already possessed. While this may seem a form of a modern sin called masochism, it also was a process requiring the collector to exercise the most subtle judgments with a consequent enhancement of the quality and interest of the collection.

The penultimate sin is that of Avarice (Avaricia). A judge is shown being paid off to rule in favor of the plaintiff who is depicted with a knowing and satisfied countenance. Avarice is certainly the sin all collectors deal with most often for it involves money and its quantity—the price. We are all, especially the spectators, a part of this routine. How boring the countless cocktail party conversations about who paid what for this or that. Or that such and such was bought for so little and sold for so much. This is not discourse about art but gossip about money. One could be a collector of money—many are—but the engravings on bills have not been illustrated in any of the standard works of the history or criticism of art. Again moderation is the measure, whether it is a proper interest or becomes a deadly sin. Price is important. Auctions can be promoted to create false values as easily as a dealer can embroider a work to his profit. Nevertheless, both auction houses and dealers have an honorable and constructive function in the art market. The extent to which they fulfill these worthwhile aims is comparable in dimension to the extent of the collectors' commitments to standards of quality and rationality in their pursuit of the perfect collection. Beware the dealer or collector or curator who continuously oversubscribes to *The Seven Deadly Sins*. If we forget that a price expressed in terms of money, rather than patience or perspicacity, is merely the means to the ends of collection and preservation, then we have indeed fallen victim to avarice.

Perhaps the most unattractive of the wicked seven is Envy (Invidia). While a burgher neighbor covets another's wife (or daughter?), the potential cuckold envies the nobleman his falcon. Below, a dog envies the bone held by the merchant though he has two bones on the ground before him. It requires no leap of the imagination to include

Fig. 3

competition in the realm of Invidia. The obvious fallacy in both competition and envy lies in diverting one's attention from the principal end of collecting—the excellent and meaningful work of art—to either matching the Jones or doing them one better. Such unattractive motivations have played a major part in the art market. The taste-makers play the tune, and the buyers dance to it. How many times has one been told "if you don't get it, what's-his-name will," or "Museum X is actively interested in this work—best act before them." Perhaps even worse is envy after the fact—the denigration of works acquired by others. The sin can only be partially combatted by the juice of sour grapes applied by the injured party. Surely envy is the least enviable of our catalog of *The Seven Deadly Sins*.

I could have provided this caprice with a positive structure drawn from the contemplation of *The Virtues*. Originally they were four in number, as Perugino depicted them in his frescos for the Collegio del Cambio in Perugia—a bank needing all available virtue. Plato's Four are Wisdom, Justice, Fortitude, and Temperance, but Sts. Ambrose and Augustine added Three—Faith, Hope and Love—thus matching the Sins in quantity. A good collector should certainly be wise and possess Fortitude. Temperance is useful in moderate amounts. Faith and Hope are noble ideas but not of much practical use in a contracting market, while too much Love can lead to grievous error. The application of Justice escapes me unless the collector has committed the unnamed sin of resorting to the law for remedy. But *The Seven Deadly Sins* are far more interesting than *The Virtues*, and further, they are modern, with strong Freudian overtones.

But Sins and Virtues alone can never accomplish the end of a great collection. There is a Goddess largely unrecognized by collectors, curators, and museum directors alike—Luck (Fortuna). Fortune must smile upon the collector. Occasionally finds are made; but more often the dealer and auction house have done the finding and the buyer has agreed to recognize their finds. But, at least in part, it is the hope of making a find that keeps one looking in out of the way places—if Fortune smiles once, the wise collector does not push his luck. He is divine if he never makes a mistake; but fortunate if he makes fewer mistakes than "finds." He is fortunate if he has enough to collect, though it can be done on little. He is fortunate if he is able to enjoy and preserve what he collects. He is fortunate to be a collector endowed with the capacity for emotional and intellectual fulfillment. A combination of much good fortune, some virtue and minimum sin is the desirable means to a good end.

They ordered these matters better in 18th century England, the time and place of the making of some of the most extraordinary art collections in history. Jonathan Richardson described the ideal in his *Two Discourses* of 1719:

> ...to be a good connoisseur a man must be as free from all kinds of prejudice as possible; he must moreover, have a clear and exact way of thinking, and reasoning; he must know how to take in, and manage just ideas; and throughout he must have not only a solid, but an unbiased judgment.

One can only say Amen! and go all of us and do likewise.

The American Museum Experience: Patrons, Patronage, and the Federal Role

J. Carter Brown

The collections of American museums have been built in a uniquely American way. Visitors from abroad to the National Gallery of Art seem incredulous when they learn (if they ever do) that every single work of art in it came to the nation through private gift. Where are the government subsidies that furnish our sister National Gallery in London, for example, with over $7 million of government acquisitions funding each year?

The American Government has, of course, participated in almost every gift to this country's museums through an enlightened tax law that grants charitable deductions for such gifts. (One unenlightened facet of the law which, since 1970, has not permitted artists to deduct the full market value of their own work, but only the cost of materials used, is under review in Washington, and perhaps will be remedied by the time this exhibition opens.)

The advantages of the American system are multiform. A principal one is the freedom from central government interference in artistic matters. The tax incentive acts on the principle of power steering. The citizen donor chooses, and the government assists his initiative.

Another great advantage is the encouragement of the American system of decentralization. Our foreign visitors are overwhelmed by the geographical diversity of our museum collections. Anyone who has seen the Chinese collections in Kansas City, the French Impressionists and Post-Impressionists in Chicago, the Japanese art in Boston, the Egyptian collection in Brooklyn, or the classical sculpture in Malibu, to name just a few, knows what we mean.

Some collections which have a policy of not lending could not be represented in this exhibition: the Gardner in Boston, the Taft in Cincinnati, the Frick in New York, or the Chester Dale paintings in the National Gallery. But enough is here to give the visitor a breathtaking view of the geographical spread which is such a healthy index of America's commitment to our visual heritage.

Here at the National Gallery of Art we are striving to help supplement this widespread interest in making available original works of art on loan, generally for renewable periods of a year, through our National Lending Service. This is over and above the educational materials that are sent out on free loan to some four thousand communities annually in all fifty states, reaching last year an audience of over forty-five million people.

The history of the growth of our museums in this country has not until quite recently had much involvement with the American Government. With the exception of the Smithsonian Institution, about which more below, the growth of our museums in this country has historically been almost exclusively through private initiative.

Although the Pennsylvania Academy may claim run-away honors for the construction of the first art museum building in the United States in 1805 and 1806, it was not to be followed until the 1830-40s. John Trumbull's gallery at Yale (1831-2) served as a personal memorial; the Wadsworth Atheneum (1842-4) housed other functions in addition to its galleries. The Smithsonian Building (1849) included one gallery designated for art and other rooms used later for displays. More ambitious yet was the first Corcoran Gallery (now the Renwick), "dedicated to art" and begun in 1859, though not completed until after the Civil War.

The decade following the war saw a national building boom and the foundation of two great city art museums, the Boston Museum of Fine Arts and New York's Metropolitan (both 1870). In the last years of the century America witnessed its first golden age of American collecting and a rapid growth of its art institutions.

When the American Federation of Arts issued its first report in 1898, it listed 42 art museums nationwide. The 1910-11 report listed 67; the 1921 report, 153; and in 1931 there were 235. Surveying that year, a handbook issued by the American Association of Museums noted that new museums were being established at the rate of one a fortnight, the great majority being in places of less than 100,000 inhabitants, with museums of art in the preponderance.

The Depression eventually took its toll, for the AFA listed only 224 art museums in 1941. After the war, the upswing resumed, slowly at first, then faster than ever. The *Museums Directory* of the AAM listed 379 art museums in the United States and Canada in 1961; 597 in 1971; and an astounding 1039 in 1982.

Attempts to establish public collections in Washington go back to the early 19th century and tell us much about the history of private and federal patronage. The first "museum" in Washington consisted of a miscellaneous collection of objects brought together about 1829 by a Mr. John Varden. In 1840, more prominent citizens, in the interest of establishing facilities for the study of science and the arts, organized the National Institute, which eventually assimilated Varden's collection and some government holdings to form a museum in the Patent Office Building. Records are spotty, but the collection contained portraits (Peale, Stuart and Copley were represented), Indian subjects by Charles Bird King and others (purchased by the Secretary of War), and about thirty-five "busts and models." The Institute's collection was transferred to the Smithsonian in 1862.

The Smithsonian Institution, a federal body with a "private side," had been established by Act of Congress in 1846, after long and bitter debate. It inherited from James Smithson about 100,000 pounds, a few personal effects (including two works of art), and the injunction to foster "the increase and diffusion of knowledge among men." The Act of Establishment anticipated the formation of an art gallery—most significantly, as we shall see below. In

1857 the Board of Regents specified the Smithsonian's museum fields as embracing natural history, ethnology and archaeology, the applied arts and sciences, and the fine arts. Paintings, sculpture, engravings and architectural designs were to be collected, and while museum displays were slowly accumulating, loan collections were to be borrowed and assistance from art associations was to be solicited.

In 1849, $3,000 of Smithson's bequest was actually expended on the purchase of a large and choice collection of prints, but this was the last active support given art for 50 years. Indeed, both artists and paintings were to suffer. In 1852 John Mix Stanley deposited 152 canvases of Indian subjects in the Smithsonian building, where they continued on display while Stanley petitioned the Institution and Congress to purchase the lot for $12,000. He was still waiting in 1865 when a disastrous fire destroyed the gallery containing his paintings and those of Charles Bird King.

The Smithsonian scientists lost any enthusiasm they may have had for art collecting. The prints and art books were sent to the Library of Congress, and arrangements were made to transfer the paintings and sculpture to the new Corcoran Gallery when it opened in 1874. It would seem that the Institution's Secretary Henry considered the privately-founded Corcoran as carrying on the functions the Smithsonian had previously been assigned as a national gallery.

It was near the end of the century, in a period when the cultural climate was changing rapidly, that the spokesmen for the Institution reexamined its role. In 1896, Secretary Langley reported to the Regents "that it is well to recall the undoubted fact that [the Institution] was intended by Congress to be a curator of the national art." In 1900, the prints having been recalled from Congress, an "art room" was set up. Meanwhile, miscellaneous works of painting and sculpture had begun to accumulate,

but, as the Secretary conceded, not to the point justifying the title "Gallery of Art."

The leap from "art room" to "National Gallery" came about unexpectedly. It was precipitated by confusion occasioned by terms in the will of Mrs. Harriet Lane Johnson, niece of President Buchanan, who died in 1903, bequeathing her collection to the Corcoran Gallery until "the Government of the United States shall establish in Washington a national art gallery." Interpreting the will, the courts found that the Smithsonian Institution had indeed been established as a national art gallery by the government in 1846, a fact that had escaped general notice, but which was then confirmed by formal decree in 1906!

The time was not yet ripe for government leadership in the arts, but patron-collectors were waiting in the wings. Charles L. Freer, the Detroit industrialist, immediately offered the Smithsonian his collection, a building and an endowment. In 1907 William T. Evans followed with his offer of a collection. When the National Museum (now the Natural History) building was opened in 1909, the central hall was given over to the National Gallery, and the Museum's director, Richard Rathbun, published an account of the fortunes of art at the Smithsonian, concluding that "the building up of a gallery of the fine arts requires considerable means for purchasing or the aid of many friends as benefactors...The Insitution has received help from neither source except to a very limited extent. Congress has declined to appropriate funds for such a purpose, and until lately individuals generally have been reluctant to contribute to what they denominate the Government, failing to appreciate that, in fact, the museum belongs to the nation."

Neither patronage nor civic pride had been effective in establishing an actual national gallery in Washington for 60 years after the need for one was recognized in 1846. Two major gifts and many minor ones came to fill the art hall of the National

Museum, and in 1920 the Gallery finally achieved the status of a department of the U.S. National Museum, with William Henry Holmes appointed to serve as its first director. Holmes was distinguished as an anthropologist and accomplished as a painter, but he was then in his 74th year. Although he campaigned nation-wide for funds to build a proper gallery building, when he died in 1933 the works of art were still wedged incongruously between natural history and ethnology. The Gallery's collections were hopelessly uneven, its staff and funding were inadequate, and it was neglected by the Smithsonian, Congress and donors generally.

The first director of the National Gallery of Art, David Finley, recounts that when Andrew Mellon was Secretary of the Treasury in the 1920s and 1930s, he was occasionally asked by representatives of foreign countries to be taken to the "National Gallery." He was forced to reply, with some embarrassment, that this country had no such collection of old masters, but that he had "a few paintings in his apartment which he would be glad to show his visitors."

In Washington of the 1920s and 1930s there were, in fact, four public collections of art, but none which surveyed the western tradition in a way comparable to the Louvre or the National Gallery in London. There was the Freer with its Oriental collection, supplemented by American paintings; the Phillips Collection of "modern art and its sources," a delightful personal collection displayed in the home of Andrew Mellon's friends Duncan and Marjorie Phillips; the Corcoran Gallery, rising proudly on the other side of the White House from the Treasury, but emphasizing the American school and thus not meeting Mellon's standards for a gallery exhibiting the finest achievements of our broader cultural heritage; and, finally, there was the curious entity within the Smithsonian which bore the title of "The National Gallery of Art." The then "National Gallery" was not remotely comparable to the Corcoran, which had flourished under more favorable conditions of housing, endowment, leadership and patronage.

It is obvious why Andrew Mellon decided that a proper national gallery of art could be established only by making an entirely fresh start, under entirely different conditions; the most discriminating and munificent patronage must be provided and attracted; national pride (and dignity) required a great building, properly administered and maintained; and every work of art must meet the high standards of the leading national art museums of England and continental Europe.

Charles Freer had shown the way a gallery might be established within the Smithsonian and yet be protected from administrative or government interference and neglect, but Freer's gallery was conceived as a personal memorial. The new gallery was to be truly national. It must have appeared to Andrew Mellon that the only way to achieve a gallery of the quality, size and independence required by national dignity was for him to lead the way by performing a definitive act of patronage on an unprecedented scale.

In December 1936, after years of patient collecting, he wrote President Roosevelt offering to give "to the Smithsonian Institution or to the United States government for the benefit of the people of this country" his art collection, an endowment and a "suitable building" which was not to bear his name.

Andrew Mellon did not leave matters to chance. His letter stipulated the architect (he was already working on plans with John Russell Pope). The site must be properly located on the Mall. His endowment would pay for the salaries of the officers of the Gallery and, if possible, for art acquisitions. The management of the Gallery would be under an independent board of trustees within the Smithsonian Institution. Future acquisitions whether by gift or purchase, would be "limited to objects of the highest standard of quality." He had already arrived at an agreement with the Regents of the Smithsonian that the new institution would assume the title of "National Gallery of Art." (The older Smithsonian bureau thus capped its bad fortune by losing its name. It was cumbersomely redesignated the National Collection of Fine Arts. More recently it has come into its own as the National Museum of American Art.)

Andrew Mellon gave the nation 132 paintings, 24 works of sculpture, a $10,000,000 endowment, and a building whose construction cost at depression prices was $15,000,000, the equivalent of over ten times that today. He also attracted great companion gifts—at the outset, those of the Kress and Widener collections, so that the first director, David Finley who was brilliantly aided in this process by his Chief Curator and eventual successor, John Walker, could write that it seemed "miraculous that, in less than three years after the National Gallery opened, it had become one of the great art museums of the world."

Many major gifts and hundreds of smaller ones have followed in the past 40 years. The government has not only strictly honored its pledge to "provide such funds as may be necessary for the upkeep of the National Gallery of Art": it has contributed substantial sums for the remodeling or construction of facilities for the National Collection of Fine Arts (now National Museum of American Art), the National Portrait Gallery, the Renwick Gallery, the Hirshhorn Museum and Sculpture Garden, and (currently) the African and Oriental Art collections of the Smithsonian. It has also provided for the operation of these facilities, together with some purchase funds. There is nothing new in principle for the support by a government of its own art museums, but it is a striking departure in practice from the period prior to 1941. The United States, unlike many European countries, has never had a federal ministry of the arts. Attempts to form an advisory committee were made during the 19th century, but these failed as the result of the traditional fear of government interference or simple congressional indifference toward the arts. Early in this century the government moved by cautious steps to the establishment, first, of a Senate Parks Commission (1901-9) to bring order to planning for the District of Columbia, then to the Commission of Fine Arts (1910) to advise on matters of design affecting the city and also—as called upon by the government—on questions of art.

Although the government sponsored many projects and employed a number of artists during the Depression, the emergency programs had expired by mid-century. At the same time, art-related activities were increasing in all departments—especially the Smithsonian, State, Defense, Agriculture, and Health, Education and Welfare. In 1951 President Truman turned to the Commission of Fine Arts, under the chairmanship of David Finley, for a survey of federal activities in the arts. The resulting report, submitted in 1953, not only surveyed activities but set many of the goals that were to be realized in the next 30 years.

First and foremost, the Commission advised, their role should remain independent and advisory, and no ministry of fine arts or bureau directing art activities should be set up. On the other hand, existing government administrations, in all their diversity, should be strengthened in their programs and encouraged to raise standards. The National Collection of Fine Arts, for example, should be given means to "promote the cultural life of communities in all parts of the country." The National Gallery of Art should be supported in the exchange of international exhibitions. Finally, the report recommended "the establishment of a music center in Washington under the jurisdiction of the Federal government."

The Commission brought a broad vision to bear

on the needs and opportunities, but there existed no mechanism for following up on its recommendations. President Eisenhower authorized the construction of a national cultural center (1958 opened finally in 1971 as the Kennedy Center for the Performing Arts) but failed to persuade Congress to establish a Federal Advisory Commission on the Arts.

In 1962 and in 1963, President Kennedy repeated the request for such an advisory commission, and both times Congress failed to respond. To bring the needs into sharp focus, he called on August Heckscher to report on "The Arts and the National Government". In May 1963, Heckscher submitted his report, stating in the introduction,

Recent years have witnessed in the United States rapidly developing interest in the arts. Attendance at museums and concerts has increased dramatically... Cultural institutions exist in numbers which would have been thought impossible a generation ago... Despite this new enthusiasm...the very demands which changing tastes have made upon established artistic institutions have strained the financial resources available to them. Older forms of patronage have not in all cases been satisfactorily replaced.

At the end of the report, Heckscher called for the creation of "administration machinery relating to the arts": a Special Advisor, an Advisory Council, and a National Arts Foundation. The President set about to establish the Advisory Council by executive order, but did not live to make appointments. It was left to President Johnson in 1964 to make the final successful effort to procure authorization for an Arts Council "to recommend ways and means to maintain and increase the cultural resources of the Nation." In 1965, legislation followed which established the National Foundation on the Arts and Humanities, along with its Arts and Humanities Endowments. The arts—under Roger Stevens—were given $4,500,000 the first year.

The Endowment for the Arts was carefully planned to prevent its becoming the equivalent of that institution Americans have always dreaded, the policy-making Ministry of the Arts. With few exceptions, it operates only through matching funds, attracting three to four dollars for each it contributes. It must by legislation extend its programs to all states and territorial jurisdictions, and it has stimulated the formulation and development of state art councils to such a degree that it has admirably "promoted the cultural life of communities in all parts of the country," to recall the words of the Commission of Fine Arts report of 30 years ago.

Within the Endowment programs, museum support was given no emphasis until 1970, when—under the active leadership of the late Nancy Hanks and her deputy, Michael Straight—the Endowment entered a period of rapid growth. By 1975-76 nearly $7,000,000 (over 10 percent of the NEA budget) went to museums. This increased to $11,296,000 in 1982. The grants are effective in upgrading museum activities, underwriting exhibitions, and assisting in the more efficient utilization of collections. Although they are not intended for routine operational support, augmenting collections, or new construction, they afford essential governmental patronage. When supplemented by other programs (the more recent Institute of Museum Services, which is operations-oriented, was appropriated $12,000,000 in 1982), they play a critical role in museum growth and even survival.

Similarly dramatic changes in private-sector support have occurred in the last 20 years. Assistance from foundations, to give one example, has substantially increased, encouraged in part by the government's participation in NEA matching grants. Again, the emergence of the corporate patron points up the trends of the times and leads to comparisons with the traditional patron-collector. Pioneering business firms bought paintings as far back as the turn of the century, but only a few of the present giants with significant holdings in art (INA, Container Corporation, IBM, Abbott Laboratories) can trace the beginnings of their collections to the 1920s and 1930s. In the 1950s, collections were begun by such firms as Mead Corporation, General Mills, and Chase Manhattan. In the 1960s and 1970s, collections sprouted everywhere and many grew to include thousands of works of art, often by prominent artists. Paintings, prints and sculpture adorned their lobbies, board rooms, corridors and offices.

The corporate patron, unlike the private collector, may help a museum purchase a work of art but seldom donates a collection. (Rare exceptions are the Fred Harvey Company, S. C. Johnson and Son, and the Meta-Mold Aluminum Company.)

On the other hand, corporations frequently help in several ways, taking out museum memberships and making large grants to projects such as traveling exhibitions. Their total contribution increased threefold between 1975 and 1980, going from less than $8,000,000 to more than $23,000,000.

The well-selected, well-presented traveling exhibitions, which are so effective in bringing art of quality and a large attendance to a number of American museums, can be related to the same basic building blocks of patronage (support), civic pride and connoisseurship which have been so keyed-in to the donations of the private collector. In fact, with the growing number of museums and the rarity of masterpieces from the past, these exhibitions fill an ever increasing need for making works of quality more widely available, in a way that even a number of wealthy and discriminating patron donors could not. The new Center for the Fine Arts in Miami, with its imaginative pioneering of state indemnity and energetic program, is a pace-setting pioneer in this particularly American development. This quick overview of newly emerging, relatively impersonal forms of museum support brings us, in the end, to the realization that a vital source has not yet been mentioned. The munificent patron and the major collector still exist, sometimes in the same person. With the proliferation of art museums, the one-to-one relationship of private patron-great museum is proportionately more rare, but the number of public spirited citizens and outstanding collectors remains impressive. Superb collections are still given to museums; museums are still being built and endowed by private fortunes; and even—as with the establishment of the National Gallery of Art nearly 50 years ago—great buildings, endowments and collections continue to spring from a single source. As this exhibition bears eloquent witness, civic pride, patronage and connoisseurship have served as the foundation stones for museums of art all over the United States, to the lasting benefit of us all.

Grand Designs in Art Collecting

Philippe de Montebello

The opening of a new art facility such as the Center for the Fine Arts in Miami provides cause for celebration, of course, but also a handy pretext for some musings on the phenomenal growth of museums and their audiences. One could start by wondering—irrelevantly in this context—how humanity managed to fare so relatively well for so many millennia without museums at all. Only two hundred years ago museums were still very much of a novelty; an examination of their complex genesis, though, would take me too far afield—suffice it to say that a good number of clues may be found in Locke, J. J. Rousseau and The Age of Enlightment as a whole, as well as in the high premium placed on objects wrought by the hand of man since the Industrial Revolution.

Pointing my musings more in the direction suggested by this inaugural exhibition, namely, collecting and museums, I shall luxuriate in a somewhat unstructured flow of thought, beginning with a highly foreshortened view of collecting. Obviously I cannot write with Joseph Alsop's exhaustive and unforgiving scalpel, so here, very summarily, I shall touch upon some aspects of the function of the modern museum and the emergence of the profession of a curator. For starters, I should note that the instinct and compelling urge to collect have existed as long as man, though collecting art qua art is a relatively new phenomenon, which has behind it "power, prestige, and wealth," as one of my predecessors, Francis Henry Taylor, put it. Further inquiry into the motives for collecting art would lead us to include love and concupiscence of a higher order—and diverse as are the motives, so are the means.

The spectrum of methods used in collecting is broad, ranging from the scientific and laboriously methodical work pursued by skilled archaeologists—especially in the days of "partage" when division of the artifacts was prevalent (the Metropolitan's own collections of Egyptian art and Nimrud ivories, for example, are the result of sharing excavated materials with the countries of origin) to the less orthodox though more expedient means of having victorious armies return with war booty. The more current and accepted mode is purchase and, in the case of museums, gifts and bequests as well.

In reviewing patterns of collecting I shall pass over the earlier phases of amassing sculptures and other creations, now defined as works of art, in the ancient Greek sanctuaries; pass over as well the church treasuries in the Middle Ages, such as that marvel of Abbot Suger's at Saint-Denis, and leap to 16th century Europe and the major collections of art formed by royal families, members of the aristocracy, and the high bourgeoisie, those collections that form the core of the great museums of Europe, many housed in converted palaces, such as the Louvre and the Hermitage.

This period of collecting also saw the first indications that caring for collections was a serious pursuit, one that required special skills. Curators in earlier eras—those to whom the treasuries of ancient sanctuaries and medieval churches were entrusted—were usually priests. They were anonymous and unremunerated; curators today still tend to be anonymous or at least behind the scenes and, they would argue with some justification, underpaid.

In 16th century France, notably at Fontainebleau, we know that the royal collections were in the care of painters, namely Primaticcio and Rosso Fiorentino. Later, Henri IV appointed a *garde de tableaux* to care for his extensive collection of Italian pictures. This curator was also a painter, a certain Jean de Hoey of Utrecht. For the first time, we are told what his duties were: "to care for the old pictures of his majesty at Fontainebleau, to restore those that are spoiled, and to clean the frescoes in the rooms." Clearly, Jean de Hoey was a combination of curator and conservator. He must have had a certain degree of sophistication, because following his recommendation, many of the king's finest pictures were transferred from the insalubrious thermal setting at Fontainebleau to the less humid climate of the Palais du Louvre.

The activities of these curator/conservators extended to cataloguing, which, in essence, is what the 17th century Flemish artist Teniers was doing when he made small copies on panel of the pictures in the Archduke Leopold Wilhelm of Hapsburg's collection at Vienna. Though the birth of the curatorial profession may thus be said to antedate the creation of the public museum proper, the role of knowledgeable advisers to the great dynastic collectors should not be overlooked. Diderot helped shape the collection of Catherine the Great which now constitutes the Hermitage. Louis XVI was well served by d'Angivillers, who was responsible for the large-scale infusion of Dutch pictures into the royal collection—a clear instance of the taste of the adviser and his concern for museological approach to completeness injecting a foreign element, so to speak, into a ruler's personal collection.

Our propensity to accept practically all styles or manners of art should not be taken for granted. Our ability to tolerate and even learn to be moved by the most troubling of images, because they represent the best of what a civilization may have produced, is of fairly recent date. It may be, in part, attributed to the increasingly comprehensive nature of art museums which put many disparate styles at our disposal—with the quasi-official imprimatur conferred by a public institution.

How recent this tolerance is is dramatically illustrated by the actions of no less than Jacques Louis David, the great neoclassical painter and regicide. For he himself placed his signature on the document which decreed the mutilation of the Gothic statues of French kings on the facade of Notre-Dame.

It should be noted, as well, that the notion that a work of art is unique and irreplaceable is also of relatively recent date. Indeed, when one of Louis XIV's curators, the painter Michelin, executed copies of the king's pictures for the monarch to enjoy in his numerous residences, he was doing nothing out of the ordinary, for the making of casts and copies of ancient statuary—to be enjoyed sui generis—was commonplace.

Works of art moved about a great deal, because they changed hands rather more frequently than the best of them do today, for when they enter museums, that is usually their last stop. I need only refer the reader to the history of the Gonzaga collection, its dispersal and the almost incredible peregrinations that followed. A large portion was acquired by Charles I of England, whose collection experienced a similar fate owing to more tragic circumstances. Charles' collection, in turn, enriched numerous others by very circuitous routes indeed, and many renowned galleries of paintings in Europe can claim great examples from this genealogical line.

Today we hear much rather smug rhetoric about the inviolability and immovability of works of art in museums. As a necessary corrective, we should consider the peripatetic existence of those works in the heyday of the grand collecting tradition. This point can be made strikingly by tracing the pedigree of *The Slaves* created by Michelangelo for the Tomb of Pope Julius II. *The Slaves* were originally given by Roberto Strozzi to Henri II. They were installed in the Louvre, which was at that time the king's private residence. Henri II then "deaccessioned" *The Slaves* giving them to Anne de Montmorency as a wedding gift (he clearly did not seek the advice of a curator or answer to a Board of Trustees). Their journey was just beginning, for later they passed into the collection of the duc de Richelieu. Ultimately, they returned to the Louvre by the infamous means of expropriation during the French Revolution.

Museum officials who hold that their grand

neoclassical buildings are the inevitable and final resting places for works of art should remember these and other provenances before declaiming too many pieties in their fine tuning of the art of recalcitrance in the granting of loans. Indeed, arguments that favor the loans of works of art to exhibitions, including this one at the Center for the Fine Arts in Miami, are better supported historically than the arguments advanced by those promoting the immovability of works of art. And I do not think I run the risk of being an apostate if I intimate that in many ways the permanent residency of works of art in museums is at best a compromise. Dare I add that most works of art would probably be less ill at ease almost anywhere else than in a museum, be it over the altar in a church or over the sofa in an apartment on Fifth Avenue or the Avenue Foch.

However, we in the art museum field should not be too ungrateful, for the birth of museums logically coincided with and in many ways may be said to have fostered the emergence of curating as a distinct profession and of art history and criticism as ligitimate fields of study. At the same time, there occurred a resurgence of interest in antiquity brought about by the archaeological excavations conducted at first rather amateurishly by Vivant Denon in Egypt with Napoleon's armies and later with increasing sophistication by Layard in Assyria and Schliemann at Troy.

We can trace, as well, the flowering of art history to loan exhibitions, which in point of fact antedate the formation of museums. Loan exhibitions, especially in the area of contemporary art, were held at the Pantheon in Rome throughout the 17th century and at the Louvre even before it was a museum, namely in the Salon Carré, whence the term, still in use, "salon." And, it is from such great exhibitions as that of paintings from English private collections held in Manchester in 1857 that the discipline of art history received its strongest impetus.

But I stray too far from my theme. If the character of many European museums is determined by the great princely collections in which they are rooted (Hapsburg for Vienna, Wittelsbach for Munich), American museums derive their personality from a multiplicity of collections of which they are the aggregation; for the Metropolitan: Havemeyer, Morgan, Altman, Bache, Wrightsman...their prodigality and that of many others account for that institution's special character. This collection spans 5,000 years of art and covers the entire globe, and consequently we refer to the Metropolitan (or Boston or Cleveland) as encyclopedic; we also term these institutions "collections of collections."

Indeed, we find the eponymous identity of many works of art most tenacious for when we speak of collections of Chinese bronzes, we quite naturally allude to the Winthrop collection at the Fogg or the Pillsbury collection in Minneapolis. Though the Kress Italian pictures are now dispersed throughout many American museums, from Houston to Honolulu to the National Gallery in Washington, the Kress identity still clings to them.

While museum professionals such as Wilhelm von Bode at the Kaiser Friedrich Museum in Berlin and Alfred H. Barr, Jr. at The Museum of Modern Art were great institutional collectors, on the whole we must admit that the greatest collections have been formed by people without institutional restraints, people free to be bold, willful, and capricious; people who have no fear, in indulging their passion, of jeopardizing their reputations—or their jobs. Private collectors are free to acquire as many works by one artist or of a type and period as they desire; they purchase for themselves and not out of some sense of responsibility to an ill-defined public need. Museum directors or curators can ill afford to be so daring or individualistic, to seek out bargains, take enormous risks, or make too many mistakes.

Whereas private collectors can purchase works of art at any price, often paying in excess of market value if they feel only that will net the prize, curators find that Acquisitions Committees tend to frown on this. To the credit of the Metropolitan's own Acquisitions Committee, though, I am happy to record that the Trustees on occasion have recommended paying more (at auction, of course) than the amount proposed by the curators and director, and I can state from my own experience that the Acquisitions Committee (and especially those members who are collectors themselves) often have emboldened a timorous curator by spontaneous enthusiasm and endorsement.

While many a curator may perceive acquisitions committees as a body of amateurs blind or even hostile to the more arcane purchases and to works of art that are not ostensibly attractive or "pretty", these committees do serve to insure that works of art be striking, in other words, that quality and significance be accompanied by a modicum of éclat. The need to secure the approval of amateurs forces curators to keep in mind the public they serve and diminishes the risk of encumbering the collection with too many works of art of purely documentary value. (Nothing is duller than the routine university museum formed by curators and academics to serve as a laboratory for the art history department).

Of course, there are instances when the documentary and more modest examples of artistic creation should be acquired; they can contribute to a deeper understanding and appreciation of related works of transcendent beauty and help to provide a more complete portrayal of civilizations whose character cannot be fully deduced from contact with only their highest achievements. Curators, like private collectors, are at their best when they are passionate in their acquisitiveness and encouraged in the expression of their strongest convictions, and ironically, curators, in truth, should be allowed some of the caprice and freedom of the private collector (which many would be if they disposed of personal fortunes rather than of public funds). To urge a curator to buy outside his primary field of interest or specialization simply in the aim of comprehensiveness, is to invite, at best, dullness—and at worst, mistakes.

In fact, we can afford to be patient. After all, another curator is bound to follow with a different field of specialization and he will, in time, redress the synoptic balance; thus, while museums are primarily an aggregate of privately formed collections, their character is also derived from a succession of curatorial biases and they may, therefore, be termed as well a palimpsest of professional specializations—all, of course, "In Quest of Excellence."

102 Benin, Hornblower, *17th century*
The Brooklyn Museum

195 *Hans Hofmann,* Goliath, *1960*
University Art Museum, University of California,
Berkeley

39

The Baltimore Museum of Art

Raphael's *Portrait of Emilia Pia da Montefeltre* was acquired by Jacob Epstein, a Baltimore businessman and collector of old master paintings, in 1925, shortly after it had turned up in the Vienna art market. A modern rediscovery, it came highly recommended by Bernard Berenson to whom the attribution was beyond dispute. Allowing for some dissention by scholars since Berenson, the painting which was bequeathed to the Baltimore Museum in 1951, is generally considered authentic and of the hand of the very young Raphael. X-radiographs and infrared photography have revealed that the neckline of the dress has been altered and that the veil surrounding the face is of a later date. Such over-painting is not uncommon and may have resulted from a change in the sitter's status (Emilia Pia became a widow in 1500) or from the need to cover damage. Conservators who have examined this oil and tempera on wood agree with scholars of Italian Renaissance painting that the portrait dates from the 16th century.

Few Renaissance courts were more famous for their elegant life style than that of Urbino. According to Vasari, the young Raphael painted three pictures for Duke Guidobaldo da Montefeltre, including one of Guidobaldo's wife, the Duchess Elisabetta Gonzaga in the Uffizi. Its frontal pose and somber expression relate the portrait of Elisabetta to that of Emilia Pia, her half-brother's wife; the elaborate detail of clothing, jewelry and landscape background as well as its better state of preservation, contrast with the Baltimore painting. Both ladies are best remembered for their role in Baldessare Castiglione's *Book of the Courtier*.

A loan moratorium at the Baltimore Museum of Art regretfully limited its representation in this exhibition to one painting.

The Walters Art Gallery

26

The champlevé enamel plaque in the Walters Art Gallery collection was once the central part of an altar cross attributed to the monastery of Grandmont workshop, outside Limoges. The so-called Grandmont enamels are the earliest and rarest of the Limoges enamels. Only two complete Grandmont crosses have survived, one in the Cleveland Museum of Art and one in Milan's Museo Poldi Pezzoli. A look at those fully preserved examples enables us to mentally reconstruct the parts missing from the Walters fragment.

The censers visible beneath Christ's hands, suggest that the angels who swayed them once appeared on the ornate potences or terminals on either end. The oval center, a typical feature of Limoges crosses, indicates that a Christ in Majesty appeared on the opposite side of the original crucifix. The drawing of Christ's chest is an anatomical variant on its more elaborate Byzantine prototype. A slight contrapposto movement and the richly detailed nimbus redeem the starkly treated limbs and loincloth. Originally, top and bottom extensions may have included angels ready to carry Christ off to heaven and St. Peter holding the keys of the kingdom.

In the 12th and 13th centuries, Limoges was a center of enamel craft and the hub of a lively trade supplying Europe with religious objects. The earliest enamel technique was cloisonné which originated in Byzantium and spread around the world as far east as China. In this technique, little fences outlined the design on a metal field. Powdered glass, mixed with the metallic oxides necessary to obtain the desired colors, was placed in the enclosures and was then fused by heat and polished to achieve an even surface. Champlevé enamel, used in this fragment, was a simplified means of achieving an effect comparable to the earlier method and it became the hallmark of Limoges. Here, in direct contrast to cloisonné, the design was dug out of the copper plate and was filled in with enamel. In a later simplification, the background only was enameled, and the figures were engraved and gilded.

Medieval art held a special attraction for Americans of Henry Walters' generation. A collector of manuscripts since just after the turn of the century, the Baltimore railroad baron turned to the unfashionable field of Early-Christian and Byzantine art, and in the last years of his life, acquired, in the words of Walters Art Gallery curator, Richard H. Randall, Jr., "the exquisitely beautiful and the ignored." The Limoges crucifix qualified on both counts and epitomized Henry Walters' taste. It was characteristically purchased from one of his favorite dealers, Henri Daguerre, who had himself acquired it at the sale of the famous Frédéric Spitzer collection in 1929.

Motivated by the conviction that illustrated books formed an integral part of the history of art, Henry Walters began acquiring illuminated manuscripts soon after coming into his inheritance in 1895. By the time of his death in 1931 he had assembled as part of the museum collection in Baltimore some 750 examples of Near Eastern and European illumination which form the outstanding nucleus of the total of c. 3,000 items in the Department of Manuscripts and Rare Books.

Of the wide range of schools of illumination represented between the ninth and early 16th century, the French sector forms a particularly important group as the result, no doubt, of Henry Walters's Francophile tendencies developed during his four-year residency in Paris as an adolescent. The representation of French medieval and renaissance devotional books is, in fact, outstanding among American collections. As far as purchase policies were concerned, the younger Walters depended largely on a handful of European book dealers who kept him informed on opportunities available and laid aside items of potential interest for him to inspect on regular buying trips abroad. His favorite stopping-off places for manuscripts were Léon Gruel's bookbinding firm on the rue Saint-Honoré in Paris and Leo S. Olschki's handsome vaulted palazzo-shop in Florence.

It was from the latter source that the Book of Hours in the exhibition was acquired shortly before World War I. Like many of these richly illuminated books for private devotion produced in great quantity for lay patrons during the 15th century, this west French example of c.1460-65 was destined for a lady as evidenced by the use of the Latin female gender for the supplicant in several prayers. Affiliation with, or at least affinity for, the Franciscan order is indicated by the inclusion of saints such as Francis, Clare, and Bernardino of Siena (canonized in 1450, only a decade or so before the manuscript was completed). This connection is further reflected in the emphasis on the suffering of Christ exemplified in the unusually full Passion cycle integrated, doubtless at the behest of the patroness, with the traditional series of Infancy scenes in the Office of the Virgin. The Entombment of Christ on view in the exhibition fully reveals the pathos of the event witnessed by the Three Maries, St. John, the Magdalen, and two scoffing soldiers in the background. The women's chalkwhite faces and veils, which match Christ's shroud, add a stark note to the rich panoply of color and gold furnished by costume and landscape.

The relatively simple but ambitious style throughout the manuscript remains to be more closely studied for links with centers of illumination, particularly in Brittany and the Loire region. At the same time, north European influence is most notably in evidence in the large border-motifs whose scale and character echo designs on engraved playing cards utilized especially by German and Netherlandish illuminators in the middle decades of the 15th century. The Walters Hours represents an outstanding early example of enthusiastic reliance on such designs in a French atelier. While at certain openings one finds exact replicas of noted playing card motifs in the borders, deviations inspired by this source also make their appearance. This is the case around the miniature of the Entombment. Of added interest here is the symbolism of selected creatures whose scale lends weight to the supposition of further meaning beyond their ornamental function. While Faith is implicit in the renderings of the two dogs, the

Resurrection is alluded to by the snail in front of the elephant and castle, a symbol of Christ tellingly positioned below the bird-allegory of the soul.

In its stylistic and iconographic complexity, the illustrative program of this French 15th century prayerbook typifies not only comtemporary taste and artistry but also Henry Walters's uncanny connoisseurship. Time and again, among the illuminated manuscripts as in other areas of his collecting interests, one is left in awe of the expertise underlying his unerring instinct for the unusual in which quality is merged with distinctiveness.

(Lillian Randall)

2

The head-cloth with regular stripes, alternately rough and polished, and the lappets that once completed it on each side, are an indication that this sculpture portrays a king. There are traces of red coloring on the rough surfaces of the gray granite. The head is broken off at the neck and at the back. Frontal damage includes the nose, later restored, and the uraeus or sacred asp on the head-cloth that served as a symbol of sovereignty. Clearly of the Late Period (663-332 B.C.), this head of a 26th dynasty king is typical of Henry Walters' interest; he began collecting Egyptian and Persian art as early as 1897, and Late Period Egyptian is now the Gallery's strength.

University Art Museum, Berkeley

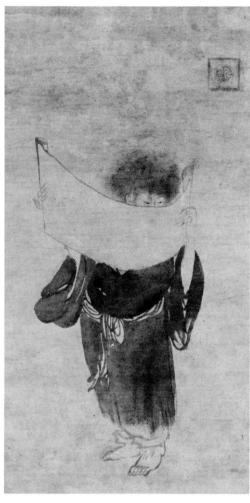

15

Hans Hofmann's profoundly effective role as a teacher of painting and his authoritative style as a practitioner of the medium, provided a direct conduit for European aesthetic theory to spill into American painting. Hofmann furnished his New York students with the textbook model of an equilibrating fusion of 20th century pictorial concepts developed in Europe—those of Matisse and Mondrian. Throughout his long life, this immigrant artist has been faithful to a self-imposed mandate to communicate in word and work the best that could be gleaned from both those artists.

Goliath, as a formal and coloristic statement, is an example of this dual orientation. With its color-saturated rectangles floating on a sea of brush strokes and spatula smears, it illustrates the flowering of Hofmann's style once he was freed from the imperatives of teaching and could embark upon the crowning phase (1958-66) of his career. *Goliath's* composition owes a debt to Cubism as did Mondrian's grid. In its orgiastic burst of color, this painting pays tribute to Matisse from his *Fauve* start to his paper cutout apogee. The tension that exists between the individual components in this shotgun wedding of the painterly and the geometric, however blunt to the observer's eye and grating on his sensibility, is exactly what the proponent of painting's "push-and-pull" theory had in mind as he deliberately steered clear of pictorial resolution. Unlike Matisse, he never compared good art to the comfort of an arm chair.

"The rectangles seem to have been squeezed out of the densely packed Hofmann surface like squared-off bubbles rising to the top of a thick stew," painter and art writer Walter Darby Bannard once graphically observed. Indeed, their back-and-forth positioning is not always readable; there is little illusion of depth, and the impression is one of superimposition and floating on the surface. With its six asymmetrically positioned rectangles of distinct hues, forward-facing and resplendent, against a churning background of coagulated paint, *Goliath* felicitously summarizes Hofmann's contribution to Abstract Expressionism at its mature stage.

Lo-ch'uang lived in the Liu-t'ung-ssu, the temple on the West Lake near Hangchow and became a follower of Mu-ch'i who resided in the same complex. Recent opinions tend to accept as genuine, the artist's seal in the upper right, previously considered a Japanese interpolation. Han-shan and his companion Shih-te were T'ang dynasty monks around whom Ch'an anecdotes and legends collected; they were among the most popular subjects in Ch'an painting. A collection of poems is attributed to the monk Han-shan, and he may be reading his own poetry in this curiously expressionistic drawing. His forward leaning, foreshortened posture, the scanning eyes visible above the scroll and the unruly hair give it power and immediacy. This impressive Late Sung ink on paper was added to the museum's Asian collection in 1970, at the persuasion of Professor James Cahill and with funds raised through the sale of lesser items from Japan.

A follower of Nicolas Poussin and Claude Lorrain, Jean-François Millet, better known as Francisque Millet, was equally enamored by the Roman countryside, the embodiment of classicist beauty for French painters of that era. We compare him with Claude because of his idyllic, rather than ideal, treatment of the landscape. Millet does not aim at topographic exactitude but his small-scale composition, *Landscape with Mountains and Plume of Smoke*, suffused with the hazy, yet luminous atmosphere of a late afternoon in the Campagna, evokes the poetic essence of a bucolic existence in a setting resonant with echoes of antiquity. The plumes of smoke coming from the mountains in the background suggest volcanic activity that must have appeared as exotic to French eyes as the stele and temple fragments past which the cattle are herded to a drinking hole. This gem of a painting encapsulates the concept of landscape in 17th century France and eminently meets the teaching needs of a university museum.

62

The Brooklyn Museum

Benin bronzes, spanning a period of at least five centuries, are a reminder of the long, artistic traditions on the African continent that have survived to our day only in those cases in which durable materials were employed. Oral tradition places the introduction of metalworking to Benin in the year 1280. Rare examples of Benin sculpture can be dated in the 16th century by the Portuguese costumes they depict. Recent casts in the old manner are not uncommon. The art of the Benin people became an instant sensation in 1897, on the return of a British expeditionary force sent there on a punitive mission to restore order after the massacre of her majesty's trade representatives. Among their treasures were the masterfully cast bronzes retired to storage from the royal palace in the 18th century.

It is to this source that the Brooklyn *Hornblower*, an attendant preceding an Oba or king, and all the world's best Benin sculpture, can be traced. Working exclusively for the court and its elaborate ancestor cult, the royal artisan maintained an appropriately decorative and remarkably realistic style. The hollow figure was cast by the lost-wax method in an alloy of copper, zinc and lead, containing tin, iron, nickel and silver as impurities. A special refinement was to enliven the eyes with pupils of iron set in the wax model before casting. The guilloche-bordering of the kilt was cast, but the other patterns of Moorish derivation were added by tooling—also called chasing—of the surface. At the time of its completion, this figure would have been placed on an altar in the palace, honoring the royal ancestors of the Benin nation.

The first exhibition of African art at the Brooklyn Museum took place in 1923. It included 1,454 objects that had been purchased in Brussels as one collection by the anthropologist Stewart Culin, first curator of the Department of African, Oceanic and New World Cultures. In the catalogue for this exhibition, Culin expressed his conviction that these objects belonged to the realm of art rather than ethnography: "The entire collection, whatever may have been its original uses, is shown under the classification of art; as representing a creative impulse, and not for the purpose of illustrating the customs of the African people....Of all the exotic arts, indeed, from which our world is seeking stimulation, the writer regards it as the most vital."

The painters who established the tradition of a national landscape art emerged in the 1820s and became known, though they were never an organized group, as the Hudson River School. An 1825 exhibition of landscapes by Thomas Cole in New York marked its beginnings. Cole was by far the most interesting painter in the group. In his grandeur of conception, power of imagination and passionate convictions, he is closer to the turbulent heart of the Romantic Movement than any American painter at that time. His work gives free reign to emotions stirred up by contemplating the wilderness, in its terror-provoking as well as in its mind-lifting aspects. By 1846, two years before the artist's death, the terribilità had subsided and the sublime had become domesticated.

The Pic-Nic, an unabashedly romantic outing of young people near the shore of a mountain lake in the Catskills, is, according to Barbara Novak, one of the artist's finest pictures in the Claudean style. Claude Lorrain, master of the calm repose, exemplified the beautiful in a picturesque sense in contrast to Salvator Rosa's preference for the sublime. Picturesque was a term introduced by William Gilpin in 1748 and it specified natural beauty as that which had been aided and abetted by the man of letters with an interest in antiquity. *The Pic-Nic* demonstrates a more pragmatic, and therefore perhaps typically American, encounter with nature; from mythic times, symbolized by ageless woods and mountains, we have pleasantly landed in human time.

In his "Essay on American Scenery," published in *The American Monthly Magazine* of January 1836, Thomas Cole wrote: "In what has been said I have alluded to wild and uncultivated scenery; but the cultivated must not be forgotten, for it is still more important to man in his social capacity—necessarily bringing him in contact with the cultured; it encompasses our homes, and, though devoid of the stern sublimity of the wild, its quieter spirit steals tenderly into our bosoms mingled with a thousand domestic affections and heart-touching associations—human hands have wrought, and human deeds hallowed all around."

This delightful pastoral scene, commissioned from Thomas Cole by James Brown, was exhibited at the National Academy of Design in 1846, the year the artist painted it. In an effort to recapture some of the great American art that had eluded it, the Brooklyn Museum, with A. Augustus Healy funds, acquired *The Pic-Nic* from the Brown family for a then record-setting sum in 1967.

The Hindu God, Vishnu, the Supreme Being, from whom the world first emanated in purity and order, is represented in his youthful manifestation as Krishna, an anthropomorphic divine savior. An example of the earliest phase of bronze casting in Nepal, this magnificent figure from the 10th century displays the characteristic features of Nepalese sculpture, youthful appearance of the figure, and a concern for surface ornament combined with a vitality of expression. In the tenth century in Nepal, the reigning Licchavi Dynasty were patrons of the cult of Vishnu, and many Vaisnava temples were erected at that time.

Vishnu's role in the world as the mediator between the antagonistic energies of the universe is symbolized by Krishnu's defeat of the serpent demon (Kaliya), who had to resign his power and withdraw to the sea, freeing the idyllic life of man from the serpent's poison. However, according to Hindu philosophy, evil power cannot be eliminated without disrupting the counterplay between destructive and productive energies. Therefore, in his mercy, and for the good of the human race, Kaliya was assigned to a more remote sphere. Vishnu, in his role of moderator, has restrained the overbearing impact of the destructive, disruptive powers.

Vishnu in his charming form of Krishna blends the god incarnate with the grandeur of his cosmic being. In his four arms he carries his four symbolic attributes. In one uplifted hand he is carrying the sharp-rimmed battle discus, the wheel (cakra) which he hurls against his opponents; the other raised arm bears his iron club (kaumodaki). In his lowered right hand he holds the lotus, which symbolizes his energy of creation; the lowered right hand bears the conch.

(Brenda Williamson)

The most important acquisition of art by an American in the Brooklyn Museum's early years, and the cornerstone of its watercolor collection, was the 1909 purchase of 80 watercolors by John Singer Sargent. When the works were shown at Knoedler, *American Art News* commented upon the circumstances of the exhibition: "The collection....represents Mr. Sargent's work for the past 20 years. He sent them to Mr. Knoedler with the instructions to sell, if he sold at all, only to some museums in an Eastern state or to some large Eastern collector, with the requirement that the collection should be kept together for public exhibition." (February 27, 1909) A. Augustus Healy, then the Museum's President, had his portrait painted by Sargent two years earlier and greatly admired the artist's work. He undertook to raise the sum of 20 thousand dollars, making a generous contribution himself, to acquire the exhibition.

In the summer of 1908, Sargent was joined on one of his climbing trips in the Swiss Alps by his old friends Alma and Lawrence Harrison and Leonard Harrison. While his companions rested, Sargent was apt to paint their relaxed poses. Here, Leonard Harrison enjoys smoking his pipe, sprawled on the bed of a simple inn. Almost monochromatic, this watercolor reveals how much subtle variety Sargent could derive from a limited range of color.

111

128

12

42

According to his notebook, John Smibert painted a portrait of "James Bodween Jnr" early in 1736, near the height of his American career. The future governor of Massachusetts, after whom the College was to be named, is pictured here with stringbow and arrow, theatrically contrived, against the backdrop of a stageset landscape. Pose and clothing of the Colonial youth were properly British and borrowed, as was the custom, from fashionable imported engravings. As a portrait painter, Smibert was modestly proficient in the court style of Sir Godfrey Kneller who dominated English portrait painting in the early 18th century. Although there is some lively brushwork, the boy's lack of facial expression and a stereotyped physiognomy suggest its author's limitations.

Smibert was among the first significant artists to emigrate from England to the New World, settling in Boston in 1730. The city's ample patronage, a lack of local competition and the social prestige resulting from his marriage, led to his establishment as the leading New England portrait painter during the first half of the 18th century. Smibert's foreign training, informally received in London, Florence and Rome prior to his coming to America, further enhanced his artistic reputation. His role extended beyond the stylistic impact of his work upon that of the local painters. Entrepreneurial in the spirit of his adoptive country, Smibert organized exhibitions of his work, sold artists' supplies and imported "the best Metzotinto Italian, French, Dutch and English Prints..."

Dupré is considered the outstanding medalist of the High Renaissance in France. His medalic activity dates from 1597 to his death in 1643. From 1604-39, Dupré was *contrôleur général* of the French mint. He seems to have been in Italy from c. 1611 to 1613, and from that date on his medals lose some of their French delicacy in exchange for an Italian vigor and robustness. The two medals on exhibition, one of Francesco de'Medici (1594-1614), brother of Cosimo II, the other of Maria Magdalena of Austria, Grand Duchess of Tuscany (1591-1631), wife of Cosimo II, are hollow cast bronzes dated 1613 and designed by Dupré, in the Italian manner, while at the Medici court in Florence.

A medal is a piece of metal, generally bronze or lead, which has been struck or cast in the form of a coin. Unlike coins, medals are commemorative in function and are not a medium of exchange. The value of a medal is determined by the quality of its design and its rarity rather than by the intrinsic worth of its material. Probably first conceived as an imitation of Roman commemorative medallions and coins, the medal is a creation of the Italian Renaissance and gained currency as a vehicle for local diplomacy and personal friendship.

The Molinari Collection of Medals and Plaquettes at Bowdoin College was given in 1966 by Amanda Marchesa Molinari in memory of her husband, Cesare Molinari d'Incisa. Notable for both its size and breadth, the collection numbering 1,500 items contains some of the better known Italian Renaissance medals and plaquettes, European medals made through the 19th century, and Northern European plaquettes.

The Molinari medals and plaquettes, with the excellent 1976 catalogue accompanying them, represent an intellectual aspect of the Bowdoin collections appropriate to a college environment. The presence of the medals attest to a scholar's pursuit, which medals by tradition have been, and demand, besides a study of history, profound knowledge of ancient and modern languages and iconography in order to be deciphered.

42 *Guillaume Dupré*, Pair of medals: Maria
Magdalene of Austria and Francesco de' Medici, *1613*
41 *Francesco Vanni*, Madonna with Infant Jesus
and St. John

51

The Bowdoin College Museum of Art boasts the country's first collegiate drawing collection, an 1811 gift from the Honorable James Bowdoin III. Friend and political associate of Thomas Jefferson, who may have aroused his interest in art, Bowdoin was commissioned minister plenipotentiary to Spain in 1804. From 1805 to 1808, he lived in Paris where Napoleon's armies were returning in those years with artistic booty from Italy and other European countries. The drawings Bowdoin bequeathed to the College were collected, in part, during his tour of duty abroad and came, for another part, from his family's purchase of the contents of the Smibert studio.

The 1811 drawing collection consists of 142 sheets, most from the 16th and 17th centuries, with Italian drawings forming its nucleus. Valued at $7.75, the two portfolios of drawings remained locked up in the library, uncatalogued, until 1881 when they were inventoried and, four years later, were incorporated into the Bowdoin Museum collections. The *Madonna with Infant Jesus and St. John*, a red chalk drawing by the Siennese Francesco Vanni, dates from the end of the 16th or the beginning of the 17th century. As a youth, Vanni went to Bologna and then to Rome, where he entered the studio of Giovanni Becchi and received advice from Federico Barocci whose style he emulated. There is a painting of the same subject in the Hampton Court collection to which the Bowdoin drawing may bear some relationship.

41

Fogg Art Museum

The Venetian painter Lorenzo Lotto, whose anarchical, confused and dreamy temperament rendered him ill-prepared to leave the 15th century, resisted the influence of Giorgione and Titian and paid a heavy price for it. After an initial journey to Rome, in 1509, he spent his life wandering from one place to another, appearing in Bergamo in 1526, in Treviso in 1532 and in the Marches in 1535. Remaining attached to Giovanni Bellini, among Venetian painters, and imitating Raphael in Rome, without much success, Lotto betrayed affinities with Flemish and German art and could be uneven, bizarre and platitudinous in his landscapes, portraits and scenes from the lives of Christ and the saints. His account book, which he started in 1538 at Ancona, is the record of a life full of setbacks and incidental commissions. One entry reads: "September 1549: To Friar Angelo Farfatti of St. Dominic, a St. Peter Martyr as large as himself in his portrait."

There is a grave and nostalgic feeling of intimacy in this portrait of a Dominican friar who wished to see himself as St. Peter Martyr. Two years before his death, Lotto entered the Santa Casa of Loreto as a lay brother. In a world buzzing with fashionable new ideas on the treatment of drapery and the rendering of landscape, Lotto represents Friar Angelo with medieval disregard for setting, characterization, adornment and true response to the torture inflicted upon the saint's head and chest. A former owner of the picture must have thought this wearily accepted martyrdom to be lacking in veracity, for the hatchet, if not the sword, was painted out and became visible again in a 1923 cleaning. Lotto's *Portrait of a Dominican Friar*, the prototypical teaching institution's "study collection picture," was given to the Fogg in 1964 by Edward W. Forbes in memory of Alice F. Cary.

Edward Waldo Forbes, the collector, is best known for the outstanding group of Italian paintings that he began to acquire in 1899, years before they became popular through Bernard Berenson's well publicized connoisseurship. His collection, generously loaned from the beginning to the Fogg Art Museum, provided material for instruction in the fine arts at Harvard University. Forbes attained prominence in conservation without ever having engaged in the practice of technical examination or treatment of works of art. His position in this field seems to have rested on his persistent appeal for attention to it. He did, on the other hand, have some knowledge of painting techniques. In his diary of 1906, he mentions how, after buying the *Saint Peter Martyr* from C. Fairfax Murray in London, that gentleman suggested he go immediately to Venice to study the art of tempera painting. In 1909 Forbes became director of the Fogg Art Museum, a position he filled until 1944. When the acquisition of some paintings proved out of reach, he found relatives and friends to help him. Mrs. Cary, his aunt, in whose memory he gave the Lotto painting, was one of these; she supplied the funds for various paintings that were acquired in the Fogg's early days.

Madame d'Haussonville (1818-1882), née Louise de Broglie, portrayed here in her late 20s, was the granddaughter of Mme. de Staël and the great-granddaughter of the financier Jacques Necker. In 1836 she married the Vicomte Othenin d'Haussonville, deputy, senator, historian and member of the French Academy. Not to be outdone by her distinguished husband, Louise d'Haussonville turned to writing, as had her grandmother, and in later years published an historical novel and two biographies, one devoted to the last years of Lord Byron. In the 1860s, the critic Prosper Merimée maliciously described the once celebrated beauty as mean, fat, balding and scarred by smallpox.

Ingres accepted the commission for her portrait in 1842, and that year painted a preliminary oil sketch for an oval portrait facing to the right. During the following three years, Ingres continued to work on the portrait; but he abandoned his original plan and began extensive studies on a new composition which culminated in the elaborate and beautifully detailed portrait finished in 1845, now in the Frick Collection. For that final composition,

Ingres reversed the Vicomtesse's pose and placed her in front of a small fireplace with a velvet valance and curtains and garniture of vases before a mirror which reflects her image.

Almost two dozen drawings exist of this attractive young woman, practically half of which are at the Ingres Museum in Montauban, testifying to the artist's thoroughness and his demand for perfection in preparing for a portrait. In this study, Ingres is concerned with the spatial arrangement of the figure and the angular placement of the console and mirror. The costume is barely sketched but the face shows great immediacy although, in the final portrait in the Frick Collection, the parted lips have closed, the stiff finger pressing against the cheek has curled under the chin and the pressure of the hips against the mantel has eased. Painting and drawing differ in that the drawing has Ingres' cool voluptuous touch without the formal conventions and restraints of the painting.

This portrait study is part of the Fogg's important group of paintings and drawings by Ingres, the largest gathering of his work outside of France. The drawing came to the Fogg as part of the Meta and Paul J. Sachs Bequest. Paul Sachs, former Associate Director and Professor of Art at Harvard, assembled one of the great drawing collections in America. A legend in his own time, his passion for drawing enlightened generations of Harvard students and inspired some of the best among them to enter upon a museum career.

In 1942, Ernest Blaney Dane, Harvard Class of 1892, and Helen Pratt Dane gave to the Fogg Art Museum their distinguished collection of Chinese ceramics, jade, and crystal in order to mark the 50th anniversary of Mr. Dane's graduation from the University. In period, quality and number, the Dane collection complements the 1943 Grenville L. Winthrop bequest of early Chinese art. The Dane gift is the largest body of Oriental ceramics ever given to the Fogg and remains the core material for late Chinese ceramic studies at the Museum. Outstanding among the fine art in the collection are more than 70 pieces of Chün-ware which date from the Sung (960-1279 A.D.) through the Ming (1368-1644 A.D.) dynasties and which constitute one of the largest collections of the ware in existence. The three small pieces are part of a group of eight cups, the character of which differs from the main portion of the Dane Chün-ware collection, which is composed primarily of planters and bulb bowls.

(Courtesy, the Fogg Art Museum)

94

14

Albright-Knox Art Gallery

In 1911, during his first stay in the French capital, Chagall painted what amounts to the earliest known version of *I and the Village*, a happy reminiscence of life in the Ukranian village of Vitebsk where he was born 24 years earlier. In 1925, after he returned once again to France, at odds with the Soviet system in which he had been allowed to play a supporting role, he settled in the village of Montchauvet, where some of the images of the past came back to him. Here he painted *Peasant Life*, also known as *Russian Village*, and several replicas of *I and the Village*, the former considered superior in composition as it puts man and beast nose to nose. Both compositions are based on a free association of images drawn from folklore, memories and the imagination, pieced together by the artist in a dream-like atmosphere.

The principal motif in both *I and the Village* and *Peasant Life*, is that of a young man and his horse—here feeding the horse carrots—suggestive of a symbiosis between man and beast, which is more easily achieved in the country's idyllic and unspoiled environment. The circular movement of foreground and background recalls not only the shape of the earth but suggests the dance of life, reinforcing the idea of natural coexistence. At the left, a family sits at a table inside a building bearing a plaque inscribed with Russian letters—presumably a shop sign referring to Chagall's mother's grocery store. The optimistic tone of the painting is heightened by the images of dancing figures and a carriage ride. Horse and man are encircled by hues of red, green and yellow, seemingly reflecting the settled and contented atmosphere of Montchauvet. It is easy to see how *Fiddler on the Roof* could draw its inspiration from a picture like this.

In 1939, through the generosity of Seymour H. Knox and his family, other donors, and under the guidance of director Gordon Washburn, a pioneering program for the collecting of contemporary art got underway. That program not only helped acquire some of the Gallery's finest pictures but indelibly stamped it with a modern character. The Room of Contemporary Art with its own purchase fund and special committee was responsible for the choice of *Peasant Life*, bought from Chagall's American dealer Pierre Matisse, in 1941, the year the artist fled to these shores from Nazi-occupied Europe.

No painting could do greater justice to the Futurists' desire to portray subjects in motion than Giacomo Balla's *Dynamism of a Dog on a Leash*, yet there is something slightly comical in seeing not the celebration of "deep-chested locomotives pawing the tracks, roaring cars that ride on grapeshot or planes whose propellers chatter in the wind," as called for in the 1909 *Futurist Manifesto*, but the demure hemline of the striding owner of a lap dog hard put to keep its mistress's pace. Balla had remained aloof from the movement until 1912, the year this picture was painted, so the Futurist rhetoric, we may presume, had kineticized his vision but not yet lifted his visors to that brand new world of modern marvels.

Balla reputedly painted this witty study of a skittering dachshund emulating the staccato steps of its half-seen mistress in May 1912 while visiting one of his students, the Countess Nerazzini, at Montepulciano. The light background with its vibrating contrasts of high-valued pink and green streaks is a proper pictoral equivalent for the white dust of the Tuscan countryside shimmering under a bright summer sun. Joshua Taylor, in his 1961 catalogue for The Museum of Modern Art, called it the first Futurist painting to display a genial sense of humor as Futurism in general tended to be quite a bombastic affair.

In 1910, before making a pictoral commitment, Balla had put his signature to the *Technical Manifesto* of Futurist painting. This document, also signed by Umberto Boccioni, Carlo D. Carrà, Luigi Russolo and Gino Severini, proclaimed that "universal dynamism must be rendered in painting as a dynamic sensation" and that "movement and light destroy the materiality of bodies." Before arriving at these statements, the manifesto argued that "a profile is never motionless before our eyes, but it constantly appears and disappears. On account of the persistency of an image upon the retina, moving objects keep multiplying; their form changes like rapid vibrations in the space through which they pass."

Balla conveys this sense of palpable dynamism through a number of devices that, while not new to painting, are applied with appealing virtuosity. Something of the Divisionists' analysis of form, as it is struck by light into a welter of pure-color dots, lingers in Balla's method of working and in that of his fellow Futurists. Intuitively, he showed himself aware of the finding of Gestalt psychology that the sensation of movement is most convincingly transmitted by a blurred image and broken outline. Antecedents for these superimposed successive images existed in the photographic experiments of the 19th century French psychologist, E. J. Marey, and the contemporary photographic parallels ranging from Antonio Bragaglia's *Fotodinamismo* to Jacques Henri Lartigue's *Grand Prix of the Automobile Club of France*, shot in 1912. Bragaglia, whose specialty was making time exposures of moving objects, befriended Balla and immortalized him as a blurred image in front of his own painting.

A. Conger Goodyear, a member of the Buffalo Fine Arts Academy's Board of Directors—the Academy was the parent organization of the Albright-Knox Art Gallery—played an important role on its Art Committee and became a founding trustee of The Museum of Modern Art in New York. He was an enthusiastic supporter of the experimental and new in art and became instrumental in the formation of the Gallery's modern collection. *Dynamism of a Dog on a Leash* is one of a number of significant paintings A. Conger Goodyear bequeathed to the Albright-Knox Art Gallery in 1964.

The Liver is the Cock's Comb, a key work in the development of Arshile Gorky's style, is the artist's most celebrated painting. Its color range may have been influenced by Kandinsky, its imagery by Miró. The arrival in New York of the Surrealists seeking refuge from the war in Europe brought the Armenian-born Gorky face-to-face with their works and theories.

André Breton took a special interest in this painter and classified him as a Surrealist even though his inspiration was in nature and his imagery was not a figment of the imagination. Of *The Liver is the Cock's Comb* Breton wrote that it struck him as "the great open door to the analogy world...hybrid forms in which all human emotion is precipitated."

To William C. Seitz "the conflated details (botanical and biological organisms) of Gorky's cryptogram confound the most curious mind." Yet Julien Levy, the artist's dealer and close friend, ingeniously suggested that whereas the Greeks consider the liver to be the seat of the soul, it is seen here "erect, proudly touched by rays of the rising sun as the cock crows." Clearly an expression of erotic ecstacy, *The Liver is the Cock's Comb* was painted when the artist, for a few short years, experienced happiness in marriage and simple country living. Immersed in nature, he seemed to look at life from within, searching for meaning and encountering a truth which for him turned out to be painful and ultimately tragic.

In her introduction to the 1981 Retrospective at the Solomon R. Guggenheim Museum, Diane Waldman put Gorky in context; "...in *The Liver is the Cock's Comb* he treats broad area in a manner that prefigures Newman; he experiments with allover patterning before Pollock; he gives disembodied color an independent life before Rothko; he exploits the physicality of paint as de Kooning, who describes him as his mentor, came to represent it. While he explores the relative values and tonalities of colors, he predicts the stain painting of Morris Louis by using thin, almost transparent washes of color."

Seymour H. Knox accounts for the Knox in what was formerly the Albright Art Gallery. Over the past four decades he has been principally responsible for the great strides forward the Gallery has made both in terms of the permanent collection, reflecting this donor's daring and courageous taste, and in terms of the physical plant's expansion with the 1962 addition designed by Gordon Bunshaft of Skidmore, Owings and Merrill.

147

187

5

13

Monet's move in 1883 to the village of Giverny, situated on the Seine halfway between Paris and Rouen, gave him a great deal of fresh subject matter. For everyday inspiration the artist turned to the peaceful countryside surrounding his home—this autumn meadow is a good example—while for more varied and dramatic material he went farther afield. The year 1886 was a dividing line in the art of the epoch as well as in the career of Monet. It marks the completion of Seurat's *A Sunday Afternoon on the Island of La Grande Jatte*, Gauguin's first stay at Pont-Aven, the foundation of the short-lived review *Le Symboliste*, and van Gogh's arrival in Paris. For Monet, it was the year of his most significant change of direction since 1880—"a reorientation," as William C. Seitz has remarked, "mysteriously in harmony with the spirit of Mallarmé, Morisot and Debussy. It could be described as a detente, a relaxation of tension; and it unquestionably reflects the graciousness of his life at Giverny..."

Meadow at Giverny in Autumn followed *Poppy Fields near Giverny* of 1885, also in the Boston Museum collection, in which Monet ushered in the avowed colorism that would become "scientific" in the hands of the Neo-Impressionists and "symbolistic" as carried forward by the painters of Pont-Aven. It preceded the thematic treatments of poplars, haystacks and the facade of Rouen Cathedral. *In Meadow at Giverny in Autumn* Monet made full use of the oppositions of spectral color that he found in nature when working *sur motif*—a progressive development from Impressionism's first, more naturalistic phase of the preceding decade.

Poplars, visible in this picture only by the shadows cast across the sunlit meadow, are a familiar feature in Monet's Giverny landscapes. The high horizon line, varied application of paint, unusual high-keyed color combinations—pink and violet autumn foliage against yellow, blue and green grass—and rhythmic pattern of shadows all minimize the sensation of depth and draw the eye to a carefully composed surface. Light reflected and light coming in from behind, shimmering, changing, filtered and partially obstructed,

shows off Impressionism at its purest and registers, in this intrinsically unspectacular landscape, season, time and weather. The artist's fluid curving brush strokes and decorative range of colors give *Meadow at Giverny in Autumn* a casual and effortless appearance.

In the mid-1920s, when a new wing of the Museum of Fine Arts was contemplated, Hannah and her sister Grace Edwards, offered, with other patrons, to bear the cost of landscaping the interior court and turning it into a garden. Their horticultural interest merged, quite naturally, with one in Impressionist painting. The death of Grace Edwards in 1938 brought into use a bequest made in 1925 by her brother Robert J. Edwards, in memory of their mother, Juliana Cheney Edwards. Under this will the museum received a fund whose income was restricted to the purchase of paintings, as well as a magnificent group of Impressionist pictures, including many by Monet. The Juliana Cheney Edwards Collection is principally responsible for the Museum of Fine Arts' fame as one of the world's great treasure troves of work by this celebrant of the landscape.

This partially intact, second century A.D. Greco-Roman copy in Greek mainland marble of a fifth century B.C. original, once completed a life-size draped statue of Zeus Ammon or a herm-bust of the type that could be found near ancient roadsides. Though not carved in the high Athenian style of its presumed prototype, the Boston head gives a good impression, nonetheless, of the sculpture by the hand of Pheidias and his followers at the time they created the Parthenon frieze. Across the centuries and indirectly, we catch a glimpse of the glory that was Greece.

This majestic head of a mature man with braided hair and full beard is characterized as divine by the remnants of two large horns and ram's ears that once projected from either side of his brow. In our copy, nose and locks are worn, chipped and weathered, but whatever damage the marble has sustained it only slightly impairs the quality of Zeus's well-modelled

features. The sharply defined contours and
the stern, somewhat removed expression
are typical of the style of its third quarter
of the fifth century B.C. original.

The cult of Zeus Ammon was adopted
by Greek settlers in Egypt, and its origins
are identified with the Oasis of Siwa in the
desert west of Alexandria where the sixth
century B.C. Egyptians worshipped the sun
god and oracle Amon-ra; from Siwa to the
Greek colony of Cyrene, Amon-ra became
Zeus Ammon. This cult, one of many
devotional imports from the Near East,
eventually found its way into the
Peloponnesus and the Greek isles. Oracles
of Zeus Ammon were established at Delphi
and Dodona as early as the fifth century.
One century later, on his march through
Egypt, Alexander the Great visited the
original oracle at Siwa. Zeus Ammon's
presence in Roman statuary is attributable
more to the Romans' identification with
Alexander than to the religious
significance of a by then faded cult.

Boston's collection of classical art is
unthinkable without the active
intervention of Edward Perry Warren
(1860-1928), an expatriate who scorned the
city of his birth and lived the greater part
of his life in England. When asked
whether he gave Greek antiquities to
American museums for the sake of the
hundredth person who might appreciate
them, or whether the ideas for which these
antiquities stood were a fundamental
challenge to American conceptions, he
replied: "For both reasons, but especially
for the latter." Warren was a born collector
whose scholarship ran not so much to
books as to objects of antiquity. His
prodigious talent for acquisition, straining
even his ample income, was turned to the
benefit of a museum which prior to
Warren's commitment had largely confined
its classical aspirations to the assembly of
plaster casts. The *Zeus Ammon*, a gift of
Edward Perry Warren, by exchange, was
acquired, following a policy of upgrading,
by the distinguished head of the
Department, Cornelius C. Vermeule whose
name is now as inseparable from the
Museum's history of classical acquisitions
as is that of its early benefactor.

Guardian deities, many derived from
early Indian sources, abound in the
Buddhist pantheon. The Shitennō, or
guardians of the four cardinal points, and
the Jūni Shinshō, or 12 guards who
accompany the Buddha of Medicine,
Yakushi, are among the better known of
these divinities. There are, in addition,
many minor guardians, all of whom wear
armor, bear arms, and have glowering
faces. Because he has no identifying
attributes, it is not possible to determine
which guardian deity this small statue
represents.

The great Japanese temples were
destroyed in 1180 by the troops of Taira no
Shigehira. One of the acts of the finally
triumphant Minamoto was the 1195
rebuilding of the Nara temples which
became the occasion for some of the
greatest sculpture that era has produced. It
set itself apart from the art that had
preceded it by advocating strength rather
than prettiness, realism rather than
formality. Particularly impressive were the
larger than life guardians of the temple
gates with the vajra or thunderbolt and
features that exhibited the terrifying
countenance of the protector Shūkongōjin.
Having a severe if not that frightening a
demeanor, the Boston *Guardian Deity*
seems to linger on the edge of the
aristocratic Heian Period (898-1185) and
its tumultuous replacement by the
Kamakura who ruled from 1185-1333.

Martin Johnson Heade, a landscape
painter who studied with Edward
Hicks and was influenced by Frederic
Edwin Church, is credited with being one
of the founders of Luminism and, past
middle age, with being the inventor of a
tropical still life genre featuring orchids
and hummingbirds. The first hummingbird
picture dates back to an 1863 trip to Brazil.
As the artist saw more of the tropics—
Nicaragua, Colombia, Panama and
Jamaica—orchids and hummingbirds
became a recurrent theme and, after 1871,
his stock image. In 1883, Heade journeyed
to Florida where he met the railroad
builder Henri Morrison Flagler who
encouraged the artist to settle in St.

114

Augustine and who became his faithful patron and supporter.

Orchids and Spray Orchids with Hummingbirds in this exhibition is a version dating from the decade of the 1880s. Ornithologists will recognize the right-hand hummingbird as a Cora's shear-tail or *Thaumastura corae*; horticulturists will identify the large orchid as a *Cattleya labiata* and the small orchids as, probably, *Aerides odoratum loureiro*. Floridians have but to go to the Henry Morrison Flagler Museum in Palm Beach in order to see how Heade, during the last 20 years of his long life, paid homage to the natural beauties of their native state.

Mrs. John Chipman Gray once remarked that the Russian Revolution of 1917 had inadvertently benefited Boston by providing husbands for local spinsters. A remarkable case in point was the concert tenor Maxim Karolik (1893-1963) who, having arrived in the United States in 1922, married Miss Martha C. Codman in 1928. In spite of considerable disparity in their ages, backgrounds and earlier lives, the Karoliks shared a common enthusiasm for the American arts of the 18th century. In 1939, Maxim Karolik and his wife donated the fruit of a decade of judicious collecting to the Museum of Fine Arts as the M. and M. Karolik Collection of Eighteenth Century American Arts. Then, with the same determination that had characterized their earlier effort, the Karoliks proceeded to put together, for the Museum's benefit, and on an equally high level, a collection of 19th century American arts, including folk art. With its extraordinary cross section of American painting, the Karolik Collection, as of 1951 installed in ten newly constructed galleries, enhanced the prestige and contributed to the study of American art as well as to the Museum of Fine Arts' reputation in that fast developing field.

65

The Art Institute of Chicago

On May 11, 1824, Delacroix noted in his diary that he was so impressed by Byron's poem, *The Giaour*, that it made him want to be a poet. Such longings were natural to youths of that era. While copying Veronese, Titian and Rubens at the Louvre, he was befriended by Richard Bonington, the English watercolorist who aroused his interest in Shakespeare, Scott and Byron, literary spurs of the romantic movement. Like all young romantics in Europe at that time, Delacroix identified with the Greeks' clamor for freedom and their uprising against the brutal Turks. Delacroix's heartrending scene of the 1822 Massacre at Chios was presented at the French Salon, in the same year that Byron lost his life at Missolonghi.

"True foes, once met, are join'd till death," Byron had written in 1813, meaning that the combat would end only after the Giaour had mortally wounded the Pasha Hassam who engaged the infidel in battle to avenge his wife's abduction. Avoiding a literal illustration of the poem, Delacroix invented the episode of the crawling swordsman trying to stab Hassam's horse. Byron's melodramatic tale is transposed into oil with a concomitant gain of visionary power and dramatic content. "At least I can express the sublimity of Byron's poetry in painting," Delacroix wrote in his diary. *Combat between the Giaour and the Pasha* was begun in 1824, the year of Byron's death, completed in 1826 and twice refused by the official Salon, in 1827 and 1828. Yet, with its lusciously painted exotic theme and expertly handled action, it is one of Delacroix's finest early works and, arguably, the best of the six known versions, spread out over a lifetime, of the Byronian combat scene.

In 1871, the then 44-year-old Quaker drygoods millionaire and playboy, Potter Palmer, married the 21-year-old Bertha Honore, an aristocratic young woman from a Kentucky family. For the balance of that century and well into the next, Bertha Palmer reigned as the queen of Chicago society and as its emissary to the world. Her indulgences were clothes, jewelry and Impressionist paintings, and the *hôtel particulier* which the Palmers kept in Paris

gave her ample opportunity to shop. Delacroix's *Combat between the Giaour and the Pasha* once adorned the walls of that Parisian residence. Acquired in 1892 (it had earlier belonged to the great French novelist Alexandre Dumas, père), this painting was one of at least five works by Delacroix in her collection. Mrs. Palmer's attraction to Delacroix must be read, as Richard R. Bretell has pointed out, in light of the view, current in the 1890s, that Delacroix, more than Courbet, was the "father" of Impressionism. On loan to the Art Institute since 1930, ownership of the painting was transferred between 1962-65 by a group of heirs and descendants of Mrs. Potter Palmer.

In Italy, the Baroque period did not witness the advent and development of an independent landscape style. The greatest interpretors of the Roman scene, and of an ideal landscape, were the Italianized Frenchmen, Nicolas Poussin and Claude Lorrain, who were guided in their chosen direction by the works of Annibale Carracci and Domenichino. In a cultural milieu in which architecture and sculpture held a monopoly, painters chose between a grand allegorical style, fitting for decoration, or a Caravaggesque realism, wedded to the studio interior and shunning the direct observation of nature. Hence, in Italian art of the 17th century, there was an association of vedute with even the most imaginary scenes.

The Lombard painter Giovanni Benedetto da Castiglione descended upon Rome in 1634. Attracted to Anthony Van Dyck's paintings and Rembrandt's engravings, he set about painting scenes from the scriptures and from classical mythology whose pastoral manner allowed for a good deal of landscape. This *Pagan Sacrifice* with its lively brushwork and color as ambitious as a painting, caught the eyes of Sir William Drake and Lord Kenneth Clark of Saltwood, two of the drawing's former owners. The late keeper of the Queen's collections, Anthony Blunt, speculated that a Christian pendant may have accompanied it. The Chicago

45

17

drawing is, without a doubt, a magnificent example of Castiglione's developed style.

The subject of this monumental drawing is the sacrifice of an ox to a pagan deity on the right, whose identity cannot be determined because he is the only lightly sketched figure in an otherwise fully finished composition. Pagan lore began to appear in Castiglione's work soon after he arrived in Rome and befriended Nicolas Poussin. The Frenchman's powerful example has clearly affected the careful construction and classical detailing as well as the subject of Castiglione's drawing. Technically, this drawing, full of literary references that would have been understood by its erudite Roman audience, belongs to a late moment in his career. Not until the mid-1650s, according to Blunt, did Castiglione produce bozzetti—colored sketches with some modelling and highlights added in opaque pigment. According to recent scholarship, Castiglione obliquely referred, in this highly finished presentation drawing—as in the drawing of a biblical sacrifice that may have matched it—to the religious syncretism then fashionable in Rome.

This sandstone votive ax in the form of a human head appears to have come from the southernmost of the three archaeological regions comprising the coastal plains and river deltas of Veracruz and Tabasco on the Gulf side of the Isthmus of Tehuantepec. In today's terms, that would make it Southern Mexican or Guatemalan. The hacha corresponds to styles centered in that area during Late Classical times (c. 750 to 950 A.D.), and it is characteristic for the Mayan civilization.

The hacha was obviously not suited for use as a hatchet and a ceremonial purpose is more likely. George Kubler has suggested that they are instruments strapped on as body gear in ritual ball-games that often ended in the blood sacrifice of winning players. The hacha forms were the most widely distributed ones of the entire ball-game panoply. The finely profiled Chicago hacha, with its naturalistic features, differs from the generally older models that seem to portray dead players or warriors in a usually more rigidly ornamental style. It bears a relationship to the reliefs of Palenque, the most notable Mayan site of that region. The detailing of the hair and the elaborately featured ear-ornament are typical of the Palenque style.

Allen Wardwell, during his tenure as curator at the Art Institute, acquired this example of the Mayan civilization through the Ada Turnbull Hertle Fund, established in 1949 by Louis Hertle, "in memory of my beloved wife, whose love of things beautiful, pure and true was outstanding."

Western Industrial is a late work, completed just four years prior to the paralyzing stroke that ended Charles Sheeler's dual career as painter and photographer. The 1950s were a busy time for him, with numerous painting and photographing commissions coming on the heels of his first retrospective exhibition, in 1954, at the University of California Art Galleries at Los Angeles. On the occasion of that retrospective, Art in America published a major article by Frederick S. Wight who quoted the artist as saying: "I favor the picture that arrives at its destination without the evidence of a trying journey rather than the one which shows the marks of battle. An efficient army buries its dead."

Sheeler can be said to have performed at least one burial when he "unlearned" his training as a realist under William Merritt Chase and, in the 1920s, aligned himself with the Precisionist group. In the mid-1940s, another, somewhat startling change took place in his painting. His palette became more intense and his viewpoint, which had been evenly balanced between realism and Cubism, leaned more heavily toward the abstract. Sharp-focus, close-up views, strongly influenced by his commercial photography and primarily concerned with industrial architecture, became his theme. To eliminate the marks of battle, he adopted a method of composing his designs on illustration board then working out color on an overlay of plexiglass before he began the final painting. His later works bear a resemblance to advertising art and may have influenced its direction. In *Western Industrial* we can see the double-image, photo-montage effect that added depth to the architecturally constructed canvases and introduced a feeling of atmosphere where none had previously existed.

This painting was among the many gifts the Institute received from Leigh B. Block and his late wife, Mary, who were long-time collectors in Chicago. As a trustee and one-time chairman of the Art Institute of Chicago board, Leigh Block has been responsible for extraordinary gifts to several of the museum's departments.

(Ann W. Heymann)

Ⅰn the last years of his life, when archivists and historians had no more use for his meticulously produced views of old Paris, Eugene Atget, then past 65, hawked his photographs around the studios of Paris, selling them to the likes of Picasso, Braque, Derain and Utrillo. He was thought of as a "primitive," as the Douanier Rousseau of the streets. Like the painter to whom they compared him, Atget appealed to the avant garde of his time. Man Ray and his assistant, the photographer Bernice Abbott, saw to it that, in 1926, four Atget prints were published in *La Révolution Surréaliste*. Three years later, the graphic design and photo journalism-oriented *Foto-Auge* came out with Atget's *Corsets, Boulevard de Strasbourg* as the first of a memorable series of 76 photo reproductions. Suddenly, the modest Atget had become a cult figure and not only did the subjective, idiosyncratic, lyrical and freely chosen photographs of the last decade of his life take on relevance for a small circle of admirers—including the photographers Stieglitz, Man Ray and Edward Weston—but the earlier images fared just as well.

It is difficult to imagine *Corsets, Boulevard de Strasbourg* (c.1905-10) being motivated, as were most of Atget's photographs, by an interest in historic preservation. These Belle Epoque trappings

on display in a working class neighborhood were, however, the perfect document of a period in France's civilization which the photographer took such pains to record. In fact, Atget may have been commissioned by the store's proprietor to immortalize his window display. We know that Atget lugged his heavy camera and glass negatives all over Paris for this purpose and sometimes took days to determine the right set-up, angle, light and mood. Because his old-fashioned apparatus was too slow to stop motion, the photographer favored the early morning when the streets were empty. That seems the moment at which he took *Corsets, Boulevard de Strasbourg*, although the door must have opened unexpectedly, turning one outside display into a blur.

This photograph of a shop window eloquently expresses the measured strength, sober dignity, covert sensuality and stealthy elegance of the French bourgeois tradition. To the Surrealists it appealed because of its erotic promise and its *horror vacui*. *Corsets* anticipates the Surrealist infatuation with the mannequin and Arman's obsessive accumulations of store bought articles. The chance imagery so richly present in *Corsets* is another occasion for Surrealist delight. As for reflections and double imagery, the angle at which Atget shot this storefront prevented the inclusion of the photographer and other sidewalk scenery, discreetly in evidence in some treatments of the same theme. Yet, morning sky and foliage loom unexpectedly in the upper windowpane and glass clearing above the door. Here, fronds seem to sprout like feathers from the neck of the mannequin displayed outdoors.

In *Memoir of an Art Gallery*, Julien Levy reminisces how Man Ray encouraged him to pay a visit to the aging Atget. The encounter was a fateful one and produced a lifelong commitment, on the art dealer's part, to preserving and exhibiting the Atget estate. *Corsets* was among the vintage prints on albumen paper Levy acquired from the photographer in 1927. With other Atget prints and photographs by Cartier-Bresson, Moholy-Nagy, Man Ray and Kertész, it entered the Art Institute of Chicago collection in 1975 as a gift from Jean and Julien Levy.

130

173

Cincinnati Art Museum

Philip IV (1605-1665), King of Spain, ascended the throne in 1621 and was married first to Isabella de Bourbon, later to his niece, Maria Anna of Austria. This portrait depicts the weary, aging king in a black, gold-buttoned coat trimmed with gold braid; a chain over his shoulders disappears beneath the starched white golilla. His senior by five years, Velazquez painted the monarch many times, in a variety of poses, while he served as Painter to the King. This bust-length was one of the most popular poses. Not idealized, as some were, the Cincinnati portrait betrays its sitter's infirm appearance at the approximate age of 50.

At the time this portrait was painted, Velazquez was at the height of his career as a loyal envoy in the king's diplomatic service and a painter at Court. His busy workshop produced portraiture, religious subjects, genre and mythological scenes. Juan Martinez del Mazo, Velazquez's son-in-law, became his principal assistant, but it is impossible to ascertain who, precisely, may have had a hand in the Cincinnati portrait. In his *catalogue raisonné*, August L. Mayer records 22 replicas and copies of the one version in the Prado. Jose Lopez-Rey, a more recent scholar, attributes it—mainly because of its unimpeachable provenance—wholly to Velazquez himself.

The King in this guise and appearance was painted some time between 1651, when Velazquez returned from Italy, and 1657, when an engraving was made by Pedro de Villafranca who obviously based himself on a variant of the Cincinnati portrait. The engraving shows the golilla, chain and Golden Fleece. The badge of that distinguished Order generally hangs below the 12th button on the jacket of this type of portrait and, indeed, the Cincinnati version displayed a Golden Fleece until a 1970 restoration proved it to be of a later hand.

This *Portrait of Philip IV* was bequeathed to the Cincinnati Art Museum by Mary M. Emery in 1927. As early as 1907, Mrs. Thomas J. Emery had provided the Museum with an endowment to make possible, in perpetuity, free admissions on Saturdays so that families could enjoy the galleries together. Besides her bequest of a collection of Old Masters, Mrs. Emery endowed a wing to be named after her.

This *Wooded Landscape with Drover, Mounted Peasants and Pack-horse returning from Market, Shepherds and Flocks of Sheep on Banks, Cottages and Distant Church*, as John Hayes identifies the Cincinnati Gainsborough in his 1982 *catalogue raisonné*, is indebted to the Dutch masters of the same genre and recalls the styles of Watteau and Fragonard in France. England's greatest portrait painter began by painting landscapes and regularly returned to that subject. Cincinnati can boast two fine examples that are essential for a broader understanding of 18th century English art.

The composition is based on two diagonals, one suggestive of the slope of the terrain and its foliage, the other indicative of the peasants' long haul back from the village. John Hayes has drawn attention to the fact that the Claudean idea of a figure pointing out some feature of beauty in the distance makes its first appearance in Gainsborough's oeuvre in this picture. Yet, as in Nicolaes Berchem's imaginary pastorals, the motif is used here quite prosaically and apparently without Claude's poetic intentions.

In 1946, Miss Mary Hanna gave the Museum 32 great paintings by French, English, Northern European and American Masters, including the Gainsborough *Returning from Market*. The same patron had donated a wing to the building in 1927, honoring the memory of her parents, Mr. and Mrs. Henry Hanna. Upon her death in 1956, a superb collection of 19th and 20th century European and American drawings, watercolors and pastels joined the earlier benefaction. Furthermore, she left the Museum Association the largest single endowment in its history.

This feline, dating from the 18th-19th Dynasties (1580-1205 B.C.), with its lustrous patina and rock crystal eyes is a

superb example of New Kingdom sculpture
and representative of what has been
referred to as Egypt's third Golden Age.
The country, once more united under
strong and efficient kings, extended its
frontiers far to the east; tremendous
architectural projects were carried out,
centering on the region of the new capital,
Thebes, and the divine kingship of the
Pharaohs was asserted by their association
with the god Amun. Akhenaten, the 18th
Dynasty's most remarkable ruler who
proclaimed his faith in a single god, also
introduced into art a more relaxed style.
The naturalism in the portrayal of this
feline and its expressive yet elegant
demeanor is typical of this loosening
attitude. In religious terms, the feline was
the incarnation of the god Bast, the "lady
of life."

John J. Emery, son of J. J. Emery whose
1910 endowment fund for art was crucial
to the Museum's early development, was
also the nephew of Mrs. Thomas J. Emery
who, in 1927, bequeathed the wing of the
building bearing her name and housing her
Old Master collection. He continued his
family's tradition of interest in the Museum
by becoming, in 1945, its fifth president. A
year later, Mr. and Mrs. Emery gave the
Museum this feline as one of many objects,
some early Persian gold among them,
with which these generous patrons are
identified.

79

1

The Cleveland Museum of Art

19

Fukaye Roshu whose seal adorns the six-fold screen, *The Pass Through the Mountains*, has only recently been identified as an Edo-period craftsman born in the 12th year of Genroku, 1699, and deceased in the seventh year of Horeki, 1755. He continued the tradition of the master painters Nonomura Sotatsu, who lived a century earlier, and Ogata Korin, still alive at the time. *The Pass Through the Mountains* illustrates the ninth section of the *Ise Monogatari*, a collection of ninth century love poetry largely of the hand of Ariwarano Narihira, popular with the Medieval Kyoto court and even more popular during the Edo (modern Tokyo) period for its decorative flourish and nostalgic atmosphere. The pass made famous by the poet leads across Utsunoyama, a mountain on the old Tokaido road between Tokyo and Kyoto. The evocation of Utsunoyama is a frequent motif in Japanese painting.

Screen paintings were commissioned to brighten the interiors of the new castle architecture of Genroku (1688-1703), a time of hedonism and intense artistic activity. The Cleveland screen is the finest of just a few known works of Fukaye Roshu. The subject's motifs—travelers, horse, mendicant priest and mountain-bound pass—are varied in color and placement though retaining the color scheme of cherry and rust, pale blue and green, and gold, peculiar to this artist.

The Cleveland Museum of Art is a relative newcomer in the field of Oriental art. Although a department was formally organized in 1914, no collections of any great distinction welcomed Sherman E. Lee when he came to Cleveland from Seattle in 1952 to assume the curatorship of Oriental art. It is a tribute to Lee's tenure as curator, associate director and director of the Cleveland Museum of Art, and to his gift for scholarship, that this museum now ranks among the world's best in the ownership and presentation of non-Western art.

In 1930, the Cleveland Museum of Art acquired six objects from the Guelph Treasure, a world famous cache of secularized religious objects, once the proud possession of the Dukes of Brunswick-Lüneburg, Electors of the Holy Roman Empire. Henry the Lion brought back with him from the Crusades relics of the Saints, among them arm bones of the Apostles which were mounted with gold and silver and precious stones. These he presented to the Brunswick cathedral, which Bishop Godehard of Hildesheim dedicated to Saint Blasius between 1030-1037. After the Reformation the Guelph treasure reverted back to the House of Brunswick-Lüneburg, which acted as its custodian until its last owner, son-in-law of the German Kaiser, put it on the market.

Cleveland's acquisition of the Guelph Treasure in which the then director, William M. Milliken, played a decisive role, made that museum, with one stroke, a ranking repository of Medieval art. The country had entered upon a depression, yet over half a million dollars was raised to afford the treasure. It "set the seal upon the future of the Museum," its bulletin proudly proclaimed. While German newspapers cried foul that art dating back to the Crusades was allowed to leave the homeland, 97,000 visitors came to see their city's newest attraction in the mere three weeks of its special display.

The *Reliquary in the form of an Arm*, one of two that have survived, has been attributed to the School of Elbertus, the famed Hildesheim goldsmith. Its most remarkable feature is a double band of figure decoration: above, circles of foliage; below, half circles within which are represented Christ and the Twelve Apostles—not embossed or in repoussé, but carved from the solid metal.

Given to fits of depression and beset by doubts about his art, Vincent van Gogh decided to consult an art collector physician who had befriended several of his fellow painters. Dr. Paul Gachet resided in the most impressive and often painted house in Auvers-sur-Oise, a little village of thatched-roof cottages on unpaved country lanes. He was a specialist in the treatment of melancholy and, himself, touched by a sadness and resignation that attracted the artist. On Wednesday, May 21, 1890, van Gogh moved into Ravoux's modest inn opposite the town hall, where room and board were three francs a day. Dr. Gachet and the innkeeper's daughter were among those who posed for the painter in the last two months of his short and tragic life.

"What excites me the most in my profession, much, much more than anything else, is portraiture, modern portraiture," Vincent wrote to his sister Will in June of that year. "I should like to paint portraits which a hundred years from now will seem to the people of those days like apparitions." He was accurate in projecting how his portraits would come across to the modern viewer. They turned out to be haunting reflections of their maker's state of mind through obsessive identification. To Gauguin he wrote, on June 20, "...I have now done a portrait of Dr. Gachet with the sad expression of our time. Perhaps it is something like what you said of your Christ in the Garden of Olives (see *Agony in the Garden*, 1889, Norton Gallery and School of Art), 'not destined to be understood'..."

Leonard C. Hanna, Jr., an industrialist whose interests included iron ore, coal, pig iron and shipping, began giving reproductions of famous paintings to the Cleveland public schools in 1925. Eleven years later he helped the Cleveland Museum of Art put on an exhibition of van Gogh paintings borrowed from the artist's estate. The sale of van Gogh reproductions broke all records to that time. Encouraged and assisted by the Museum, Leonard Hanna formed one of the finest Impressionist and Post-Impressionist collections in the Midwest. When he died, in 1957, Hanna left his paintings, including *Mlle Ravoux*, to the Museum. Reports at the time called it a minor part of the total bequest which amounted then to the largest single gift ever received by an American art museum, making Cleveland second only to the Metropolitan Museum of Art in the size of its endowment.

124

Columbus Museum of Art

Albert Gleizes may not be one of the "essential Cubists" whose 1907-20 contribution to the history of painting was the subject of last spring's Tate Gallery exhibition organized by the redoubtable Douglas Cooper, but his work is steeped in the Cubist vocabulary and expressive of the Cubist spirit. He entered that historic arena with Metzinger and Le Fauconnier, after Braque, Picasso and Léger, and before Duchamp and Gris. In 1912, Gleizes and Jean Metzinger co-authored *Du Cubism*, a proclamation of the new aesthetic's aims and antecedents. His 1913 *Paysage* in the Ferdinand Howald Collection at the Columbus Museum of Art, is representative of the artist's mature style and a credit to the visual ideas of the 'abstract-decorative' wing of the Cubist movement.

Daniel Robbins has written that, unlike Braque and Picasso, "Gleizes never set out to analyze and describe visual reality. A mandolin, guitar, pipe or bowl of fruit—all more or less neutral objects from daily life—could not satisfy his complex idealistic concepts of true reality. He always stressed subjects of vast scale and of provocative social and cultural meaning." (*Albert Gleizes*. New York: The Solomon R. Guggenheim Museum, 1964) For Gleizes, as for Delaunay in a more spectacular way, Cubism led to pure abstraction. Theoretically, he was more attuned to Mondrian and Kandinsky than to Braque and Picasso. Gleizes took part in *La Section d'Or*, Cubism's first watershed in the fall of 1912 and, defying Picasso's leadership, he wrote that Delaunay, in 1913, had best defined the movement's goal.

In February 1927, John Quinn's vintage collection of modern art went on the auction block. Another early collector of modern art (there were only a handful then), Ferdinand Howald, the owner of a mining fortune in Columbus, Ohio, took advantage of the occasion by buying several Quinn pictures, Gleizes' resplendent *Paysage* among them. In the auction records it was listed as *Landscape at Toul*, but that constituted an anachronism as Gleizes never saw that fortress city until he was mobilized and stationed there in the winter of 1914-15. Although the viaduct in this composition should be a good enough clue, historians of Gleizes' work have not attempted to locate it. We know that the artist painted one of his last pre-war suburban landscapes in Montreuil. Robbins has drawn our attention to the similarity between the Columbus painting and the landscape background of the Kröller-Müller's *Sewing Women* of 1913, a representation of the artist's mother and two sisters at the family home in Courbevoie. Most likely, Paysage is a composite of landscape impressions and not tied to a single place.

Ferdinand Howald's benefaction of the Columbus Museum of Art has been compared, in size and nature of collections, with the Cone sisters' gift to the Baltimore Museum of Art. They dared buying modern when few collectors did, they played favorites, they plunged, and if they liked something they bought a lot of it. A bachelor patriarch with a big house in Columbus and an apartment in New York, Howald began buying the work of American artists at the time of the 1913 Armory Show. He eventually concentrated on French painting but stopped at the time of the Crash. Prompted by William Hekking, director of the then Columbus Gallery of Fine Arts, Ferdinand Howald contributed a substantial part of the money required for a new building and, before his death in 1934, donated his pictures to the people of Columbus.

George Bellows, himself, ranked *Polo at Lakewood* among the best of his early paintings, and Robert Henri, his teacher at the New York School of Art, on seeing it completed, pronounced it the finest picture Bellows had yet created. The painting was executed from sketches made on a visit to Lakewood, New Jersey, where the artist and sports enthusiast had seen polo for the first time. In a letter to a friend, Bellows wrote: "The players are nice looking, the horses are beautiful. I believe they brush their teeth and bathe them in goat's milk. It's a great subject to draw, fortunately respectable."

Fortunately respectable, was of particular significance after the experience of having one of his less accepted paintings and those of others of "The Eight" relegated to a "chamber of obscenities" by the directors of the Carnegie Library where Bellows arranged an exhibition in 1911. Only adult males were admitted to the bolted and guarded room in which pictures of partially or completely unclothed human forms (boxers in an arena and some nudes), were sealed from public view as a compromise to calling off the show altogether. "As if to compensate George for the offense of hiding Knockout from the eyes of the "innocent," the Columbus Art Association purchased *Polo at Lakewood* for nine hundred dollars, almost double the price he had received for his most expensive painting barely a year earlier. The local boy had made good in his home town." (Donald Braider. *George Bellows and the Ashcan School of Painting*. New York: 1971)

Franz Huntington, head of the Columbus Art Association at the time, had seen the expedience of purchasing the work of an artist whose value would soar not many years later. Acquisition of *Polo at Lakewood*, along with Robert Henri's *Dancer in a Yellow Shawl*, constituted the beginning of a favored interest in American art at the Columbus Museum of Art, generously swelled by the contributions of such patrons as Frederick W. Schumacher, Ferdinand Howald and Francis C. Sessions.

(Ann W. Heymann)

The church interior in Dutch painting was a genre unto itself. Stark, spiritual and elegant, it receives light from above which is partially absorbed, partially bounced off pillars, walls and floor. Its spatial order and architectural geometry had a particular appeal to the members of the Dutch Reformed Church and writers have suggested that the influence of Pieter Jansz Saenredam, the undisputed pioneer of the genre, is found, transcended, in Piet Mondrian's Neoplasticist abstractions. The genre's other master, less enigmatic and more scenic, was Emanuel de Witte, twenty years younger than Saenredam and active first in Amsterdam, then in Delft. Once the church interior was a well established subject, by the middle of the 17th century, it attracted a new generation of painters, among them Cornelis de Man, better known for his domestic scenes than for the odd dozen church interiors ascribed to him.

In 1981, the Columbus Museum of Art acquired the signal work by this artist, *Interior of Oude Kerk, Delft*. A cleaning revealed the signature at the base of the column to the left and suddenly a model exists by which other examples of the hand of this heretofore little known painter can be measured. A smallish oil on panel of almost the identical view but populated with different figures, in the Museum der bildenden Künste in Leipzig, is now recognized as a version of and not the prototype for the Columbus picture. Other views of the Oude Kerk in Delft can be found in the Hessisches Landesmuseum, Darmstadt, in the Trafalgar Galleries, London, and in a private collection in West Germany. As a result of the stylistic clues the Columbus picture provides, an Oude Kerk in Delft interior at the Art Institute of Chicago, given to Gerard Houckgeest, should, according to Walter A. Liedtke, be reattributed to Cornelis de Man.

The hand of a painter is identified as often by what it cannot do correctly as by what it typically does well. Cornelis de Man, a dry and eclectic painter, can be spotted by his stiff representation, precise contours and simple local tones which seem to emphasize patterns for their decorative effect. Such hackneyed modelling may have been the artist's shortcut to a more simplified style much as the atmospheric portrayal of daylight is sacrificed to an emphasis of light as shape. There are flaws in the perspective treatment and detailing of architectural elements that suggest a pictorial ability falling somewhat short of that of de Man's closest rival, Hendrick van Vliet whose interior of the same church painted that same year, now in the Metropolitan Museum of Art, provides an instructive comparison.

143

53

Lowe Art Museum

All through the age of art's mechanical reproduction, the medium's practitioners have clung to the myth of manual creation while suspecting some of their more brilliant brethren of ignoring the age-old injunctions against making direct molds from the human body and painting on or from photographs. Rodin may or may not have been guilty of such charges leveled against him but we know what good use Delacroix, Manet and Degas made of the photographer's art. Once artists began owning up to such practices, the taboo was lifted. Credit for that goes to a belief championed by Marcel Duchamp, that art resides as much in the inventive brain as in the crafting hand. Duane Hanson's *Football Player* is a good case in point.

Realistic sculpture, from Rodin to Segal, is an attempt to face the subject squarely and portray it with candor. It neither distorts nor adorns but it admits selectiveness and, ultimately, aspires at poetry. Veristic sculpture, practiced most interestingly today by John de Andrea and Duane Hanson, is not so much different in essence as it is in degree—the same basic attitudes apply, but with a vengeance. If excessive logic leads to the madhouse, obsessive realism ends up at the cabinet of curiosities. This road has been traveled at different times in history and, in the late 18th century, literally led to the waxworks. But who will deny that there is a strange fascination in man's ability to make cherries look so real that birds swoop down to eat them? Veristic, then, means inclusive beyond considerations of beauty and ugliness, total appropriation of the ready-found, and voluntary forfeiture of the artist's traditional prerogative to form as well as edit at will.

Hanson's work compares to Segal's the way a technicolor movie full of ultra realistic details and special effects, like *The Exorcist*, compares to the black-and-white, almost abstract Fritz Lang classic M. Hanson has gone beyond Segal inasmuch as he has perfected the art of casting from live models and dispenses with environmental indices to buttress his compositions. He implicitly rejects abstraction (to which Segal continues to

adhere) and aesthetically aligns himself with what has come to be known as photo-realism. Flaunting his skillful use of polyester, fiberglass and color, Duane Hanson is hard-hitting and shamelessly self-assured as he dazzles the art world with an astounding cast of lowbrow characters ranging from the cheerfully ordinary to the painfully pathetic.

Why is Hanson's art so popular that it draws record crowds to museums everywhere? Consider the Lowe Art Museum's *Football Player*. It is apprehended as reality, not as sculpture. The admiration it attracts centers on how cunningly it fools the eye. Its mimetic power is so strong that, much as we cannot behold the sun for its blinding aura, so we have trouble focusing on this work's primary figuration *as art*. It appears to have no style, yet with time the characteristics of our era will reveal themselves just as surely as Hanson's selective eye and expert hand. Doubters should reflect on the styleless figures at Madame Tussaud's. Despite claims of veracity, they are poorly made; they require history (mostly ghoulish) and anecdote (mostly trivial) as crutches; they belong to neither the time they simulate, nor to the time in which they are seen. Finally, and most important, they are not proposed and accepted *as art* in the context of a museum *for art*.

The Virgin in this Northern Renaissance panel painting is seated, shown to just below the knee, holding the nude Christ Child on her lap with her right hand and delicately touching a little bouquet of flowers with her left; the golden rays of saintliness and godliness leap forth from the heads of mother and son. Mary's demure head is crowned with flowing curly hair and her gown has borders richly jeweled in a late Gothic style. Sitting on a white cloth the Child touches the wing of a a parrot with his right hand and reaches for the flowers with his left.

The diptych shares a window looking out upon an Italianate seaport surrounded by mountains; this vista is balanced by a leaded glass window pane on the left side

and, on the right, a lavabo and towel in a niche, presumably referring to purification (Ephesians 5:26). The donor, in half-length, his hands folded in prayer, wears a quilted doublet under a sleeveless, fur-collared robe. His young face betrays awe and uneasiness and the legend on the period frame makes it clear, in old Flemish, that this was the way he looked, at age 32, on February 16, 1513.

This diptych was thought to be by Albrecht Dürer until shortly before 1831, when it was re-attributed to an anonymous Lower German master. In his authoritative *Die altniederländische Malerei* (1934), Max J. Friedländer gave the picture to Adriaen Isenbrandt, noting that it was copied after Jan van Eyck's *Van der Paele Altar* (1436) in the Musée Communal in Bruges. The current attribution to Isenbrandt is consistent with the works that are accepted as his.

This classic serape, known as the "Spiegelberg Serape" for the Santa Fe family which first collected it, represents the pinnacle of Navajo weaving. Navajo textiles present a powerful presence. Visually appealing, they display the high quality of technical control and aesthetic design that separates art from mere craft. Women were the weavers among the Navajo. They owned the sheep, sheared and spun the wool, dyeing it with natural dyes. Around 1840, Europeans introduced wool trade cloth in red and other colors and that was ravelled to be rewoven. The women worked on an upright loom, the work progressing from the bottom up. Thus Navajo weaving seemed to emerge from the earth, as legends of the people say the Navajo themselves did.

In the creation of a classic serape, the women found their greatest freedom to express individuality and artistic capability within a weaving tradition. The finest classic serapes were produced between 1840 to 1860.

Alfred I. Barton spotted his first Navajo blanket in a Santa Fe store window in the early 1940s. A man not only of sophistication and taste who recognized the

34 *Adriaen Isenbrandt*, Diptych: Madonna and
Child with a Hillensberger Donor, *1513*

106 *Navajo*, Classic Serape (The Spiegelberg
Serape), *1840-60*

6 *Chinese*, Kuang-ting, *Shang Dynasty*

intrinsic artistic value of Native American
weavings, he had the intellectual curiosity
to seek the outstanding scholar in the field,
H. P. Mera, to educate and refine that taste.
Barton assembled a collection of the best
examples of 19th and 20th century Navajo,
Pueblo, and Spanish weavings by
purchasing works from private collectors,
antique dealers and trading posts. He
presented his superb collection of
Southwestern textiles and other American
Indian artifacts to the Lowe Art Museum
between 1956 and 1962.

(*Dorothy Downs*)

For twenty-one years until his death in
1978, Stephen Junkunc III, a resident
of Chicago, was the principal contributor
of Oriental art to the Lowe Art Museum.
Junkunc preferred to "encourage new
schools and art centers which really would
make use of the material for exhibition and
educational purposes." His gifts, which
include bronzes, jades, ceramics and
paintings, form the core of the museum's
holdings in Chinese art.

The Anyang Period Kuang-ting was one
of the first gifts he made to the Lowe in
1958 and remains a cornerstone of the
museum's Chinese collection. Made for
ritual purposes, it is a unique hybrid form
which combines the elongated neck and
cover of the kuang (wine-server) shape with
the round lower body of the three-legged
ting (food-cooker) shape. It bears a one
character inscription "fu" on both the
inside of the cover and the bottom inside
of the bowl. ("Fu" indicates that it was a
ritual vessel belonging to an emperor's
consort.) The zöomorphic creature
depicted in relief on the cover combines
certain feline and serpentine traits. A band
of stylized birds decorates the lower part of
the vessel.

(*Brian Dursum*)

34

106

6

Dallas Museum of Art

Along the Pacific coast and in the Andes mountains of South America, a number of sophisticated cultures developed. Unlike the high civilizations of Mesoamerica, they did not communicate through the written word and monumental architecture or stone sculpture were relatively less important. The geographic nature of Peru, with its narrow river valleys separated by deserts, made trade and communication between areas difficult. Widespread empires are a late development in Andean history. The Inca had dominated Peru for less than a hundred years at the time of the Spanish Conquest.

The emphasis in South American art was on small ceramics, textiles and goldwork, as opposed to the large-scale art of Mesoamerica. The level of craftsmanship was superb and goldwork was of dazzling quality and intricate technique. The majority of surviving works have been found in graves. When the Spanish conquered Peru in the 16th century, they were overpowered by the mass of gold used to decorate the Inca palaces and temples, such as those at Cuzco in the Andean highlands. The finds of gold in Peruvian graves suggests this ceremonial grandeur.

The Museum has a collection of 34 gold cups from a single Lambayeque Chimú grave at Batán Grande, dating from between 700 and 950 A.D. The frog is a motif frequently found in Inca iconography but the lack of written documents makes it hard to interpret the character of their symbols. Frogs, birds, pumas, jaguars, hawks, eagles, whales, seals, fish and snakes are all part of the sacred repertory of the Inca.

The Chokwe belong to the important Lunda group scattered throughout the region east of the upper Lualua River and southeast of Katanga, a narrow area extending from the Kasai River to the Kwilu River, north of the Angola border. As a tribe they fell under the influence of the Lunda as early as the 17th century. They gathered wealth by trading ivory and slaves for European articles and built a remarkable political organization which continues today. In the mid-19th century, the Chokwe pushed northward and, about 1885, invaded the heart of the Lunda empire and killed their great chief. The aristocratic society the Chokwe subsequently built has favored the development of art, a dynamic art for comfort and adornment and one that is distinguished by the carving of multiple figure compositions.

A love of decoration is widespread among the Chokwe. There is virtually a grammar of style, with many geometric motifs applied with a good deal of imagination. Chokwe carvers are less concerned with volume than with working the surface of masks and objects of common use. Chairs were not a normal part of African life but a European import and an emblem of authority. Chokwe carvers retained the basic European model—an archaic, Spanish type of carved wood and tooled leather—but adorned back and stretchers with intricate scenes that represent the spirits of ancestors and sometimes zoomorphic motifs rarely found in African sculpture.

The Clark and Frances Stillman collection of Congo sculpture was assembled over a period of almost 40 years and is recognized as one of the finest in its field. It came to the Museum in 1969 through the enthusiastic interest and generosity of Eugene and Margaret McDermott.

For a museum collection to do justice to the Russian contribution to avant garde art in our century is well-nigh impossible because of the scarcity of the available material. The Bolshevik Revolution and the rise of the proletariat provided the impetus for artists to practice in the public domain what had come to fermentation in intense exchanges with their counterparts in the West. But the realities of a society in upheaval dampened individual ambitions, ideologists sowed the seeds of dissent and commissars condemned as bourgeois what they and their constituents failed to comprehend. Proscribed, stifled, neglected, seized and relegated to inaccessible "study collections," Constructivist and Suprematist art has not, as has, Cubist or Futurist art, found its way into the market place, into the hands of discriminating collectors and, eventually, into the worlds' museums. What has come out of Russia escaped with its makers in the 1920s and early 1930s, or it traveled secret, semi-official conduits which, in the cold war years, filtered out just enough material to feed the scholarly world's growing interest in that heroic and innovative period in Russian art.

Kazimir Severinovich Malevich (1878-1935) has been regarded primarily as a painter and theorist, rather than as a graphic artist in his own right. Yet, the lithographs he produced between 1913 and 1930 are among the Russian avant garde's most exciting creations. They graphically extend the artist's Suprematist theories as just one of many outlets for his boundless energy—political advertisements in streetcars, banners for May Day parades, sets and scenery for avant garde theater and porcelain designs. Malevich attempted to expand Suprematism into a universal doctrine of artistic creation, into a system that transcended the barriers between "pure" and "applied" art. Maiakovsky's famous exhortation that the artist "make the streets his brushes and the squares his palette," was particularly appropriate to Malevich who designed both front and back cover of this important revolutionary era book.

The *Congress of Committees on Rural Poverty* appeared just after the congress itself had convened in Petrograd on November 3-9, 1918. Lithographed in only ten or 12 copies by the 15th State Printing House, it contains instructions to the village and country Soviet, a speech by the head of the party for Petrograd, Grigorii Zinoviev (an ally of Trotsky who was expelled from the party in 1927 and shot in 1936), and another one by Anatolii Lunacharsky, Commissar for Popular Enlightenment. John E. Bowlt, America's premier scholar of the Russian avant garde ascribes the extreme rarity of this book with its Malevich design to the fact that all but a few copies were destroyed, mutilated or concealed in the wake of the political purge of its principal author.

The Museum was fortunate to acquire
the largest single collection in this country
of printed materials designed by Kazimir
Malevich and other members of the
Russian avant garde. An interest in
geometric abstraction at the Museum was
fostered by one of its most distinguished
patrons, James H. Clark. It was fitting,
therefore, that the Russian avant garde
acquisition was dedicated to the memory of
that recently deceased collector of works
by Mondrian and Vantongerloo.

164

145

Dayton Art Institute

105

During the early sixth century of the Northern Wei Dynasty (386-535), Buddhism was recognized as the official state religion in China. The archaic Buddhist sculpture, dominant from the fourth century into the third quarter of the sixth, drew strong influence from the styles of the kingdoms of Central Asia along the road traveled by Buddhism from India to China. The first predominately Chinese style of Buddhist sculpture is found in a series of cave temples in the cliffs of Yungang, not far from Tatung, the first capital of the Northern Wei Dynasty. The cave temples were built near important trade routes in order to be easily accessible to Buddhist pilgrims.

The idea of cave sculpture came from India and probably suggested the inner search for holiness. Colossal Buddhas, the largest measuring over seventy feet, filled the atrium while the cave walls were covered with thousands of figures of smaller Buddhas and accompanying figures of Bodhisattvas, disciples and celestial musicians. Bodhisattvas are those who have foregone entrance into nirvana to help all sentient beings attain enlightenment. This painted sandstone *Head of a Bodhisattva* derives from the caves at Yungang. Its expression is one of meditative contemplation and in the center of the head ornament is a figure of Buddha. In the line of the lips can be discerned the archaic smile derived, by way of India, from archaic Greek art.

The foundation of the Asian collection of the Dayton Art Institute was established by Jefferson Patterson's donation of his considerable collection of Chinese art to the Institute which his mother had built. Mr. Patterson was a career diplomat and inveterate collector, who served in China in the U. S. Consular Service between 1922-1924.

(Brenda Williamson)

The "Bird of Paradise" coverlet is one of approximately 250 examples of American, European, Asian and Pre-Columbian textiles, all of which entered the Dayton Art Institute's collection as gifts. The coverlet, which was recently identified as the work of Portsmouth, Ohio, weaver Don Purcell, is a much admired example of the designs achieved by cottage weavers of the mid-19th century who, although working from accepted patterns, imbued their products with marks of individuality. Aided by a Jacquard attachment (a set of punch cards used to control the rise and fall of the warp threads), the weaver was able to create intricate curvilinear patterns in the bird and floral motif so popular during that era.

The Jacquard also made it possible to enhance the architectural border design with waving palm trees and fluttering American flags complete with 28 stars and 13 stripes. In this case, the corner squares are all devoted to diamond shaped floral designs rather than to a signature block which was often woven into one of the corner squares. As was the method in handloomed coverlets before the arrival of mechanized looms, the "Bird of Paradise" was woven in two sections sewn together down the middle. Only one end of the coverlet is fringed, a characteristic more common to Indiana coverlets than to Ohio ones, and a peculiarity which adds another element of distinction to this Ohio coverlet.

(Ann W. Heymann)

Unlike a historic subject, a genre picture does not generally refer to a written text. It relates, instead, to the popular, often crude and simplistic, metaphorical interpretation of an era's daily life. A simple situation is, through the introduction of key symbols, turned into a moral example. In the Low Countries, the new genre painting emerged in Haarlem and, from there, spread to Leiden and to Utrecht where, in the work of Hendrick ter Brugghen and Gerrit van Honthorst, it acquired a unique character. These two painters, unlike their colleagues in Haarlem and Leiden, spent many years in Rome where they adopted the style of Caravaggio and his circle. Instead of using small figures in a spacious setting, they crammed large-size figures into a tightly cropped and usually dimly lit space. Although the illumination comes from candles, oil lamps or torches—giving these Utrecht pictures their special attraction—there is some evidence that Jan Vermeer van Delft looked at Honthorst's work in an early stage of his career.

Theme and treatment suggest that the painter shows us a brothel scene. Two young men are allowed to watch but keep silent as the establishment's owner, characteristically a shrewd old hag with spectacles, stages a flea hunt that allows clients to inspect, unobserved, their prospective bedmate's generous endowments. As is often the case in Dutch genre pictures, the scene may reflect a popular proverb or expression. The Dutch poet and moralist Jacob Cats, a contemporary of Honthorst, whose extremely popular works were a virtual index to the symbolism in genre painting, spoke of painting's "pleasing obscurity" and noted that one could decipher such hidden meanings only after a proper period of reflection. *The Flea Hunt* predates by four years a more worldly instance of matchmaking, *The Procuress* (Centraal Museum, Utrecht) in which the same old woman is featured and the proverbial reference is as clear as the candle on the table.

For the Dayton Art Institute *The Flea Hunt*, acquired in 1980, adds an equally notable Caravaggesque work by a Northern painter to a collection strong in the period of the Italian Baroque with important representations of Mattia Preti, Bernardo Strozzi, Guercino, Manfredi and Saraceni. Partial funding for this and 57 past acquisitions was provided by the *Art Ball*, a fundraiser originated in 1958 by the Junior League of Dayton and, since 1965, an annual function of the Associate Board of the Dayton Art Institute.

46

75 Marcos Zapata and Cipriano Gutierrez y Toledo,
Adoration of the Magi, c. 1750
The Denver Art Museum

84

89

The Detroit Institute of Arts

Venetian by birth and training, Tiepolo blended the tradition of Baroque illusionism with the pageantry of Paolo Veronese. At the height of the 18th century he covered the walls of palaces and the ceilings of churches from Venice and Bergamo to Würzburg and Madrid, with the luminous vortices of his enormous frescoes. Tiepolo's art is of a brilliance and expansiveness far in excess of that of his French Rococo contemporaries. As he looked back at and found inspiration in the work of his 16th century Venetian predecessors, Giorgione and Titian, so, in turn, he impressed Fragonard and Goya with the grace and daring of his own compelling style.

Girl with a Lute (Pandorina) is exceptional for its consummate handling of the subject and for its freedom from decorative conventions. Virtually unknown before entering the Detroit collection, it now ranks as this master's most beautiful portrait in America. Tiepolo biographer Antonio Morassi ventures that *Girl with a Lute (Pandorina)* constitutes the artist's ideal of female beauty and that the sitter was, in all probability, his favorite model, Cristina. We see her tuning a twelve-string lute, prototype of the Neapolitan mandolin, while looking dreamily at whomever caused her to neglect the music at hand.

The tender sensuality of the pose is matched by the luscious undulations of the draperies. From the woman's opalescent skin to the light blue, yellow, pink and orange of her accoutrements, the palette is as purely Tiepolo as is the theatrical swirl of clothing ready to slip down and reveal more skin. Stylistically, this painting can be safely dated between the artist's return from executing his famous ceiling in the Episcopal Palace in Würzburg, in 1753, and the 1757 decoration of the Villa Valmarana.

The Detroit Institute of Arts has developed one of the country's finest collections of Italian art, from a rare group of early sculpture, assembled for the most part by W. R. Valentiner, to the Eleanor Clay Ford bequest of Italian Renaissance painting. This splendid portrait is a 1957 gift from Mr. and Mrs. Henry Ford II.

96

43

On the tide of recognition accorded the breakthrough accomplishment of Gustave Courbet and the Realism he proposed, ancillary artists, such as Breton and Bonvin, have recently surfaced from the oblivion to which they had been relegated by historians more concerned with movements and their star representatives than with the competent rank and file. While nobody would claim that this revisionist attitude threatens to reverse established value judgments with regard to the 19th century, it does challenge our reading of that era based only on a knowledge of mainstream art.

The revisionists' limitation is their implicit equation of social with morphological significance and their favoring—the old tug-of-war—of content over style. Be this as it may, Gabriel P. Weisberg deserves credit for bringing back to life Courbet's friend, François Bonvin, a painter of workmanlike domestic genre scenes and a luminist who, in his better moments, aspired to be a 19th century Chardin. *La Femme de l'Artiste Lisant*, acquired by the Detroit Institute of Arts in the wake of the Realist revival, is a fine example of how, as through a special magic, charcoal can squeeze light from the paper to which it is expertly applied.

The struggle of these two noble specimens of creation unto a certain and tragic death has been the subject of heroic portrayals from antiquity to Delacroix. At the height of the Mannerist era, a young artist from Douai, Jean de Boulogne, went to Italy for further training and stayed to become, under the Italianized name of Giovanni da Bologna, the most important sculptor in Florence during the last third of the 16th century. Wilhelm von Bode, in his *Italian Bronze Statuettes*, credited Giovanni da Bologna with the invention of a subject listed in contemporary accounts as *Il cavallo ucciso dal leone*. Antonio Susini, a fellow Florentine, was authorized by Bologna to make casts of his originals, and the Detroit example of *Lion Attacking a Horse* bears the signature of Susini on its base. This 1925 purchase with funds made available by the City of Detroit, then enjoying its first automotive boom, was typical of the interest in developing an Italian Renaissance sculpture collection which W. R. Valentiner brought to the Institute during his productive directorship.

This religious subject painted in the grandiloquent manner of the French Academy, was attributed to Noël-Nicolas Coypel when the Detroit Institute of Arts acquired it at auction in 1978. Now thought to be of the hand of Jouvenet, it has become a touchstone for determining the artist's interpretation of aesthetic canons set forth by Charles Lebrun, the Academy's founder. Jouvenet's powerfully realistic style broke through academic formulas and carried on Le Brun's conventions, not in facile procedures, but in a more vigorous vein. He never had an opportunity to travel to Rome and thus did not fall under the spell, as was customary for his colleagues, of the great Italian masters. It lent a "modern" tone to Jouvenet's oeuvre in which that spirit of enthusiastic enterprise and boundless ambition so characteristic for the reign of Louis XIV transpires without restraint.

It is difficult to date *Adoration of the Magi* but, considering its self-assured and accomplished style, it appears to have been painted after the artist's 1674 admission to the Academy. Before 1705, the painting gained enough recognition to become the subject of an engraving by Alexis Loir, and a comparison between the original and its faithfully engraved mirror image leaves no doubt about Detroit's correct attribution. In the literature about Jouvenet (Antoine Schnapper. Paris: 1974, p. 202-203) two painted versions of this subject are mentioned, two ostensibly preparatory drawings, the engraving by Loir and at least four 18th-19th century copies. The Detroit painting is the larger of the two known versions. It appeared on the German art market in 1953, and may be the one executed in 1694 or 1695 for the main altar of the Jesuit Church of Rennes.

83

The Denver Art Museum

The Denver Art Museum has traditionally been strong in Native American art and in the arts of the Americas, both pre-Colombian and Spanish colonial. The circle of artists who founded the museum, then called the *Artists' Club*, shared an enthusiasm for regional "folk art" which insured the eventual acceptance of a broad spectrum of art forms under the umbrella of a New World Art Department. In the wake of several gifts and bequests that included rare Southwest Santos and Mochica ceramics, the Museum acquired, from Engracia Freyer and her children in 1969, the widely published and exhibited Frank Barrows Freyer Memorial Collection of 17th and 18th century Peruvian colonial art. Assembled by Mrs. Freyer in Peru during the 1920s while her husband was Chief of the United States Naval Mission, the collection received special dispensation to leave the country in recognition of Freyer's singular contribution to the Peruvian nation. The Freyer paintings, furniture, woodcarvings, tooled leather objects and silver, illustrate the lavishly ornamented Cuzco style and are considered among the finest New World interpretations of Spanish baroque art.

Considered by Mrs. Freyer as one of the top three paintings in her extensive collection, the *Adoration of the Magi* was found by her in 1923 in the public market of Cuzco "where it had been relegated to the use of a pillow to cushion the onion vendor from the cold hard pavement." Mrs. Freyer's find proved to be a picture by Marcos Zapata and his assistant Cipriano Gutierrez y Toledo, a prolific team, active between 1748 and 1764, to whom over 200 works have been attributed. Because engraved reproductions of his work were readily available, Peter Paul Rubens had a profound influence on Spanish colonial painting. This Cuzqueño composition is based on a 1631 engraving of an adoration scene painted by Rubens in 1628. Changes such as the outdoor setting, the substitution of llamas for camels, and the use of overlaid gold, however, are characteristic of colonial adaptations by artists indigenous to the Andean mountains.

Like Jasper Johns and Larry Rivers, members of an older generation whose basic inventions and permissions underscore his work, Jim Dine is a beneficiary of Willem de Kooning's expressionistic figuration, Pollock's and Sam Francis' painting field explorations and the Dadas' radical- promiscuous intermingling of words and images, real objects and their representations. Contrary to Rauschenberg who went from collage to combine to environment, between 1956-66, Dine started out with the creation of kinetic environments (Happenings), pressed that essential experience into a static, more two-dimensional frame and moved closer to pure painting. Loosely associated with Pop Art in the 1960s, Dine rejected Rauschenberg's and Warhol's use of mechanical reproduction and Lichtenstein's, Rosenquist's and Wesselmann's slick appropriations and exploitations of modern consumer culture. In his celebration of the painter's trade, tools and medium, he occupies a pictorially isolated and poetically aloof middleground between 1950s-style painting and its current expressionistic revival.

Colour of the Month of August is part of a cycle which the artist termed (and headlined in this canvas) "Painting Pleasures." The color patches, like daubings on a palette, are allowed to run freely, giving them the insouciant air of massively released balloons and the literary connotation of a thousand flowers blooming. Interspersed with the oval color patches and moving from the upper right to the lower left like a shower, is a rain of scribbled words—the names of colors mostly, but also those of friends, *Ileana* (Sonnabend) and (Ron) *Padgett*, and of nouns, *water* and *noodle*. A large-scale free-association picture, *Colour of the Month of August* harks back to its 1961 predecessors in the way real objects butt into the pictorial arena. "My paintings are involved with 'objects'," Jim Dine has said. "At a time when the consumption of same is so enormous I find the most effective picture of them to be not a transformation or romantic distortion but a straight smack right there attitude. I am interested in

their own presence." Indeed, he leaves the viewer with a cloth to wipe, paint to throw, bricks to support and, ultimately, an ax to destroy his beautiful picture. They render an ambiguous testimony to the creative person's state of mind as he waivers between acceptance and rejection.

Between 1894 and 1973, the Museum, in its original and present formation, sponsored 74 juried and invitational exhibitions of work by artists west of the Mississippi, and through purchase awards, built a nucleus of contemporary, mostly regional art. With the 1971 opening of a new building designed by internationally renowned Gio Ponti, the Museum began to collect contemporary art—actively and on a broader scale. Accession funds were set aside in 1976 and, in 1978, a special department was created. The first gallery to permanently display the Museum's collection of contemporary art was opened in 1980, one year after Dine's *Colour of the Month of August* was acquired with a grant from the National Endowment for the Arts, matching private and corporate gifts.

The art and culture of the native Americans was radically changed by the 18th century introduction of European trade goods. This Southeastern Indian beaded pouch, attributed to Cherokee origin, is a superb example of the people's adaptability, creativity and craftsmanship. The women readily used the European materials in new ways, fashioning clothing or other objects from European styles. This pouch was copied after the bandolier bags worn by British soldiers on the American frontier. The style is typical of a Southeastern pouch—square with a triangular flap, held by a long strap that ended in tassels. It was made of woolen cloth and decorated with shiny glass beads, embroidered in designs that can be traced to prehistoric native pottery and shell designs. Indian men wore these pouches for dress or battle, and they contained ammunition and sacred "medicine" for protection.

The Denver Art Museum was the first art museum to recognize the aesthetic

value of such objects, collecting and
displaying them as art, not ethnographic
material. Miss Anne Evans was the
foremost proponent of this cause,
assembling a nucleus collection. The
Department of Indian Art was established
in 1928 and the first curator of Indian art
was appointed. The second curator was
noted scholar Frederic H. Douglas, who
established the ongoing curatorial efforts of
assimilating the most representative
collection of every definable regional style
of art produced by our native people.

(Dorothy Downs)

198

108

Des Moines Art Center

144

Morris Louis' *Untitled #189*, a spectacular "Veil" of 1959, was acquired in 1972 with funds received from de-accessioning a small painting by Renoir donated 13 years earlier by Gardner Cowles, whose father founded the *Des Moines Register*. The donor had written a letter volunteering his agreement beforehand to have the work sold with the proceeds to be used for the acquisition of contemporary art. Cowles' sophisticated point of view and generosity of spirit enabled the Art Center to acquire the Morris Louis as well as an important watercolor by Claes Oldenburg.

The generic term *Veil*, designating the paintings executed both in 1954 and 1958-1959, originated with William S. Rubin, an early supporter of the work of Morris Louis and the former owner of *Untitled #189*. All of the *Veils* exhibited during Louis's lifetime were given unique titles, most of which were suggested by the critic Clement Greenberg who helped the artist secure exhibitions. The Des Moines *Veil*, bearing the widow's authentication, ML, and the estate number on the reverse, came to light, among other *Veils*, after the artist's death at age 50, in 1962.

Diane Upright-Headley who has prepared the artist's oeuvre catalogue, sees five compositional type *Veils*: "triadic," "split," "monadic," "vertical" and "Italian." *Untitled #189* should be classified as a "monadic" *Veil*, showing an internal continuity unmarred by dramatic divisions and paint swirls. The *Veil* chronology, established by Greenberg on the basis of just the slightest of clues (Louis was neither writer nor record keeper), places most of the 80-odd paintings of that type in 1958. "It is evident," Upright-Headley argues, "that the more colorful "monadic" paintings on larger canvas, such as *Untitled #189*, are properly dated 1959.

Ballet Girl in White, a particularly beautiful 1909 painting by Robert Henri, was purchased directly from the artist by the Des Moines Association of Fine Arts, predecessor of the Des Moines Art Center. "The Eight" had a strong following in the Midwest where taste in painting had often been formed by realists of the Barbizon School. The Henri ballerina had hung in the Des Moines Public Library among works by Luks, Sloan, Bellows and Glackens before it caught the eye of local art patrons. With a Bellows, it now leads off the Des Moines Art Center's modern but primarily postwar art collection.

American dancers, notably Loie Fuller, Isidora Duncan and Ruth St. Denis, were all the rage on Europe's cultural stage in the years preceding World War I. Our own painters, John Sloan, Morgan Russell and Robert Henri painted them with sensitivity and admiration. Sloan portrayed Isidora Duncan in performance; Russell incorporated her rhythms in his Synchromist compositions, and Henri spoke of her dancing as an instance of creative "seeing." While Henri worshiped Duncan, and in 1919, painted an uncommissioned portrait of *Ruth St. Denis in the Peacock Dance*, it seems clear that *Ballet Girl in White* represents a model striking a pose rather than a dancer of note. We are reminded of Manet and, in Henri's own oeuvre, we see a striking resemblance, in subject and treatment, with the identical size *Masquerade Dress: Portrait of Mrs. Robert Henri* of 1911 in the Metropolitan Museum of Art. It is tempting to speculate that the artist's beautiful wife stood for both pictures.

Alberto Giacometti's life-size *Man Pointing* (1947) appears to us like a phantom whose bulk has shrunk to skeletal proportions and whose arms are frozen in mid-gesture. A rhetorical expression of post-World War II existentialist feeling, it also renders timeless testimony to man's quixotic attempt at orchestrating the world about him as he stands on the edge of the abyss. A similar aura of suspended time, eerie space and halted motion pervades the artist's group compositions, such as the 1948 *City Square*, in which the same aimless wanderer stalks four mirror images of his disappearing self.

It has been said that toward the end of

his life, fragile, ashen and covered with plaster dust, Giacometti began to resemble his sculptures. The distracted intensity of his wanderers across city squares appeared to be the artist's own. James Lord quotes Giacometti about the hurried way in which *Man Pointing* was finished so it could be cast in bronze: "I did that piece in one night, between midnight and nine the next morning. That is, I'd already done it, but I demolished it and did it all over again because the men from the foundry were coming to take it away. And when they got here, the plaster was still wet." The artist had intended *Man Pointing* to be part of a two-figure composition. After he completed the second figure in plaster four years later, he exhibited the two together in Paris. Unhappy with the result, he destroyed the second figure and decided that the original sculpture should stand alone.

The major source of revenue for Art Center acquisitions, which have visibly grown in distinction during the present directorship, came from the estate of Winnie Ewing Coffin. Mrs. Coffin's will provided for the purchase of works of art in memory of her husband, Nathan Emory Coffin, through the Coffin Fine Arts Trust. *Man Pointing*, a major acquisition in the Art Center's history and one of the finest sculptures Giacometti ever made, now stands in the I.M. Pei-designed interior sculpture court, a 1968 gift of the Gardner Cowles Foundation.

176

Hood Museum of Art, Dartmouth College

When *Guitar on a Table* entered the Dartmouth collections, it was dated 1912-13 and came with the instruction that it be hung vertically, as, indeed, it had been in *Four Americans in Paris* at The Museum of Modern Art in 1970. Research by Pierre Daix and Joan Rosselet has pinpointed the date as autumn 1912. A comparison with two preparatory works as well as the irrefutable photographic evidence that in Gertrude Stein's home the painting hung horizontally, settled the intended direction. The painting's subject, a table stacked with books and a guitar, should be clear. The subtleties of its genesis are less so as they unravel. In the *Catalogue Raisonné* covering Picasso's Cubist Years, 1907-1916, we learn that Braque's first *papier collé* of September 1912 and Picasso's own sheet-metal and wire Guitar of that spring were at the base of a series of formal experiments Picasso conducted in December, and that they acted as catalysts for the development of his style.

The open-form guitar with inverted volumes formally preceded Picasso's painting which, itself, caught up, that autumn, with the papiers collés. The papiers collés had their start in Braque's gluing strips of artificially wood-grained wallpaper into a *Still-life with Fruit-dish and Glass* at a time Picasso was off on a visit to Paris. No sooner had he returned than he began on a series of works on paper, as well as on canvas, in which he moved from actual pasted papers to painterly imitations of the wood-grained wallpaper Braque had used, in combination with mixing sand in his glazes for heightened surface effect.

Guitar on a Table is one of these experiments. Its sketchy outlines suggest that the artist may have considered finishing this picture to a higher degree. The guitar on the table is Picasso's own sheetmetal rendering (note the hole at the center of the picture) and the perpendicular surface does not represent a table but Picasso's painterly imitation of a wood-grained surface. In other words, this picture is twice removed from an observed reality, and its author, while pictorially recording his own prior transformation of it, probed even deeper into Cubism's perceptual paradox.

Guitar on a Table was acquired in 1975 as a gift of Nelson Rockefeller, the College's most distinguished alumnus. Fulfilling a pledge to his Alma Mater for an amount inferior to the market value of this Picasso, and offering to redeem this pledge through the gift of some indifferent outside sculpture, he was successfully persuaded to increase his commitment to the College, allowing a Picasso painting that was targeted for The Museum of Modern Art to go to Dartmouth instead. Thus, what would have been another star in a crowded firmament was now fated to become a small college's prime example of what Douglas Cooper has recently termed "the essential Cubism."

By 1975, the Dartmouth collections had become rich in paintings by Bernard Buffet, spread around campus offices with such effect that their temporary custodians had grown fiercely possessive of them. In skillful negotiations, four paintings were pried loose, and through the good offices of J. J. Aberbach, their original donor, disposed of at auction in order to enable the College to acquire one important painting by Jean Dubuffet. An additional gift by Mr. Aberbach secured *Topographie au nid de pierres*, a large and sumptuous canvas by France's premier postwar painter.

In his meticulous way, Dubuffet has explained that at the end of 1957 he started "a cycle of large paintings celebrating the ground." In a memoir on the development of his work, written for the catalogue of his 1962 exhibition at The Museum of Modern Art, Dubuffet elaborated: "My idea was to obtain large paintings by means of assemblages...What I had in mind was to portray these surfaces without using lines or forms. I meant to evoke any area of bare ground—preferably esplanade or roadway—seen from above, that is, a fragment of a continuous unit, perhaps vaguely divided into zones...What captivated me in the first place was the opportunity afforded of composing paintings by the simple method of juxtaposing textures on which there were no objects with clearly defined contours, and which gave one the same impression as looking down at a vast expanse of ground that could be endlessly prolonged. I decided to call these paintings Topographies."

193

Dartmouth College's oldest treasure, a veritable holy grail, on a par, somehow, with Daniel Webster's 1818 dictum ("This may be a small college but there are those of us who like it") is the silver Monteith, given to the College in 1771 by Governor Wentworth and Friends to President Wheelock. It heralded the beginnings of a collection of colonial silver that through the more recent generosity of Frank L. ('24) and Louise C. Harrington of Worcester, Massachusetts, has grown into a cornerstone of the Dartmouth collections. Always interested in fine craftsmanship, these dedicated patrons focused their collecting on the crafts of New England silversmiths of the colonial period and, more particularly, on the work of Paul Revere, father and son.

In its lean and elegant shape the water pitcher by the son of patriot-craftsman Paul Revere embodies the sensibility of New England silversmithing. Transfer-printed creamware jugs, exported from the region around Liverpool, gained popularity in the States after 1800 and undoubtedly inspired its proportions. Paul Revere made at least two other pitchers for his family's use with the same simple lines and plain surfaces as this one. Several other Revere pitchers with smooth or strap handles are known; each has a bottom mark that shows REVERE in a clipped-cornered rectangle or a script R in a medallion.

Traditionally, a set of beakers by Benjamin Burt, another fine New England silversmith, have been paired with the Revere pitcher. They both carry the mark B BURT in a rectangle on the base and predate the pitcher by seven years. Major John Bray, their first owner, whose name appears on the beakers as well as on the pitcher, is supposed to have given one to each of his eight daughters.

73

72

The Museum of Fine Arts, Houston

109

27

At the time this portrait was reputedly painted, Paul Cézanne had successfully absorbed the lessons of Pissarro. He now sought to impose the Impressionists' free brush work and high-keyed color seen in natural light onto indoor subjects in which individual elements are reordered to fit an attempt at classical composition. Once Cézanne felt that he understood Impressionism, he held it necessary to go on, to go further: "I don't hide it, I have been an impressionist." But as he wrote to Maurice Denis, he wanted to make of it "something solid and durable as is the art in museums...In the fleeting quality of everything...it is necessary to now put a solidity, a framework."

In *Madame Cézanne in Blue*, Cézanne retains that generally naturalistic point of view characteristic of his bourgeois age, yet ventures beyond it by drawing the viewer's attention to an almost abstractly treated unity of form and color. While the blue of the sitter's bodice bounces about and can be spotted on face and furniture, the brown of the background intrudes upon the blue. Favoring surface over depth, the artist has deliberately flattened the space and brought the subject right up to the viewer. The slight tilt of the sitter's posture, repeated in the door ajar, occurs in other Cézanne portraits and became an affectation in early XXth Century art, particularly in the work of Modigliani and Soutine.

Hortense Fiquet, a tall and handsome brunette with whom the reclusive artist had lived since 1869 and by whom he had a son, officially became Madame Cézanne around the time this and several other portraits of the placid and withdrawn 36 year old woman were painted. The sad truth was that the couple no longer got along. *Madame Cézanne in Blue* seems to have been painted during a short reprieve in their relationship when the artist asked Hortense to join him in Gardanne on the outskirts of Aix-en-Provence. The weary, almost vacuous expression on Hortense's oval face betrays delicate submissiveness and an often tried patience. But the artist has treated her not without tenderness as though he chose to transfer to his wife the repressed nature and shyness for which he himself was known.

Beginning in 1947, the Robert Lee Blaffer family gave a number of important paintings to the Museum that added significantly to its European art collection. The same family enabled the Museum to increase its space, thus joining the Cullinan and anticipating the Brown families' generosity with regard to the Museum building which, from its inception in 1926, grew in stages—1953, 1958 and 1974.

Edward Hicks was a Quaker preacher as well as a sign and coach painter in Bucks County, Pennsylvania. His most famous works are the more than one hundred versions of *The Peaceable Kingdom*, painted between 1845 and 1849. Based on the 11th chapter of Isaiah, Hicks transferred the biblical scene to the banks of the Delaware River, and more often than not, combined his pastoral with a view of William Penn signing his famous treaty with the Indians.

The Bayou Bend example is one of the earlier versions of the theme and one of a small number which incorporate a frame embellished with verse variations of the biblical text. In the corner squares, Hicks has painted the Lamb of God and the dove of peace, accompanied by the words *Innocence, Meakness* and *Liberty*.

The earliest examples, according to Alice Ford in her 1952 study of Edward Hicks, are based on a painting by Richard Westall, R. A., which was reproduced in print form in a number of bibles and prayer books published during the 1820s, while the treaty scene was based on H. B. Hall's engraving of the subject by Benjamin West.

A gift to the Museum in 1957 made by Miss Ima Hogg, an oil heiress, of her stately home, Bayou Bend, culminated a series of grand donations that began with her 1939 gift of 100 important works on paper and included her 1944 gift of a large collection of American Indian artifacts. Resplendent with a first rate collection of American painting and decorative arts, the Bayou Bend Collection of the Museum of Fine Arts opened to the public as a branch museum in 1966.

Houston's small panel, attributed by Bernard Berenson, Lionello Venturi and John Pope-Hennessy to Fra Angelico himself rather than to a follower, is probably a fragment of a larger work. Pope-Hennessy has stressed its similarities to the *Penitence of St. Julian* in Cherbourg and has suggested that both pieces may originally have been parts of the same predella.

Influenced by Massaccio's innovative ideas and particularly by his frescoes in the Brancacci Chapel at S. Maria del Carmine, Florence, Fra Angelico adopted this painter's new conception of volumes and space but converted them to the spiritual aims that confer upon his own work their ethereal quality and mystical significance. The pivoting motion of St. Anthony as he turns away from the temptation of a heap of gold placed in his path by the Devil and the aerial perspective of the luminous horizon are advanced Renaissance aspects of the painting, while the schematic rocks and out-of-scale buildings are deliberate archaisms.

(*J. Patrice Marandel*)

The most important gift in the Museum's history to that time came in 1944 with the acquisition of the Edith A. and Percy S. Straus Collection. It numbered 83 works and consisted primarily of Italian bronzes, Trecento and Quattrocento paintings, Northern Renaissance paintings and works from the 18th century.

Constantin Brancusi's *View of the Studio: Endless Column, Bird in Space* is a particularly fine vintage print by a photographer who is best known as one of this century's greatest sculptors but who was no innocent in the use of a camera. The list of artists who have made a contribution to photography is long and impressive and runs from Edgar Degas and Thomas Eakins to David Hockney and Robert Rauschenberg. What sets Brancusi apart is his single-minded concentration on just one subject—the interior arrangement of his studio and the works in it.

Brancusi began to photographically

record his sculpture in 1902. Visitors to the artist's studio have noticed how he was always busy with a camera. It is not known whether Brancusi was familiar with the work of Eugène Atget, the great French photographer then working in Paris in almost total obscurity, but they did share a compulsion to take visual inventory. Brancusi knew Edward Steichen who became one of the American promotors of his work, and he was even closer to Man Ray who helped him set up a darkroom. A rising tide of interest in photography swept up what might have remained a distinguished but marginal pursuit for the Romanian sculptor.

Precisely what distinguishes a print like *View of the Studio*, is its spontaneous-looking but highly controlled presentation of the artist's sculpture, and its evocation of stillness, the visual corollary of silence. This recurring image, in its many variations, always devoid of human presences, unfairly contributed to the myth of the solitary genius and inaccurately reflected Brancusi's gregarious life style.

In paying so much attention to his studio's appearance, Brancusi created, as Sidney Geist has pointed out, the idea of the artist's studio in our time—"at once a temple and laboratory of art, the site of a confrontation of man-made order and natural chaos"—worthy to be preserved as such within a museum context. Millions have been exposed, with benefits unknown, to this prototypical experience of the artist's private battleground as they visited the less than successful recreation of Brancusi's Impasse Ronsin studio at the Centre National d'Art et de Culture Georges Pompidou in Paris.

In 1975, Target Stores, a division of the Dayton-Hudson Corporation well known for its leadership in corporate philanthropy, made an initial gift with annual supplements to the Museum of Fine Arts. This has provided it with the means to collect photography on a scale comparable to that of the better museum collections in that medium around the country. As a result, new donors have been attracted allowing the Museum to conduct a highly professional program of photography exhibitions.

151

Indianapolis Museum of Art

With its elaborate theory, rigorous abstraction and mechanical technique, Neo-Impressionism was a reaction in the name of modernity against the transient effects, naturalism, personal response and sensuous surfaces of the Impressionists. Maximilien Luce adopted the style of the new aesthetic's undisputed leader, Georges Seurat, around 1886 and soon became one of the group's more prominent representatives. From 1887 on, he exhibited with the Neo-Impressionists at the Société des Artistes Indépendants. More naturalistic than Seurat and Signac, he can be compared, in his interpretation of the group's orthodoxy, with Henri-Edmond Cross. Luce developed a close relationship with Camille Pissarro, who had converted to the new experiment in painting in sympathy with his son Lucien's beliefs.

La Rue Mouffetard, executed in the latter part of 1889, is one of Luce's classic statements and a highlight for Neo-Impressionism. The choice of subject suits the group's interest in contemporary urban life as well as the artist's own deep concern for the ordinary man. This very Parisian street is a busy artery of a working-class neighborhood located, as the large department store advertisement suggests, not far from the Pantheon. Luce's studio on the Rue Cortot was nearby and so were the offices of La Révolte, the anarchist newspaper to which Luce and his friends regularly contributed illustrations. The scientific optimism of the 19th century offers more than one example of avant garde art and political ideology making common cause. The view chosen by the artist is the one opposite the church of Saint-Médard; the elevated viewpoint allows for the full rise of the three and four story houses in that street at the expense of the sometimes truncated foreground figures.

Luce's palette was unusual among the Neo-Impressionists in emphasizing the purple hue that pervades La Rue Mouffetard. In the pale yellow sunlight of late afternoon, the indirect blue light takes on a greater prominence, which intensifies the purple tones. It is broken down into dots of its components, blue and red placed throughout the canvas and diluted with varying amounts of white to alter their values. Through complementary contrast with red, its color opposite, an intense green in the foreground further strengthens the juxtaposed purples. The complexity of the palette is further enhanced by a great variety of intermediate colors. The color dots establish an optical vibration which, rather than depicting visual reality, is intentionally anti-naturalistic, for the Neo-Impressionists believed that their "scientific" approach was true to a higher reality.

As a critical example of Luce's work, La Rue Mouffetard remains an important historical, thematic and stylistic document of Neo-Impressionism and one of the masterpieces of the Holliday Collection. W. J. Holliday, who made his fortune in coal, was attracted to French painting of the late 19th century in general and Neo-Impressionist pictures in particular. At a time when that movement was not exactly in fashion, he amassed 100 or so examples which he bequeathed to the Indianapolis Museum of Art in 1979. The collection is now the most comprehensive of its type in an American public museum.

(adapted from Anthony F. Janson)

Two cultures, Flemish and French, combined to inform the genius of Antoine Watteau, destined to become the standard bearer of Rococo art. Born and raised in Valenciennes, a town that Flandres had ceded to France, he studied for a few years with a local artist who had been trained in the Flemish traditions of Adriaen van Ostade and David Teniers (see Tavern Scene on loan from the Memorial Art Gallery at the University of Rochester). In 1695, at the age of 17, Watteau went off to Paris where Claude Gillot took him in as an apprentice and introduced the young provincial to the commedia dell' arte. In the summer of 1709 Watteau failed to win the Academy's prize trip to Rome and, disappointed, he left Paris and went back home. There he found Louis XIV's troops encamped all about the countryside. The maneuvers and the entertainment provided by camp followers gave Watteau plenty of opportunity to add to his repertoire.

La Danse Champêtre was painted about the time of his return to Valenciennes. A relatively early work, it shows the artist's continuing debt to Dutch 17th century genre painting. A. F. Janson, the Indianapolis Museum of Art's senior curator, believes that the picture's main source lies in the work of Pieter de Hooch whose example provided the refined poses and aspirations to upper class elegance. "The supreme occupation of Watteau's parties is love..." wrote Pierre Schneider in a 1967 study of that artist's world. "Dance, music-making are mere pretexts or preludes; soon the gathering splits up into pairs and the great game of amorous persuasion and reticence begins." La Danse Champêtre proves Schneider's point. To that game the child who stumbles upon the scene and demands its distracted nursemaid's attention is the only outsider. Tired of dancing the gavotte, one couple has already gone off into the bushes. The waiting is for the music to stop and either love or duty to prevail. The question left hanging is to which of the three gawking flautists the flirting tambourine player will accord her favors.

Radiographs at the Indianapolis Museum of Art have revealed numerous changes in the underpainting, making it unlikely that we are dealing with a copy after Watteau. The picture's originality is further corroborated by Pierre Dupin's engraving of the identical subject in Jullien's 1726 L'oeuvre (gravée) d'Antoine Watteau. The appearance just five years after his death of this publication devoted to the artist, attests to Watteau's considerable reputation. In fact, he made his fame in just the last five years of his short life, from 1716-21, with a series of fêtes galantes he neither attended nor observed but invented in every courtly detail.

La Danse Champêtre was acquired in 1974 as a gift from Mrs. Herman C. Krannert. While still known as the John Herron Art Institute the Museum began to receive important gifts of art from the Krannerts in the 1950s. Herman C.

Krannert became chairman of the board in 1960 and when, in 1967, the 54-acre Lilly estate, Oldfield, with its landscaping by Olmsted, was given to the Indianapolis Art Association, he made a matching grant offer that eventually brought about the construction of the present building. After her husband's death in 1972, Mrs. Krannert has continued to be one of the Museum's principal patrons.

Rufus is similar to Table III in Stubbs' book *The Anatomy of a Horse*, published in 1766 and based on detailed drawings he had executed during 1758-59. The book marks an important turning point in English animal painting, for it was the first scientifically accurate investigation of equine physiology. In *Rufus*, however, Stubbs' objective description is accompanied by an unusually sympathetic rendering. Thus, the painting is a fully individualized portrait in both appearance and character. Unlike earlier British sporting artists, Stubbs had little interest in capturing the excitement of a race or hunt, and he omitted the background from our picture, except for the shadows anchoring *Rufus* in space. Later in his career, Stubbs invested his paintings of animals with nearly human action and emotion. Moreover, he did a series of drawings for a book comparing the anatomy of man to animals. His scientific curiosity and comprehensive approach fall squarely in the Enlightenment, which sought to unite all knowledge into a single rational system and coherent philosophy.

(A. F. Janson & A. I. Fraser)

Rufus, one racing picture Eli Lilly reputedly was proud of having snatched up before Paul Mellon got hold of it, was given to the Museum by Mr. and Mrs. Eli Lilly in 1947. With its gift of the Lilly estate and the Josiah K. Lilly, Jr., mansion (now the Lilly Pavilion of Decorative Arts) as well as with major gifts to the Museum's collections and endowments, the Lilly Family has become the institution's premier benefactor.

84

78

Wadsworth Atheneum

49

Ere becoming the land of political freedom and economic opportunity, America loomed large in the eyes of Europeans as the continent of the noble savage, unspoiled by civilization, at peace with the animal kingdom and living off the fat of the land. A foil, in other words, for the frustrated imagination to roam freely if not exactly Dr. Pangloss's "best of all possible worlds." Meissen porcelain makers had no more global knowledge than what had been spelled out and illustrated for them in the accounts of adventurers— one-eyed sailors, Jesuit missionaries and wooden-legged soldiers of fortune. Their aristocratic clientele, from Bohemia to the Baltic, ensconced in drafty palaces and creaky castles, watched the rabble's every move from their clerestory windows but had a painted teacup notion of foreign parts. After two millenia they still borrowed from Antiquity allegorical impersonations and literary allusions to keep the exotic unknown from intruding upon their feudal comfort. Man, woman, child and servant, they would lustily embark upon a boat trip to the isle of Cythera, yet would not dream of being hemline to waterline with the New World's crocodile-infested swamps.

This Meissen porcelain allegory expressing *The European Vision of America*, traveled in a special exhibition to honor the Bicentennial of the United States from Cleveland to Washington to Paris. Combination Vanitas (Christian) and river goddess (pagan), this buxom Saxon rides the wrong animal and holds the wrong bird, as connoisseurs of indigenous species would have it. In its bombastic display of craftsmanship and outlandish imagination, it fitted the opulent taste of the great financier and patron J. P. Morgan whose son donated it to the Wadsworth Atheneum in 1917. Factory records indicate that two sets of *Continents* were produced at Meissen in the 1740s, from similar models, but different in size. The model for this larger version seems to have been the joint work of Johann Joachim Kändler, Johann Friedrich Eberlein and Peter Reineke. Another example of the large *America* on a different, rocky platform is in the Porzellansammlung, Dresden. Examples of the small version are in the Bayerisches Nationalmuseum,

Munich, and in the Cooper-Hewitt Museum, New York.

Between 1908 and 1910 and again in 1916, the original Atheneum was expanded with a mammoth wing, designed by Benjamin Wistar Morriss of New York in a Renaissance Revival style. This space was given by J. Pierpont Morgan, Sr., in memory of his father, Junius Spencer Morgan, financier of Hartford. The Morgan Memorial personified the powerful and sometimes rapacious collecting habits of the Morgans. To help fill this new wing, J. Pierpont Morgan, Jr., gave a portion of his father's collection after the latter's death in 1915. This included a superb group of French and German porcelains, 17th century gilt objects, paintings from the Italian Renaissance and uniquely valuable Greek, Roman and Early Christian bronzes. Although many spectacular items in the collection went to the Metropolitan Museum of Art in New York, the material received by the Wadsworth was significant enough to propel it into the front ranks of museums, as the largest repository of Meissen figurines outside of Europe.

This portrait of the dapper Joseph Coymans at age 52 is as good and typical an example of the mature style of the Haarlem painter as one is likely to encounter. It epitomizes the recent rise to wealth and social prominence of a burgher class, smugly adopting the aristocrat's escutcheon and confidently flaunting expensive silks and velvets. The sitter's family fortune reputedly derived from the textile trade and banking. The three cow heads in the obligatory coat of arms signify that his name, in Dutch, meant cattle handler. His type is familiar as that of so many staunch regents of almshouses and orphanages whose sober miens, individually or collectively, bear witness that pictorial survival is charity's sweet reward.

Hals was advanced in years but at the height of his powers—the standard bearer of realist painting in Haarlem—when he painted *Joseph Coymans*. The flamboyance of his youth had given way to a more composed style and solemn mood. Gone are the robustness of Rubens and the drama of Caravaggio that mark his more youthful paintings. But the bravura brush stroke is still evident in glove, collar and coiffure while the artist's knack for highlighting surfaces keeps our eye riveted on Joseph Coymans' smartly woven coat. The austerity and depth of feeling Hals's mature paintings display move them closer to those of his Amsterdam rival, Rembrandt Harmensz van Rijn.

76

Goya executed his first independent commissions, a series of cartoons for the Royal Tapestry Works of Santa Barbara, in 1775. Having just returned from Italy, he leaned heavily on the virtuosity of the Neapolitans, Luca Giordano and Corrado Giacquinto, who appealed to his Spanish taste. Also, as a recent Madrileño, Goya could not have avoided falling under the spell of Giambattista Tiepolo whose ceiling fresco in the throne room of the Royal Palace represented the height of European Rococo.

The Forge (c. 1820) in the Frick Collection, was Goya's last major painting before he went into voluntary exile. In just 50 years, this remarkable artist had gone from an affirmation of the age of elegance to an embrace of the new proletarian values. "Living simultaneously with and against the dominant trends of his time," (Fred Licht), Goya had one foot solidly planted in the 18th century while with the other, he strode into the next. World political upheavals and their repercussions in Spain visibly affected the artist's work. But, of greater consequence and the real *caesura* in Goya's career, was the 1792-93 illness that brought him close to death and left him deaf for life. A new depth of feeling and a new seriousness of commitment mark his every artistic effort from then on.

Gossiping Women looks back to the past rather more than forward to the future. In a compressed horizontal space, determined by its having been commissioned, in all likelihood, as a salon decoration, two women hold counsel. The picture's most salient feature is the women's position while

112

talking to one other—one turning away and illuminated, the other facing the viewer but looming from the dark. This Manichaean arrangement underscores the nature of the verbal exchange and evokes, across the centuries, the ancients' consultation of the oracle, customarily a woman who is heard but not seen. While atypical of Goya's representation in American collections, *Gossiping Women* caught the eye of Atheneum director A. Everett Austin, Jr., who, consistent with his promotion of Russian ballet and Surrealist art, brought late Baroque painting back into fashion.

At the time he painted the Hartford picture, Goya rode the crest of his popularity as a designer of contemporary pastorals, many of which can be seen at the Prado Museum. A member of the Academy of San Fernando, he was named painter to the court in 1786 and, in 1789, the year of Charles IV's coronation, he was promoted to *pintor de camera*. A look at paintings and cartoons commissioned by the Versailles and Schönbrunn courts, reveals how stubbornly independent and, indeed, *modern* Goya was even then. Venturing a comparison, only Pietro Longhi's sly and realistic depictions of Venetian high and low life come to mind. Goya did visit the Laguna city, but his portrayals of elegantly attired young people in garden settings show less staging and instead of indulging the viewer's voyeuristic instinct from afar, make, through a much more close-up positioning, direct and sometimes insolent contact with him.

A key event in the Atheneum's history was the establishment, in 1927, of the Sumner Fund to create the Ella Gallup Sumner and Mary Catlin Sumner Collection. The bequest of $2 million came from the estate of banker Frank C. Sumner, a man who had no interest in art. His wife, Mary, his brother George and his sister-in-law, Ella, influenced his choice of the Atheneum, and a welcome choice it was, coming at an economically propitious time for that institution. It provided the dashing Austin, a Harvard-trained disciple of Paul J. Sachs, with funds to embark on a buying spree. The Sumner Fund has allowed subsequent directors to add yet greater paintings to the Atheneum's distinguished collection.

James Abbott McNeill Whistler is often referred to as our country's most celebrated expatriate. Born in Lowell, Massachusetts, in 1834, he joined his father, a military specialist in railroad engineering, in St. Petersburg at the age of nine. After spending his youth in Russia and aborting his career in the military by flunking chemistry at West Point, the aspiring artist picked up some engraver's skills and, in 1855, headed for Paris, never to return. In the French capital he entered the studio of Gleyre where he befriended Henri Fantin-Latour. With Fantin and Manet, Whistler shared the distinction of being rejected by the jury of the 1859 Salon. Louis Bonvin took their canvases into his studio where a realist colleague, Gustave Courbet, dropped by to see them. According to Fantin, Courbet was struck with Whistler's *At the Piano*, a somber composition in contrasting blacks and whites, now in the Taft Museum in Cincinnati, which had shocked the jurors not so much because of its modernity but because it was conceived as a harmony of masses modeled in close tones without the aid of lines.

That same year, 1859, Whistler traveled to London where a half-sister lived. He began a series of etchings and exhibited *At the Piano* in the 1860 Royal Academy show. Going back and forth between France and England, Whistler became a link between the French avant garde which included both Courbet and Manet, and the Pre-Raphaelites in England. A close neighbor of Dante Gabriel Rossetti in Chelsea, he befriended the beautiful Johanna Heffernan, an Irish girl with flaming red hair, who seemed born of the Pre-Raphaelite imagination. She stood for the two versions of *The White Girl* and prominently posed for a number of pictures Courbet painted in 1865 when she and Whistler joined him, Monet and Boudin in Trouville. There did not exist in France, as in England, a tradition of painting near the seaside. Whistler was among the first to do so, on the deserted coast of Brittany, in 1861. *Alone with the Tide* as *Coast of Brittany* was called, in that era's maudlin fashion, when exhibited at the Royal Academy in 1862, is Whistler's first

painting of a seascape. We are strongly reminded of Courbet—without the coarse impasto—and we catch an early glimpse of Monet at Honfleur. Yet, Whistler competed with neither of these artists and, in later years, would regret ever having heeded Courbet's call to nature. His increasing penchant for tonal harmonies, limited contrasts and flat horizontal zones of color, is barely kept in check by the exigencies of this natural subject with a Breton peasant girl reclining as its sole motif. Another pictorial dichotomy, indicative of the artist's relative inexperience and inability to control his setting, is a lack of atmospheric integration between the smoothly rendered sea and sky on the horizon and the sketchily treated rock-littered beach.

160 Ernst Ludwig Kirchner, Street Scene, 1926-27
Milwaukee Art Museum

175 Walt Kuhn, Lancer, 1939
The Currier Gallery of Art, Manchester

The Minneapolis Institute of Art

This large and handsome painting represents a superb example of collaboration between two artists. It is likely that Hobbema painted the entire landscape but left the figures to the hand of another painter. Even in the 17th century, specialization was a well-established tradition, and Hobbema recognized his limitations when it came to the human form. His gifts for landscape, however, are quite evident in this work.

Unlike other artists who reveled in the angry side of nature, Hobbema preferred her more placid face. His colors are lush and soft; the old watermill quietly goes about its business, and only a few unlucky ducks are threatened with any harm at all. If we avert our eyes from the scarlet-coated hunter, we may retreat into the woods, into a world where stillness and peace reign supreme.

This is the golden age of Dutch art. A 30 year war had finally won Holland her independence from Spain, and her merchant navy now dominated the seas, reaping large profits from her colonies. Her wealthy (and largely non-Catholic) burghers wanted art to decorate the walls of their homes rather than their churches, and the art of Hobbema was in justifiably high demand.

William Hood Dunwoody was president of the Washburn-Crosby Milling Company and one of the original contributors, in 1910, to the Minneapolis Institute of Arts' building construction. When he died, four years later, he bequeathed to the Institute one million dollars as an art puchase endowment. Masterpieces by Titian, El Greco, Rembrandt, Poussin, Tiepolo, Chardin, van Gogh, Gauguin, Cézanne, Pissarro and Matisse were acquired through the William Hood Dunwoody Fund, in addition to Meindert Hobbema's *Wooded Landscape with Watermill.*

(Samuel Sachs II)

115

7

The name Pillsbury has become synonymous with Chinese bronzes and archaic jades of the highest quality and the Minneapolis Institute of Arts is famous for being their repository. Alfred F. Pillsbury, a past president of the Minneapolis Society of Fine Arts and collector of Chinese art, acquired this exquisitely crafted bronze tsun in the shape of an owl shortly after its excavation in the 1930s. In 1950 he bequeathed it, along with 125 other bronzes, to the Institute.

Animal form vessels such as this tsun are exceedingly rare, and they are considered a unique vestige of ancient Chinese civilization. The tsun is a ritual vessel used as a wine container during ceremonies honoring the ancestors. In this example the bird has one front and one back flange, with alternating straight and L-shaped scores, the former ending just under the beak, the latter continuing to the top of the head. The tail forms the back support for the vessel; the feet are very realistically formed, whereas the rest is strongly stylized. The whole bird is covered with rows of scales, the only exception being that the shoulder line (expressed by a vigorous spiral) and the wing quills are designed by bands filled with antithetical spirals. A flawless brown green patina adds to its distinction.

In his celebrated image, *Graveyard, Houses and Steel Mill, Bethlehem, Pa.*, Walker Evans portrays the environmental clutter of the American industrial landscape with its grim repetition of tombstones in the foreground, telephone poles in the middle distance and smokestacks on the horizon. Graveyard was shot with an 8 x 10 view camera in November 1935 under the auspices of the Resettlement Administration of the Departments of the Interior and Agriculture.

Within a group of talented photographers who travelled the length and breadth of the United States to document, record and preserve the American scene, Walker Evans was clearly the artist-with-the-camera who set a standard of perfection for others. He had a unique vision of America that was already fully developed when he joined this government sponsored program. It did not really suit his style or temperament; he refused to "politicize" with his camera and he felt that it was "extremely difficult for an artist to work for anyone else's use."

After two years of itinerant photography on the government payroll he was fired in 1937. Walker Evans associated, in Greenwich Village in the early 1930s, with men like Ben Shahn, Hart Crane, Lincoln Kirstein and James Agee, before he joined what was best known by its subsequent designation, the Farm Security Administration. The only photographer in whom Evans showed any interest then was Ralph Steiner whose 1936 *The Plow That Broke The Plains* (with Paul Strand) was financed by the same agency.

D. Thomas Bergen, the donor of this image, is an international businessman and avid collector of German Expressionist prints and drawings, as well as, more recently, vintage American photographs. His generosity has been directed primarily toward the Minneapolis and Chicago Art Institutes.

The Norwegian fin-de-siècle painter, Edvard Munch, is as famous for his graphic oeuvre as he is for his paintings. Munch's search for a distilled, elementary form and image that could speak for all of human experience is best understood within the framework of late 19th century art. *The Kiss* is symbolist in style but almost abstract in its interpretation of the lovers wedded into a unitary composition. A gradual abstraction of this theme can best be observed by comparing the woodcut with paintings (including a variant that turns lover into vampire) and an 1895 etching. All environmental references are omitted; there is no depth, modeling or perspective. A few white areas and incised lines separate the black hulk from a vertically striated background.

Munch developed his highly personal technique of wood cutting in Paris. He employed long-cut timber and, like Gauguin, exposed the grain of the wood itself, a method which suited the primitivism of his imagery. *The Kiss* is made up of two blocks: the figures are cut from one, over which is printed an uncut rectangle of coarsely grained, lightly inked pine.

Herschel V. Jones, owner and editor of the *Minneapolis Journal*, was an early supporter of the Society of Fine Arts. He came by his interest in the graphic arts quite naturally. Appointed a trustee in 1914, Jones was responsible for establishing the Institute's Department of Prints and Drawings. Upon his death in 1928, he left half of his collection of old master prints to the Institute with the other half coming as a bequest from his daughter in 1968.

169

126

The Nelson-Atkins Museum of Art

From ambiguous, biomorphic beginnings that characterized the work of the first generation Abstract Expressionists, Mark Rothko, a delicate colorist of poetic sensibility, developed in the mid-1950s what E.C. Goossen called an "omnibus image,"—an image of his own, dependent on nothing already clotted with associations, simple without being simplistic, precise but open-ended, asserting the primacy of the purely visual, yet serving as a vehicle for private emotion and universal spirituality. "We favor the simple expression of the complex thought," Rothko wrote in a 1943 manifesto cosigned by Adolph Gottlieb. Professing a spiritual kinship with primitive and archaic art, Rothko searched for a hieratic image within a reductive format.

Untitled #11 is painted in the warm, somber colors characteristic of the "Seagram Paintings" of the late 1950s. Having had an exhibition at The Museum of Modern Art and having just completed a series of murals for Harvard University, the artist's energies were sapped and he produced very little work that year. As his fame grew, so did his uneasiness about having reached a dead end in his painting. Brooding and depressed, he developed an increasing bias in favor of dimly lit presentations and his style evolved toward ever-darker paintings. The colors loom and define themselves to the eye with the slowness with which we recognize the configurations of a darkened room.

Rothko used to sit in his studio long after the light had died down, contemplating the memory of color. This probing beyond the visible, this plunging into an abyss of color dimmed by the absence of light, is indicative of a culminating move from youthful humanism to a tragic awareness of his Jewishness in later life. Rothko thought of his paintings as dramas. For every work he painted, Rothko had a chapel in mind. The diaphanous fields of color, suspended like veils before a void, dramatize Judaism's injunction against the graven image. The chapel was not long in coming. Within a year from this picture, Rothko was preoccupied with a commission from Dominique and John de Menil to execute murals for an interdenominational chapel in Houston on an octagonal floorplan designed by Philip Johnson.

Untitled #11 was bought from the artist in 1964 by the Friends of Art, a support organization which doubles as the Nelson Gallery-Atkins Museum's membership association. The Friends of Art was founded in 1934 to buy works of contemporary art for the museum because a clause in William Rockhill Nelson's will precluded the use of money from his trust for purchase of any work of an artist until he had been dead for thirty years. Such provisions are not uncommon in our older museums, and they became a challenge for outside groups to see to it that newer art forms would not remain unrepresented in an institution's permanent collection.

In the battle between the Classicists and the Romantics, Théodore Chassériau, for a time one of Ingres' most prominent pupils, left his master and went over to the camp of Delacroix. About a final discussion with Ingres, the much younger Chassériau confided to his brother with a sense of shock: "(He) has no comprehension of the ideas and the changes which have taken place in the arts in our day. He is completely ignorant of all the poets of recent times." The year was 1840 and the Romantic Movement was at its apogee. Relentlessly Ingres pursued the fight of line against color which was to be for many years the chief topic wherever artists met. When Paul de Saint-Victor introduced his newly arrived cousin, John La Farge, at Chassériau's, the American student was startled at being questioned immediately, as if it were of first importance, about the position he held with regard to Ingres and Delacroix.

Historians and poets of the 19th century glorified the victories of indigenous populations over their foreign oppressors and in doing so stirred up nationalist feelings everywhere. Faith triumphant, pitiless savagery, soul-stirring gallantry and the sacrificing love of the hero for the heroine were the themes writers shared with painters and examples abounded from Aeneas to Vercingetorix. As in Chassériau's *Roman Battle Scene*, an uneven hand to hand fight between the well-armed, rampaging soldier and the intrepid young champion of the downtrodden and defenseless, was grist for the romantic mill and a subject frequently encountered in the work of Delacroix and his followers.

Drawings by Chassériau are relatively rare outside of the Louvre and Petit Palais because one of the artist's descendants, Baron Arthus Chassériau, devoted his life to collecting the works of his great granduncle and bequeathed them all to the state. Both its quality and rarity recommended this drawing for purchase by the Nelson-Atkins Museum.

Ceramics in China are not to be considered as merely adjuncts to decorative arts in general or as service utensils alone, but rather as a distinctive category within the arts. Spanning almost four millennia from the painted neolithic pottery of about 2,000 B.C. to the delicate, decorated porcelains of the 19th century, the art of the Chinese potter possesses qualities of creativity, diversity, technical perfection and aesthetic worth that set it apart from the ceramics of any other culture.

Glazes date back to prehistoric times. About 1200 B.C., during the Shang Dynasty, potters introduced a high-fired porcelaneous stoneware with traces, probably fortuitous, of ash glaze. By the fifth to third century B.C., fully glazed pottery was common, and during the Han Dynasty the constantly growing demand for cheap pottery imitations to be buried in the tombs as substitutes for the far more valuable bronze and lacquer vessels stimulated the ceramics industry to ever greater production.

During the second century B.C., fantastic accounts of a breed of "heavenly horses in a land to the west" were reported to the Han court. Excited by these accounts, the Chinese sent expeditions to Ferghana in Central Asia to secure these fabled beasts. Hardier and larger than the native horses, the steeds were eagerly sought for military purposes. By the eighth century, the Chinese were breeding enough of their own stock with the help of Central Asian grooms, yet they continued to send expeditions to import the Ferghana horses which were highly prized by the aristocrats of the T'ang Dynasty for intelligence as well as for fine appearance. Worth about 40 bolts of silk, a Ferghana steed became a status symbol, and sculptors of the T'ang Dynasty (618-906) obviously delighted in capturing the spirit and grace of these superb animals in models that went with the wealthy to their burial sites.

The Horse and Rider in this exhibition is a fine example of the Nelson-Atkins Museum's world-renowned oriental collection, brought together, in large part, by its director emeritus Laurence Sickman over a long life of dedication to that institution.

95

10

Los Angeles County Museum of Art

11

"Images for Magritte attest to the fact that there is something other than our rapport with the real. They serve as springboards to the attentive mind for use as instruments of knowledge and *liberation* (italics are mine)," Suzi Gablik wrote in 1965 when Magritte's star began its tardy rise. If images set us free, what then are we to make of those key, glass, bird and pipe silhouettes cut from the canvas behind which this weary traveler hides his head and chest? Is he a soothsayer who speaks in riddles and lifts the host of knowledge? From the late 1920s on, Magritte has explored the theory of reality and illusion and has, much like the Austrian linguist-philosopher Wittgenstein, questioned the way in which everyday language disguises thought. His 1930 *The Key of Dreams* launched one of the most significant and intellectually difficult of Magritte's pictorial themes—one that cropped up, again and again, in later paintings.

The Liberator goes back, in Magritte's oeuvre, to a 1937 photograph of a seated man (the artist in disguise?) whose body and head are covered by a canvas with a blanket thrown over it and topped by a hat; the legs are showing, and the left hand rests on a cane. Its title, *God on the eighth day*—presumably the one after he beheld his handiwork, considered it well done and took a rest—is pregnant with some unspoken post-creation promise. Departing from this facetiously staged photograph, Magritte did several versions of what he came to call *The Healer*, sometimes replacing the silhouettes with a birdcage in which two turtledoves "watch over the health of the healer." The silhouettes in *The Liberator* are a repetition of the four symbols in Magritte's 1935 *Alphabet of Revelations*; the leaf has become a bird, which is no real difference because, in the artist's language, they interchangeably crop up as the hybrid "leaf-bird." Thus it would seem that *The Liberator*'s connotation is one of revelation through language. The most puzzling and surreal feature of *The Liberator* is the pearl-studded facial mask held in his right hand like a monstrance containing the transubstantiated body of the Redeemer. In Christian ritual the Host heals the sick and liberates the recipient from evil. There is, however, another, bizarre and unexplained connotation. In several paintings and gouaches dating between 1946-50 and, again, in *The Healer with a Face of Pearls* (1953) in *Le Domaine Enchanté*, Magritte's panoramic summation of earlier themes at the Casino of Knokke-Le Zoute, the facial mask is referred to as that of *Sheherazade*, the woman who managed to stay alive by never finishing her story. Thus, in one convoluted image, the artist bares himself as a faceless traveler who sits down with his hat in the clouds telling us a story that is all images and riddles and, as in The Arabian Nights, will never reach its conclusion.

In 1952 when few collectors paid the Belgian Surrealist heed, Bill Copley, a patron of such artists as Magritte and Man Ray, a one-time art promotor through his Copley Gallery in Beverly Hills, and a successful painter in his own right (signing CPLY), presented the Los Angeles County Museum with *The Liberator* as his gift.

This portrayal of the River Goddess Ganga and her attendants originated in Central India or Rajasthan in the ninth century A.D. The red sandstone fragment, while purchased by the Associates in 1972, forms part of the Nasli and Alice Heeramaneck Collection, a distinguished representation of Indian art at the Los Angeles County Museum and justly considered one of that museum's greatest assets. The Heeramaneck collection was 40 years in the making when the Museum acquired it in 1969.

Ganga personifies India's most sacred river, the Ganges. In Hindu mythology she figures prominently in the life of Siva. In representations of this incarnation of Vishnu, Ganga sometimes rises from the tangled hair of Siva as a fifth head of Brahma. When the gods consented to the descent of Ganga, the heavenly river, the weight of the mass of water would have engulfed the earth, if the god with the trident (Siva) had not offered himself to lessen the shock. Falling into his tangled hair, Ganga wandered about the god's head for several years without finding an outlet. Finally Siva had to divide her into seven streams so that she could descend on earth without causing a catastrophe. In this representation of Ganga we see her simply enjoying the bountifulness of the river and what grows through its life-giving power.

B ecause of its later adoption as almost a cliché image of speediness in delivery, Giovanni da Bologna's *Mercury* now automatically comes to mind when we think of Italian Renaissance bronzes. That time designation is misleading, though. The sculptor from Douai who Italianized his name arrived on the scene in Florence after the second elegant phase of Mannerism had reached its apogee with the goldsmith Benvenuto Cellini. Giambologna became, during a life in art that stretched into the 17th century, sculptor *sans pareil* to the Medici. A 1978 Arts Council of Great Britain exhibition documented his extraordinary production and addressed, without necessarily offering a solution, the many problems that have arisen around the famed *Mercury*, its original design, several known variants and countless copies.

The same iconography underlies all versions. Mercury is shown in flight, naked but for his winged hat. His right arm is raised and the index finger points upward. In his lowered left hand he holds the caduceus, the herald's staff with two entwined snakes and two wings at the top Wings also sprout from each of his ankles. What appear to be variations may also be misinterpretations of a later date or uncorrected losses. The Los Angeles *Mercury* with its impeccable pedigree of having been in the collections of Vincent Astor and Sir Thomas Gibson Carmichael, turns his torso and stretches his neck, as he looks upward, in a way that differs, however slightly, from the accepted originals. More obvious differences are the pouch (?) in his right hand and the absence of a caduceus which, indeed, may have been removed or simply lost from his left hand. The base which Mercury's left foot just barely touches in the original casts, has been replaced in the Los Angeles cast by a less effective cupped stand and stem. Finally, the facial features differ just enough to suggest that another intermediary may have been involved in this presumably 17th century copy after the original.

The literary source for Giambologna's *Mercury* is Homer's Odyssey (Book V, p. 45-46); as origin of the messenger's pointing gesture, Leonardo da Vinci's *Annunciation* has been suggested. The first mention of a *Mercury in Flight* by Giambologna in Vasari (1568) expressly stated that it was sent to Maximilian II of Austria. It is likely that the artist, at the behest of the Grand Duke Cosimo I, conceived the figure specially for this purpose (what more fitting symbol to send?) and that the statuette of *Mercury*, formerly in the imperial possession, now in the Kunsthistorisches Museum, is the actual bronze presented to the Emperor in 1565. The Vienna *Mercury* differs from a variant that was sent to Ottavio Farnese in about 1579 and can now be found in the Capodimonte Museum in Naples. Most scholars agree that the *Mercury* in the Museo Civico in Bologna is a preliminary model. As for its best known version, a life-size variant in the Bargello, it has Mercury gliding on the head of Zephyrus and it dates from as late as 1580. While a statuette traceable in Dresden from 1587 is closest to the Vienna *Mercury*, most of the numerous other replicas are based on the Naples variant. Antonio Susini, whom Giambologna took into his workshop in the second half of the 1570s, may have had a hand in the casting and finishing of three of the four existing original versions.

39

The Currier Gallery of Art

Walt Kuhn deserves to be known for more than his role as one of the organizers of the 1913 Armory Show. A realist, like Hopper and Guy Pène du Bois, he has left us with a picture of America at a more innocent age, gay as the circus or the Fourth of July, yet haunting because of its implied make-believe. *Lancer* with its military parade trappings and horsehair plume forcing the composition into a surging tizzy, is a sad and sober picture in which the "act" parades as the joyless model's only true reality.

The arrangement of the figure and the vertically stretched background, featuring rather than just accommodating the lancer's headgear, are carried off by an effective use of color. Working within narrow ranges, the painter achieves surprisingly rich and varied effects. The color scheme stresses the patriotic primaries with an addition of white and grays for proper balance. The woman's closely fitted costume is ultramarine blue tempered by slight variations of the same color and accented by the introduction of an intense vermillion into the bodice. Red is used again in the neckband and in the hat. Gold braid, tassel, badge and epaulets, and a white belt and gloves complete the costume. Essential to offset the subject's coloristic grandstanding are the pallid flesh tones and the mauve tonality of the background.

The artist's daughter has preserved for us the trivial but endearing details surrounding this painting. In the year of the New York World's Fair, Kuhn engaged a nightclub performer by the name of Lorraine Roe to pose for him in this strutting costume in his East 18th Street studio. Once on intimate terms with the world of clowns, acrobats, jugglers and bareback riders, Kuhn looked behind the eye shadow and defiant pose to find the vulnerability and deeper humanity of his subjects. Yet, he is neither maudlin nor given to social criticism. His intense involvement with painting's intrinsic demands of color and composition makes him tackle even that most dangerous of themes, the circus clown.

The personality, life and work of Lorenzo Costa remain paradoxical. Modern art historians consider him a lesser master, but contemporary critics called him the Apelles of his time. Born in 1460 in Ferrara, Costa was probably a pupil of Cosimo Tura. As a young man he went to Bologna, and is usually identified with that city. He set up a workshop with Francesco Francia and painted many religious scenes for the Bentivoglio, Bologna's ruling family. When in 1506, the Bentivoglio were driven from the city by the forces of Pope Julius II, Costa hastened to accept the invitation of Isabella d'Este that he come to Mantua as court painter in place of Andrea Mantegna who had recently died. Costa remained in Mantua until his death in 1535.

The Currier *Portrait of a Lady* is neither signed nor dated, but its traditional attribution to Lorenzo Costa, by Adolfo Venturi, Wilhelm von Bode and Georg Swarzenski has been accepted by recent art historians. Its close resemblance to the artist's *Portrait of a Lady with Lapdog* in the Royal Collection at Hampton Court served as a potent argument. The signed and dated painting that most closely resembles the Currier portrait is the *Pala Ghedini*, Costa's masterpiece of 1497. Until John E. Schloder questioned the picture's date and the identity of its sitter, in an article in the Currier Gallery of Art Bulletin of Fall 1978, it was generally considered to be a likeness of Eleanora Gonzaga, painted about 1506.

Whoever she may be, the sitter in the Currier portrait is certainly a lady of rank and fortune; her clothes, her jewels and her noble bearing leave no doubt. The brilliant juxtaposition of clear, vigorous colors is as typical of Costa's work as is the geometrical anatomy of his model. Her captivating, enigmatic expression is reminiscent of Leonardo da Vinci and his school. The prominent shading and coloring of the costume which gives the bows and the jewels the semblance of applied ornaments, contrast with the delicate modeling and subtle tone gradations of the sitter's face. Her costume shows the Spanish influence that first entered Italy through the Aragonese court

of Naples about 1480. Even her coiffure, tightly drawn into two smooth waves encircling the cheeks, betrays the Spanish style although its regularity is relieved by filiform strands of hair that fall in capricious waves of gold on either side of the smoothly drawn crown.

Moody Currier was the very model of a successful American in the 19th century. School teacher, lawyer, newspaperman, industrialist, banker and politician, he found time to publish poetry and serve his state as Governor. While not a collector of art, he directed in his will that an art gallery be erected on the site of the Currier mansion, leaving to others the task of filling and endowing his creation. The Gallery's first professional director, Gordon M. Smith, reasoned that one masterpiece was more to be desired than a roomful of run-of-the-mill paintings. So in 1947, he acquired the Lorenzo Costa portrait which heralded the beginning of the Currier's distinguished painting collection.

Known as *Grand Nu Assis, Bras Levés*, this largest and perhaps most important of all of Henri Matisse's bronzes, dates back to 1923-25 when the artist began to make his permanent home in Nice. It evolved from his visits to the School of Decorative Arts to study a cast of Michelangelo's *Night*, one of the pair made for the Medici tomb in Florence and it combines the indolence of the painted odalisques with an extraordinary vitality and tension borrowed from that High Renaissance example. The massive torso, leaning sharply backward with arms locked behind the head, is like an architectural cantilever anchored by the left foot firmly tucked under the right knee. Visualizing his model in a pose that would be extremely fatiguing to sustain, Matisse brought arms, legs and torso, straining as they try to pull away from each other, into a powerful plastic relationship. The fact that the thighs and legs are unusually short compared with the torso may have its origin in the painter's habit of optical foreshortening.

The head of *Seated Nude*, stripped of

recognizable facial characteristics and disproportionately small for the fleshy bulk of the body, anticipates later works. Matisse deals with the elongated body as the main theme and the head as almost an unavoidable afterthought in two versions of his 1931-33 *Dance* (Musée d'Art Moderne de la Ville de Paris and Barnes Foundation) as well as in the documented 22 stages of the Cone Collection's *Pink Nude*. *Seated Nude*'s pose is strikingly similar to that of the *Odalisque with Raised Arms* (1923) in the Chester Dale Collection, *Nude on Blue Pillow* (1924) in the Sidney F. Brody Collection, a number of 1924-25 lithographs and, most intriguingly, the *Rape of Europa* (1929) in a Chicago collection. Matisse admitted to having difficulty with the latter and to reworking it over a period of three years. Was the thought of transferring his model from a comfortable armchair to the back of a swimming bull already on Matisse's mind when he precariously balanced her languorous form on no more than a Moroccan pillow?

31

159

Milwaukee Art Museum

140

In 1904, four young student painters of the Dresden Institute of Technology came to know each other—Kirchner, Heckel, Schmidt-Rottluff and Bleyl. In 1905, they founded an artists' association which they called Die Brücke. Two years later they were joined by Pechstein and Nolde. They painted in shouting, luminous colors and with great spontaneity, taking their motifs directly from nature. The spirit of van Gogh, the decorativeness of the Jugendstil, the expressionism of Edvard Munch and the evocative powers of Oceanic sculpture all passed into the vocabulary of these young painters. Since their objectives ran parallel to those of the French Fauves, it was only natural that artists of Die Brücke entered into contact with their French colleagues.

In 1911, Kirchner, Heckel and Schmidt-Rottluff transferred their activities to Berlin where Pechstein had already moved in 1908 and Otto Mueller had espoused their cause in 1910. A new and final Brücke style now developed in the circles of the New Secession. In Berlin, Kirchner painted one of his grandest pictures, *The Street*, 1913, in the collection of The Museum of Modern Art. That Cubism had become a factor for the Berlin group is apparent, but the overriding impression is one of hectic note-taking, restless interlacing of space, colors grating on each other and acute awareness of life on the edge of the abyss.

Ernst Ludwig Kirchner who became a patient in Davos in 1917, experienced the broadest development and left the most moving legacy of any artist in Die Brücke. A city dweller at heart, he became deeply involved, nonetheless, with the heroic quality of the Swiss mountain scenery and with the rural rituals of its inhabitants. In the winter of 1925-26, Kirchner broke out of his isolation and revisited the cities he had known—Frankfurt, Dresden, Chemnitz and Berlin. From this trip he brought back sketches of urban scenes which he translated into paintings that bore an eery spiritual resemblance to those he painted just before the outbreak of the war. On closer inspection, we realize that stylistically they are of the 1920s, fitting more comfortably in the context of postwar German realist art or of Kees van Dongen's late Fauve pictures than in the rhythmically agitated and symbolically pregnant Brücke milieu at its heyday. With its quick-stepping metropolitan pulse and its garish Bengal light coloration, *Street Scene* is a fine example of German Expressionism revisited at a time when majestic mountain scenes almost monopolized the painter's attention.

In 1967, Mrs. Harry Lynde Bradley, a Milwaukee art collector who had long been the Art Center's major patron, indicated that she wished to leave her collection in Milwaukee provided suitable facilities could be created. With her monetary incentive as well, the Center embarked on a building campaign, and in 1975, a new structure, four times the size of the old one, was opened to the public. Featuring the Bradley Family Foundation paintings, the re-named Milwaukee Art Museum now boasts an in-depth representation of 19th and 20th century art. from Degas to Warhol.

The interaction of two figures in the primordial "game of life" preoccupied Archipenko, and allowed him to explore spatial relationships within and between forms in motion. The void, or what we might call "negative form," actual or merely suggested through concave and slanted planes, became this sculptor's lifelong fascination. Despite his protestations, he did *take from* and not just *add to* the Cubist vocabulary. That should be clear in the faceting of these headless boxers, reminiscent of bodies and limbs so treated by Picasso and Braque in their 1908 paintings. Yet, to their pictorial vision he added a strong sense of architecture and a "Gothic" rhythm that reflected the different cultural tradition whence his work sprang. Archipenko's ambition and that of Duchamp-Villon, Boccioni and Lipchitz with whose contemporaneous sculptures *La Lutte* should be compared, was not just to reduce form to its crystalline essence but to eliminate frontality by substituting a dynamic for a static point of view.

Alexander Archipenko was born in Kiev in 1887, son of a mechanical engineer and grandson of an icon painter. He entered art school in 1902, went to Moscow in 1906 and, just before his 21st birthday, took a train for Paris, never to return to his native country. In Montparnasse he associated with Modigliani and Gaudier-Brzeska and at the Louvre he looked at archaic Mediterranean and early Gothic sculpture. When the Section d'Or was formed, Archipenko became one of its members and, from 1912-14, exhibited with that group which included most of the Cubists. The Folkwang Museum in Hagen offered him his first one-man exhibition, and Guillaume Apollinaire consented to write the catalogue. In 1913, Archipenko was represented by four sculptures and five drawings in the Armory Show in New York and, like Duchamp's *Nude Descending a Staircase*, one was ridiculed in a newspaper cartoon. *La Lutte*, created in 1914, was the artist's most abstract sculpture up to that date.

H aitian art, like Inuit art, has suffered greatly from the attempts of idealistic, well-intentioned outsiders to help its practitioners achieve recognition and recompense for their unique visions. It is impossible to say how those arts might have developed, if at all, had the artists not been encouraged to repetition and over-production and, as a consequence, lost the original motivations which made the work exciting. The art of Hector Hyppolite was spared at least some of the influences of commercial exploitation because he died in 1948, having produced, according to various estimates, between 250-600 paintings within two years.

Prior to his involvement with the Port-au-Prince art colony, Hyppolite had made his way in the world as a houngan (voodoo priest) and house painter, occasionally using his talents to decorate buildings. He is unanimously considered the foremost artist among Haitian painters. Alone among that group, his work retains the direct, untutored expression of the

Haitian synthesis of French and African cultures—the integration of Christian and Voodoo religions in a style that imbues the real with the unreal. Pierre Apraxine wrote: "The Haitian mind grasps everything as having a meaning other than, or in addition to, the literal meaning of the image," and only the Haitian mind has references with which to decipher those hidden meanings.

In *Adoration of Love*, a crucifixion, Hyppolite combines an image of Christ on the cross with five worshipers dressed in the white robes of hounsis, those who assist the houngan during voodoo ceremonies. Serrated patches of light define the figures and indicate the melding of man and god which takes place during voodoo "possession." The mask-like faces with their transfixed expressions also refer to the possessed state as well as to the ceremonial masks in which Haitians delight.

Richard B. Flagg, an active member of the museum board of trustees and major benefactor to all the arts in Milwaukee, recognized the importance of Haitian art long before it became fashionable. He assembled the Flagg Tanning Corporation Collection of Haitian Art which is considered one of the most important collections of that form in the United States, preserving, as it does, the uniquely Haitian images of the original painters. Mr. Flagg's contributions and loans to the museum, as well as his participation in its ongoing development, make him stand out among the supporters of the arts in Milwaukee.

(Ann W. Heymann)

185

Walker Art Center

American sculpture of the 20th century has two uncontested geniuses, Alexander Calder and David Smith. With the majestic, stainless steel *Cubis*, Smith reached the zenith of his creative powers, made the best sculpture this country had ever seen, and delivered the epitaph to a prodigious career. In *Terminal Ironworks*, the artist's biographer Rosalind E. Krauss, sees the *Cubis* as the culmination of Smith's experience with drawing in the 1950s. To him they had a basic geometric form, already "found," composed of such pre-existing shapes as squares, triangles and circles, and he "drew" them across a continuous plane. This reinforces their frontality, which is at odds with the very nature of the sculptural experience, yet, in the case of the Cubis, does not diminish their authority as sculpture.

Cubi IX was acquired by the Art Center one year before the sculptor's death and chosen from among 28 odd works in that series; most of them were still standing on the grounds of Bolten Landing. It remains one of the best ones—a superb example of Smith's artistry. Demonstrative of the artist's preoccupation with properties of light and mass, *Cubi IX* does not appear heavy because of its extraordinary balance and the manner in which its brushed surfaces absorb the light. About this and other Cubis, Smith has said: "The metal (iron or steel) itself possesses little art history. What associations it possesses are those of this century: power, structure, movement, progress, suspension, destruction, brutality..."

For a 1950 exhibition on the theme of black and white at the Kootz Gallery, the leading artist-spokesman for and practitioner of Abstract Expressionism, Robert Motherwell, wrote: "There is so much to be seen in a work of art, so much to say if one is concrete and accurate, that it is a relief to deal on occasion with a simple relation. Yet not even it, no more than any other relation in art, is so simple." The challenge is still there and the warning has lost none of its poignancy, 30 years after Abstract Expressionism's heroic phase, as we now look at an elegiac, beautifully resolved summation of those earlier heroics. In reply to the present owner's request for relevant information about subject and ideas expressed, the artist simply stated: "It is basically a very mysterious painting. Let it stay that way." In a postscript Motherwell made clear that the painting should not be "overlit," no doubt wanting to retain for it, as Mark Rothko had earlier for his increasingly dark shapes floating on dark backgrounds, that aura of gradual self-definition that only daylight, even fading daylight, lends.

Untitled, 1971, was painted the year Motherwell moved to Greenwich, Connecticut, and it was acquired the year thereafter by Walker Art Center, a museum that takes pride in being on top of contemporary developments. The two major themes that have dominated Motherwell's painting, *The Elegies to the Spanish Republic* and *The Open Series*, show the full measure of this prodigious talent as he masterfully elaborates on what are, in essence, visions of an archetypal nature. The former is bold and related to the gestural nature of that movement also referred to as "Action Painting." The latter is subtle and more akin to the color field orientation of Rothko and Newman. They occur simultaneously throughout the artist's career although the emphasis now seems to lie on the latter. *Untitled*, 1971, with its solid black and open red contraposition, seems to derive from both but stylistically belongs to *The Open Series*.

Confirming one of history's ironies, American born Lyonel Feininger, when turning 60, was given, as a tribute to his art and teaching, a major retrospective exhibition at the Kronprinzen Palais in Berlin in 1931 and then, just six years later, saw his work included in the infamous *Entartete Kunst* exhibition which the Nazis staged at the Haus der Deutsche Kunst in Munich. *Church of the Minorites (II)*, 1926, was painted the year Feininger moved with the Bauhaus, where he led the graphic arts workshop, from Weimar to Dessau. The artist was at the height of his

200

reputation. He had exhibited at the Berlin
Secession, at the prestigious Galerie der
Sturm and he had joined Jawlensky,
Kandinsky and Klee in the *Blue Four*, in
1924. The newly painted picture was
acquired by a German museum but in the
1930s it, too, found itself banned. It was
acquired by the Walker Art Center in 1943
in that institution's first modernist phase.

At the end of the first decade of this
century Lyonel Feininger, then
approaching middle age, discovered van
Gogh and Cézanne and switched from the
drawings and cartoons with which he had
made a minor reputation, to painting
proper. On a visit to Paris, in 1911,
Cubism appeared to him as something he
had "intuitively striven after for years."
Not too fond of labels, he later joked that
his own brand of Cubism might be called
"Prismism" and, indeed, the sharply
faceted forms and limpid colors of *Church
of the Minorites (II)* have the quality of a
picture seen through faceted glass. Its
shifting, interpenetrating planes introduce
the viewer to a sense of motion and time
in a way that relates Feininger to the
painters of the Section d'Or in Paris. The
first version of this same subject, the
Gothic "Barfüsserkirche" in Erfurt
(Thuringia), of 1924, is owned by a private
collector in Wuppertal.

142

Founded through the munificence of T.
B. Walker in 1879, the Walker Art
Center, in it first building (1927-1968) as
well as on its new premises designed by
Edward Larrabee Barnes (since 1971), has
consistently functioned as a patron of the
new. Regional art and design played a
major role in the 1930s and 1940s but as of
the 1950s, the Center was on a solid
contemporary course, continuing its design
focus and broadening its perspective to
include international art. All major
purchases have been made with Walker
funds and when, in 1976, the Center
became a public institution, the T. B.
Walker Foundation transferred to it all
works of art that had been, heretofore, the
Foundation's property.

The Newark Museum

153

Georgia O'Keeffe was the solitary woman among Alfred Stieglitz's distinguished American modernists. She met the photographer and promotor of painting in 1916 when visiting "291" to show him her work. "Finally, a woman on paper," Stieglitz is said to have exclaimed. He gave O'Keeffe her first exhibition, took charge of her career and married her in 1924. From the 1930s on, the painter spent her winters in New Mexico; the desert landscape, with its stubborn vegetation, bleached skeletons and adobe buildings became the source of her inspiration. Like Arthur Dove before her, O'Keeffe gave biomorphic abstraction an individual inflection rooted in observation and experience, never straying far from the world of visible phenomena.

White Flower on Red Earth, No. 1 was painted in New Mexico and exhibited at *An American Place*, the New York gallery which Alfred Stieglitz, then separated from O'Keeffe, directed until his death. Reputedly, Beatrice Winser, assistant and successor to John Cotton Dana, the Newark Museum's founding director, selected this painting for purchase in consultation with Alfred Stieglitz. The flower's magnification in this close-up and its tight fit within the picture plane, anticipate, by several decades, Ellsworth Kelly's graphic and Jack Youngerman's abstract treatment of floral motifs, as well as their straight use by Andy Warhol and Lowell Nesbitt. Its modest size and its delicate facture, however, clearly identify this work as hewing the line of 1940s painting.

Among John Cotton Dana's most important contributions to the development of contemporary museum policy and practice were his active support and purchase of American art and his championship of good design and industrial art at the Newark Museum. In 1912, in cooperation with Karl Ernst Osthaus, the director of the German Museum for Art in Commerce and Industry at Hagen, Westphalia, and the Deutscher Werkbund, Dana organized the pioneering exhibition,

Modern German Applied Arts. Dana's philosophy in championing industrial art and design was pragmatic, democratizing and educational. Newark was essentially an industrial city and he wanted the museum to serve, inform and lead. "The modern movement in the decorative arts is really a movement toward machine art...," Dana wrote in 1927, voicing the philosophy that, within a few years, would elevate the machine to the level of art.

When Dana bought objects from the applied arts exhibitions at his museum, he tended to select the small, simple and common—in line with his "good objects of low cost" leaning. That habit failed to take into account the more opulent taste of one of his most dedicated patrons, Louis Bamberger, founder of a department store chain and collector of English and Continental silver. Bamberger shared Dana's interest in craftmanship and fine design, and he could be counted upon to finance higher priced acquisitions for the museum's applied arts collection. In 1922, he purchased and donated a silver compote designed and commercially introduced by George Jensen in 1918. Its chalice shape and vine ornaments are typical of a late 19th century revivalist taste that spawned the so-called *Jugendstil*—also known as *Art Nouveau* and *Liberty Style*. The compote retains those characteristics even though the style that gave rise to them was well past its prime.

The Copenhagen atelier for the design of silverware, founded in 1904 by George Jensen and still in existence today, began to gain its international reputation as early as 1910. In tune with crafts innovators all over Europe, Jensen set out to restore to the manufacture of silver objects for daily use, the simple virtues and manifest qualities lost in machine tooling and mass fabrication. In Denmark, where the influence of William Morris and the English Arts and Crafts Movement with its revival of Celtic ornament was more noticeable than that of the Austrian Jugendstil, the renewal was referred to as *Skönvirke*. In the Jensen workshops, silver was treated with a renewed interest in the metal's properties; chasing was out, hammering and embossing were in. The shape of the object became the essential feature and decoration became a symbol of function. Details were first modelled and then applied to merge with an object's basic shape. In a state of tension between surface and ornament, form, in Jensen's hands, became intrinsically ornamental.

Because of the innovative accomplishments of its own designers Hector Guimard, René Lalique and Emile Gallé, France was sensitized to modern craftsmanship early on and accorded it high honors. In 1913, Jensen was represented in the Salon d'Automne in Paris, and in 1914 a compote, prototypical to the one in this exhibition, was shown in the Salon de la Société Nationale des Beaux-Arts and was subsequently acquired by the Musée des Arts Décoratifs in Paris.

Tibetan Art is best known by the tanka. The tanka, however, is not created primarily for aesthetic enjoyment, but as Giuseppe Tucci has said, "as a picture the tanka opens up vistas for him [the devotee]; but it presents also, in a preliminary form, the experience of vision." In Tibet prior to 1959, the words "religion" and "culture" were nearly synonymous. There are five principal sects in Tibetan Buddhism, and this 17th century image of Guru *Drag-po-che and Retinue* is a deity of the Ningma-pa school.

The frequency of sexual symbolism in Tibetan art may appear puzzling to the Western mind. Eleanor Olson in *The Art of Tibet* has noted that sexual symbolism is almost a prerogative of mysticism. In esoteric Buddhist thought the sexual embrace symbolizes the essential unity of an apparent duality. These yab-yum images were not for general display, and only the initiates were introduced to their esoteric significance.

The word "tanka" literally means "something that is rolled up." According to Olson, the tanka originated in India, but the frequent mountings of Chinese brocade reflect the contribution of China to external form. Several artists usually work on a tanka—the master, who draws, and his assistants who apply the paint. No Tibetan tanka is signed, and only a few are dated. The support of a tanka is usually cotton or linen, and the vegetable, mineral and animal pigments are applied after the surface is prepared with a ground of chalk and glue.

The important Tibetan collection in the Newark Museum resulted from a 1910 shipboard friendship between Edward N. Crane, a founding trustee of the Newark Museum, and Dr. Albert L. Shelton, a medical missionary who had been stationed in the town of Batang, east of the then-existing Sino-Tibetan border. Territorial disputes between China and local Tibetan rulers had resulted in widespread destruction, including the 1905 razing of the great Batang monestary. Many Tibetan objects were sold to Dr. Shelton in order to obtain funds to buy back land from the Chinese. Traditionally, these sacred objects had seldom been permitted to pass into foreign hands.

Mr. Crane arranged for the 1911 exhibition of the approximately one hundred fifty Tibetan objects at the then fledgling Newark Museum. The "exotic" exhibition was surprisingly successful, and when Crane suddenly died in 1911, his family purchased the entire collection from Dr. Shelton and presented it to the Museum as a memorial. In 1913, the Museum commissioned Dr. Shelton to continue to collect Tibetan "curios." By 1919, Dr. Shelton was able to return with 250 additional artifacts, again with valuable supporting documentation.

(Brenda Williamson)

66

92 *French*, Portrait of a Young Woman Called
Mademoiselle Charlotte du Val d'Ognes, *c. 1800*
The Metropolitan Museum of Art, New York

136

Yale University Art Gallery

Fox Trot B, painted in 1929, belongs to the artist's "classical" period (1928-1932) when the iconic summation of *Neo-Plasticist* theory had reached its intended perfection. The ordering principle is a horizontal-vertical rhythm. Within a square space, rectangular planes in primary colors, bounded by black lines, run parallel to the framing edge. Its stability derives from the near-square at the center of the composition which anchors, with the aid of a solid black and yellow base, the red, black and blue planes running across the top and into the left segment of the picture. One may visualize these planes as well as the lines that frame them, transgressing the rim of the image. The fixed center thus becomes a nucleus and conceptual starting point of a higher pictorial order, capable, in the artist's aesthetic, of being given unlimited physical and spiritual extension.

Katherine S. Dreier started the Collection of the Société Anonyme as a private Museum of Modern Art in 1920 with the gift of six paintings by Walter C. Arensberg's cousin, John Covert, who decided to toss over art for a career in business. Assisted by the peripatetic Marcel Duchamp as her secretary, Miss Dreier borrowed pictures from artists with the stated purpose of exhibiting them in furtherance of the cause of modern art and for the educational benefit of Americans not yet exposed to ideas that, with the 1913 Armory Show, had begun to gain currency in some circles. In 1926 she visited Mondrian in his studio in the rue du Depart and bought from him the diamond-shaped canvas which she later bequeathed to The Museum of Modern Art.

Some time in 1930, Katherine Dreier selected two loans for the Collection of the Société Anonyme, *Fox Trot A* and *Fox Trot B*, which Duchamp was charged to ship to her in New York. After they had been traveling in Société Anonyme exhibitions for seven years, friends prevailed upon Mondrian to turn them into a gift. In 1941, the Collection of the Société Anonyme was deeded to Yale University but its donors, Katherine Dreier and Marcel Duchamp, continued adding to it while George Heard Hamilton became its distinguished curator and author of its catalogue.

An issue touched on by Mondrian scholars but not clarified should concern us here. Why is the artist's 1929 square referred to as *Fox Trot B* while the diamond-shaped canvas Miss Dreier selected along with it, carries 1930 as its date on the front and is clearly marked, *Fox Trot A*, in Mondrian's own hand, on the back of the stretcher? The President of the Collection of the Société Anonyme was known to take liberties with titles but there is sufficient evidence that Mondrian determined the titles of both pictures while making a rare exception to his habit of labeling everything Composition.

Since there is ample precedent for pictures taking years between inception and completion because of the artist's proclivity to reconsider and repaint, I submit that *Fox Trot A* was far enough along in 1927 for the artist to identify it on the stretcher frame but that, possibly between Miss Dreier's visit and its pickup for shipment, Mondrian made a few last minute changes and, accordingly, affixed his initials and '30 to a surface that was not yet signed. This hypothesis is corroborated by Michel Seuphor's listing *Fox Trot A* in his classified catalogue as having been painted in 1927, ostensibly on stylistic grounds but possibly as the result of privileged information.

More weight is adduced by correspondence between Mondrian and the architect J. J. Oud that has recently come to light. In March 1927, Mondrian wrote to Oud that 20 freshly painted pictures, referred to as groups of importance in his evolution, had been scuffed and punctured as a result of careless handling by a Dutch artists' association in Paris. He was forced to repaint them but thought their quality had improved in the process. As oeuvre catalogues list no more than a dozen paintings for 1926-27, and as no pictures of that year have been recorded lost, we must assume that almost half of Mondrian's production of the winter of 1926-27 was painted over, to some degree, at a later date and carries the dates of completion.

The reference to these paintings as

139

158

71

being important in his evolution would suggest their being, for a good part at least, the diamond-shape challenges to Theo van Doesburg's Elementarist heresy. Thus *Fox Trot A* would retain its place in E. A. Carmean, Jr's, 1979 sequence of the Diamond Compositions between *Painting I, 1926*, Katherine S. Dreier's bequest to The Museum of Modern Art, and *Composition I-A, 1930*, Hilla von Rebay's bequest to the Solomon R. Guggenheim Museum. Stylistically, it clearly relates to its predecessor, rather than to its successor in the series.

The Fox Trot, an American dance of Negro ancestry, became popular from about 1913 onward. Dancing was Mondrian's favorite relaxation and he engaged in it, according to contemporary witnesses, with religio-scientific fervor and all the grace of a wooden slat. In his studio he kept a red phonograph and an extensive record collection for practice and impromptu parties. Despite his meager income he took dancing lessons, and when the Dutch papers attacked the Charleston, he jumped to its defense. Visiting friends took Mondrian to such night spots as the *Jockey Club*, the *Bal-Bullier* and *La Cigogne*, all in Montparnasse. In the *Internationale Revue i 10* of December 1927, Mondrian published an article on "Jazz and Neo-Plasticism" in which he justified the latter in terms of the former's spiritual ambitions and in which the bar becomes the crucible of man's baser instincts held in check by jazz's purifying rhythms.

After the birth of his son Paulo in February 1921, Picasso rented a comfortably bourgeois villa at Fontainebleau. The domestic atmosphere of the place did not agree with him but he threw himself into his work and completed several major paintings. On the one hand, he undertook large compositions in a neoclassical style, on the other he recapitulated, on an impressive scale, the basic tenets of Synthetic Cubism. *Dog and Cock*, according to William S. Rubin, was painted in Paris either just before or just after the summer at Fontainebleau. Its

fluency of form and the autumnal tone of the artist's palette suggest that it followed rather than preceded the two versions of *Three Musicians*. An additional argument might be the freer articulation of table legs, dog and table contents in a breezily handled late Cubist way—freer, that is, than the way in which he put *Three Musicians* together.

The dichotomy, in Picasso's work at this time, between the plumply portrayed women pursuing men and nursing their offspring and, chastely within the late Cubist idiom, their flattened male counterparts harmonizing in a commedia dell'arte setting, may reflect the artist being pulled between family and professional demands. In *Dog and Cock* Picasso returns to the cherished Cubist still life tradition but introduces, unlike anything he has ever done before, the antagonistic ingredient of a live dog (the artist pulling at his leash?) threatening the life-like victuals of a domestic existence.

Dog and Cock is an elegant summation of Synthetic Cubism. It recapitulates, in a seemingly effortless way, the basic inventions of that style. Table, dog and repast are distributed across the surface at an angle perpendicular to the viewer. Their organization in narrow, vertical planes, overlapping and interlocking with each other, recalls the *Papier collé* origin of the Synthetic Cubist morphology and is, although more broadly conceived, reminiscent of the 1916-17 pointillist manner. With a combination of formal wit and decorative savvy, Picasso uses a sawtooth outline to show the dog's panting, neat rows of ferns for the cock's plumage and dots and cross-hatch marks for the wicker basket. The narrow format is well-suited to the small dinner table on high legs, energetically pushed upward by the motions of the ferreting dog. Alfred Barr's argument that this format is too narrow for decorative comfort is untenable in light of its age-old use for painted corner decorations in a wainscoted formal room— a room such as his rented quarters at Fontainebleau may well have had.

Stephen Carlton Clark and Robert Sterling Clark (who endowed Williamstown with his collection of

Impressionist paintings and English silver) were sons of the founder of the Singer Sewing Machine Company. Stephen C. Clark erected the National Baseball Hall of Fame in Cooperstown, New York, served on the boards of trustees of both the Metropolitan and The Museum of Modern Art and left, upon his death in 1960, a significant collection of mainly 19th and 20th century paintings to Yale University, the institution from which he graduated.

This cherry and pinewood dressing table from East Windsor, Connecticut, is a fine example of late 18th century cabinetry; it can be attributed to Eliphalet Chapin (1741-1807), who was trained as a cabinetmaker in Enfield, Connecticut, spent his apprenticeship in Philadelphia, and returned to East Windsor where he opened shop in 1771. The influence of his Philadelphia training is evident in the design of this dressing table, although it lacks the more elegant Philadelphia detailing and substitutes cherry for black walnut.

The Mabel Brady Garvan Collections at the Yale University Art Gallery consist of an initial gift, in 1930, by Francis P. Garvan, Class of 1897, of an outstanding representation of early American art which, since that time, has doubled in size to comprise 10,000 examples of Americana. A memorial to the late Mabel Brady Garvan, who supported the American Arts program at Yale for half a century, the quality and wealth of these materials placed in trust with the Gallery by their one-time owners, make New Haven a place of pilgrimage for lovers of early American decorative arts.

Fascinated by the process of evolution, Brancusi repeatedly examined the same motifs in order to mine the possiblities of formal and technical variation and refinement. Mlle. *Pogany II* is the second in a series of three discrete yet evolutionary interpretations of a subject Brancusi had

first treated in 1912. The original *Mlle. Pogany* derived from sketches and clay busts of Margit Pogany, an Hungarian artist who had posed for Brancusi in the winter of 1910-11. In the second and third versions conceived in 1919 and 1931 respectively, Brancusi placed progressively greater emphasis on attenuated verticality and simplified formal elegance, thus moving the work farther away from the realm of actual portraiture into that of abstract, decorative design.

The Katharine Ordway Collection's *Mlle. Pogany II*, cast by the artist in 1925, is one of four polished bronzes of the 1919 version. The mouth, eyes and chignon of the 1912 work have been replaced by accentuated arching brows and an elongated, stepped swirl of arched curls. The arms and hands which, in the earlier sculpture, were held to the left cheek in an attitude of prayer, are now joined into a single tapering column. Brancusi's new, sparer design, with its precise contours and sharply defined but sinuous lines, establishes a rhythm of smooth transition between parts. In combination with the work's spiralling rather than frontal orientation, this rhythm invites the viewer to move around the sculpture. The resulting multiplicity of aspects is reinforced by the highly polished surface which denies one's sense of mass and weight by reflecting light and mirroring the work's environment.

Mlle. Pogany II's contemplative pose, and the sacrifice of individually articulated features in favor of a more concentrated unity, suggest that Brancusi intended the work to represent the artist's muse, the source of his creative inspiration.

(*Lesley K. Baier*)

Katharine Ordway began collecting in the 1920s, exercising her own judgment and showing remarkable independence and foresight. She saw Brancusi's *Mlle. Pogany* while it was still in the studio and, in 1925, bought it directly from the artist. A major benefactor of the Yale University Art Gallery, her collection once housed in New York and Weston, Connecticut, was bequeathed in 1979 to go on public view in the Katharine Ordway Gallery.

152

The Solomon R. Guggenheim Museum

Surrealist sculpture, whether practiced by Giacometti or Picasso, Arp, Miró or Ernst, trades on a found object appearance. In 1934, Max Ernst stayed for awhile with Giacometti in the Swiss village of Maloja where he worked on egg-shaped stones from a nearby river bed and received, from his host's intensely original vision, the impetus for his own sculpture of a later date. There is little doubt that Giacometti's fully developed formal language, from the 1926 *Spoon-Woman* to the 1934-35 *Hands Holding the Void*, profoundly affected his German contemporary who until then had never seriously considered the medium of sculpture. After a ten year incubation, that influence leaped to the surface as though by accident.

In the summer of 1944, Max Ernst, then living with Dorothea Tanning, had rented a rambling house in Great River, Long Island, which he offered to share with Julien Levy, a friend and, incidentally, Giacometti's dealer. Having gone ahead, he sent Levy a postcard reading "No chess set available at the village store." When Levy arrived in Great River he found Ernst, completely diverted from painting, making a chess set by pouring plaster of Paris into molds. These ingenious molds, of the most startling simplicity and originality to Levy's unsuspecting eyes, bore the shapes of garage tools and kitchen utensils. One evening, Levy recalled, Ernst picked up a spoon from the table, sat looking at it for awhile, then carefully carried it to the garage where it would serve as the mold for the mouth of *An Anxious Friend*, one of several large sculptures related to the chess set.

Collectors and art patrons Dominique and John de Menil assembled the world's premier private collection of works by Max Ernst and sponsored that artist's scholarly *catalogue raisonné*. Besides their involvement with institutions in Texas, they took an active interest in The Museum of Modern Art and the Solomon R. Guggenheim Museum. In 1959, Mr. and Mrs. de Menil gave The Guggenheim #5 of nine casts of *An Anxious Friend* made in 1957 by Modern Art Foundry from the original 1944 plaster.

It was in Munich shortly after the turn of the century that Vasily Kandinsky made his historic breakthrough to abstract painting. At that time, Munich was an international art center and the home of Germany's Jugendstil movement. Peg Weiss, the chronicler of Kandinsky's formative years in that city, has convincingly argued that Kandinsky's breakthrough to abstraction was, more than anything else, the result of a convergence of strong Jugendstil tendencies toward abstract ornamentation with a symbolist thrust toward inner significance and spiritual revolution.

The year 1909 was rich in events for the 43-year-old Russian painter. He founded and was elected president of the *Neue Künstlervereinigung Müchen*; began work on stage compositions such as *Der Gelbe Klang*; moved with Gabriele Münter into a house in Murnau; saw a large exhibition of Japanese and East-Asian art; began painting on glass; published a series of woodcuts; participated in exhibitions in Paris, Munich and Odessa. His themes were landscapes, landscape improvisations, figurative scenes and beginning abstractions, all intensely colorful in a manner that relates them to the *Fauves* in France.

Group in Crinolines is steeped in the fairy-tale atmosphere so dear to Russian artists of that generation. Four gentlemen in morning coats and four ladies in crinolines move about in a park-like setting at the height of the Biedermeier era which was then enjoying a modest revival. Kandinsky was preoccupied with Biedermeier style and costume, as is evident from his sketch books, another version of *Group in Crinolines* in the Tretiakov Gallery in Moscow, *Pastorale* of 1911 in the Guggenheim, and a 1916 series of 14 watercolors. Kandinsky's *fête champêtre* may have been inspired by an Adolf Münzer mural, *Luxus*, shown at the 1900 Glaspalast exhibition; a comparison between the two works shows how a great painter can turn a trivial source into an enchanting new vision.

Solomon R. Guggenheim's role as collector and museum founder stands most glowingly revealed in the superb representation of the oeuvre of Vasily Kandinsky. With the help of his curator and the Museum of Non-Objective Art's first director, Hilla von Rebay, Guggenheim brought together a collection of works by this great painter, matched only by that of the Gabriele Münter Stiftung in Munich.

New Harmony (*Neue Harmonie*) is one of only 25 works recorded in 1936 when the artist was plagued with illness. It contains the colored rectangles or "magic squares" that first appeared in Klee's painting in 1923 as an expression of his color theories. Even the title belongs with those works he designated "Architecture, Harmony and Sound." This last of Klee's independent color-rectangle compositions reflects, like so many before, the artist's study of musical harmony.

Klee must have felt or intended specific points of contrast between this painting and his "old harmony," the *Alter Klang* of 1925 in the Kunstmuseum Basel. The most obvious difference is the brighter, heightened chromatism of the later work; in *New Harmony*, light is distributed more flatly and evenly across a surface held firm by dark underpainting; there is also a more uniform distribution of compositional interest.

Andrew Kagan who has argued that Klee found models for his pictorial compositions in 18th century polyphony, sees *New Harmony* governed by the principle of bilateral, inverted symmetry. The cross correspondence of color units with their respective weights opposing and balancing each other create what Klee himself referred to as a "dynamic equilibrium." The term must have had the currency in the 1920s and 1930s that Hans Hofmann's "push and pull" possessed two decades later. A contradiction in terms, Mondrian used it frequently and to him it meant a reconciliation of opposites.

With its 12 tones of color, *New Harmony* may well be a covert tribute to Arnold Schoenberg even though a tranquil Mozartian inspiration is more readily in evidence. Klee's reverence for Mozart, whom he regarded as the greatest creative artist of all time, is well known. What is less generally known is Klee's lifelong preoccupation with musical theory and its potential for providing visual artists with the key to the perfect picture. Klee's painting may deserve a new look in light of the music he knew, played and liked.

From his 1961 appointment to the directorship of the Solomon R. Guggenheim Museum until the present, Czech-born, Harvard-trained Thomas M. Messer has been responsible for an exemplary program of mutually supportive acquisitions and exhibitions. Building from strength and respectful of the existing collection, he organized definitive exhibitions of the work of Kandinsky, Mondrian, Klee and other artists whose historic accomplishments the Guggenheim was meant to enshrine. The knowledge gained from such exhibitions was properly channeled into what amounts to the most authoritative and ongoing permanent collection catalogue of any museum of 20th century art. This, however, has not slowed down the museum or its professional staff, including the director, in exploring the broader parameters of art in our time.

133

181

143

The Metropolitan Museum of Art

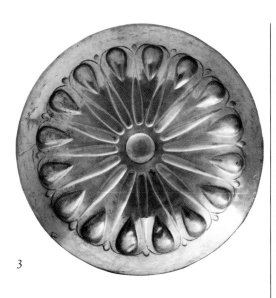

3

Pictures about which a mystery hangs never cease to intrigue the viewer. The young woman in her late teens, fashionably dressed in an Empire gown, peering at us with sultry eyes set in a perfectly oval face crowned by curly hair held together in the back with a stickpin, has never yielded who painted her or when, nor what particular incident the broken window pane and couple on the terrace refer to. Quite evidently, she is sketching whoever painted her yet nobody has suggested that it might be a self-portrait in the mirror. The frank contact this painter has the model make with the viewer, and her portrayal against the light, render this c. 1800 painting unabashedly modern of pose and observation. The starkness of the room in an era that may have been austere but not devoid of decoration, and the scene beyond the window with its involuntarily surreal implications, remove this painting from the realm of Empire portraiture in the style of (and once thought to be by) Jacques-Louis David and relegate it to the no-man's (and no-woman's) land of art that resists attribution.

A press release, contemporaneous with the 1917 acquisition by the Metropolitan Museum of Art of the *Portrait of a Young Woman called Charlotte du Val d'Ognes* as a gift from Isaac Dudley Fletcher, stated: "As one of the masterpieces of this artist, the Fletcher picture will henceforth be known in the art world as 'the New York David,' just as we speak of the *Man with a Fur Cap* of the Hermitage, or the *Sistine Madonna* of Dresden...Mr. Fletcher is said to have paid $200,000 for this great David." Why David? Beyond a mere resemblance, there is a record of a portrait by David of Mademoiselle Charlotte du Val d'Ognes having been exhibited at the Ecole des Beaux-Arts in Paris in 1897.

About that picture, M. Tourneaux, in a Gazette des Beaux-Arts article of the same year, observed that the sitter was supposed to have been a pupil of David and that the portrait was painted in 1803 in a hôtel particulier on the Rue de Lille. There was nothing to substantiate that location, and the date is definitely suspect. On greater evidence, it can be assumed that this portrait had already been exhibited in the Salon of 1801, as an engraving by Monsaldy and Devisme and a preparatory drawing by Monsaldy recording the pictures exhibited at the *Muséum Central des Arts en l'An IX* (as the Salon of 1801 was then called) have convincingly proved. The fact that David painted a portrait of another member of the family, the young Edouard du Val d'Ognes, in the Carroll Tyson Collection, does not, by itself, make a case for the artist. Suffice it to add, in this connection, that prominent pictures offered for sale to prominent collectors, never suffer from a lack of prominent, although not always convincing, attributions.

In 1950, the eminent art historian, Charles Sterling, presented a detailed argument for reattributing the so-called portrait of Charlotte du Val d'Ognes (the sitter's name was never in doubt as the picture had come down in the Val d'Ognes and Hardouin de Grosville families) to Constance Charpentier, née Blondelu (1767-1849), a pupil of David known for having painted portraits of women and children and for having exhibited at the Salon between 1795 and 1819. Just prior to Sterling's assertion, doubt had already been cast on the David attribution by Otto Benesch (1944) and by Georges Brière (1945-46). While it was conspicuously absent from the 1948 David exhibition in Paris, André Maurois, nonetheless, called it "the most astonishing feminine portrait by David...a merciless portrait of an intelligent, homely woman...with color worthy of Vermeer...perfect, unforgettable."

Sterling may not have been aware that he played right into the hands of feminist art historians two decades hence. Charlotte du Val d'Ognes found herself on the cover of the January 1971 issue of ARTnews in which Linda Nochlin asked the rhetorical question, "Why have there been no great women artists?" Wisely, she does not embroil herself in the David vs. Charpentier controversy for, as Robert Rosenblum has stated in his note on Constance Charpentier in the 1975 Grand Palais catalogue *De David à Delacroix*, the portrait's identification with Charpentier, in general, and its listing as no. 60 in the Salon of 1801 specifically, "must remain a mere hypothesis." A fuller comparison with other paintings by Constance Charpentier is clearly needed and, the trend toward unearthing more historic information on women artists should produce, Rosenblum believed, the additional evidence to shore up Charpentier's authorship of the portrait of Charlotte du Val d'Ognes.

Recent opinion no longer favors the worthy but obscure woman painter. Daniel Wildenstein, in a 1977 letter on record at the Metropolitan Museum of Art, stated that he and his father have always been convinced that this painting was by Gérard; he thought that he could find a document showing that Gérard exhibited it at the Salon although it did not appear in the catalogue. In a further verbal communication to curator Charles Moffett, Wildenstein claimed that same year having bought the picture which is actually Mme Charpentier's portrait of Charlotte du Val d'Ognes, and that the Metropolitan's picture may, indeed, be by Gérard. Reflective of the department's belief in Daniel Wildenstein and Sir John Pope-Hennessy's arbitration of the issue, the portrait has reverted back to being that of a "Young Woman called Mademoiselle Charlotte du Val d'Ognes," and the authorship, on the label, is listed as "unknown."

Metal vessels are among the most distinctive and splendid of the artistic productions of Achaemenian Persia. Made of gold or silver, in a wide variety of shapes, they were used at royal banquets and brought in tribute to the King of Kings. Achaemenian vessels were influenced by the arts of many people in the region, comprising, besides Iranians, the earlier Sumerians, Assyrians and Scyths. The silver bowl in the Department of Ancient Near Eastern Art, was used for libation, a form of sacrifice which was performed by first pouring wine from a jug into the libation bowl and then tilting the bowl to pour the wine onto the ground. It is decorated with a stylized open lotus-like flower whose petals radiate from a central circle. Sixteen drop-shaped motifs are sunk into the surface of the bowl, forming a

circle concentric with the rim. No information is available on the site where it was found but stylistic analysis suggests that it can be dated from the fifth century B.C.

These two limestone heads of a male and a female Votary date from the fifth century B.C. and were found on the isle of Cyprus where the Metropolitan Museum's first director, Luigi Palma di Cesnola, conducted a massive archaeological dig. The better preserved male head shows traces of the paint that enlivened its eyes. Its regal facial features include an archaic smile and a hairdo, coiffed in ringlets like the beard, and surmounted by a laurel wreath. The female head is distinguished for its elaborate coiffure and jewelry. Purchased by subscription in 1874-76, the Cesnola collection provided the nucleus for the Museum's Department of Antiquities.

4

This Renaissance maiolica plate, made in Caffaggiolo, a center of the ceramic industry, between 1510-20, bears the image of David with the sling in his hand and the head of the slain Goliath at his feet. The theme was fashionable with the rulers and inhabitants of the city states and allowed many a champion of freedom and liberator from oppression the thrill of identification. This finely painted and well-preserved plate once belonged to William Randolph Hearst, a Goliath rather than a David of the newspaper industry, and was owned by Robert Lehman before his entire collection was donated, in 1975, to the Metropolitan Museum of Art.

Representative of a popular type of object probably used in private devotion, and a fine example of works produced in such prominent centers as Paris and Cologne in the Gothic period, this mid-14th century diptych holds an important place in the Metropolitan's encyclopedic collection of Medieval ivories. One of the specialties of

32

64

the Parisian ivory-carving ateliers of that time was diptychs of the Passion. Frequently one or more scenes from Christ's early life were juxtaposed with one or more scenes from his Passion. The reliefs of this diptych show *The Nativity and the Crucifixion* beneath trefoil arches framed within crocketed arcades. The compositional complexity and mannered exaggeration, coupled with the expressive physiognomies, contrast with the restrained lyricism of the 13th century figure style. The rudimentary bucolic landscape in the Nativity reflects the same interest in nature that appears in contemporary manuscript illumination.

(*Adapted from C. Gómez-Moreno*)

The coat of arms, six fleurs-de-lis surmounted by a ducal coronet, is that of Pier Luigi Farnese, first Duke of Parma and Piacenza from 1545 until his assassination in 1547. Members of the Farnese family were among the grandest patrons of the Renaissance, commissioning artists throughout Italy. A Farnese commission was a sure guarantee of high quality; both Michelangelo and Titian worked for Pope Paul III, founder of the family's fortunes. The Farnese also lavished their attentions on the decorative arts. The Milanese art of damascening in the Persian manner, exemplified by this casket with its delicate patternings in gold and silver, appealed particularly to Farnese tastes. No fewer than twenty examples are recorded, though none is described, in the 1653 inventory of the family's Roman palace.

(*James D. Draper*)

The parade shield and helmet once thought to have been made for Louis XIV, are now more conservatively dated as having been crafted well into the realm of the Sun King's successor, Louis XV. They belong to a period when armor had all but ceased to be worn for protection in battle and was rarely used even on ceremonial occasions. The great weight of these bronze pieces suggests that they were not worn at all but rather were intended to be carried

and displayed in courtly processions and theatrical productions with themes borrowed from classical antiquity. Material, construction and form indicate decorative and symbolic functions.

The bowl of the helmet, burgonet in heraldic terms, and oval of the shield, are formed of hammered bronze sheet, the exterior of which is silvered. The silver has now oxidized to a deep blue color but it may originally have been polished mirror-bright. The ormolu mounts, particularly the dragon crest and lion head at the front of the burgonet, and the head of the Medusa on the shield, demonstrate a quality of casting and chasing equal to contemporary French furniture mounts of the best workmanship. Helmet and shield are designed in emulation of antique Roman armor and come at the end of a tradition, begun during the Renaissance, of parade armor *alla romana*. The wearer's valiance and intrepidness as well as his aristocratic kinship to the ancient demigods was implicit in the iconic portrayal of the gorgon Medusa slain by Perseus whose father Zeus sired him by inflicting himself upon an earthly creature, Danae, in the form of a shower of gold.

Douglas Newton, the eminent scholar of New Guinea art, has described the relatively recent discovery of the Sepik River and its astonishingly diverse art: One day in May 1885, a German ornithologist and ethnographer, Otto Finsch, secretly employed by a trading company, chanced upon a great muddy stain in the offshore waters of northeast New Guinea. He had found the mouth of an enormous river, mentioned in travel accounts but never previously explored by a white man. Not thinking it very promising, Finsch turned his back on the river after having gone thirty miles upstream. The German Colonial Office and the museums of Berlin and Hamburg as well as of Chicago thought otherwise and dispatched scientific and collecting expeditions to the area. Although the Brücke artists were stirred by what anthropologists brought back from that region, appreciation for the art of the

Sepik grew more slowly than that for African art. An understanding for the complex systems of religious symbolism took even longer; through his writings, Douglas Newton has importantly contributed to that understanding.

This monumental image of a spirit-patron of war and hunting is one of a group of about a dozen such figures dating to the late 18th century. It was collected from the Sawos people who live in the grasslands north of the river, in the village of Yamok, which is part of the East Sepik Province and is generally referred to as Middle Sepik. As wood is a notoriously unstable material in the tropics and as missionaries were wont to destroy whatever related to pagan ritual, these carvings for the village's spirit house were rarely more than a century old. With its wonderful symmetry and hieratic posture and with scarification marks that include a zigzag on the torso and inverted crescents on the chest, this sculpture is one of the most impressive in the Museum's collection of Papua New Guinea art. Nelson A. Rockefeller acquired it for the Museum of Primitive Art in 1959. In 1979, it entered the Michael C. Rockefeller Memorial Collection, installed in its own wing, at the Metropolitan Museum of Art.

25

35

161

122

In her introduction to *Georgia O'Keeffe, A Portrait by Alfred Stieglitz*, the painter muses about the photographer: "Stieglitz photographed me first at his gallery '291' in the spring of 1917...two portraits of my face against one of my large watercolors and three photographs of my hands...My hands had always been admired since I was a little girl—but I never thought much about it. He wanted head and hands and arms on a pillow—in many different positions. I was asked to move my hands in many different ways—also my head—and I had to turn this way and that...I was photographed with a kind of heat and excitement and in a way wondered what it was all about."

O'Keeffe was to find out soon enough, and the world has recognized, in these poetic poses, some of the finest photography of the twentieth century. Stieglitz's idea of a portrait was not just one photograph but a series of photographs that would form a portrait of the many aspects of a person. They combine observation and memory: their first meeting was in 1908 when O'Keeffe came to see the Rodin drawings at '291;' it took another eight years before they became close. In 1917, Stieglitz offered the then 30-year-old woman her first solo exhibition. The following year, the two began to spend their summers together at Lake George, as O'Keeffe had then come to live in New York, under contract with '291.' With the young painter as both source of inspiration and model, Stieglitz produced, over a period of years, a series of photographic portraits and figure studies that, arguably, constitute the greatest tribute to a woman ever accomplished in that medium.

The Schulte, Strand and Wertheim gifts of 1928 constitute the first accession of photographs into the art collections of the Metropolitan Museum of Art and mark the beginning of that or any American museum's collecting master photographs. The untitled 1918 silverprint by Alfred Stieglitz, featuring the right side of O'Keeffe's face, her right arm and shoulder and her two hands poised as though she were playing an invisible harp, was a 1928 gift from David A. Schulte.

Although Guardi painted imaginary landscapes with ruins, marines, figure pieces and portraits, he is famous primarily for his views of Venice. The dating of his works is difficult because there is little documentary evidence. Guardi was not highly regarded by his contemporaries, who considered him a mere follower of Canaletto, another painter of Venetian vedutae, and he was not admitted to the Academy until he was 72 years old. From the little that is known about his life he seems to have been employed principally by Englishmen living in Venice. Although Guardi's style closely follows the rococo formula, in recent times, he has been considered more of an innovator and a forerunner, almost, of 19th century Impressionism.

This view of the Grand Canal showing the bridge of the Rialto with the Palazzo dei Camerlenghi and the Erberia (vegetable market) on the right, is a pendant to the view of Santa Maria della Salute in the Metropolitan Museum Collection, but pictorially more intriguing. In composition it is closely connected with paintings by Canaletto. Guardi repeated this composition in a signed and much larger canvas now in the collection of the Earl of Iveagh. The Iveagh version is very likely the one that was exhibited by the artist in the Piazza San Marco on April 24, 1764. The style of the Metropolitan painting shows clearly the characteristics of Guardi's early period. Its likely date is between 1760-65.

Guardi's *Venice: The Grand Canal above the Rialto* was among the first works of a collection purchased in 1871 by a board of trustees presided over by John Taylor Johnston—a purchase made before the Metropolitan came into physical existence. That core of the collection consisted predominantly of Dutch and Flemish paintings, many of which are no longer owned by the Museum.

82

The Museum of Modern Art

166

Born in Greece, of Italian parents, Giorgio de Chirico was confronted from a tender age, with the remnants of our classical heritage. In Munich, during the first decade of this century, he attended the Academy of Fine Arts and became imbued with the fashionable pessimism of Schopenhauer's and Nietzsche's writings and Boecklin's and Klinger's imagery. From such experiences, de Chirico fashioned, just prior to World War I, the "metaphysical" paintings that would become a contributory influence on Surrealism's representational direction. The works he completed between 1911 and 1917 have long assured him a prominent place among the masters of modern art.

Before moving to Paris, as any aspiring artist at that time would feel obliged to do, de Chirico visited Turin where his hero Nietzsche had written *The Antichrist*. In the vast arcaded piazzas and public statuary of that city the painter found "a strange and profound poetry, infinitely mysterious and solitary (that was) based on the mood of an autumn afternoon when the skies are clear and the shadows are longer than in summer...." Those well-paved squares across which Nietzsche took such pleasure strolling and the stuccoed buildings with their sheltering arches became, in de Chirico's "metaphysical" paintings, paradigms of 20th century anxiety and foreshadowings of the end of civilization.

In his recent monograph on the artist, William S. Rubin has called de Chirico a "great composer of paintings as well as a great poet within painting," whose plastic power functioned in perfect harmony with his poetic imagination. Too singularly considered a haunting image-maker, de Chirico assimilated the formal canons of abstraction more thoroughly than had been understood heretofore. In particular, the artist's manipulation of perspective contributes to the unsettling impact of his enigmatic dream imagery with its strange juxtaposition of unrelated objects from everyday life seemingly propped up by invisible architectural designers.

On de Chirico's "metaphysical" stage the mannequin or dummy replaces the actor. James Thrall Soby has written that of all the paintings in the 1915 mannequin series *The Duo* is the most moving and tender. "The lovers stand out against their elegiac setting like figures seen through a stereoscope. Behind them a green sky frames a rose tower whose soft color and bland texture recall the frescoes of the Italian Renaissance artist Piero della Francesca. The artificiality of the potted shrub is conveyed with such acuteness that it appears more real than nature itself." Soby should know, for he once owned this painting, and in 1955, organized an exhibition of de Chirico's early work for The Museum of Modern Art.

Ever since the Industrial Revolution, machines have exerted a fascination far beyond their function. Critics have invested them with moral attributes, viewing them as either despoilers or benefactors of society. Where some have seen harsh ugliness, others have found beauty. From the early 19th century, with paintings such as Turner's 1843 *Rain, Steam, and Speed—The Great Western Railway*, artists have attempted to capture the force and excitement of machines. Machine-inspired imagery has turned up again and again in paintings, music, and literature, reaching a peak in the second and third decades of the 20th century with the bold experiments of the Futurists and Constructivists. But beyond the increasingly widely held belief that the machine was a fitting subject for the artist, there grew a conviction among some that machines themselves, pure and simple, were art, that they did not need the eye and hand of the artist to interpret them, that taken raw they were beautiful.

This attitude was summed up in an ambitious exhibition presented by The Museum of Modern Art in 1934 called "Machine Art". It included a wide variety of industrial objects, ranging from springs, insulators, cable sections, and propeller blades through kitchen wares to scientific instruments and laboratory glass. It was accompanied by an illustrated catalogue, at the front of which were printed three epigraphs: quotations from Plato's *Philebus*, St. Thomas Acquinas's *Summa Theologiae*,

and L.P. Jack's *Responsibility and Culture*.
The Plato, printed in both the original
Greek and English translation, stated:
"by Beauty of shapes I do not mean, as most
people would suppose, the beauty of living
figures or of pictures, but, to make my point
clear, I mean straight lines and circles, and
shapes, plane or solid, made from them by
lathe, ruler, or square. These are not, like
other things, beautiful relatively, but always
and absolutely." The cover of the catalogue
bore a photograph of this ball-bearing which
seemed to epitomize pure, Platonic
geometry; its sleek polished spheres and
concentric rings of gleaming steel having all
the inevitability of fine sculpture.

In fact it had been designed by a young
textile engineer in an effort to overcome the
serious power losses that resulted from
misaligned line shaftings in textile factories.
In his effort to solve a practical problem
and, so far as is known, with no thought of
aesthetics, Sven Wingquist came up with a
solution of such compelling visual logic that
it has become a potent symbol of
modernism. *(J. Stewart Johnson,* Looking at
Design, *to be published by The Museum of
Modern Art)*

O ne year after André Breton, in his
Surréalisme et la peinture, described Joan
Miró as "possibly the most surrealist of all of
us," the painter obliged with a series of four
"imaginary portraits," of which the *Portrait
of Mistress Mills in 1750* is his masterpiece.
As late as 1959, Miró confided to James
Thrall Soby, the then owner of this
important picture, that he had chosen his
subject from an engraving without knowing
the identity of the original artist. We now
know that this portrait of a singer by British
painter George Engleheart was engraved by
John R. Smith. This leads us to speculate
that Miró slanted his metamorphosis of the
original just enough to transform a reader's
into a performer's pose, a beribboned hat
into a string instrument, a bustle into a
horn, and a letter into a sheet of music.
There certainly is a bravura to the Miró
painting that its sedate model does not
possess.

177

178

168

Why did an artist with Miró's capacity for invention need this fashionable engraving as a visual crutch? William S. Rubin explained that old master reproductions served Miró as a substitute for doodling ("automatic writing" in Surrealist language), and were a means of getting the picture started. His point is well taken as one looks at the pencil sketches preceding *Portrait of Mistress Mills in 1750*, in which the original is gradually transformed and abstracted into Miró's vision of the subject. However, what he retains, and in fact elaborates on, is the ornamental character of his 18th century model.

An affinity has been pointed out, by James Thrall Soby, between this painting's biomorphic shapes and those appearing earlier in the canvases, cutouts and reliefs of Hans Arp, Miró's close neighbor on the rue Tourlaque. Yet Arp denied that he ever influenced his younger friend and colleague, and countered that Miró arrived at his style by observing the art of children and by looking at the early Catalan frescoes of his native land. As for the latter, Miró did admit to Soby that the rich chocolate browns, reds, yellows, greens, purples and blacks of his *Portrait of Mistress Mills in 1750* were inspired by and can be traced back to those Catalan frescoes.

Especially identified with the Miró collection at The Museum of Modern Art, the finest and most complete of this artist's work in public or private hands, has been the painter's long-time friend James Thrall Soby (1906-1979). A curator, department director and trustee of the Museum for half a lifetime, this farsighted collector and perceptive writer organized Miró's 1959 retrospective and authored the classic monograph that served as its catalogue. Instrumental in acquiring a number of Mirós for the Museum, he donated four important works while alive and left others he owned, the *Portrait of Mistress Mills in 1750* among them, as his bequest. Of Soby as a critic, the late Paul J. Sachs, art historian and one of the founding trustees of The Museum of Modern Art, wrote in 1957: "By actual experience as well as intellectually and emotionally, he has earned the right to describe (and he does so with gusto) the artistic revolutionary thoughts and techniques of the 20th century."

The *Minotauromachy* etching was the highlight in a relatively barren year of Picasso's creative career. In it we see the fierce and savage exiled man-bull returning from the sea with a gigantic pack on his back. A female matador, modeled on Picasso's then-pregnant mistress, Marie-Thérèse Walter, is slung across the back of her disemboweled but still agonizing horse. At the left, a little girl with the profile of the artist himself, carries a lighted candle and a bouquet of flowers. A symbol of innocence (?), she remains calm about the intrusion, confident, perhaps, that the artist's noble impulses will win out over his baser drives and that the monster, in fact, will turn tame. At the far left, a bearded man who resembles the artist's father, scrambles up a ladder. Two young women contemplate the drama from the safety of their window ledge. Many critics have noted the similarity between the imagery of this print and that of *Guernica*, created two years later. In both instances, we probably deal with a basic vocabulary of images which reflects the impact of certain early experiences indelibly imprinted on Picasso's memory—images which surfaced in his art whenever he became particularly impassioned and, thus, even more emphatically autobiographical in his references. (*Adapted from Mary Mathews Gedo*, Picasso. Art as Autobiography. *Chicago: 1980, p. 161-2*)

To Mrs. John D. Rockefeller, Jr., who had financed the purchase but disliked Picasso's *Minotauromachy*, Alfred H. Barr, Jr., the Museum's first director, wrote in a letter dated January 15, 1947: "Some kinds of art should be restful and easy—as Matisse said, like a good armchair. Other kinds, like Picasso's, challenge and stimulate us. They are often hard to understand at first but, like our minds and muscles, our artistic sensibilities are strengthened by exercise and hard work. I have never thought of art as something primarily pleasant—but as something which stirs us to a fresh awareness and

understanding of life—even of the difficulties, confusions and tragedies of life as well as its joys.

"I myself do not fully understand the Picasso *Minotaurmachy* but I believe it to be the greatest single print thus far produced in our century. I have looked at it literally hundreds of times as it hangs in our living room. It has never worn thin or lost its fascination...the Picasso allegory seems to me to reveal dramatically and poetically something of the mystery, the groping paradox, the pathos of man's nature—half beast, half angel—a subject for art which is both immediate and eternal." (*The Museum of Modern Art Archives*)

This rare gelatin-silver print by the Constructivist painter, pioneer photographer and designer whose singular accomplishment has only recently come to the world's attention, is titled on verso by hand in Russian, "Chauffeur. A.M. Rodchenko, 1933." There exists at least one other print of the same image, entitled *Taxi Driver*, shown at the Museum of Modern Art, Oxford, in 1979. Although this photograph did not enter into the Museum's collection until 1970, it is indicative of the institution's long standing interest in the pioneering movements in Eastern Europe shortly after the October Revolution. Alfred H. Barr, Jr. traveled to the Soviet Union in 1927-28, met Rodchenko and accepted several 1918-20 gouaches, water colors and crayons from the artist as a gift to the Museum; they were shown in the 1936 exhibition *Cubism and Abstract Art*.

Ever since Jan van Eyck slyly introduced himself into the Arnolfinis' bridal chamber by way of a convex mirror, artists have been tempted (and photographers have had ample opportunity) to include their own likenesses in their work—thus unobtrusively inserting a second signature or visual authentification. An ingenious camera angle has given Rodchenko two shots at being seen in *Chauffeur*—a highly complex image, not easily read or understood. Half in focus, half out of focus it derives its interest from the simultaneous

inclusion of a car mirror and a pipe taken at close range. The driver of that car, whilst also smoker of that pipe, is reflected in the mirror—a secondary reality more piquant and not without sinister overtones. As in a spy story, we are made suddenly aware that the grimly confident driver observing us (but only in the mirror) is himself observed, photographed and thus rendered harmless.

Rodchenko moved from painting to photography in the conviction that photography, in post-revolutionary Russia, was more attuned to society's needs. "Once a brilliant painter, today a committed photographer," wrote Ossip Brik in 1926, "Rodchenko's main task is to move away from the principles of painterly composition of photographs and to find other specifically photographic laws...." Ironically, instead of giving up the circles, diagonals and perspective twists that characterized his paintings with their slants and tilts, he reintroduced these same compositional principles in his photographs. He favors urban scenes as they reveal themselves through the window of a trolley car, from the roof of a building or askance from street level. His perspective is cinematic, and as he presses several angles of one and the same subject into a single frame, Rodchenko paraphrases the analytic sequences of snapshots and the photo collages that were his other contributions to modern photography. Such eccentric interpretation of the medium had him branded as a formalist in 1931, and caused his expulsion from the "October Group."

The Pierpont Morgan Library

20

23

In 1910, Pierpont Morgan seized upon the opportunity to purchase the Charles Fairfax Murray Collection of old master drawings from all European schools and periods. With that purchase, he brought to America the first important classic collection which forms the core of the Morgan Library's extensive current holdings. Albrecht Dürer's *Design for Mural Decoration* was in that 1910 purchase. Considered to have been executed on his return from a sojourn in the Netherlands, this pen drawing with wash is thought to be a design commissioned in 1521 for the Nuremburg Town Hall council chambers. The size and shape of the Town Hall windows substantiate that premise. The drawing shows a partial design for the ten south wall windows, but it is not certain that it was ever employed for the decoration.

Dürer's theme, the power of women over men, was a popular one in Northern Europe during the late Middle Ages; it reflects a prevailing negative attitude toward women. In the roundels at the top of the design are scenes of David and Bathsheba, Samson and Delilah and Aristotle and Phyllis, the latter demonstrating that even the wisest of men is susceptible to a woman's wiles—to his detriment, of course. Another roundel which may have been originally on this obviously trimmed sheet could have included a scene of Solomon's idolatry, a representation often depicted in conjunction with this theme. The ornamental motifs of trailing grape vines swirl around smaller figures beneath each roundel and seem to show, in contrast, what would have been considered a more wholesome relationship between man and woman—that of producing and caring for the young. To the serenade of his pipes, the satyr's mate nurses their child while a nesting pelican pierces her breast to feed her young, symbolizing Christ's sacrifice—a theme used by Dürer on a book cover also owned by the Morgan Library.

(Adapted from Helen B. Mules)

Although there is no documentary evidence to corroborate the story,

tradition has it that Saint Bartholomew, one of the Apostles, spread the word of Christ all the way to India. On his return trip from that exotic land, he was martyred in Armenia by being flayed alive. His story is all too graphically portrayed in four miniatures from the Morgan Library collection. These illuminations from one leaf of a picture book of scenes from the New Testament were assembled to correspond to the original format after they had been removed and trimmed. The major part of the book from which they were cut is in the Vatican.

The product of a court atelier and illuminated by Bolognese and native Hungarian artists of the first half of the 14th century, the *St. Bartholomew* scenes show the strong influences of Italian style with decidedly Balkan details in costumes and iconography. The top scenes show Saint Bartholomew baptising and preaching in foreign lands. The two lower scenes show the martyrdom in all its goriness from flaying to burial. Details of architecture, fabric patterns and furnishings identify the oriental character of the land where the story unfolds, and each background of highly burnished gold is completed with a border of tiny tooled rosettes. The individual illuminations are enclosed in a frame of scrolls, leaves and a variation of the egg and dart design.

(Adapted from Meta Harrsen)

Enameled book covers such as this splendid example from the Pierpont Morgan Library seem to have been produced in a flourishing enamelwork industry that sprang up in Limoges after the middle of the 12th century. Continuing into the 14th century, the Limoges workshops produced many types of liturgical objects including champlevé decorated covers for altar books. Most of the remaining examples of the book covers are of one size, made of copper mounted on wood and prepared with sunken compartments to receive the enamel. It is probable that the Limoges covers were made in pairs—the upper cover representing a crucifixion and the lower cover, Christ in majesty. With only one known exception (that of the complete altar book from the monastary of Saint Gall), the Limoges book covers are separated from their original codices—most likely by 19th and 20th century dealers who wanted to sell them as art objects rather than as rare books. In this example of the crucifixion, the small figure seen at the feet of Christ is said to be Adam rising, restored to life by the savior's blood.

(Adapted from Paul Needham)

Related in style to Byzantine mosaics and frescoes, and particularly to the mosaic of the Last Judgment in the cathedral at Torcello in the Venetian Laguna, this *Single leaf from an antiphonarium depicting the Last Judgment within an initial A* is the work of a 13th century Central Italian miniaturist. The leaf may have originally served as the frontispiece for a hymnal (the musical notations on the back of the leaf were a 16th century addition).

The full-page illumination describes the letter A within a rectangular frame of chain border design. The interior space of the A has been horizontally divided into three sections: the top section shows the seated Christ flanked by Mary and Saint John the Baptist, who are in turn flanked by the Archangel Michael on the right, and on the left, an angel bearing the instruments of Christ's passion; the middle section is devoted to a presentation of the seated 12 apostles, 10 of whom hold open manuscripts on their laps; in the lower section, two groups of standing elect await their calling. The miniaturist may, himself, be present in this last group in the form of the small bearded figure on the right, a position and size often favored for the presentation of donor portraits.

(Adapted from Meta Harrsen)

Giovanni Battista Piranesi's *Gondola* is one of more than 130 sheets that came to the Morgan Library from the collection of Mrs. J. P. Morgan. A design for a ceremonial gondola or "bissona," it was executed in 1744-45 during the artist's brief sojourn in Venice following his first residence in Rome. The influence of Giovanni Battista Tiepolo, in whose studio Piranesi is believed to have worked at that time, is seen in the lightness and inventiveness of the drawing, and its fluid, flickering line also suggests Francesco Guardi. It is an outstanding example of the artist's Venetian Rococo period. Shortly after the artist returned to Rome, Andrew Robison has shown, Piranesi adapted this fanciful design for a gondola to that of a carriage in the foreground of his etching *Veduta della Basilica e Piazza di S. Pietro in Vaticano*.

(Adapted from Helen B. Mules)

80

40

Ever since *Mountain Landscape* was first exhibited in the galleries of Messrs. Obach in London in 1908, this extraordinary drawing has been associated with the name of Jacques de Gheyn. In 1932, the late J. Q. van Regteren Altena discussed its relationship with the forgotten artist Jan van Stinemolen (1518—after 1582) and with the close version, inscribed *de Gheyn*, in the National Museum at Stockholm. He proposed the possibility that both drawings were copies of a lost drawing by Stinemolen, the Morgan Library's by de Gheyn, the Stockholm sheet by Goltzius. The Dutch art historian more recently wrote that the Morgan drawing "can hardly be anything else than a genuine De Gheyn drawing." The catalogue of the Royal Academy's 1953 exhibition, in which the Morgan drawing—then owned by James Murray Usher—was shown, records A. E. Popham's preference for the attribution to de Gheyn.

Whatever the attribution, the drawing is a magnificent cosmic landscape, encompassing a sweeping view over a tremendous expanse of rugged mountainous terrain. In the immediate foreground, in an effect of bold repoussoir, the accomplished draftsman records eroded forms of rock and earth, tufted with leafy growth. The pen stroke, rich and varied, modulates with finesse until it fades out in the distant mist.

(Adapted from Felice Stampfle)

Whitney Museum of American Art

Although Stuart Davis' association with the Whitney began earlier, it is Edward Hopper who is most closely identified with this institution. Little support was given Hopper's work; he earned a living through commercial art and illustration. His first one-man exhibition of paintings was held at the Whitney Studio Club in January 1920, and Mrs. Whitney's patronage was carried on by the Museum from its founding until the artist's death in 1967.

Seven A.M. is one of several mature paintings that were purchased from the artist during his lifetime. Lloyd Goodrich, long-time director and organizer of the artist's 1964 retrospective, was instrumental in securing the entire artistic estate for the Museum upon the death of Mrs. Hopper in 1968. The Hopper bequest is the largest of its kind ever made by an artist to a public institution in this country. It contains early works and works on paper which, together with the purchased works and gifts from other sources, show the full range of Hopper's uniquely American achievement.

Edward Hopper is generally considered America's major 20th century realist. The sober quality of his composition, the severity of his forms and the magic of his light put him in good standing with proponents of abstract art as well. For a short moment in the 1960s Hopper was held up as a champion of Americana with an avuncular relationship to Pop art. The Whitney's sharing of the Hopper bequest with the country and with the world in numerous recent exhibitions, and the writings of Lloyd Goodrich, Brian O'Doherty and Gail Levin, published since the artist's death in 1967, have shed light on every aspect of his work. Yet, standing in front of one of his paintings, we are not interested so much in Hopper's subject, whether an office at night or a hotel room in the morning, but how that subject, rendered with a genius for understated but pregnant portrayal, evokes in us every corresponding emotion, from guilt to loneliness and from contentment to nostalgia.

Seven A.M. presents a storefront at the cutting edge of night—a dense and impenetrable neck of the woods—and day—an open and welcoming place of business, bathed in light and ready to receive its first customers. The hour is felt in the violet shadows and confirmed by the clock on the wall. Though empty of people, their appearance is as certain to occur as that of the actors on a stage. Hopper trades on that theatrical expectation. Waiting is as natural a condition for his subjects as is solitude and what appears to be gentle despair. There is always more than meets the eye, thoughts and feelings are conveyed by way of shadows falling through an open window, the green of a train compartment or curtains set aflutter. Times of day are made palpable and carefully chosen for mood or effect.

Stuart Davis was among an early group of artists who exhibited their work at the Whitney Studio Club, parent organization of the Whitney Museum of American Art. The artist's 1917 exhibition at the Club adjoining Gertrude Vanderbilt Whitney's sculpture studio began an association which was to span his entire career. When in May of 1928, Juliana R. Force, a co-founder of the Club, bought several of Davis' paintings, that sale permitted him to go to Paris and live there until August of the following year. It was during this French period that Davis became involved with lithography and produced some of his most light-hearted paintings. *Place Pasdeloup* is among the more ambitious and carefree of his Paris cityscapes. It was acquired by Mrs. Whitney shortly after the artist's return from Europe. The Whitney Studio Club became the Whitney Museum of American Art in 1930, and Davis was subsequently given three one-man exhibitions there. His work has been collected in depth; eight paintings and 13 paintings and drawings are now owned by the Museum.

Stuart Davis' *Place Pasdeloup* represents an idyllic reprieve from that serious pursuit of a modernist style that had been so evident in the 1927-28 Eggbeater series. In that series which heralded abstract geometric art in America, Davis nearly eliminated, as John R. Lane has explained, the imitation of natural features in favor of his own invented geometric forms. In Paris, Davis painted many local street scenes but while he applied the structural lessons gained from his work on the Eggbeaters, naturalistic detail with an emphasis on the picturesque carried the day. Gallic insouciance, the levity of the cabaret, Irving Berlin and Gershwin's *An American in Paris* were all reflected in these stage-set cityscapes trivialized by subsequent commercial adaptations. Davis anticipated, in *Place Pasdeloup*, those celebrants of the vernacular, Andy Warhol and Roy Lichtenstein, to whom, however, good old America proved as colorful as France.

For an artist who is so well represented in the collection of the Whitney Museum of American Art, Alexander Calder's involvement with this institution was late in starting and slow to develop. Calder's art was shown for the first time in the Museum in its 1942 Annual Exhibition—a full 16 years after the artist had had his first one-man exhibition in New York City. Nine years of inclusion in Whitney Annual Exhibitions preceded the Museum's first Calder purchase. In 1983 the Whitney can boast 25 works by Calder; several more have been promised, and a number are on loan from the Howard and Jean Lipman Foundation. Beyond collecting this artist's work with an unmatched commitment, Jean Lipman has organized two Calder exhibitions for the Museum and written the accompanying catalogues. Great American collections are built in this manner and today, as a testament to the inspired support of the Lipmans, the Whitney Museum of American Art owns the most comprehensive public collection of Alexander Calder's sculpture.

A link between the European avant garde and the American artisan's tradition, Alexander Calder is the most flamboyant sculptor of the machine age. He acquired an early fame in Paris with circus marionettes made of wire, followed by wire portrait sculptures. A chance encounter with Mondrian called his figurative orientation

into question and he began to experiment
with abstract shapes and primary colors.
Hans Arp, a friend of Mondrian's and of the
young American, saw these stationary
abstract sculptures and called them
"stabiles." Then, when Calder first
introduced movement into his art, another
colleague, Marcel Duchamp, obliged by
proposing the term "mobiles." Mobile and
stabile were as gracefully combined into one
as were their constituent materials, metal,
wood and string.

Cage Within a Cage borrows from the
artist's own early wire versions of an
aquarium with goldfish as well as from
Giacometti's "open" Surrealist sculptures.
The flexibility and resilience of the wire
medium lend themselves to the insertion of
parts and the affixation of levers that shake,
vibrate and wiggle. Quite in contrast to the
free-swinging metal cutout mobiles, these
early wire sculptures are self-contained,
withholding and tentatively rather than
aggressively involved with space.

172

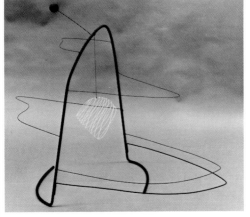

180

Smith College Museum of Art

Edwin Romanzo Elmer's *Mourning Picture*, reputedly is the most asked about and reproduced painting in the Smith College Museum of Art's entire collection. At The Museum of Modern Art, Andrew Wyeth's *Christina's World* holds a similar record. Both institutions boast far greater treasures, yet none with greater appeal to the popular imagination. Is it the Easter Seal mentality of a child-centered society? Or perhaps the vicarious attraction of misfortune—one lovely girl has gone to her heavenly reward, the other is crippled yet struggling her way up the hill? Some people are just plain grateful when art displays common emotion and gives them an opportunity to identify with another person's sorrow. The clapboard Victorian mansion reassures those who live in an unstable world in much the same way as in *Christina's World* the family farm appears to be the only safe haven. *Mourning Picture* was conceived as a memorial to the artist's beloved daughter. The stiff poses of the mournfully attired parents and the cutout isolation of the child with her toys betray a not entirely successful yet captivating integration of period photographs and Sunday painter's craft into one elegiac composition.

When Henry-Russell Hitchcock was director of the Smith College Museum of Art, from 1949-55, he enthusiastically shared an interest in American 19th and early 20th century art of his assistant, Mary Bartlett Cowdrey. A 1950 lecture by Alfred Frankenstein on the *trompe l'oeil* still lifes of John Frederick Peto, which she organized, fortuitously attracted a woman by the name of Maud Valona Elmer. She astounded the museum's staff when pulling out some paintings by her uncle. Edwin Romanzo Elmer (1850-1923), a totally unknown artist, had lived and worked in Ashfield and Shelburne Falls, hilltowns of the Eastern Berkshires, no more than 25 miles from Northampton. He showed his pictures only once, at the Shelburne Falls, Massachusetts, Post Office, in November 1890. Hitchcock and Cowdrey recognized his original talent and immediately began planning an exhibition for the fall of 1952. Frankenstein devoted a short article to Elmer, and in 1953, *Mourning Picture* was acquired for the museum's permanent collection.

Old Man Writing by Candlelight was painted c. 1627, the year Peter Paul Rubens, traveling through Holland, commented that "looking for a painter he had found but one, namely Henricus ter Brugghen." Like the Utrecht painter, Rubens had absorbed the lessons of Caravaggio and that may have been the reason why he showered such praise on his Dutch colleague. Terbrugghen and Honthorst (see *The Flea Hunt* on loan from the Dayton Art Institute) are known as the "Utrecht Caravaggists" and they each spent ten years in Italy. While a high-keyed realism, noticeable in the old man's face and hands, firmly connects Terbrugghen to the native tradition, the picture's plastic qualities from night cap to writing paper and the subject's dramatically lit clothing, would have been unthinkable without its author's Italian experience. Seen from the waist up and in closely confined quarters, the *Old Man Writing by Candlelight* has an immediacy rare in Dutch genre painting, and anticipates, by not too many years, the night scenes of Georges de La Tour.

Hendrick Terbrugghen in America, a 1965 exhibition organized by the Dayton Art Institute, occasioned a debate about this picture's date and antecedents. Dated incompletely on the writing paper and with no radiographic evidence that the digits beyond 16.. ever existed, this may be, it has been suggested, the uncommunicative artist's practical joke on posterity. Stylistic comparisons place the picture somewhere between 1626 and 1628. Closest in subject and treatment to the Smith College painting are a *Magdalen* in Pommersfelden and a *Concert* at Eastnor Castle. The type goes back to early 16th century Flemish portraiture, most notably a portrait of Erasmus of Rotterdam attributed to Quentin Massys in the Palazzo Barberini. Another precedent is provided by the candlelight rendering of a *Saint Jerome* in the Rijksmuseum, assigned to the 16th century School of Leyden. Portraits of the same general type occurred in the joint workshop of Terbrugghen and Baburen, another Utrecht School painter. The motif of the intensified light passing through the eyeglass lens seems to have been first utilized by Baburen in 1622. Nocturnal effects were the general province of Honthorst whose fame with that particular genre earned him the name Gherardo delle Notti in Italy.

That Smith College ought to have a collection of original works of art was the conviction of its first President, L. Clark Seelye, and in 1879 he bought 27 paintings by contemporary Americans such as Eakins, Homer, Bierstadt and J.G. Brown. Thus the students at the College were given a chance to learn from original works of art. Among these early graduates were two sisters, Caroline R. ('96) and Adeline F. ('98) Wing, who became, towards the end of their lives, generous and active supporters of the Museum. Natives of Bangor, Maine, they wintered each year in New York City where they regularly visited the art galleries. Their gifts, some eighteen paintings, drawings and sculptures, came in part from their own collection; the majority, however, were chosen by the museum's directors and funded by the Misses Wing.

In the case of the Terbrugghen, Robert O. Parks, director from 1955-61, whose acquisitions reveal him to have had an exceptionally good eye, found the picture at Cramer's in the Hague. He had been asked by two other generous donors, Eleanor Lamont Cunningham ('32) and her husband, Charles C. Cunningham, then director of the Wadsworth Atheneum, to find works from which they might choose a gift in memory of Alphons P.A. Vorenkamp, a distinguished member of the art history faculty who was very popular with alumnae but who had gone back to Holland after the war. When the Cunninghams eventually chose another work, the Wing sisters came to the rescue and allowed Parks to acquire this very fine Terbrugghen.

In his catalogue introduction to a Juan Gris exhibition at The Museum of Modern Art in 1958, James Thrall Soby called 1914 "the great year of Gris' *papiers collés*." Although no original invention—Braque and Picasso had been pasting papers since the fall of 1912—Gris' inclusion of various and sundry clippings in at least three dozen compositions that can be dated between April and December, was brilliant, nonetheless, and gained him the sobriquet of "a Cubists' Cubist." On the eve of the European cataclysm, life looked promising to Juan Gris and his work expressed that optimism. Daniel-Henry Kahnweiler had signed him on, and Gertrude Stein was telling everybody how highly she thought of him. The first five months of 1914 were spent in Paris; from June till September, he passed his holidays with his wife in Collioure. There he saw a great deal of the older Henri Matisse, who had owned a villa in that small fishing village in the Pyrenées Orientales since his 1905 Fauve days. Then, suddenly, the war broke out and Gris, cut off from his dealer and considered an alien, squeaked through the fall season with the help of Matisse and Gertrude Stein.

Glasses and Newspaper is closely related in theme, still life paraphernalia and composition to *Book and Glasses*, owned by Gertrude Stein at one time, now in the Goulandris Collection. It followed by one week (if *Le Journal* can be trusted) the magistral *Tea Cups* in the Kunstsammlung Nordrhein Westfalen. Gris' collages are far more colorful than those of Braque or even Picasso. Clearly, they demonstrate a painter's ambition. One rightly suspects subtle signals and cryptic references contained and sometimes concealed in the printed matter Gris integrated in pictures that were meant to be, in the artist's own words, "the very opposite of trompe l'oeil." In "Picasso and the Typography of Cubism," Robert Rosenblum has identified the folded paper as *Le Journal* of May 3, 1914, carrying on its front page a diagramed illustration and story of the explosion of the dirigible *l'Adjudant-Réau* near Verdun. "This illustration," Rosenblum argues, "formally analogous to the checkerboard squares to the right, shows us the lower part of a dirigible, whose swollen arc seems to hover under the base of a wineglass that, with an almost Futurist path of movement, floats up to the left-hand corner, as if propelled skyward by this fragment of an airship."

The New York dealer Joseph Brummer acquired *Glasses and Newspaper*, as near as we can tell, at the first of four Kahnweiler sales between 1921-23. The original Kahnweiler Gallery had gone out of business in 1914, and the French State requisitioned its stock. In 1920, Daniel-Henry Kahnweiler returned to the profession by using the name of his French backer for the Galerie Simon which he opened in the rue d'Astorg. The fact that between 1921-23 Brummer presented the College with five works by Juan Gris (the first, for sure, to enter a museum collection anywhere), suggests that he had acquired them advantageously at the above-mentioned auction sale. The Museum's director, from 1920-32, was Alfred Vance Churchill, a painter and art historian with a special interest in 19th and 20th century art. A friend of Feininger, he acquired in 1922, for the sum of $200, the first sculpture by Wilhelm Lehmbruck to ever enter an American public collection. On a foundation laid by Churchill, Jere Abbott, his successor in 1932, purchased the Museum's first Picasso, an imposing 1919-20 still life, *Table, Guitar and Bottle*.

New Orleans Museum of Art

170

103

Brilliant but often overlooked, Rococo painter Charles Natoire was responsible, along with Noël-Nicolas Coypel, François Boucher and Jean-Marc Nattier, for the creation of the Louis XV style. His extremely productive years, 1730 to 1750, were spent executing a series of richly decorative fresco programs in and around Paris at such historic landmarks as Marly, Versailles, Fontainebleau and the Hôtel de Soubise.

The Psyche story, based on the *Golden Ass* of Apuleius, provided the inspiration for a number of French decorative schemes by two artists, Boucher and Natoire. While the Psyche story inspired Boucher to render a series of paintings and tapestries, this theme moved Natoire to execute frescoes for the Hôtel de Soubise. The exclusion of the episode, *Toilette of Psyche* from Natoire's original decoration, prompted him to adopt the subject later as a single theme.

The original grisaille sketch for the tapestry episode of the *Toilette* by Boucher comprises all the essentials that Natoire used in his 1745 *Toilette*: a baldachin bed, a palace interior with columns and a pool with nymphs. In addition, Natoire provides a garden, perhaps suggested by a reading of the specific stage directions for Moliére's tragi-comedy *Psiche*, which describes a garden scene visible from the palace. One significant difference is that Natoire presents us with an ambiguous space, neither indoors nor outdoors.

(Adapted from Joan G. Caldwell)

The tradition of collecting art is not new to the Crescent City if one considers an important early collection assembled by New Orleanian James Robb. Included in this group were 15 works purchased from the collection of Joseph Bonaparte, older brother of Napoleon and ex-king of Naples and Spain, who brought his entire collection to the United States after he lost the Spanish throne and Napoleon was defeated. Robb acquired the large *Toilette of Psyche* in 1845 at the sale of Joseph Bonaparte's estate in Bordentown, New Jersey, near Philadelphia and hung the painting in his palatial Garden District villa, which was decorated with frescoes painted by the nephew of "the great

Canova," Dominic Canova. The Robb collection of 67 paintings was dispersed at auction in 1859. Among the works sold was the Natoire which, after passing through other local collections, was put on loan at the then Isaac Delgado Museum of Art when it first opened in 1911. The painting eventually came into the Museum's possession through the bequest of Judge Charles F. Claiborne in 1940.

(William A. Fagaly)

Photographer Clarence John Laughlin is to the Mississippi valley what Eugène Atget was to turn-of-the-century Paris and Ansel Adams is to the high sierras; they all championed those aspects of life and nature upon which modern civilization was seen to be rapidly encroaching. Deeply enamored with his native Louisiana, Laughlin has photographically recorded the vanishing remainders of its glorious past, cemetery monuments, plantation houses and trees that have fallen victim to river bank erosion. The past, for Laughlin, is a visual obsession, more imagined than real; a nostalgic backward glance tinged with romantic overstatement; the child's dilapidated playground filled with omens and haunted by ghosts. The photographer's captions, on which he insists, praise, in elegiac prose, the "land of the writhing, ever-coiling bayous, whose passages are lined with the grey, dolorous membranes of moss," and the "great crumbling masses of wood, brick and stone...their walls cracked by the resistless and feverish searchings of plant roots, stained by the hot caresses of the rain..."

Darkness in Daylight is a mourning tribute to a tragic queen among plantation houses, Belle Grove, near White Castle, Louisiana. Built by Henry Howard in 1857 in the Greek Revival style with elegant Palladian touches for a sugar baron who was soon to lose his wealth in the war between the states, this antebellum mansion was plagued by the misfortunes of its successive owners and, in 1952, succumbed to a ravishing fire. Laughlin photographed Belle Grove from 1939 on, painstakingly recording its progressive

demise. This image, the ominously shaded
ruin of an only partially erect house,
suggests Civil War, not recent destruction.
It evokes memories of George N. Barnard's
visual reports from the battlegrounds of
Charleston and Atlanta once the enemy
had moved on. But, as the illusion comes
under closer scrutiny, melodrama rears its
head and *Darkness in Daylight* flattens into
a stageset for *Gone with the Wind*.

When John Bullard was appointed
Director of the New Orleans Museum of
Art in 1973, he began assembling a
photographic collection which, in just ten
years, has achieved national recognition.
NEA purchase grants for the work of living
American photographers as well as gifts
from the Edward Steichen Estate and from
the New Orleanian Clarence John
Laughlin, boosted a collection developed
through judicious selection by the
standards and criteria of art history. The
collection numbers over 8,000 images and
is strong in American documentary and
post-World War II photography, German
and East European photography of the
1930s and in the history of Louisiana.

Traditional art from the Hawaiian
Islands is extremely rare. The way of
life it reflected was eradicated a generation
or two after Captain Cook's arrival in
1776. Scarcity and beauty go hand in
hand. "If we were forced to choose a single
specimen to represent the characteristic art
of Polynesia, it might well be one of the
extraordinary wooden gods of Hawaii...,"
wrote Henri M. Luquiens in 1931. "Here
the wooden images of the gods speak for
themselves, up to a certain point, owing to
a kind of transparent realism in their
conception." Fewer than 150 of these
extraordinary creations survive today, most
of them collected by visiting Europeans
prior to 1819 when Kamehameha II
denounced the old religions and had all
idols destroyed.

One of the earliest known wooden
images from Hawaii is that now in New
Orleans, collected by James Cook on his
third voyage to the island in 1778-1779. It
has an impeccable pedigree, and it has

70

been the subject of extensive research, most recently by Adrienne Kaeppler of the Bernice P. Bishop Museum in Honolulu. She has suggested that the New Orleans image, and a likely mate now in the British Museum, may have been part of a sculpturally adorned picket fence from Hikiau heiau that Cook's men removed and chopped up for firewood. The third surviving war god guardian of the sacred precincts around the platforms on which the Hawaiian temples stood is a large, impressive but presumably later example in the Peabody Museum of Salem, Massachusetts.

The stance and appearance of the temple figure bespeak its protective function. Thrusting and aggressive, it faces the viewer with a grotesque expression reinforced by a figure-eight mouth, snub nose and enormous, slanted eyes not unlike those we encounter in Japanese war deities. The tall, serrated headdress makes the stocky little warrior god look more formidable as it represents half of the post from which he has been carved. The sturdy neck, sloping shoulders and bulky arms and legs carry the marks of the adze with which they have been hewn. Taut and contained, the form of this temple figure is powerful and very sculptural in conception. We are reminded, particularly in the treatment of chest, hips and knees, of early Cubist (1909) painting which illustrates primitive art's hold on the imagination of Braque and Picasso.

In 1977 the New Orleans Museum of Art received the single most important donation of works of art in its history with the bequest of 17 major paintings and sculptures by eight European and American artists, together with 180 African and Oceanic sculptures, from the Estate of Victor K. Kiam. The donor, a prominent financier, had grown up in New Orleans and studied at Tulane University before moving to New York. His friendship with Picasso and Miró may have inspired his interest in Oceanic and African art. The *Temple Figure* attests to the seriousness of that interest and is one of several extraordinary objects in the Kiam bequest.

John Singleton Copley was the most skillful artist practicing in the American colonies before the Revolution. He had two careers, one in the colonies and one in England where his loyalist sympathies led him to settle in 1774.

By the middle 1760s Copley had secured a reputation as a portraitist to the elite of Boston. His artistic growth can be traced through the steady development of an ability to achieve a softer, more rounded modelling of the human figure and an increased use of chiaroscuro.

By 1768 the *Portrait of Colonel George Watson* indicated a change in Copley's style toward a more sombre palette, along with a shift in the level of his patronage. As the impending Revolution became felt, Copley began to paint a new breed of men: politicians, professionals and financiers.

Watson, like Copley, was a loyalist, an elected member of His Majesty's Council in the colonies. Six years after the Watson portrait, a midnight crowd appeared at Copley's house demanding to see the loyalist "villain" Colonel George Watson whom they believed to be visiting the painter. Watson had left Boston a few hours earlier so Copley's home was spared destruction by the rebellious mob, but the incident helped confirm Copley's decision to move to Royalist England.

(Adapted from Joan G. Caldwell)

Sarah Watson, daughter of George Watson, married Martin Brimmer of Roxbury. Their grandson, Martin Brimmer III, owned the portrait until 1892 when it passed into the hands of Henderson Inches of Brookline, Massachusetts.

In 1966 the Women's Volunteer Committee of the Museum inaugurated the First Annual Fund Raising Ball. During its 17 year history, the *Odyssee Ball's* revenues have exceeded one million dollars, giving the professional staff means to acquire important art objects. In 1967, the "Arts of the Americas" program was proposed as an area of concentration for the Museum's permanent collection. The Copley *Portrait of Colonel George Watson* was acquired in 1977 with Women's Volunteer Committee funds.

(William A. Fagaly)

164

168

Philadelphia Museum of Art

In *William Rush Carving His Allegorical Figure of the Schuylkill River*, Philadelphia painter Thomas Eakins transformed a historical subject into a genre painting. The story of the early Philadelphia sculptor who sought a model to pose nude for him had a special meaning for Eakins as it symbolized his own struggle against a prevailing puritanism in the city of brotherly love. Milton W. Brown has written that in all of Eakins' work there is no more sensuous painting than that of the buxom nude and her clothes scattered on the chair. The frankness of the naked (a word he preferred to 'nude') model is far removed from the erotic ideality of his teacher, the admired salon artist Gérôme, and completely new to American painting. Still in his 30s, Eakins, with this 1877 picture, established himself as the greatest painter in the United States.

In preparation for the work, Eakins appears to have done careful historical research: studying other examples of Rush's work (his figure of George Washington in Independence Hall can be seen in the painting); copying fashion plates and paintings as sources for the costumes; borrowing a Chippendale chair to assure accuracy of the furnishings, and visiting Rush's workshop near the Delaware waterfront. The historical interest awakened by this work and by demonstrations of colonial life at the Centennial must have inspired Eakins' series of paintings and sculptures showing women in period costumes, spinning, knitting (as the chaperone in this painting), or simply lost in reverie. The Philadelphia Museum of Art acquired this and many other Eakins' works remaining in his studio in 1929, as a gift from Mrs. Thomas Eakins and Miss Mary A. Williams.

Rodin's name was already so well known in Latin America in 1894, that the city of Buenos Aires chose him to make a monument in honor of Domingo Faustino Sarmiento (1811-1888), author, educator, diplomat and Argentina's president from 1868-1874. Rodin accepted the commission although he was in poor health and embroiled in a controversy about his monument to Balzac. He decided to return to a compositional scheme that had served him well for his monument to Claude Lorrain—one in which the hero is portrayed in stride on top of a pedestal carrying symbolic representations. Rodin relied on photographs for a physical likeness of the man he had never known, but he failed to impress its authenticity on those who remembered Sarmiento and they denounced the result. As that is hardly a measure of the portrayal's merit *as sculpture*, Rodin deserves credit for having created a fully clad—vs. the nude Balzac—figure of a public personage, in a reserved dramatic manner and a robust impressionistic style. The medium-size study of *President Sarmiento* in Philadelphia shows a rather more energetic pose than the final version but comes without a sculpted pedestal.

The Rodin Museum and its collection were given to the City of Philadelphia by Jules E. Mastbaum, a leading figure in the motion picture industry and one of Philadelphia's best known philanthropists. On a visit to Paris, just three years before his death, Mr. Mastbaum bought a small bronze by Rodin which so fired his enthusiasm that he conceived the idea of establishing a Rodin Museum "for the enjoyment of my fellow-citizens." Bronzes were purchased directly from the Musée Rodin in Paris and the collection was virtually complete in two years' time. Housed in a building Jules E. and Etta Wedell Mastbaum erected in Fairmount Park, the collection was transferred to the administrative authority of the Philadelphia Museum of Art in 1939.

The painting depicts an event from the Old Testament: "And all the congregation of the children of Israel journeyed from the wilderness of Sin, after their journeys, according to the commandment of the Lord, and pitched in Rephidim: and there was no water for the people to drink. Wherefore the people did chide with Moses, and said, Give us water that we may drink. And Moses said unto them, Why chide ye with me? Wherefore do you tempt the Lord?... And the Lord said unto Moses, Go on before the people, and take with thee the elders of Israel; and thy rod, wherewith thou smotest the river, take in thine hand, and go. Behold, I will stand before thee there upon the rock in Horeb; and thou shalt smite the rock, and there shall come water out of it, and the people may drink..." (Exodus 17:1-7)

Surrounded by the throng of his followers, Moses stands in shadow, his arms outstretched and his eyes turned heavenward in acknowledgment of the Lord's miracle. The Israelites, so recently doubt-ridden and rebellious, rejoice as they rush forward to quench their thirst. Jan Steen depicts the Children of Israel as an exotic and diverse people, yet unmistakably more related to the Dutch of all social classes than to the inhabitants of the Near East. The lush and hilly landscape is a far cry from the wilderness and cannot possibly have lacked water. In medieval thought, the water Moses drew from the rock was interpreted as prefiguring the sacrificial waters of baptism. Although typological meanings no longer were the rule in the 17th century, Steen, nonetheless, probably thought of Moses, at least in one sense, as the forerunner of Christ. Most scholars concur in calling *Moses Striking the Rock* an early work of about 1660-61, when the painter worked in Haarlem.

The John G. Johnson Collection at the Philadelphia Museum of Art contains over 1,300 paintings collected by their donor before his death in 1917. John Gaver Johnson, in his day, was considered by eminent judges to be the greatest lawyer in the English speaking world, and his scholarship and knowledge in the field of painting was hardly equalled by any of his American fellow collectors of the turn of the century. Born in Philadelphia in 1841 as the son of a blacksmith and a milliner, Johnson grew up to become one of the country's top corporate lawyers whose clients included Henry O. Havemeyer and John Pierpont Morgan. Stimulated by the 1876 Centennial Exhibition, Johnson began collecting in the 1880s, mostly

101

Italian, but Flemish, Dutch and English paintings as well. He bequeathed his collection to the City of Philadelphia to be exhibited in his home, but safety required that it be transferred to a wing of the Philadelphia Museum of Art.

For those familiar with Léger's work but seeing *Composition 1923-27* for the first time, two questions leap to mind. How do we explain the peculiar dating, and what subject should we read into it? It is clear that this sober two-color painting was conceived in 1923 as it fits Léger's style of that year to a tee. The later date is perplexing. Curious, to say the least, is a palette far more limited than we are accustomed to seeing in the artist's work of the 1920s.

A clue may be given us by a drawing that came to light only recently. In his 1983 *Fernand Léger*, Peter Francia reproduces a drawing identified as *Untitled 1923* (dimensions and whereabouts unknown) that in all but the minutest details 'blueprints' the Philadelphia painting. It is signed F.L.23 in a location to the left instead of to the right of the black vertical anchoring the image. As the author neither describes nor refers to this drawing in his text, we are again left wondering. Léger dated the Philadelphia painting 27 on its front and there is no doubt that he painted it after the 1923 drawing. A close variant of the Gallatin picture is *Composition in Blue* in the Charles H. and Mary F. S. Worcester Collection at the Art Institute of Chicago. Its size is identical but, dated 1921-27, the spread of years between conception and execution is even greater. The two almost monochromatic pictures may have been commissioned from a drawing to serve, individually or together, a specific decorative purpose of the period.

The year 1923 was an eventful one in Léger's life. He tried his hand at making a film, *Le Ballet Mécanique*, and he designed costumes and décors for the Blaise Cendrars and Darius Milhaud ballet *La Création du Monde* which premiered in October of that year. At Léonce

Rosenberg's Galerie de l'Effort Moderne where Léger had exhibited since 1919, the Dutchman Theo van Doesburg, recently settled in Paris, presented an exhibition of *De Stijl* architecture that fall. In his paintings, Léger features tugboats, machinery, and architecture. While the great archetypal image of the modern metropolis can still be gleaned, a Purist flavor begins to assert itself.

If, for a moment, we eliminate from this composition, those smoothly curved terra cotta colored volumes, shaded in dark grays to accentuate their roundness, we are left with a scaffold. "The vernacular architecture of Léger's native Normandy with its timbered and mortar farmhouses, invariably painted black and white, provided a ready-made equivalent analogy to the formal structure of De Stijl paintings," Peter de Francia has written apropos of the open-ended grids firming up Léger's semi-abstract compositions of those years. They do indeed remind us of Vilmos Huszar's cover design for the magazine *De Stijl* and Theo van Doesburg's 1917 *Composition IX. Card Players*, then in the artist's Paris studio, now in the collection of the Gemeentemuseum, The Hague. There is every reason to assume that Léger was familiar with and, with reservations, showed himself open to, as he would with Ozenfant and Jeanneret, the tectonic qualities in the Dutch artists' work.

The formalist reduction in this 1923 composition of the visible world from which Léger drew his inspiration, has left so few recognizable motifs intact that we are obliged to guess what it specifically portrays. There seems to be just the merest hint of a human figure while everything else reads like chimneys, cowlings, horns, boilers and bent metal sheeting. There is a wisp of smoke or clouds and we easily imagine the tugboat environment. A poem by Blaise Cendrars comes to mind: "At dawn I went down to the engine room/ I listened for the last time to the deep breathing of the pistons/ The mauve sky was cloudless." (*L'Aube*, 1924)

Reality is paraphrased rather than represented. Léger did not imitate machinery but echoed its prominence in modern life through imaginary, purely pictorial forms. While his work's components are static, they suggest with their bulging, elliptical and rounded shapes, the barely contained dynamics of a boiler factory. Within an ambiguously scaled space, solid objects are jammed together without fully surrendering their individual identities—just enough to tempt us into multiple readings.

Albert Eugene Gallatin followed hard on the heels of pioneer collectors John Quinn, Arthur Jerome Eddy, Gertrude and Leo Stein and the Cohn sisters of Baltimore, in acquiring and promoting avant garde art. The pictures he began buying in the 1920s were made available to students and artists in a hall of New York University and effectively became, as of 1927, the city's first publicly accessible collection of contemporary art. Known as the *Gallery of Living Art*, the Gallatin Collection functioned as a training ground for young artists and a rallying point for the founders—Gallatin prominently among them—of the American Abstract Artists group. When the university administration needed the space for another purpose, the Philadelphia Museum of Art offered Gallatin, who was born in a suburb of that city, its premises instead. On loan since 1943, the Gallatin Collection was deeded to the Philadelphia Museum of Art at the owner's death in 1952.

54

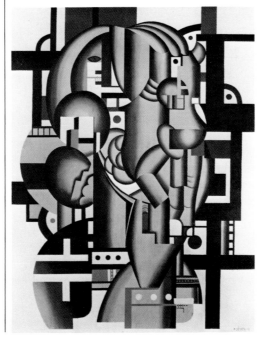

149

Allen Memorial Art Gallery, Oberlin College

By 1645, when de Heem had become a master in the Antwerp guild and when this elegant display of fancy foods and tableware may have been painted, the basic genre was fixed, in contents as well as form: a table against a black background, without clear spatial definition, and on the table objects of visual and gustatory delectation portrayed with minute attention to color, light and texture. Clearly, they served to demonstrate that their owner was a person of means, taste and distinction. Who else could afford Mediterranean crustaceans and fruit not indigenous to the Low Countries? Antwerp was a port of transfer with a thriving commerce that drew craftsmen of every stripe to cater to the whims and pleasures of a prospering merchant class. The Dutch language has a fitting term for this type of still life: *pronkstilleven*, meaning, literally, a still life with which to impress and show off.

The Oberlin still life was proposed as a worthwhile acquisition by the late Wolfgang Stechow, a member of the College's faculty with an international reputation as a scholar of Dutch painting. Dr. Stechow identified it as having come from the Winter Palace and, subsequently, the Hermitage in Leningrad. Up until World War II, the Soviet government quietly sold off art through Western dealers—ostensibly to make up for a disastrous economy. The same paraphernalia in a different arrangement are found in a still life by Jan Davidsz de Heem, dated 1645, in the Emile Wolf collection, New York.

Mrs. F. F. Prentiss (1865-1944), the daughter of Louis Severance, an early partner of John D. Rockefeller, was the former Mrs. Dudley Peter Allen. When Dr. Allen died in 1915, his widow assumed the cost of building the Art Museum as a memorial. Twenty years later, Mrs. Prentiss donated a new wing to the Art Museum and she bequeathed a portion of her estate as an endowment. The *Still Life* by de Heem was acquired in 1954 through the Mrs. F. F. Prentiss Fund.

Known for its superb drawing collection, the Allen Memorial Art Museum has reason to be proud of Filippino Lippi's *Lament at the Tomb*, an important work from a significant moment in the artist's career. Even though the subject is relatively rare in Filippino's work, there is, in the Kress Collection at the National Gallery, a painting by Lippi, entitled *Pietà*, of the same composition and approximately the same dimensions. Scholars from Bernard Berenson to John R. Spencer have drawn comparisons between the two works and attempted to date them. In the *Allen Memorial Art Museum Bulletin*, (Fall 1966), Spencer made a conclusive argument for attributing the drawing to the artist's middle career. As for the predella in the National Gallery, Spencer hypothesizes that it belonged to a lost altarpiece painted around 1495, and that the Oberlin drawing of about 1485, itself treated in a very painterly way and pricked for transfer, was used by the artist first as a study for the Matthias Corvinus altarpiece for the Church of Our Lady in Budapest, Hungary, and again as a cartoon for the Washington predella. The ten year interval accounts for the minute but noticeable differences in style and composition.

Filippino Lippi ranks as one of the great masters of the Florentine Renaissance. According to Giorgio Vasari, who wrote a chronicle of the talented and the famous of his time, Lorenzo the Magnificent liked Lippi so much that he would not "exchange him for any of the painters that lived in ancient Greece."

R. T. Miller, Jr., in whose name the Filippino Lippi drawing was acquired, graduated from Oberlin in 1891 and, after working as a newspaper reporter and attending the Harvard Law School, founded a correspondence school "for the purpose of giving practical home study for wage earners." From the time of his retirement and until his death in 1958, he gave the Art Museum a generous sum every year with which to buy works of art.

With his famous dictum "aesthetics is for artists like ornithology is for the birds," Barnett Newman, artist and birdwatcher, warned us that whatever meaning we attribute to his art, it is our problem and of little concern to him. Newman's severe paint surfaces with their monosyllabic vertical articulations elude critical interpretation. They are paradigms of the "toughness" for which the best of Abstract Expressionist painting is famous. The vertical "zips" in Newman's work are stopped short by the canvas's physical termination and could theoretically go on forever. Even in a small painting, that implicit vastness is crucial to Newman. With color as his subject (and not a mere attribute), Newman claimed for himself, in Harold Rosenberg's words, "an art entirely liberated from residues of visual experience," which, in effect, made him a knight errant of painting in search of the holy grail.

"As a young man," Thomas B. Hess has written, "Newman had sensed the nature of the aesthetic experience in Spinoza's apprehension of the nature of God; as a mature artist, he found stimulation, resonance and (if the old-fashioned word still has a meaning) inspiration in the writings of the Jewish mystics." Art should be ethics and not aesthetics, Newman claimed. He gave credence to that belief by devoting his single most important cycle of paintings to the "Stations of the Cross," a tribute to the New Testament that left members of his faith at a loss for explanations. The curious title *Onement* suggests wholeness, harmony, but also, as Newman himself pointed out, refers to At-*onement*—Atonement, the events of Yom Kippur, which is a day of remembrance of the dead, but for the Kabbalists, also the ideal moment for meditation on the Messianic secret, on rebirth, new life—in a word, Creation.

28

189

Joslyn Art Museum

199

Jules Breton's pastoral visions of rural France earned him critical accolades, official honors and the affection of the public throughout his long career. American collectors, with that Victorian tendency to romanticize life in the country, bought his work long before they became aware of the Impressionists. As late as the 1930s, visitors to the Art Institute of Chicago voted *Song of the Lark* America's favorite painting, while the Joslyn Art Museum received, from the Friends of Art, *The Vintage at Château Lagrange*. For well-nigh half a century this artist's work could be found only in museum basements until, in the 1970s, the pendulum of taste and scholarly concern began to swing back, selectively, to the heyday of realist painting. The Joslyn Art Museum made a signal contribution to the reevaluation of that period in general and the knowledge of Breton in particular, by organizing the impressively documented 1982 exhibition *Jules Breton and the French Rural Tradition*.

In 1862, Breton, then 35, received his most important commission to date. The Count Duchâtel, former Minister under Louis-Philippe, now retired to his family estate in the Haut-Médoc, asked him to record the grape harvest at Château Lagrange. Breton made two trips south on which it rained; he was forced to observe the harvesting peasants through a telescope from one of the chateau's towers, and he had to avail himself of the services of a local photographer to help document his composition. Numerous drawn and painted preparatory studies later, the painting was completed in 1864 and shown in the Salon that same year. It was well received by the critics. Théophile Thoré praised its underlying classicism and recognized prototypes for this subject in the bacchanals of Titian and Poussin; Théophile Gautier found that the ox-drawn cart gave the scene "a kind of antique majesty." Hollister Sturgis, the Joslyn curator to whom we owe this detailed knowledge, has explained how Breton embraced the Realists' progressive conception of large-scale genre painting (e.g., Courbet's *Burial at Ornans*) even as he persisted in academic stylistic conventions.

Wine lovers may wish to take note that Château Lagrange, situated in the Commune of St. Julien, was classified a Third Growth in 1855 after significant improvements for which the Countess Duchâtel is credited. In the late 19th century, Lagrange was the largest Classified Growth in the entire region with 750 acres of vine. Allowed to go downhill in this century, the vinyard has improved within the past few years, and at 137 acres is now considered good by some critics.
(Alexis Lichine, *New Encyclopedia of Wines and Spirits*, 1978 ed.)

Times Square is a strange meeting place for the human race. Segal went there with a camera to record the sights and the oddities, the telescoping of space, the refraction of light, the overlay of images. The painter in him was coming out again, craving to get involved in this marvelous kaleidoscope of color. Could he show it all and yet fit it into his sober and exacting frame? He realized that he could do it only by creating a direct relationship with its real-life model—unambiguous, specific and head-on. The mode of activity that would fit the situation was not hard to choose. It had to be loitering. One man walking is a loner, two men walking are the beginnings of a crowd. From the start there was a logic to *Times Square at Night*, a clear sequence to the artist's decisions that built up to a successful conclusion. As this writer was asked to pose for and became a physical part of the sculpture, he had privileged access to the artist's thinking at the time.

Segal's figures have been routinely described as life-like. They may well have seemed that way when first encountered in the 1960s but continued usage does not make the description accurate. Life is mimicked in these figures—not reproduced—and they should remind us of art more than of life. To associate whiteness and art is irrepressible. Whiteness not only connotes art but also creates aesthetic distance. It does so in conjunction with a space equally well articulated by the artist. Despite its naturalistic portrayal, *Times Square at Night*

is an abstract of reality, related more to
Hopper and Minimalist sculpture than to
Pop art and its derivations.

When Sarah Joslyn established the
museum in 1932, she did not prohibit the
acquisition of work by living artists, she
just confined herself to artists living in the
region. In those days, acquisition funds
were spent on older art that would allow
the new institution in Nebraska to catch
up with its sisters back east. Even though
the first major work by a living American
artist came into the collection as the result
of Peggy Guggenheim's 1949 gift to the
Joslyn of Jackson Pollock's *Galaxy*, the
board did not adopt a policy to expand in
that direction until 1970. Significant
contemporary acquisitions, effectively
supported by exhibitions have distinguished
the Joslyn Art Museum in recent years.

60

One of 30 pictures from the 17th
century in the Joslyn collection,
Claude Lorrain's *Rest on the Flight into
Egypt* offers an excellent example of an
idealized pastoral landscape. The
composition is in many respects
conventional—there is a dark foreground
with two silhouetted framing elements, or
repoussoirs (the palm tree and the mass of
rocks and trees on the left), enclosing a
distant and lighter vista. A convincing
illusion of space and atmosphere is created,
however, by the careful gradation of tone
and color from the foreground to the
peach-tinged luminous horizon. One of
Claude's contemporaries described him
going into the fields at different times of
the day to mix paints approximating the
actual tints of sky and land, then carrying
them home to apply to his canvases. The
Joslyn painting, whether or not a direct
result of this unusual practice, certainly
reflects Claude's study of light in
landscape. If Röthlisberger's proposed
dating of 1634-35 is accepted, this is an
early formulation of the paradoxical
combination of carefully arranged and
conventional composition with astonishing
atmospheric realism that Claude was to
refine and perfect for the rest of his career.

(Hollister Sturges)

Museum of Art, Carnegie Institute

171

In a country that routinely allowed foreign cooks to wield their utensils in its art kitchen, Pierre Bonnard comes across as a French chef with uniquely French recipes. Mixing colors in a china plate on his studio table, he once boasted about the quality of his pigments and explained: "I hope that my pictures will keep without cracking for I would like to arrive before the young painters of the year 2000 on the sheer wings of a butterfly." Bonnard's colors, while derived from the Impressionists, have the violence Delacroix strove for in his paintings. A picture by Bonnard is like a tropical fish bowl in which the fish are magnified, their colors intensified, and always off to one corner where they are skewered with the greenery and coral rock. This intentional massing to one side while leaving large areas open, first observed in Degas, seems to have had its origin in real or imagined photographic close-ups.

Originally dated 1908-12 and identified as a race along the Seine when *Fête sur l'Eau (Regatta)* was acquired by the Museum of Art in 1963, it now has been correctly identified as having been painted in Hamburg where Bonnard took a trip with his friend Edouard Vuillard in 1913. Clearly, we are in the middle of the city and before us a group of boating enthusiasts on a balcony or terrace pays casual attention to a regatta presumably on the Aussen-Alster during the jubilee of the Kaiser. Time and place are corroborated by the presence of a kindred picture, *Le Crépuscule au Fahrhaus D'Uhlenhorst Hambourg*, in the Kunsthalle of that city. The telescoping and foreshortening of the foreground figures, pressing them all into more or less the same plane, reminds us of the flat decorative patterns in Bonnard's graphically oriented art of the Nabis period. It is tempting to speculate that Bonnard also might have been impressed with German Expressionist art, then at its apogee and certainly in full evidence in cosmopolitan Hamburg.

Sarah Mellon Scaife, daughter of Richard B. Mellon and niece of Andrew W. Mellon, initiated the only large-scale, precisely focused collecting campaign in the Museum's history. Through her generosity it was able to acquire, beginning in 1961, important French Impressionist and Post-Impressionist paintings, including major works by Monet, Pissarro, Cézanne, Gauguin and van Gogh. As she had a special love for Bonnard, the Museum saw itself enriched with four exceptional examples of that artist's work. Following Mrs. Scaife's death in 1965, her family and foundation carried on her commitment to the improvement of the Museum's 19th and 20th century collection. The same family also financed the construction of the Sarah Scaife Gallery after a design by Edward Larrabee Barnes. Completed in 1974, it was the first major addition to the Carnegie Institute since the early 1900s.

The life of W. Eugene Smith as a journalist started at age 17 as a reporter for both the *Wichita Eagle* and *Wichita Beacon*. A brief stint with *Newsweek* ended when young Smith broke the house rules by taking a miniature camera on assignment. In 1939, he signed on with *Life*, that era's haven for photo journalists, and while covering World War II in the Pacific theater, was severely wounded on Okinawa. During the postwar years the veteran photographer contributed to the development, and became a prime author of, the so-called "photo-essay." His 1954 *Man of Mercy*, a pictorial on Albert Schweitzer, triggered a dispute about artistic control between the photographer and his employer. Smith left *Life* and joined the Magnum group. Having outgrown the photo journalist label and become a humanitarian with a photo eye, Smith found himself without a mass circulation outlet or a commercial sponsor. Yet, he embarked on his most ambitious undertaking ever—a photo essay on Pittsburgh for which the John Simon Guggenheim Memorial Foundation awarded him a fellowship in 1956.

About *Pittsburgh, a Labyrinthian Walk*, W. Eugene Smith has written: "To portray a city is beyond ending; to begin such an effort is in itself a grave conceit. For though the portrayal may achieve its own measure of truth, it still will be no more than a rumor of the city—no more meaningful, and no more permanent." Rumor has it that Pittsburgh was a city of blast furnaces and smoke-filled skies at one time. Today, that stigma has almost disappeared. While the photographer's 1955 "truth" is "no more permanent," his deeply moving record of that one time truth has found permanency as art. If, as Lincoln Kirstein once put it in an homage to W. Eugene Smith, "the photographer's greatest service is the seizure of the metaphorical moment," then this remarkable photographer not only captured but, for generations to come, retained the image of Pittsburgh as a metaphor for America's industrial past.

W. Eugene Smith went beyond his original assignment to make photographs for Stefan Lorant's *Pittsburgh, Study of an American City* (1964) to eventually produce nearly 10,000 negatives and more than 400 master prints that capture the city's people, industry and institutions. In 1982, the Museum of Art received a group of over 500 black and white photographs, many of them Smith master prints, which were transferred from the Pittsburgh Photographic Library of the Carnegie Library of Pittsburgh in a project generously supported by the Howard Heinz Endowment. Through the Vira I. Heinz Fund of the Pittsburgh Foundation, additional master prints, including *Smoky City*, were acquired to complement this major collection of photographs by W. Eugene Smith.

117

In making plans for the first International in 1896, the fine arts committee of the Carnegie Institute decided to "offer a prize of $5,000 for the best picture painted by an American artist in the year 1896 and publicly exhibited for the first time in the Carnegie Gallery, and which shall be adjudged worthy of the prize by the committee, the picture to become the property of the board of trustees of the Carnegie Fine Arts and the Museum Collection fund." Winslow Homer had promised two paintings for the first International, an invitational art

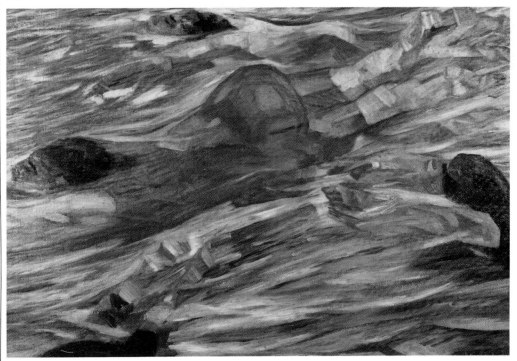

146

179

exhibition destined to identify Pittsburgh with the championship of modern art. But, in September 1896, he wrote: "I have decided to send but one picture to your exhibition, but that is the best one I have painted this year." Before the exhibition's closing, *The Wreck*, for which its maker had not set a price, was declared best in the exhibition and acquired for the predetermined amount. Homer, by all accounts, was satisfied and always cordial to the Carnegie Museum of Art. When John Beatty, the Museum's first director, visited the Maine coast, Homer was his guide and host. He was "Cousin Winslow" to Homer Saint-Gaudens who succeeded Beatty. After serving on the jury of the second International in 1897, Homer was subsequently honored with two one-man exhibitions at the Carnegie Institute.

After he settled in Prout's Neck on the Maine coast in 1884, Homer's paintings nearly always dealt with the drama of the sea. Although painted in 1896, *The Wreck* is based on a sketch the artist had made of a disaster which befell a three-masted vessel off the coast of Atlantic City ten years earlier. The wrecked ship itself is not depicted but the drama is quite clearly conveyed by the urgent figures conducting the rescue operation. Yet, originally Homer had included evidence of the sailing vessel. There are traces of the masts, just above the dunes, at the point between the two groups of spectators where a light seems to flare up. Lloyd Goodrich in describing the painting writes: "*The Wreck* is one of his finest chromatic achievements. Leaden sky, dun-colored sand, brown bushes, slate-gray oilskins, make up a harmony of grays and tones close to gray. Almost a monochrome, it is so subtly varied, so exquisitely related, that the effect is one of great depth and strength of color, and one is hardly conscious of how close its range is. Its sombreness suits perfectly the grim sense of storm and foreboding that fills the picture and makes it one of Homer's most impressive works."

When Andrew Carnegie founded the Carnegie Institute in 1896, he shaped its art program around the concept of an annual international exhibition. From these shows, he contended, the museum would have an opportunity to purchase the best in contemporary painting so that a permanent collection of masters of our time might be acquired. Possibly he was the first art patron in the country to conceive of a museum of modern art. With Homer's *The Wreck* as its very first accession and cornerstone of the collection, the Museum of Art went on to acquire, from the Internationals, paintings by Whistler, Pissarro, Sisley, Puvis de Chavannes, Sargent and Childe Hassam.

Futurism did not grow out of the discovery of a new formal language, as had Cubism, nor does it represent a style. Instead, it could be called an impulse—translated into poetry, the visual arts, music and eventually into politics. When the *Manifesto of Futurist Painters* was defiantly proclaimed from the stage of the Politeama Chiarella in Turin on March 8, 1910, there was as yet nothing that could be distinguished as Futurist painting. In May or June of that year, according to Carlo D. Carrà's 1956 recollections, he exhibited a freshly finished painting entitled *Nuotatrici* in an exhibition of *Indipendenti* at the Padiglione Ricordi, Milan. That exhibition, in fact, was called *La Mostra d'Arte Libera* and it opened not in 1910 but on April 30, 1911. Then, in February of the following year, *Nuotatrici* was exhibited in the famous Futurist exhibition at Bernheim-Jeune in Paris.

Possibly taking a suggestion, as Joshua C. Taylor has argued, from Libero Altomare's poem "Swimming in the Tiber," recited by Marinetti with great effect at many Futurist presentations, Carrà created a painting in which the forms and colors of the swimmers and the flowing water mingle in a single continuous pattern. "Light and motion are the two forces that tend to destroy the concreteness of form," Futurist theory claimed. In *The Swimmers*, the bright ripples of the water, the broad patches of divisionist color, break up the forms that are already made angular and elongated through motion. Taylor observed that the painting as a whole still relied on the persuasive continuous rhythm of Art Nouveau, luring the viewer to follow rather than to place himself in the midst of the scene.

This observation may have led Sharon Latchaw Hirsh to question, in an article in *Arts Magazine* of January 1979, the picture's Futurist credentials. She points out that between its exhibition in Milan in April 1911 and in Paris in February 1912, the artist painted over an earlier version of *The Swimmers* in a pre-Futurist symbolist-divisionist style that no longer lived up to the Futurist rhetoric and that, he was afraid, might not curry favor with the Paris critics. Indeed, there is evidence of overpainting and the article's author offers compelling arguments including a cartoon portrayal of Carrà standing in front of *The Swimmers* at a Futurist evening in Milan on June 17, 1911, in which the figures appear to be nude. Basically, the argument goes, Carrà had conceived this picture in the symbolist manner of Gustav Klimt's *Bewegtes Wasser* and other works of the period that showed sinuously moving women engulfed in flowing waters, correlated arching nude bodies with climaxing waves and emphasized rather than masked the sensuality inherent to the Art Nouveau theme. So what was Carrà to do in light of the Futurist ridicule for paintings done from the nude and after having been rudely confronted, on an exploratory visit to Paris, with the Cubists' cool, intellectual manner and advanced explorations of form? He turned his bathing nymphs into strapping amazons by adjusting their physiognomies and clothing them in fashionable tunics, and he updated his divisionist technique by geometricizing and faceting major parts of the composition. With Carrà's hurried but brave revision in the fall of 1911, a couple of frolicsome 19th century bathers became the "dynamic, violently revolutionary" and very 20th century *Swimmers*.

G. David Thompson, a self-made financier, was Pittsburgh's leading collector in the 1940s and 50s. During his lifetime, he donated more than 90 works to the Museum of Art including paintings and sculpture by De Kooning, Dubuffet, Arp, Noguchi, Metzinger and Carrà's *The Swimmers*, in 1955.

The Saint Louis Art Museum

The farmer's son from Ornans, friend of the socialist philosopher Proudhon and future Communard, Gustave Courbet never rid himself of a chip on his shoulder about the rich and the famous. Musing about getting even with the Superintendent of Fine Arts, Count Nieuwerkerke, over an unkept promise and perceived slight—Courbet continued a letter to his sister Juliette, by telling her that he had "given in to the insistent invitation of the Count of Choiseul to come and stay with him at his seaside villa." Trouville and Deauville, on the coast of Normandy, had been made fashionable in the 1850s by the Duchess of Morny and the Count of Choiseul. Not only Courbet, but Whistler, Monet and Boudin accepted invitations there and painted the novel scenery. As he had done the year before, in the company of Whistler and his Irish girlfriend Jo, Courbet spent the September and October months painting landscapes, seascapes, portraits and, perhaps in recognition of the hospitality received, *The Greyhounds of the Comte de Choiseul*. Did the fashionable beach resort of Deauville turn Courbet into a society painter? Had the vulgarian been converted to Sir Edwin Landseer's vision of canine beauty?

Though we do not know what Courbet thought of that beautiful Russian breed of greyhounds, he did confide to his sister how impressed he was with their master's home: "Here I am living in an earthly paradise, alone with this young man (Eugène-Antoine-Horace Comte de Choiseul) who is really charming. He has the genuine grand manner and distinction of the most courtly era in France...The routine of our life here is very simple but extremely luxurious. There are six servants to wait on us...The table is laden with dishes and cutlery of chased silver...Every wine imaginable...The walls of the salon and other rooms are hung with silk brocade... There are canopies over the beds, toilettes in white marble...basins for hydrotherapy...perfumes are burnt several times a day by a woman thoughout the house... Complicated flower-decorations... Every morning, as I leap from bed, a dressing gown is handed me...For the day, a carriage is always ready, harnessed to take me on excursions..."

The finely groomed greyhounds have been called, by Courbet's biographer André Fermigier, "the most Second Empire of all his pictures." Indeed, when we compare this stately pair, so clearly posed for the occasion, with the many animals and hunting scenes Courbet painted since 1858, then we must admit the singularity, even oddity of the subject. It is as though the artist had transferred the awe in which he held the villa, its trappings and its servants, to these two proud and primping beasts, not seen from above and in a kenneled environment but like creatures of myth, portrayed on the seashore, from an ascending point of view and with faraway Britain as their presumed backdrop. The umbre, blue and white colors add their aristocratic reticence and the light, unlike that of Courbet's native Franche-Comté, has the cool and silvery clarity one associates with Ingres. Exhibited in the artist's second private exhibition in a pavilion at the Rond-Point de l'Alma in 1867, *The Greyhounds of the Comte de Choiseul* was owned by the artist's sister Juliette well into this century. Acquired by Mrs. Mark C. Steinberg for her private collection, it was given by this patron, whose family's generosity also benefited the Washington University Gallery of Art, to the City Art Museum of Saint Louis in 1953.

Heavy loan demands, impairing internal operations, have forced the Saint Louis Art Museum to curtail its representation in this exhibition.

99

The Phoenix Art Museum

85

Summers spent at his Three Spear Ranch in Dubois, Wyoming, took Ivan Albright from the city made infamous by the Bugs Moran and Al Capone gangs to the one-time operating grounds of Butch Cassidy and his outlaw band. There is some evidence that the latter's 1900 robbery of the Pacific Express in Wyoming's Red Desert provided anecdotic inspiration for *The Wild Bunch (Hole in the Wall Gang)*, 1950-51, a Western still life which devotees of the genre have claimed for "cowboy art." Albright, who rejected every sound or spurious label art writers suggested in the last 50 years, preferred comparison with near-namesake Albrecht Dürer, the German Renaissance painter he admired for his scientific curiosity and fastidious technique.

In the manner in which the Dutch had damask, pewter and edibles spill off a table, *The Wild Bunch* amasses a panoply of shooting irons, leather goods and ammunition, all lit, in a cold, metallic way, from a window no larger than a hole in the wall. Color is smoked on rather than painted, and the surface glows with a charnel luminosity. "The reason I use an extremely minute technique is to tie down, to fuse, to crystallize various discordant elements so that my painting has a composite feeling," Albright confided to this writer. To our eye, such observation and rendering of detail appears grotesque because normal vision does not probe that closely, nor is it capable of such sustained and undivided concentration.

Painting at an average rate of one-half of a square inch each five-hour working day, Albright defied the law of general optics, driving home the anti-naturalistic point that what we are looking at is not really what we are looking at. His method was the opposite of that of the 19th century trompe-l'oeil painter who by flattening his space brought objects forward; however shallow we know them to be, Albright's pictures suggest a depth in which objects recede, float and turn about unhampered. The effect on the viewer can be quite unsettling. He feels tossed around in every direction and has no clue whether to visually enter the painting upward, downward, or sideways. The over-all impression is one of contrived chaos in which everything exists in a state of suspended gravity and halted animation.

The making of cloisonné enamels in China can be traced back to the Mongols of the Yuan Dynasty (1279-1367). Through the intermediary of the Near East, Turkey in particular, Byzantine enamel techniques reached China across the famed silk roads. Allowing for some minor technical innovations in the 17th and 18th centuries, the basic process of cloisonné manufacture has not changed much. It depends on the skillful manipulation of metal and glass. Glass, in the form of powdered enamel, is laid into tiny cells formed by wires affixed to a metal base and is then fired. The result is a mosaic of colors separated by gilded wires, concealing the metal beneath.

In 1982, the Phoenix Art Museum acquired as part purchase, part gift from Robert H. Clague, a collection of nearly 100 fine examples of Chinese cloisonné enamel, ranging in date from the early 16th through the late 19th century. Indicative of the vagaries of collecting, Chinese cloisonné enamels elicited widespread interest until about 1925, when museums in the West virtually abandoned the field to private collectors. Recently, however, this situation reversed itself and cloisonné has regained the legitimacy it once enjoyed.

This *Champion Vase* from the Qing Dynasty (1644-1911) combines gilt-bronze sculptural forms with cloisonné enamel surface on a heavy cast-bronze base. The shape has its origin in a double-bronze vessel probably conceived as a trophy and based on the archer's quiver. On the front, between the two vessels, a falcon with outstretched wings subdues a feline monster, visible from the rear on the other side. Above, a curled dragon with bifurcated tail serves as a handle for the double lid. On the reverse, above the tail and hindquarters of the monster, another dragon unifies the two cylinders and preserves the compact silhouette by spreading to either side.

In the Clague vase, a Ming-style color

scheme prevails, dominated by red, yellow and cobalt blue against a turquoise ground. The lotus scrolls, too, conform to the classic lotus pattern of Ming decorative arts. The splayed ring foot of each cylinder bears a pattern of lotus panels, a device common in blue-and-white porcelains of the Ming and Qing Dynasties. A comparison with works in other collections would suggest the first half of the 18th century, or the last decade of the Kangxi reign, as the proper time in which to date this vase.
(*Adapted from Claudia Brown*)

If Henri Rousseau did not already exist, a retired customs collector aspiring to paint like Ingres, Picasso and the painters of the *bateau lavoir* would have had to invent him. In a metropolis teeming with literary and pictorial talent, Rousseau was that paradox, a folk artist of genius. Poor and beset by troubles, he was commissioned, just a year before his death, to paint the portraits of the poet Guillaume Apollinaire and his mistress, the painter Marie Laurencin. *La Muse de Guillaume Apollinaire* (The Muse of Guillaume Apollinaire) in the collection of the Phoenix Art Museum is derived from two double portraits Rousseau completed in 1909, one in the Pushkin Museum in Moscow, the other in the Kunstmuseum Basel. This much smaller picture, painted in all likelihood after the first and before the second, constitutes the aging artist's tribute to his friend and promotor's 24-year old fiancee. A handsome young woman, noted for her delicate features, Laurencin could hardly be pleased (and neither, we know, was Apollinaire) with the broad impassive face, dour and unsmiling, and with the country widow dress in which Rousseau committed her to posterity.

Staid and erect between symmetrically arranged trees, Laurencin is receiving inspiration from a blond and angelic creature, identical to the figure of Liberty in Rousseau's 1906 *Liberty Inviting the Artists to the Twenty-second Exhibition of the Independents*, and reminiscent of the Angel Gabriel in traditional Annunciations. Is there, perhaps, the allusion—the celestial messenger has wings, carries flowers and makes the sign of the cross—that the poet's bride is about to conceive, in some divine way, art destined for greatness? As in those religious pictures, all of nature pays homage; at the muse's feet a row of flowers sprouts, poet's carnation or sweet william, to remind us of the unseen groom. The landscape, an essential complement to the portrait, is visionary despite the mundane touches of a black dog nearby and a gardener in the distance. Rousseau never knew more about the tropics than what he observed on visits to that Parisian institution, the Jardin Botanique. On such second hand experience he based a genre, the "portrait paysage," of haunting authenticity.

The Phoenix Art Museum has received many of its finest pictures as gifts, over the years, from winter residents Henry R. and Claire Boothe Luce. These include, beside the Henri Rousseau, paintings by Boucher, Delacroix, Diego Rivera, Reginald Marsh and Richard Diebenkorn.

131

Portland Art Museum, Oregon

141

One of the lesser known but more exquisite paintings by Camille Pissarro in America is *The Red House* of 1873, bathed in the limpid light so typical of the Ile-de-France and Pontoise where this picture was painted. The town stands on an escarpment overlooking the valley of Montmorency and the river Oise to the northwest of Paris. From 1866 on, Pissarro gathered a small band of companions to paint there—all younger men, Cézanne among them, who looked to him for guidance and advice. They set up their easels in the fields and painted "sur motif," trying to capture, under ever-changing skies, whatever fleeting impression the landscape would yield. *Impressionists* was the name they acquired when Pissarro and 30 kindred spirits exhibited in a studio vacated by Nadar in 1874.

The contemporary critic Théodore Duret credited Pissarro with an intimate and profound feeling for nature and a power of brush that lent definitiveness to his pictures. "There was in Pissarro's approach to nature a humility which the other Impressionists did not seem to possess to the same degree," wrote John Rewald in his authoritative study on the subject. The artist's placid character and undramatic life style may have hindered the growth of his Parisian reputation. He has been referred to as a "painter's painter," whose greatness in art as in life, lay in his modesty and intransigeance, his unswerving attachment to truth without ostentation (Françoise Cachin). In 1874 Pissarro began to sell his work, thanks to the efforts of Durand-Ruel and the breakthrough the exhibition at Nadar's provided. It would take more than a hundred years, though, for art history to do justice to the "father" of Impressionism with a large scale retrospective in 1980 from which *The Red House* was omitted.

Winslow B. Ayer, a founding trustee (1892-1928) of the Portland Art Association, a generous donor, in 1930, to the capital campaign for the present building and a collector in his own right, left Pissarro's *The Red House* and 28 other paintings to the Portland Art Museum in his will. In addition, he set up a purchase fund named after his wife, Helen.

In an age when donations on the grand scale are rare and no longer likely to occur, Portland merchant Evan H. Roberts enabled the Museum, at one fell swoop, to assemble a representative collection of 20th century sculpture. The selection process, begun in 1970 under Francis J. Newton, involved donor and museum staff. Andrew C. Ritchie acted as a consultant in locating and recommending works for purchase. Donald Jenkins, in 1981, saw the project through completion with the installation of an interior sculpture court.

Lipchitz's *Spanish Servant Girl*, acquired for the Roberts Sculpture Collection, formally relates to *Bather, Standing Figure* and *Detachable Figure (Dancer)*, all of 1915. Ostensibly released by the sculptor in an edition of two casts and shown for the first time at the Marlborough-Gerson Gallery in 1968, it reappeared the year of its Portland purchase, in an edition of seven, in *Jacques Lipchitz (1891-1973) Sculptures and Drawings from the Cubist Epoch* at the Marlborough Gallery. Deborah A. Scott in her 1975 dissertation, *Jacques Lipchitz and Cubism*, was as little aware of the existence of this sculpture as this writer had been in his 1960 *Museumjournaal* (Amsterdam, July 1960) article, "Lipchitz als kubist."

Judging from two sketches that have recently surfaced, *Spanish Servant Girl* materialized in 1914-1915, immediately after the artist was forced by the outbreak of hostilities to return from an inspirational visit to Mallorca and Madrid. The sculpture retains the rounded shapes reminiscent of Art Nouveau, African tribal carvings, Boccioni and Archipenko that characterized his 1913-14 production. The hinged and flattened limbs betray knowledge of Braque's and Picasso's *papiers collés*.

Despite a revelation in Mallorca that precipitated his understanding of form in terms of nature, for Lipchitz, Cubism was an acquired stylistic mode and not yet a personal accomplishment. He pays homage to synthetic Cubism in each of his 1915 sculptures and then, just a year or two later, we see him return to the analytic phase of Braque's and Picasso's Cubism for a truly sculptural interpretation of what had been essentially a painter's art.

In 1948 the Portland Art Museum acquired the Northwest Coast Indian art collected, with rare scholarship and discrimination, by Axel Rasmussen. The information that came with the objects provided a primary source of research material on tribal custom and tradition. Through judicious trading, new purchases and the acceptance of gifts, the Rasmussen Collection at the Portland Art Museum continues to grow in stature.

The carved mask of a young girl with braids, dating back to the turn of the century, but possibly older, is striking because of a naturalism that takes away from its intended ceremonial character; it could almost pass for contemporary portraiture. The Tsimshian Indians of British Columbia were particularly adept at these sensitive facial renderings full of compelling realism. The painted features are dramatically offset with human hair; the pendants depict eagles with outstretched wings; the wings are hinged and, when opened, reveal a design of wing feathers in black on white. The mask is reputedly from a settlement on the Nass River, called Niska, and the likeness is referred to as that of *Bella Coola.* A highlight of the Rasmussen Collection, this mask would be a star in any exhibition of Northwest Coast Indian art.

107

The Art Museum, Princeton University

Arion on the Dolphin in the Art Museum, Princeton University, and *Vertumnus and Pomona* in the Columbus Museum of Art, are said to have been commissioned from François Boucher by the Crown as two of a projected set of four paintings, presumably overdoors, symbolizing the Elements. Boucher never completed the series beyond *Water* (1748) and *Earth* (1749). Intended for the Château de la Muette, these pictures never hung there but were acquired by a Parisian collector of Boucher and Fragonard. Since the stories of Vertumnus and Pomona and of Arion were well known to Boucher's public, and their symbolic aptness to Earth and Water self-evident, there is no need to seek a specific source for either in classical literature. The immediate inspiration for *Vertumnus and Pomona* was, in fact, not classical but contemporary. On January 15, 1749, a ballet by that name, with sets designed by Boucher, was performed at Versailles with Madame de Pompadour cast in the title role. The legend of Arion and the Dolphin, though seldom used to symbolize Water in earlier Baroque painting, became popular in 18th century France, no doubt because the real hero of the story is not Arion but *le dauphin*, (title given to the eldest son of a king of France). The appropriateness to a royal commission of this exotic creature whose actual appearance was evidently unfamiliar to Boucher, is underlined by the fact that, in *Vertumnus and Pomona*, Earth is watered by a *dauphin* carved in stone.

Arion of Lesbos, a son of Poseidon and the Nymph Oneaea, was a master of the lyre and invented the dithyramb in Dionysus's honor. One day his patron Periander, tyrant of Corinth, reluctantly gave him permission to visit Taenarus in Sicily, where he had been invited to compete in a music festival. Arion won the prize and his admirers showered him with so many gifts that these excited the greed of the sailors engaged to bring him back to Corinth. The captain threatened to kill his rich shipmate and Arion begged that he be permitted to sing a last song. Dressed in his finest robe, Arion mounted the prow where he invoked the gods with impassioned strains, and then leaped overboard. His song had attracted a school of music-loving dolphins, one of which took Arion on his back and carried him safely back to Corinth. Apollo later set the images of Arion and his lyre among the stars.

In Boucher's version of the seventh century B.C. Greek myth, Arion is surrounded by a panoply of saviors other than the dolphin carrying him—three tritons, three nereids and at least one more dolphin swimming along. The drama is gratuitously heightened by the stormy sky and sea and by the foundering galleon on fire in the background. The story does not mention an outbreak of Zeus's anger but relates that the captain and crew made it back to Corinth where they were confronted with their misdeed and executed on the spot. Boucher's *Arion on the Dolphin* is a fine example of the "King's Painter's" rococo style and treatment of a playful subject meant to please the aristocratic taste of the Versailles court.

The Olmec lived, from pre-Classic times onward, in the deltas of the rivers of southern Veracruz and Tabasco, on the Gulf side of the Isthmus of Tehuantepec. The term signifies the rubber-people, the dwellers in Olman. Archaeological knowledge of Olmec culture is restricted to the formative period (Olmec I, 1300-700 B.C.) and has been imparted through excavations at Tres Zapotes, northwest of Potrero, San Lorenzo in Veracruz and the island of La Venta in the Tonalá River on the boundary between Veracruz and Tabasco. Primarily a sculptural style, Olmec is best known for its majestic heads of a distinct ethnic type—pear-shaped, with thick everted lips, broad noses and elliptical eyes. But, it has also produced, on a much smaller scale, veristic sculpture with faithfully transposed appearances and often incised with glyph-like notations representing body designs. Olmec culture on the Gulf coast is marked by a preference for durable materials such as jade and basalt, permitting the sculptor to investigate kinds of form that are not easily available to the potter. It not only furthered a realistic technique but it permitted experimentation with the visual effects of skin texture and surface engraving. A common form is that of the figurine with legs folded, upper torso leaning forward and hands grasping the knees.

The Princeton stone figure of a *Shaman in Transformation Pose*, while obviously of superior quality, is unrecorded in the literature. Dated 800 B.C., it mostly resembles the style of La Venta. The figure has been rubbed with cinnabar except for an area which would indicate the presence at one time of clothing resembling shorts in perishable materials. A chin beard, probably cermonial, has been broken off and the eye sockets may have once contained precious inlays. Most revealing is the outline of a frog incised on the figure's shaved pate. The interpretation has been put forward that the priest-like figure has taken a hallucinogen derived from the frog which has put him in a position of readiness for transformation induced by the drug. Hence, the title *Shaman in Transformation Pose.*

The Italian drawings section in the graphic collection at Princeton is outstanding in number, variety and quality and, with close to 1,000 sheets, constitutes almost a quarter of its entire holdings. Such splendors are owed in huge proportion to two pioneer collectors, Dan Fellows Platt, a lawyer and connoisseur, and Frank Jewett Mather, Jr., an art historian and director of the Art Museum. Platt graduated from Princeton in the class of 1895, studied art at the American School of Classical Studies in Rome, took up law but practiced little of it, helped elect Woodrow Wilson, felt guided by Bernard Berenson in his preference for Italian art before Raphael, and wrote a book on his travels through Italy with car and camera. His collection of drawings did not begin until several years after World War I, extending through a period approximately from 1920-37.

The *Caricature of a Boy Wearing a Broad-Brimmed Hat* by Giovanni Francesco Barbieri, named Il Guercino, came from an album of caricatures which Dan Fellows Platt acquired, in 1928, from the London Dealer P.W. Holoway. At that time, nine leaves had already been removed by a previous dealer but Platt was able to hunt them down and restore them to the original series. In past exhibitions, the album has been shown opened on the brown ink and wash drawing of the insolently posed, big-mouthed and plump-nosed urchin. A hand-lettered preface to the album, presumably of the 18th century, heaps praise on Guercino: "One of his particular gifts was making certain portraits that our painters call caricatures, a kind of thing in which he was one of those few gifted with the vivacity and intelligence that this sort of thing requires..." Its once having belonged to Sir Joshua Reynolds lends additional interest to this spirited record.

44

16

86

This gentle, luminescent portrait of a peasant girl from the Savoy was painted in 1873. Its circumstances and the identity of the sitter are unknown although a good deal about the painter's life and activities of that year has been recorded. In the fall of 1872, Degas accompanied his brother René to New Orleans where their mother had been born and where his two brothers had established themselves as cotton merchants. In the bayou city he painted the famous interior of a cotton dealer's office (that of his uncle Michel Musson), and obliged his hosts by painting their portraits. Particularly moving is the one of Mme René De Gas, née Estelle Musson, his blind sister-in-law, in the Chester Dale Collection, bearing a clear and direct relationship to *La Savoisienne*.

Having returned to Paris, Degas, through his dealer Durand-Ruel, sold his first work, a pastel, to Louisine Waldron Elder, the future Mrs. H.O. Havemeyer. Her attention had been drawn to this artist by her friend Mary Cassatt, a young painter from Pittsburgh. "The first sight of Degas' pictures," Cassatt would later write, "was the turning point in my artistic life." That autumn, Degas was deeply affected by the burning of the Paris opera, which for some time deprived him of his favorite haunt. Then, on December 27, the artist signed the charter document of an anonymous society of artists committed to exhibit their work in April of the following year. To that exhibition, Degas contributed ten paintings, drawings and pastels of racers, dancers and laundresses, but repeatedly cautioned his friends not to exclude painters of a more academic persuasion; he tried unsuccessfully to rally Manet to their cause. When this exhibition, in the just-vacated studios of Nadar on the Boulevard des Capucines, drew ridicule from the critics and was derisively referred to as "Exposition des Impressionistes," Degas, compromised by association, was branded a traitor to tradition. Degas' later reluctance to join the Impressionists and the anger it provoked among his conservative friends is a measure of the painter's ambiguous allegiance to the conflicting aesthetics of his time.

As *La Savoisienne* demonstrates, Ingres and not Delacroix or Courbet, was his inspiration. "Draw lines, young man, many lines; from memory or from nature, it is in this way that you will become a good artist," Degas remembered Ingres admonishing him. That lesson was never forgotten and never renounced. Such discipline agreed with Degas' character and natural inclinations. Contemporaries described him as cold, caustic, reticent, disdainful and obstinate. Born into a wealthy family whose aristocratic name he spurned, the painter of young women of the working classes is generally described as a misogynist. Considering this drawback, Degas admirably acquitted himself in the Savoy peasant girl's portrayal. The lassitude in the budding woman's face is touched upon with tenderness, her skin has the dewy, unaided complexion that comes with life in the country, and her costume offers the painter that same pleasure in flimsy white fabrics he indulged in his treatment of ballet dancers' tights and tutus. The cool light suffusing this smoothly painted portrait—one Ingres might have approved —recalls the clarity of Degas' Louisiana pictures, and suggests that the experience of the Gulf Coast's luminosity temporarily affected his work.

The Princess and her Attendant, one of several similar paintings in the collection of the Rhode Island School of Design, is a very good example of how the themes and techniques of Mughal painting spread throughout the provinces of India. It was painted after the Empire itself had declined, and its court-supported art studios were no longer in existence. Artists at this time worked on a freelance basis for lesser nobles, plying their trade wherever they could find interest. This painting was intended to be included in an album, which probably indicates that it was done for a provincial nobleman rather than as a traveler's souvenir.

Carefully done in naturalistic, muted palette, replete with gold accents and heavy shadings, it retains to some extent the Persian influences which dominated illuminations at the beginning of the 200-year span of Mughal court art. There is an attention to detail in the decorative patterns of fabrics, jewelry and architectural elements. However, these are less ornate than they would have been at the height of the style and show the Indian propensity for larger masses and simplified forms. There is no inclusion here of the flora and fauna which were an integral part of most earlier works. Even in chamber scenes such as this, an open door usually permitted a view of the outside. Here we see only access to another chamber on the right, and on the left, a stairway rendered in primitive perspective.

The Princess (or Nayaka lady, as she is also known) kneels on a low couch while she selects jewelry to adorn herself—hinting at an imminent meeting with her lover. Her attendant holds a mirror, thus giving the artist a means of presenting his sitter in both profile and three-quarter views. Her light skin and transparent garments define her social status. With this choice of subject matter, the artist (or artists, since more than one often worked on a painting) has combined two of the three important subjects of Mughal painting: portraiture, subtle erotica and historic battles. Mughal art concerned itself not at all with religious symbolisms; therefore, we can read no more into this painting than that it is a popular excerpt from daily life, painted to please some wealthy noble—perhaps the lady's husband.

(Ann W. Heymann)

The most important German bronze factory at the time of the Northern Renaissance was that of the Vischer family, active in Nuremberg between 1453 and 1554. The identity of the workshop as a whole is more clearly defined than that of the work of individual family members. Their activity ranged from church monuments to inkwells, plaques and medals. When *Fertility*, presumed to have been made by Georg Vischer, was acquired in 1920, it was referred to as *Eve* by Peter Vischer the Younger and it was dated between 1508-28. E. F. Bange, in his 1949 study devoted to 16th century German bronze statuettes, proposed Georg, Hans Vischer's oldest son, as the likely maker, dating it proportionately later and suggesting the more probable pagan theme.

The Rhode Island bronze ranks as one of the most Italianate figures produced by the Vischer workshop. The slender and elongated form, the flexed knee accentuating the roundness of the opposite hip, the long and delicate fingers encircling the left breast, offer a sharp contrast to the squat and angular poses and that mixture of late Gothic sensibility and Flemish realism that seemed to characterize most of the Vischer workshop's production. The difference had come with the spread of Italian Renaissance ideas and travel by members of the family (Peter journeyed to Northern Italy as early as 1507) from their advantageously located city. Yet, for a modern observer, this healthy young maiden could not possibly have hailed from Florence or the Romagna. Her bone structure, high forehead and slightly inelegant stance reveal her Germanic origin and relate her to a sorority that includes Cranach's Graces no less than those melancholy nudes by Lehmbruck, Kolbe and Marcks.

L. Earle Rowe came to the Rhode Island School of Design as President in 1912 and, by 1917, took on the additional responsibility of directing the Museum. During his tenure, the Museum expanded into the current building and greatly increased its collections both through purchase and donations. From money bequeathed to the Museum by Miss Lyra Brown Nickerson, an Appropriation Fund was established for the purchase of important works of art. All three loans from the Rhode Island School of Design were acquired, between 1917 and 1923, with the aid of that fund. Dr. Rowe summarized the collecting goals of the Museum of Art: "The function of the modern art museum is that of inspiration to artist and public...fortunate indeed is that institution which has buying committees or private benefactors who, like Napoleon, demand the best."

(Bulletin of the Rhode Island School of Design, Vol. 8, no. 4, October 1920)

38

189

Memorial Art Gallery of the University of Rochester

David Teniers, referred to as The Younger, was born to a family of artists that had come to prominence in the early 17th century in the city made famous by Rubens. When he married a daughter of the genre painter Jan Bruegel, nicknamed The Velvet, Peter Paul Rubens was his witness. Again, it was the illustrious Antwerp painter's intercedence that landed Teniers the deanship of the Guild of St. Luke and brought him to the attention of Archduke Leopold William, Governor of the Spanish Netherlands, who made him Groom of the Chambers, court painter and director of the picture gallery installed in the Palace at Brussels. Our painter bought one of Rubens' former residences but a further ambition to be elevated into his country's aristocracy met with a condition too untenable for the vainglorious burgher—that he stop accepting payment for his pictorial services. In great public demand for his Flemish kermesses, allegories and tavern interiors, Teniers lived a long life and his work continued to be so popular that it commanded higher prices than Rembrandt's at auctions throughout the 18th century.

There may be some irony in the aspiring nobleman's embrace of low life subject matter but the genre held enormous appeal ever since Adriaen Brouwer had moved from Haarlem to Antwerp in 1631. A much praised figure of a smoker in a tavern, now at the Louvre, gained Teniers entrance to the painter's guild. The Rochester *Tavern Scene* includes elements of the Louvre Smoker but relates in greater detail to a tavern interior at the Alte Pinacothek in Munich. Most remarkable in these pictures is the silvery brown light that filters into the cavernous space and the adroit rendering of human detail. Clay pipe smoking seemed as passionate a form of recreation in Flemish taverns as drinking ale and making light of it in a dark corner. While stray animals and heads popping in through shuttered windows are part of Teniers' standard repertoire, the most intriguing telltale is the drawing pinned against the wall in each of the artist's taverns. Instead of the human head that usually appears in these drawings, this one

shows an owl (symbol of wisdom) and a candle (instrument of illumination), which may allude to the Dutch proverb: "when drink enters man his wisdom dims like the flame of a candle." The date, 1680, on the drawing marked the artist's 70th year, in which he chose to repeat a favored theme associated more readily with his earlier career.

Tavern Scene entered the Memorial Art Gallery collection as part of the 1955 Buswell-Hochstetter bequest including items given by Bertha Hochstetter Buswell and her brother Ralph Hochstetter, both of Buffalo, New York. The bequest consisted largely of European sculptures and decorative objects but also included Dutch and Flemish 17th century paintings. Of the latter category, Teniers' *Tavern Scene* is a shining example.

Beginning in 1912, the work of Picasso and Braque is based on the radically new principle that the pictorial illusion of reality, as in *Nature morte à la pipe*, takes place upon the physical reality of an opaque surface rather than in a fictional space behind a transparent plane. As of the same date, Analytic Cubism with its dissection of light, line and plane, gives way to Synthetic Cubism, which no longer explores the anatomy of nature but creates a new anatomy less dependent upon the data of perception. Whereas there is an about-face in the Cubists' relation to nature, their independence of nature is more often of degree than of kind. Illusionistic depth has been further obliterated and the artist's pictorial re-creation, through line, plane, color and texture, of the subject before him, results in its becoming more of an object. Braque favored the oval format as it mocked directional imperatives, eliminated the last vestiges of a horizon and dealt with compositional weight and balance in a centrifugal way. He used lettering because it belonged to his still life ingredients, because it appealed to him for its modernity and because it contained equivalences, like echoes or rhymes, of his geometrized subject matter.

The compositional structure of *Nature morte à la pipe* leaves no doubt that the artist thought in terms of overlapping planes and the layered effect of the pasted papers he used, intermittently, from September 1912 on. The angular, cut-up forms and the shifts in surface textures reinforce that impression. There are no ovals, in Braque's oeuvre of those years, of corresponding dimension nor are there subjects of more than passing similarity. With its pipe, goblet, ace of spades playing card and fragment of the newspaper *L'Echo de Paris*, this almost monochromatic picture shows the coloristic restraint of an earlier period, yet may, on stylistic grounds, have to be dated 1913-14 instead of 1913 according to Nicole Worms de Romilly in her 1982 oeuvre catalogue of the artist.

Nature morte à la pipe was acquired in 1954 through the Marion Stratton Gould Fund, a memorial bequest of the late 1930s for the purchase of paintings.

The small rectangular châsse or reliquary box with hinged gabled cover and cusped bail handle in the Memorial Art Gallery collection is a typical product of the Limoges enamel workshops and can be dated, with some certainty, between 1220 and 1230. Stylistically, it is similar to and can be compared with the slightly larger châsses portraying the *Martyrdom of St. Thomas à Becket*, in the Schütgen Museum, Cologne, and the *Adoration of the Magi*, in the Royal Ontario Museum, Toronto. The Rochester châsse represents the stoning and reception in heaven of St. Stephen, Christendom's first martyr and the patron saint of Limoges cathedral. Its manufacture is relatively primitive; the bodies are reserved in the metal, with drapery folds and features realized by incising; the background and decorative elements are fashioned in enamel; only the heads on side and roof panel are wrought in relief. The two end panels are engraved with medallions of angels and the back part is enameled with rosettes of two alternating types set within a trellis framework. The colors range from lapis blue, light blue, turquoise and green to red, white and yellow.

On the lower front panel St. Stephen is seen kneeling and facing his executioners who approach him with stones in hand. Typical of the medieval craftsman's *horror vacui*, the scene's background is filled with colored rosettes and small almond-shaped stones that fall around the supplicant saint. On the roof panel of the châsse, we see the nude, half-length figure of St. Stephen rising from clouds, raising his arms in an orans gesture and framed in a nimbus carried by angels. The drama of the stoning, following the narrative in the Acts of the Apostles (7:54-60), held a special appeal for Christians of the year 1200 and many churches all over Europe, dedicated to the saint, treasured the obligatory token of his mortal remains. The iconographical arrangement of this reliquary box represents a hierarchy of scenes that suggests ascending realms of existence. The châsse not only displays an identifying narrative of the saint whose relics are preserved within, but is itself a kind of cosmic edifice, possessing an ordered structure of decoration with distinct terrestrial and celestial zones.

This champlevé enamel on gilded copper châsse was acquired for the Memorial Art Gallery by Director Gertrude Herdle Moore and Curator Isabel Herdle (daughters of founding director George Herdle) at the famous Joseph Brummer Collection Sale in New York in 1949, with the aid of the R. T. Miller Fund. The Herdle sisters' expertise being in medieval art, many fine sculptures and decorative objects entered the Gallery's collection during their tenure.

137

22

191

Washington University Gallery of Art

98

During the period 1900-13, nearly every significant modern American artist traveled to Europe. There they felt at first hand the impact of abstract art and the lure of such new movements as Fauvism, Cubism, and the Blue Rider. America had not yet firmly established its visual traditions and was not ready to launch and sustain new movements or innovative concepts. The achievement of early American modernists was in individual expression rather than in forming schools. Although Marsden Hartley started out conservatively, after his first one-man show at "291" in 1909, his early supporter Alfred Stieglitz commented that the painter's interpretation of nature strove for a decorative rather than a realistic effect. With Stieglitz's encouragement and support, Hartley went abroad in 1912, and instead of settling down in Paris, he chose Berlin because he felt attracted to the high-keyed colors and the inspirational abstractions of the Blue Rider group. By 1914, Hartley had developed a personal style of decorative Cubism, expressing emblems in a fluid, intense spectrum akin to Kandinsky's first abstract manner. His Berlin pictures coloristically and iconographically prefigured Pop painting of the 1960s.

In her 1980 book on the artist, Barbara Haskell has given us a detailed account of Hartley's second Berlin period, from March 1914 until December 1915. On his trip over he stopped off in Paris where Robert Delaunay's Orphist abstraction, *Homage to Blériot*, at the Salon des Indépendants notably impressed him. He began to work in bright colors, laid down flat within discrete boundaries in contrasting tonal fields. Elements in these paintings were derived from American Indian culture to which he felt nostalgically attracted and which, in turn, was hugely popular in Germany.

The onset of war was accompanied by personal tragedy for Hartley. Within a few months time, he lost his father as well as his cherished friend von Freyburg, a young officer in the Royal Guards. Obsessed by masculine beauty throughout his life, Hartley looked on the dashing von Freyburg as a classical embodiment of handsome youth. When the boy was killed in action, his image became an icon for Hartley. He turned to work and created a series of powerful canvases equal to any produced by key artists in the European avant garde. Recognizable for their war motifs, these canvases reflect his simultaneous repulsion and fascination with war. Haunted by the tragedy of his friend's death, he was magnetized, nonetheless, by war's pageantry and reckless energy. Despite their expressive breakthrough, the style of these War Motif paintings owed a great deal to American Indian imagery, the intentional primitivism of the Blue Rider painters, the vocabulary of Synthetic Cubism and the symbolic use of numbers and letters then in vogue with poets and writers.

The Iron Cross in the Washington University collection, devoted to von Freyburg who had served in the 4th Cavalry Regiment and was posthumously awarded the imperial soldier's badge of valor, is one of the two or three prime examples of Hartley's War Motif series. The heraldic colors of the Hohenzollerns, red, yellow and black, can be conveniently assigned those other meanings of spilt blood, fiery grenades in lethal trajectories and the dark night of death and mourning. Checkers, lozenges and wavy lines derive from the Indian weaver's vocabulary and the whole composition with its stitch-like brush strokes and opaque pigments leaves a patterned, almost quilted impression. Juxtaposed or overlapping in the manner of a Cubist collage, *The Iron Cross* treats us to snippets and fragments of Prussian military heraldry—insignia, badges and a cockade, pressed into a tightly knit, emblematic format.

Hartley's *The Iron Cross* was a 1952 University purchase from the Bixby Fund. William Bixby established a fund for the purchase of American paintings which he envisaged to be American Impressionists. After World War II a fresh interpretation was given to Mr. Bixby's original intentions to allow the acquisition of paintings in the American modernist tradition.

Gustave Moreau has a strong claim to
being the greatest of French Symbolist
painters. He forms a direct link between
Delacroix, whose pupil he may have been,
and Matisse who was his student. Admired
by Oscar Wilde and Proust's painter Elstir in
Remembrance of Things Past, Moreau felt
little sympathy for the "decadent" literary
movement which considered him its doyen.
He aspired to the honors customarily
bestowed upon an Establishment painter.
Yet it is the personalized eclecticism of his
fluid Romantic style, his obsession with the
conflict between moral idealism and sensual
passion, the transcendent poetry of his
mysteriously embroidered themes, not his
allegiance to any one school or aesthetic
that have guaranteed him an enduring
niche in the pantheon of 19th century
French art. Responsive to the psychological
truths of classical mythology and the
architectonic harmonies of Christian
iconography in equal measure, this shy and
solitary artist did not commit himself to the
world of his contemporaries and remained
essentially a prisoner of his own feelings.

Orpheus in the Washington University
collection is a version of the larger work
which Moreau exhibited at the Paris Salon
of 1866 under its long title *Orpheus—a girl
reverently gathers up the head of Orpheus and
his lyre borne on the waters of the Hebros to the
shores of Thrace.* The story of Orpheus was a
popular one at the time, partly due to the
1858 revival of Gluck's *Orpheus and
Eurydice* at the Paris Opera. According to
Greek myth, Orpheus, a Thracian, was
dismembered by Maenads who mocked his
single-minded obsession with Eurydice.
Incensed, they flung his head and lyre into
the River Hebros whence they floated down
to Lesbos. Caught in a fissure of rock, the
divine singer's head delivered oracles for
many years. The scene portrayed in
Moreau's *Orpheus* suggests a Maenad's
momentary remorse before setting head and
lyre afloat. Her bloody deed accomplished,
she mournfully gazes at the immobile,
serenely reposing head. Typical of the
Symbolist Movement's syncretic
imagination, Moreau must have chosen this
psychologically arresting but invented
episode in the Orphic myth because,
cradled by the arms of a beautiful woman,

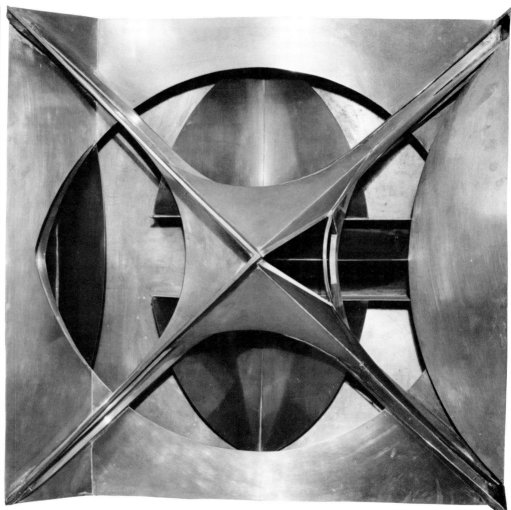

165

193

the waterborne head of Orpheus on a lyre dramatically resembled St. John the Baptist's on a platter. The seductively striding Salome, carrying the severed head of the desert preacher who scorned her, was Moreau's favorite subject and the archetype, we assume, for the Thracian maiden's contemplative pose.

Moreau's *Orpheus* has a meaning that transcends the episode portrayed. The great musician of Greek legend symbolizes creation through divine inspiration. While the turtles in the lower right-hand corner refer to the mythical origins of the lyre which Hermes fashioned from that animal's shell, and while a shepherd perched high on a promontory entertains his companion with music from a pipe, the center stage is held by a woman who has cruelly, if regretfully, decided on the musician's fate. The Thracian's ambiguous attitude reflects that era's ambivalent notion of woman who, on the one hand, is a spiritual guide and life's companion fostering creativity, and, on the other, the temptress who through her sexuality condemns her consort to creative annihilation. There may even be a biographic twist to Moreau's painting. Several authors have remarked that the Thracian maiden resembles portraits of the artist's mother found in his studio-turned-shrine on the Rue de la Rochefoucauld. Was it a tribute, or an accusation in disguise, by the late-blossoming artist to the mother who reigned supreme in his affections and who, reputedly, was the sole inspiration of his life and art?

Acquired as a University purchase through the Parsons Fund in 1965, Moreau's *Orpheus* complements the Gallery's collection of 19th century European and American painting. In large part, the formation of that collection and its bequest to Washington University were owed to Charles Parsons, a bellwether among tastemakers in late 19th century St. Louis and the Gallery's first major patron.

Two decades before western art historians began putting skin and flesh on the skeletal reputation to which Russia had confined Constructivist sculptors Tatlin and Rodchenko—one decade before Picasso, at age 85, stood revealed as having been this century's greatest inventor of sculpture, and Marcel Duchamp, at age 77, its greatest challenger—the Pevsner brothers, Antoine and Naum Gabo, were the scions of vanguard experimentation in sculpture and the staple of books on the subject. New discoveries, shifting scholarly interests, and the artist's decision to leave the bulk of his work to France's National Museum of Modern Art when, unfortunately, that institution was ill prepared to do it justice, all conspired to dull the once shining reputation of the Russian-born, Paris-based Antoine Pevsner. There is some comfort in the cyclical progress of history and one day Pevsner may again attract the critical acclaim accorded him in the late 1950s.

Pevsner's finest hour arrived when, with his younger brother Gabo, he exhibited his work in an orchestra shell on Moscow's Boulevard Tversky in August 1920, and when together they launched the famous *Realist Manifesto*: "The realization of our perceptions of the world in forms of space and time is the only aim of our pictorial and plastic art...we shape our work as the world its creation, the engineer his bridge, the mathematician his formulas of a planetary orbit." In 1921, Pevsner found his studio suddenly closed without explanation. Before long, he followed his brother Naum Gabo to Berlin where his paintings had already been seen in the *Erste Russische Kunstausstellung* at the van Diemen Gallery. In October 1923, Pevsner moved on to Paris, gave up painting and launched himself on a sculptural career by copying Gabo's constructions as an exercise. Free-standing and relief constructions with multi-faceted and transparent planes in twisted configurations constituted Pevsner's belated contribution to Constructivist sculpture and established his fame in the French capital.

During the 1920s, Paris was a center of interest in machinery, which prompted the art world to adopt its *Style Mécanique*. In the 1925 *International Exhibition of Modern Decorative and Industrial Arts*, mechanical inventions shared the spotlight with works of fine art. About that time, Pevsner created a series of constuctions in which brass and bronze are cut and joined in flat sections, welded or held together by screws. Washington University's *Sunken Bas Relief* is exemplary of a serious sculptural concern at the core of the Art Deco style. Works of this type attracted the attention of the Société Anonyme's Katherine Dreier and Marcel Duchamp, and in 1942, Peggy Guggenheim exhibited *Sunken Bas Relief* at her Art of This Century Gallery. H. W. Janson, then chairman of the Washington University Art Department, acquired this sculpture for the Gallery's collection from Peggy Guggenheim, in 1946, through the W. N. MacMillan Fund. That distinguished scholar's eye for modern and contemporary art, his control of the Gallery's acquisition purse strings and his ability to persuade the University administration to allow the deaccessioning of paintings that were never on view resulted in the institution's enrichment with works by Braque, Gris, Miró, Klee, Ernst, Beckmann and Tamayo.

57 *Peter Paul Rubens*, Portrait of the Archduke
Ferdinand, *1635*
The John and Mable Ringling Museum of Art,
Sarasota, Florida

197

San Francisco Museum of Modern Art

Most of Matisse's portraits in the wake of his Fauve period are scarcely portraits by strict definition. Like Cézanne, Matisse was more interested in formal and coloristic accomplishment than in psychological characterization. One cannot even assume that the physiognomy of the model who sat for *La Fille aux Yeux Verts* has been accurately recorded. "Exactitude is not truth," the artist was fond of saying. The ten or so images of women Matisse painted between 1908-10 form a consistent series in which the composition of the figure in relation to the background and to the rectangle of the picture, as Alfred H. Barr, Jr. has pointed out, is carefully studied and brilliantly solved. The sequence moves from compositions in which a figure is elaborated against a plain background, through paintings in which the sitter competes with the background, back to portraits in which the figure completely dominates the canvas. Clearly, the San Francisco painting belongs in the middle category.

One of Matisse's subjects has described how long it took the master—ten sessions of three hours each—to paint her 1908-09 portrait. Whenever he altered a color he felt forced to change the whole color scheme. Yet, despite the many changes, the result appeared freshly and fluently painted. Between sessions Matisse would go off to the Louvre for consolation and new inspiration. While it may not show, similar attention must have been bestowed upon *La Fille aux Yeux Verts*. She is demurely posed, slightly off center, in a bright orange embroidered Chinese robe against a red and green background. On an elongated neck, a pale oval-shaped face is crowned by auburn hair and a fashionable hat. Albert Elsen has identified the sculpture standing next to the ornamented vases as the fragmented Parthenon pedimental figure known as the Ilissus. It reappears as the central motif in Matisse's 1908 *Still Life with a Greek Torso* and is indicative of the artist's lifelong interest in sculpture.

The 1963 discovery of a Bernheim-Jeune bill of sale dated November 23, 1908, established that year as the execution date of *La Fille aux Yeux Verts*. It appears that Harriet Lane Levy, a well traveled and cultured young San Francisco woman who had been responsible for introducing her friend Alice B. Toklas to Gertrude Stein, acquired the picture through Gertrude's brother, Michael. The purchase was an act of courage, for two years later the "green-eyed girl" caused such a furor in London that critics equated her with "an intentionally outrageous daub." Michael and his wife Sally Stein had been the first to transport Matisse's work westward when, for the benefit of their San Francisco friends, they carried three of his canvases in their luggage on a visit to inspect damage to their property following the 1906 earthquake.

After having been placed on loan there for many years, *La Fille aux Yeux Verts* was bequeathed to the San Francisco Museum of Modern Art in 1950. The terms of her bequest, including works by artists she knew through the Steins in Paris, specify Miss Levy's intentions: "While I place no legal or equitable restriction of any kind or nature upon said gift, the same being intended to be outright, it is my hope that they may either serve as a nucleus for or as an addition to the collection of modern French art, and that they will be kept together as a unit as a memorial to and under the name of Harriet Lane Levy with the privilege of, from time to time, using said paintings, sculpture, lithographs and engravings, singly or in groups, for exhibition purposes, provided that the major portion of such collection shall be exhibited free to the public of San Francisco for a period of at least fifteen (15) days once in each calendar year."

Clyfford Still's association with the San Francisco Museum of Modern Art began when that institution offered the then 39-year-old painter his first retrospective exhibition in 1943. Three years later, Douglas MacAgy invited Still to teach at the San Francisco Art Institute, an association that lasted until 1950. A student of those days described his response to "these potent, utterly original oils" as one of "disbelief, then shock, then admiration...Most of us, veterans of the Second World War, had stern convictions as to the nature of modern painting; it must be Mondrian, Miró or Picasso...Still's images were organic, his colors and surfaces had nothing in common with what we had learned to regard as 'good' modern painting...His works were marked by a violence, a rawness, which few of us were prepared to recognize as art. Here was painting that instructed even as it destroyed: the School of Paris had died quite suddenly for us..."

Untitled 1960 was shown privately in the artist's studio at 128 West 23rd Street in New York, the year of its completion. On his 55th birthday, just months before, Gordon Smith had given Still a retrospective of 72 of his paintings at the Albright Art Gallery in Buffalo. In a letter to Smith, published in the exhibition's catalogue, Still wrote: "It was never a problem of aesthetics, or public or private acceptance, that determined my responsibility to the completed work. Rather, it was the hope to make clear its conceptual germination of idea and vision, without which all art becomes but an exercise in conformity with shifting fashions or tribal ethics...I held it imperative to evolve an instrument of thought which would aid in cutting through all cultural opiates, past and present, so that a direct, immediate, and truly free vision could be achieved, and an idea be revealed with clarity." Such high moral standards were reiterated, again and again, by an artist whose writings are marred by colossal arrogance, petty sorties, cruel invectives and misplaced comparisons. Yet, the work has a majesty that bespeaks sheer pictorial aspiration on a larger than human scale, sprung free even from the mind that conceived it.

In May, 1975, Clyfford Still presented to the San Francisco Museum of Modern Art, a gift of 28 paintings dating from 1934 to 1974, contingent upon their permanent installation in an exclusive gallery. *Untitled 1960*, then on loan to the museum from Mr. and Mrs. Harry W. Anderson, was the trigger. The artist came to revisit this splendid canvas with its cascading brown, red, blue and yellow, and requested to see

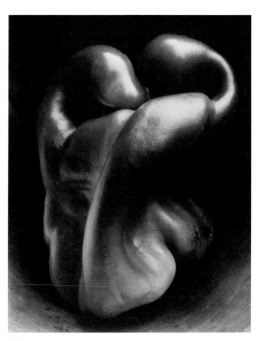

167

the director. The ensuing visits, back and forth, led to the artist's decision to make San Francisco, as once he had Buffalo, a shrine for a carefully selected number of paintings to be shown on his terms. Until his death in 1980, Clyfford Still refused to have his pictures entered into group exhibitions, and he routinely rejected one-man exhibitions. Thus, the Still room at the San Francisco Museum of Modern Art, takes on an important informational dimension. Just prior to the Still gift becoming effective, the Andersons graciously added *Untitled 1960* to the museum's unique representation of the work of this solitary genius of Abstract Expressionism.

Pepper #30 is one of a series of images Edward Weston created in 1929-30. The photographer was a vegetarian whose eye, sensitized to formal equivalences, delighted in the swelling volumes and organic shapes of these gleaming peppers. Despite the magic he achieved, Weston's working methods were straightforward. Using a classic 8 x 10 view camera and previsualizing the outcome because he eschewed cropping or trimming, Weston paid particular attention to light-fall and enhanced its effect on his subjects. His concern with the quality of light was fanatical. In his Carmel studio he utilized the cross light from a set of French windows and experimented with home-made reflective devices. Apparently, one of Weston's most successful methods was to put the pepper in a large tin funnel which would diffuse light around and behind it. Everything in this image is sharp and precise. Weston feared loosing that quality in his work to the extent that he rejected enlarging his negatives and stuck to the aperture that inspired his West Coast followers to name their 1932 photographic society "Group f.64."

In her 1975 review of the Edward Weston retrospective at The Museum of Modern Art, Janet Malcolm commented on the metamorphic character of "peppers like clenched fists, thighs like shells, shells like vulvas"—forms that Weston saw

because he had seen modern art. Malcolm believes Weston's work presents one of the strongest cases there is for viewing photography not as a primary but as an ancillary art form tied to painting and sculpture but always a few steps behind them. This argument deserves credence since Weston, when he expressed himself on his aims as a photographer, reverted to the language of the painter. He told his colleague Minor White, that neither the nudes nor his monumental series of shells, squash and peppers, had any but the purest abstract intent.

Mexico's contribution to art in the 20th century was the populist monumental style of its three muralists, Diego Rivera, Jose Orozco and David Siqueiros. Their activity in the United States during a period of economic hopelessness and government concern for the arts, did not fail to affect our painters, in particular those committed to a realist point of view and a Marxist notion of progress. Rivera, a Mexican Picasso, had earned his battle scars in the Cubist theater and rose to fame with a style related to his Spanish hero's pictorial gigantism. The Fords and the Rockefellers invited him to Detroit and New York where he painted murals that preached the ideals of social revolution and the evils of capitalism. Such masochism on the part of our captains of industry can be explained only by surmising their guilty consciences at the depth of a worldwide depression. Rivera became a public presence in San Francisco through the mural he painted for the local Stock Exchange.

In 1935, Albert M. Bender commissioned Rivera to paint a picture that would serve as a memorial to his close friend and fellow art patron, Caroline Walter. Bender wrote to Rivera on March 29 of that year, "I am exceedingly anxious that the tribute to Mrs. Walter be the work of a man of genius, and equally anxious that it be a representation of your work at its finest and best." The Mexican obliged his American patron with a textbook example, painted in the burnished tones and earthen pigments of his native land, of an Indian brought down on all fours by the burden of free enterprise and suffering an additional blow to the male ego as charity attempts to shift his burden. The message must have been lost on its recipient for there is no other record than that of high praise for Rivera's monumental simplicity, hieratic composition reminiscent of Giotto, and pleasant reiteration of the decorative scheme made popular by his frescoes. *The Flower Carrier* was one of the first gifts the San Francisco Museum of Modern Art received when it opened in 1935.

179

The Fine Arts Museums of San Francisco

With the war ended and the Dutch having wrested their water-logged country from Spain, sentiment and pride poured forth to stimulate a new contemplation of the landscape. In Haarlem, a city between Amsterdam and the North Sea dunes, this pride originated the Dutch landscape painting tradition. Busy waterways bound by horizons dotted with windmills and Reformed Church towers reflected the Republic's pride in its newly secured future. Never before in the history of Western civilization was landscape given such prominence as a painterly subject. Topography was not the issue in these pictures, and painterly demands took over from whatever faithfulness to locale was required.

With Jacob van Ruisdaël and Meindert Hobbema, Jan van Goyen represents Dutch landscape painting at its finest. Only Rembrandt, in his infrequent forays into this genre, achieved greater transcendence of the subject's generally humble ingredients. In his almost monochromatic greyish-brown riverscapes, van Goyen carried the prototypically Dutch genre beyond what Jan Porcellis, Esaias van de Velde and Simon de Vliegher had accomplished in their marine views. He excelled in the rendition of atmospheric light and in doing so proves what Constable would say a century and a half later: "The sky is the chief organ of the sentiment in a painting."

For van Goyen, who was capable of confining his sweeping views and arching skies to the deceptive format of a cabinet picture, *The Thunderstorm*, painted at the height of his career, is extraordinarily large and commanding. The artist took obvious delight in pitching a cloud-laden sky against windswept water in this view of an inland waterway. As sunlight struggles free from its cover, wavelets, ship sails and seagulls bathe in an eery silver hue. The threat of bad weather bursting forth is more imagined than real as the waters are shallow and the shore is within reach. The farm houses, village church and distant windmill do not offer clues to their precise locale but we may assume it to be near the mouth of the Rhine River.

A rare example of public funds being applied to the purchase of art, this painting was acquired by the City and County of San Francisco in 1948 for the M. H. de Young Memorial Museum.

The Maori of New Zealand were among the most prolific artists in Polynesia. Their style was characterized by elaborate curvilinear surface ornamentation which, in that culture's ancestral and mythical carvings, expressed itself in ornate patterns of facial and body tattooing. As much of Maori art was devoted to architectural decoration, a number of gable ornaments, support posts and threshold boards have been preserved, fully sculptured or covered with reliefs. The fierce courage of the Maori warrior is legendary; his preoccupation with battle, revenge and the status accrued to the victor is reflected in the magnificence of his weapons and canoes. The Maori holdings of the Fine Arts Museums of San Francisco constitute an historic area of strength with a nucleus of important pieces acquired at the time of the 1894 Mid-Winter Fair.

The San Francisco *Gable Figure for a Chief's House (tekoteko)* from the central part of North Island, probably pre-dates the development of the meeting house of about 1840 and is a superb example of its type. Typical for these gable and support post figures is an oversized head with symmetrical facial tattooing and frontal pose with the hands to the abdomen. Late 19th century archival photographs of tribal chieftains confirm that the carvers followed pre-existing tattoo patterns. While every phase of the carving process, according to Kathleen J. Berrin in her article "Maori Art and Artistry" (Apollo, February 1980), "called for strict and formal artistry, the ability to treat the finally dressed wood with a deliberate and named pattern (such as 'waves', foliage', or 'basketry') was a talent much admired." The artist's decision to leave the marks of the stone-bladed adze upon the wood as intrinsic to the object's aesthetic enjoyment is reflected in this compelling portrait of a much-esteemed ancest

104

"Vastness on a small scale," was the way in which pioneer historian of American painting, E. P. Richardson, recommended the purchase of Thomas Moran's *Grand Canyon of the Yellowstone* to John D. Rockefeller III. The Far West, to Moran, was a romantic expanse of untrammeled and grandiose nature. According to Robert Rosenblum, Moran perpetuated the sublime landscape tradition of the German Romantic Kasper David Friedrich. Thurman Wilkins, his biographer, called Moran "painter of the mountains," whose life-long career as a western artist began in 1871. In her *Nature and Culture*, Barbara Novak has argued that Thomas Moran "merged Claude's composition and Turner's atmosphere in baroque compositions that quote the 17th century traditions. Humboldt...had spoken of the necessity for 'exalted' forms of speech, worthy of bearing witness to the majesty and greatness of Creation." At another point in her book, Novak quotes Walt Whitman to whom the "beauty, terror, power" of the West were "more than Dante ever knew," as he described the atmospheric effects Moran had already painted:"...these mountains and parks seem to me to afford new lights and shades. Everywhere the aerial gradations and sky effects inimitable; nowhere else such perspectives, such transparent lilacs and grays..."

Related to the San Francisco painting is a much larger view of the Grand Canyon of the Yellowstone, commissioned in 1893 by the Chicago Columbian Exposition and now owned by the Smithsonian Institution. Between 1872 and 1912, Moran painted several versions of what ranks, then and now, as one of America's greatest natural sights. The collection of American art assembled by Mr. and Mrs. John D. Rockefeller 3rd, given by them to the Fine Arts Museums of San Francisco in 1979, is of such quality and importance that it has made that institution, with one stroke, the prime repository of American painting on the West Coast.

116

The Santa Barbara Museum of Art

Benjamin West, the first painter from the American colonies to reap fame in Europe, was born ten miles from Philadelphia on what is now the campus of Swarthmore College. Showing signs of precocious talent, he was taken to the city by an uncle and apprenticed to a British artist. From August 1756 to April 1760, West was reputedly active as a portrait painter in Philadelphia where the eminent patriot, Stephen Carmick, was one of his sitters. In 1760, a group of the city's businessmen sponsored West's voyage to Rome and this put the young artist on a course that would lead him to London where he became a founding member of the Royal Academy and then, after the death of Sir Joshua Reynolds, its distinguished president. Forever proud of his New-World background, Benjamin West ended up making an important contribution to the growth of the Romantic movement.

Stephen Carmick (1719-1774) was a Philadelphia merchant and importer of Scottish descent. He assumed an important role in the colonies' early efforts for independence as evidenced by his membership in the "Sons of Liberty," a radical group organized to protest the British imposition of the infamous Stamp Act of 1765. In addition he holds the distinction of being laid to rest in Christ Church Cemetery, not far from Benjamin Franklin's grave site.

For the viewer who may wonder about the mannerisms of these colonial portraits, it is instructive to know that their painters had frequent recourse to popular mezzotint engravings, imported from England, as up-to-date guides to current fashions and notable personalities among British royalty and gentry. These engravings also provided our artists with ideas for formal poses and pictorial props. It was customary for a portrait painter to have a selection of such prints from which a potential client might choose a desired pose or favored costume. As we know that West's brother-in-law was a dealer in engravings, he must have been well aware of the practical uses of such aids to the provincial imagination, particularly during these formative years. In this *Portrait of Stephen Carmick*, the outstretched arm, the hand placed firmly on the hip, the three-quarter pose which shows off the face's profile with its fine aquiline nose, and the heavy drapery are all conventions used in British portraiture that can be traced back at least to the first half of the 17th century.

A 1960 gift to the Santa Barbara Museum by Mrs. Sterling (Preston) Morton, the Benjamin West *Portrait of Stephen Carmick* is now part of the Preston Morton Collection of American Art, a focus of the museum's strength and on permanent display in the Preston Morton Gallery.

Dali painted *Honey is Sweeter than Blood*, a key work as it came between the artist's Surrealist and classicist phases, in the winter of 1941, less than a year after his arrival from war-torn Europe. With his wife, Gala, he had found refuge on a Virginia horse farm as guests of Caresse Peabody Crosby, an international hostess, collector of artists and self-proclaimed inventor of the brassiere. As snow covered the rolling hills, Dali ordered a model, forgot he had done so, kept her waiting in the studio and painted her, or so the story goes, after the poor girl's skin had turned blue.

The picture shows us a faceless, bluish nude, cushioned by billowy clouds and leaning on a crutch cradled in her armpit. Pensively pressing her left nipple with narrow, emaciated fingers, she appears to have been left behind by her ravisher, a cocky centaur who is seen fleeing the scene in the right hand corner. Olive trees grow from the horse's hindquarters and one branch lingers, like a peace offering left in the passage of the centaur who defiantly carries off one of the woman's crutches as a trophy.

Technique was an obsession with Dali and he particularly admired the Dutch artist Vermeer's ability to create an illusion of atmospheric space. While his style showed aspirations toward Ingres, the results look more like Meissonier. Nor would Dali's cumulus clouds have passed muster with the 18th century ceiling painters who transported Saints and Olympians in that mode. Just as Parker Tyler thought that Mae West looked like a woman imitating a transvestite's imitation of a woman, so Dali appears to emulate 19th century emulations of the classical Italian Renaissance paintings he admired.

More interesting than the academic illusionism of his style, was the dream-inspired content of Dali's paintings. However hermetic he may have thought them to be, Freud disabused the artist of an illusion: "In classic paintings I look for the subconscious—in a Surrealist painting for the conscious." Dali's "paranoiac-critical" method of linking forms in nature to concepts of the hallucinating mind is not impervious to rational analysis. The cliché of blood, an especially hispanic substance, suggests virility and passion. Honey, on the other hand, has connotations of the female gender such as sweetness and the power of seduction. Dali explained this picture to its first owner succinctly and unambiguously: "Life is good and war is hell." This leaves no doubt that he saw the abused woman (a metaphor for Europe?) as an embodiment of life enduring, the centaur as death stalking the world with masculine insolence. He thought himself in possession of a binary personality, and signed this picture Gala Salvador Dali.

The centaur is a cloud-image or phantasmagoria. In his writings Dali has specifically referred to Aristophanes's comedy *The Clouds* in which they appear to the playwright in the shape of women and centaurs. Hybrid beings in which riders merge with their mounts, centaurs conjure up, in classical mythology, images of rape and rampage. Dali used them in several of his war-related pictures. A more pervasive (1933-1941) and even more enigmatic image is that of the crutch, a phallic symbol in disguise. Invariably, it supports phantom limbs protruding, weakened or gone soft. A rampant sight in Europe, after the Great War, the artist seems to associate the crutch with the helplessness of Europe in the 1930s. When writing: "….(the crutch) would be useful for life and at the same time for death, something to push with and to lean on: a

183 *Salvador Dali*, Honey is Sweeter than Blood,
1941
182 *Henry Moore*, Three Figures in a Setting, *1942*

weapon and a protection, an embrace and
a caress," Dali comes close to explaining
the meaning of a detail and the whole into
which it fits as well.

Exhibited at the Julien Levy Gallery in
April 1941, *Honey is Sweeter than Blood*
was sold by the artist to the Dalzell
Hatfield Galleries in Los Angeles when he
himself lived in Pebble Beach. Mr. and
Mrs. K. W. Tremaine who owned the
painting since 1945, gave it to the Santa
Barbara Museum in 1949.

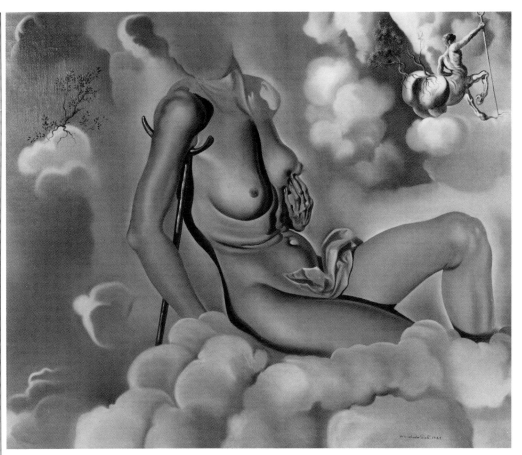

183

T*hree Figures in a Setting* relates to but
does not necessarily illustrate the
scenes Henry Moore, as an official war
artist, recorded while depicting life during
the 1940-43 bombings of Great Britain.
Residents of such target cities as London
literally went underground, living and
sleeping in basements and subway tunnels
during the air raids which devastated the
cities above them. Recorded in David
Sylvester's 1957 edition of *Henry Moore.
Sculpture and Drawings 1921-1948*, the
Santa Barbara drawing spatially articulates
a 1939 drawing in the collection of E. C.
Gregory, Esq., London, and shows a direct
relationship to a 1942 drawing in the
collection of Paul Magriel, New York, both
referred to as *Figures in a Setting*.

Symbols of repose and endurance, rather
than persons of a specific type, these
females of statuesque proportions in their
prison-like setting, thoroughly reflect
Moore's sculptural preoccupations at the
time. His shapes can be seen as archetypal
images, embodiments of man's collective
subconsciousness, in which the significance
of form depends on countless associations
of the individual as well as of the race and
for which the artist finds the appropriate
plastic expression. It is easy to see why, in
the 1940s, the Surrealists recruited Moore
for their cause. Peggy Guggenheim, with
her customary frankness called Moore "a
very direct simple man from Yorkshire
whose wonderful Surrealist drawings I like
better than his sculpture."

Santa Barbara owes its superb drawing
collection to the continuing generosity of
Wright Ludington, a great museum patron.

182

The John and Mable Ringling Museum of Art

61

When handsome, blond Ferdinand sat for his portrait in 1635, he was 26 years old, an important member of the Hapsburg Dynasty (his brother was King Philip IV of Spain), a cardinal since the age of ten, and a successful general who had routed the Swedes at the Battle of Nördlingen the year before. The Pope had made him a "Defender of the Faith" in the belief that he would lead the Counter-Reformation forces to victory over the Protestant armies. When he painted Ferdinand, Rubens was 58, one of the most famous artists of Europe, a successful diplomat knighted by the Kings of Spain and England and a grand seigneur living in a splendid Antwerp townhouse. He was also at the height of his artistic prowess, creating rich, powerful paintings with a bravura brushstroke reminiscent of the late Titian whose works he had admired on trips to Italy and Spain, earlier in his career.

Ferdinand arrived in Antwerp in 1635, ready to assume the governorship of the Spanish Netherlands. The city honored him with a grand triumphal entry designed by Rubens, who supervised the execution of complex temporary arches and facades lauding the Archduke-Governor. Commissioned soon after, the Ringling portrait met the need for an official likeness of the handsome, gracious, humanistic prince-general. Popular with the Antwerp citizenry, who saw their new governor as a Baroque Apollo, he was the ray of hope that would dispel years of political confusion and economic decay. The life-sized equestrian portrait of the Archduke Ferdinand at the Battle of Nördlingen in the Prado and a modello for that painting in the Art Institute of Detroit show heads and upper bodies so close to the Ringling portrait that it is reasonable to assume that they were based on and, indeed, more recent than this apparent study from life.

The state portrait of the *Archduke Ferdinand* is a magnificent example of Rubens' late portrait style and the first purchase made by the Ringling Museum after John Ringling's death in 1936. It had belonged to another grandee of painting, Sir Joshua Reynolds, and had passed through the collection of the fastidious J. Pierpont Morgan, before that most flamboyant of museum directors, A. Everett Austin, Jr., bagged it in 1948, for the museum to which he had been recently appointed. Reminiscing in 1957, after 'Chick' Austin's life had been cut short by a heart attack, Sir Osbert Sitwell professed a special interest in the genial museum director who, after 18 years at the Wadsworth Atheneum, had come to Sarasota to serve the Ringling as its master of the revels: "He once told me that the chief formative influence on his taste had been the books of my brother Sacheverell on the baroque and the rococo, which came out when Austin was a very young man...As well as being a director of the museum, Austin was also a born impresario of genius like Diaghilev." During his tenure at the Ringling, Austin wrote the only existing study on the mysterious Baroque painter called Monsù Desiderio, moved an 18th century theater from Asolo near Venice to the Florida Gulf Coast and presented the arts of music and drama on a par with the visual arts, thus making culture blossom in Sarasota as it never had before.

Late in life and during a relatively brief period, John Ringling, circus entrepreneur extraordinaire and millionaire patron of the arts, amassed a collection of European paintings that reflected his admiration for the continent whence his family had come. Like any other collector of his time, Ringling was well advised, but he did exercise his own taste and judgment. As there are few spectacles more baroque than the circus, it stood to reason that his acquisitions leaned toward Italy and Spain at the height of their respective pictorial powers. Yet the art of the Spanish Netherlands or French painting inspired by Italy were just as likely to catch the circus master's attention.

Propitious was Ringling's first meeting, in 1922-23, with the Munich art dealer Julius Böhler who came to Florida in 1924 and again in 1925 to discuss the decoration of a hotel that Ringling planned to build. They went to Italy together to scout for decorative sculpture and, during their last few days in Naples, Ringling broached the idea to Böhler that he help him build a collection as well as a museum.

In July 1929, with Böhler as his intermediary, Ringling bought 23 paintings from the Earl of Yarborough sale at Christie's. Lot 70 was a Nicolas Poussin, *The Holy Family with the Infant Saint John* (1655), rumored to have been painted for the Duc de Créqui, France's Ambassador to the Holy See at the time of Poussin's residence in Rome. Included in the 1960 exhibition at the Louvre on the authority of Anthony Blunt, the painting was belatedly accepted as authentic by Thuillier when its 1978 exhibition in Rome prompted him to call it an example of the artist's mature style. A pictorial homage to Raphael, the Sarasota Poussin is the last of four known paintings of the Holy Family, one of which can be found at the Toledo Museum of Art. The quality of the execution, the subtlety of palette and the great delicacy and softness of tone all lend veracity to this picture's attribution to the French classicistic Baroque painter.

In a concerted effort to exhibit and collect contemporary art, the State-operated John and Mable Ringling Museum of Art organized, in 1983, a retrospective of John Chamberlain's "modern baroque" sculptures and acquired, from that retrospective, a 1975 relief, *Added Pleasure*, with money provided by a private Acquisition Trust Fund.

John Chamberlain's *Added Pleasure* recapitulates formal and coloristic conventions of the late 1950s. Scrapped fenders in a broad spectrum of fashionable colors are whipped into a frenzy of jagged shapes and affixed against a flat plane. The result suggests the freewheeling energy of sparks flying off an anvil or spatters off a loaded brush. Forms flex their muscle within the confinement of an armature. Colors leap forth like flames from a smoldering hearth.

The aesthetic procedure keeps the myth of *Action Painting* alive as it flaunts its *Abstract Expressionist* derivation. The artist admitted at one time that his sculptures could be read as "self-portraits revealing the force of (his) anger." Spiritually akin to Franz Kline and Willem de Kooning, John Chamberlain, temperamentally as well as stylistically, belongs to that earlier generation—one in which painting eclipsed sculpture. Singularly bent on a structural permutation of found forms and colors for almost 25 years, the author of *Added Pleasure* has vindicated that iniquity by realizing, with great bravura, his predecessors' inchoate ambition.

Few sculptors have dealt with implicit kineticism and implied speed more effectively than Chamberlain whose freestanding and relief constructions resemble Futurist expressions of modern life's elemental impulses. In *Added Pleasure*, a centripetal force draws forms on the sculpture's periphery towards its hidden center. As their shapes bend and fold over crevices and inner passages, these scrounged components attain a morphological balance in which the brute process of their assemblage is successfully disguised. The gestural velocity with which he "throws together" forms "so they stick," is as important now to Chamberlain as once it was to the Abstract Expressionists.

202

Seattle Art Museum

Mark Tobey was born in Wisconsin, spent time in France, England and the Orient, and died, an expatriate, in Basel. Yet, journalists referred to him as "the sage of Seattle" and that city on the Pacific was the hub of Tobey's universe. He went there in 1923 to teach at Miss Nellie Cornish's progressive school of art, music, dance and theater. Teng Kuei, a Chinese student he met at the University of Washington, was Tobey's Virgil. His question, "Why do Western artists paint fish only when they are dead, and why does Western painting resemble holes in the wall?" shook the aspiring painter's faith in Renaissance concepts. A convert to the Bahá'í World Faith since 1918, Tobey got his chance to visit China and Japan in 1934. At a Zen monastery in Kyoto, he studied calligraphy, meditated and wrote poetry. The artist's style, later known as "white writing" developed from that experience.

Their allover approach to the canvas notwithstanding, few artists living in the same time and country are more dissimilar than Mark Tobey and Jackson Pollock. Their race is that of the turtle and the hare. If Pollock painted from the shoulder, Tobey painted from the wrist. If one had a swaggering sense of individualism, the other, through lifelong discipline and concentration, willingly submerged it. Eschewing the need to rebel against tradition, Tobey never allied himself with an avant garde bent on wiping the slate clean. He honed a talent for visual poetry that spoke in a whisper, and developed into an abstract miniaturist whose quiet sense of magic bears comparison with that of Klee. *Parnassus*, resonant with Apollonian Mountain associations, was painted when the artist, at 73, had savored the triumph of major exhibitions in Paris and New York. Its immensely large scale pushes "white writing" to the brink, yet an even, musical rhythm is sustained throughout. Painted in whites, blacks, reds, browns and yellows, its chromatic effect is that of a tan surface shimmering with vibrant pink. Teeming with energy, *Parnassus* is not merely a covered surface but a void that has swallowed the world.

Dr. Richard E. Fuller was one of Tobey's early patrons. His consistent acquisitions resulted in the Museum's extensive holdings of work by this artist. Parnassus was acquired from the Willard Gallery by Mr. and Mrs. Bagley Wright of Seattle and given to the Seattle Art Museum in 1974 through the Virginia Wright Fund. The Wrights' support for the Seattle Art Museum ranks second only to that of the founder's family. Their initiative, in addition, has enriched a consortium of Washington museums with 20th century American drawings, and is turning the State University campus at Bellingham into an obligatory stop for enthusiasts of monumental sculpture.

Some abstract forms have origins that precede recorded history yet never cease to fascinate. Outside the Seattle Art Museum in Volunteer Park stands a donut-shaped, Brazilian granite sculpture by Isamu Noguchi, carved in Japan in 1969. To the sculptor it is the dark sun of the afterworld and the unconscious. "Like a coiled magnet it aims its energy to the West—which is really the East—and when the sun sets in America and it becomes dark, that same sun rises in Japan." Noguchi helps us understand the magic inherent in another work in the Museum's collection—an archaic Chinese *Pi-disc*. By some considered a symbol of heaven, this brownish green jade dates back to 771-476 B.C., the Spring and Autumn Periods. Not much is known about its presumed ceremonial use, less yet about its geographic origins.

Dr. Richard E. Fuller, president and director of the Seattle Art Museum from 1933 until 1973, was a geologist by training whose knowledge of minerals gave him a keen appreciation of jades. An enthusiastic traveler to the Orient, with access to that network of agents and procurers helping American museums build their fabulous collections until the 1940s, Fuller accomplished his dream and that of his mother, the Museum's co-founder, to give fellow citizens a first-hand experience of non-Western art. It was the mysterious beauty of the stone and the ingenuity of the workmanship which moved the reticent Fuller to take a personal interest in jade and to create a collection known throughout the museum world for its excellence and diversity. This exceptionally large Pi-disc with its two opposed and stylized dragons carved in slight relief, was acquired by Dr. Fuller in 1939 for the Eugene Fuller Memorial Collection in tribute to his father.

The Bakota, or Kota, are not a homogeneous people. They appear to be a number of tribes which, during the course of their migrations, banded together under pressure from the Fang and are related through the customs and cultural systems that they evolved in common. They came from the Ogooué River and straddle the frontiers of the Republic of Congo and Gabon in West Africa just below the Equator. Bakota art is one of the most famous types of tribal art. Abstract forms are mastered, masses flattened out and surfaces and lines combined into taut compositions. Their formal and expressive quality recommended Bakota guardian and reliquary figures to Picasso whose 1907-08 concave, striated faces reflect his familiarity with what was then among the first types of "Negro" Art to fall into artists' hands.

The *Bwete Guardian Figure* in the Katherine White Collection at the Seattle Art Museum was found on a refuse site in Ojibwa, Gabon, by the anthropologist Hans Himmelheber in 1937 and, in all likelihood, dates back to the 19th century. Its first owner, Charles Ratton, had the lower portion restored. All guardian figures terminate somewhat awkwardly because they were once affixed to baskets containing the relics of the tribe's distinguished dead. The "guardian" is an image which is always highly stylized and relies entirely on the face to make an impact. Its body is merely a support, either straight like an ax handle or lozenge-shaped to suggest arms and legs. Its face is a slightly concave, truncated oval with nose and eyes in low relief and an almost non-existent mouth. The most distinct ornamental aspect of these wooden guardian figures is their hammered, embossed, cut and engraved brass and iron surface dressing.

Katherine Coryton White was no ordinary collector of African art. A some time poet and patron of the arts in Los Angeles, she respected, preserved and actively researched its context. Robert Farris Thompson's 1974 *African Art in Motion*, a study of the relation between "icon and act," was not only based on the White collection but was made possible, in part, by the collector. Mrs. White moved from Los Angeles to Seattle where she died in 1981. Through a combination of purchase and bequest, the Seattle Art Museum fell heir to the Katherine White Collection of many hundred objects of African art covering at least 67 cultures.

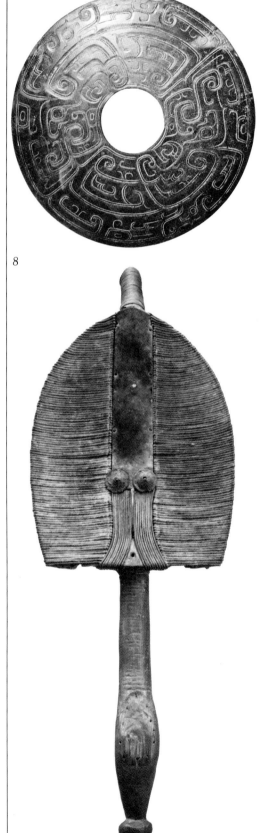

8

135

213

The Toledo Museum of Art

77

Outside of Corning, New York, the Toledo Museum of Art treats viewers to the largest art glass collection in an American public institution. The museum, in a sense, is the house that glass built and it would be inappropriate, therefore, not to have made glass one of this exhibition's choices. The Toledo Museum of Art was founded in 1901 by a small group of citizens under the leadership of industrialist Edward Drummond Libbey, whose successful glass company and its successor companies have formed the economic cornerstone of the city for many years. When Mr. Libbey died in 1925, he not only left an art collection but a residuary estate earmarked for art acquisitions. Florence Scott Libbey, his widow, continued the couple's interest in the museum and, at her death in 1938, bequeathed her estate as well. With these funds and in her name, Mrs. Libbey's interests in decorative arts and American painting have been favored in subsequent acquisitions.

René Lalique was the leading glass maker of Art Deco, the period that received its name from the 1925 *Exposition Internationale des Arts Décoratifs et Industriels Modernes* in Paris—presumably because of a typographic break in the word Déco-ratifs on the poster announcing the exhibition, but more likely because nobody could commit a title of such length to memory. Then 65, Lalique had built his reputation with jewelry, collaborated with the Danish porcelain manufacturers Bing and Gröndahl, designed perfume bottles for Coty and Worth, and led the move toward machine production and mass marketing. The rare blue-green "Tourbillon" vase with its deeply molded scroll design is of the very type by which we identify Art Deco as a style. Its designation comes, literally, from the whirling column in a fireworks display. It is pressed from an elegantly designed and expertly crafted mold and then acid polished. Colorless glass vases with black enamel outlines are the more commonly found products of the same c.1925 mold.

It is fashionable to belittle academicians, for who does not like to knock pomposity off its pins? "The best that can be said of (Sir Joshua) Reynolds," the late H. W. Janson was willing to allow, "is that he almost succeeded in making painting respectable in England as a liberal art...but at what cost! His *Discourses*...inhibited the visual capacity of generations of students in England and America." What then does Sir Joshua have to redeem himself? As a collector—the Rubens painting and Guercino drawing in this exhibition once belonged to him—he obviously valued and respected the work of others. Sympathizing with fellow artists, he encouraged and defended the Swiss visionary John Henry Fuseli who must have been one of the stranger painters around. Students at the Royal Academy (and future abstractionists everywhere) he advised that "the beauty of form alone, without the assistance of any other quality, makes of itself a great work." Was that, perhaps, what the art historian Janson objected to? Yet, how Reynolds implemented his *Discourses* was a different matter for all to see.

Miss Esther Jacobs, a lovely lady by any account, goes beyond "the science of abstract form," and would not be in this exhibition, had not her painter heeded more than "the beauty of form alone." In fact, his style is indebted to Titian and Van Dyck in greater measure than his theoretical pronouncements would lead us to believe. Despite an academic approach to art acquired during a two year residency in Rome, and despite a weakness for history painting in the grand manner, Sir Joshua was eager to compete, in his society portraiture, with the lofty grace of Thomas Gainsborough, his principal rival on the London scene. In this portrait he combined the reticence of the British with the elegance of the French and an Italian taste for luxurious adornment. About 1890, W. C. Whitney acquired the painting in England as a complement to the ballroom paneling of his spectacular New York mansion. Mrs. Samuel A. Peck, a Whitney descendant and heir, donated *Miss Esther Jacobs* to the Toledo Museum of Art in 1953.

Following the war years when practically no European art had been acquired, the Toledo Museum of Art began collecting again in 1946 with funds that had accumulated and with the greater yield of the Libbey endowments. As a lucky coincidence, many great works of European art came into the market at prices not yet inflated by the decline in value of most international currencies. Dutch 17th century paintings, of which Toledo could boast only a few examples, belonged to a category of art not extensively sought at that time and therefore reasonably valued. Otto Wittman who arrived at the Museum in 1946 after completion of military service in World War II, shared Director Blakemore Godwin's interest in Dutch art and was importantly responsible, as has been his successor, Roger Mandle, for the consistent attention Dutch art has received at the Toledo Museum of Art in the last 35 years.

Acquired at the Delft Art Dealers Fair, fondly remembered for its quality offerings in the postwar period, Melchior d'Hondecoeter's barnyard subject was, however superbly painted, not exactly the type for which museum directors were prepared to kill. Yet, just as at the time d'Hondecoeter painted his roosters, capons and turkeys, no stately dining room lacked its formal portrayal of the good earth's bounty, slaughtered or on the hoof, so today no collection of Dutch 17th century art is complete without one such brilliant display of domestic fowl. Working in Utrecht, The Hague and Amsterdam in the second half of the 17th century, d'Hondecoeter was a son and grandson of landscape and bird painters of the same name and studied for awhile with his uncle, the famed painter of hunter still lifes, Jan Baptist Weenix. His style varied little over a lifetime, nor did his subjects, of which the Toledo picture is a colorful example.

56

National Gallery of Art

Rembrandt's *Joseph Accused by Potiphar's Wife* is one of the outstanding examples of European painting included in Andrew Mellon's original bequest to the nation in 1937, the year Congress established a National Gallery of Art. Although his collection numbered only 132 pictures, these masterpieces, spanning a period from the 13th to the mid-19th centuries, set a standard for the subsequent acquisition policies of the Gallery. One of the great strengths of his collection was the nine paintings by Rembrandt. As with the *Joseph Accused by Potiphar's Wife*, a number of these were among the 21 masterpieces which Mr. Mellon acquired from the Hermitage in the early 1930's.

The story told in this painting comes from the book of Genesis, chapter 39. Joseph, who had been sold to Potiphar, an officer of the pharoah, came to be trusted and honored in Potiphar's household. He was, however, falsely accused by Potiphar's wife of having tried to violate her when her repeated attempts at seduction had failed. When he fled from her, she held onto his robe and eventually used the robe as evidence against him. In Rembrandt's painting Potiphar's wife is pointing to Joseph's red robe which is draped over her bed post. Potiphar is listening to the story while Joseph stands quietly on the far side of the bed.

Rembrandt's scene differs from the biblical text in that it depicts all three protagonists together at the time of the accusation. Joseph's presence is not mentioned in the Bible. Iconographically, the presence of Joseph is also unusual. One precedent Rembrandt might have known, is Jan Pynas's painting of the same subject. Rembrandt may have arrived at this conception as a result of viewing Vondel's play of *Joseph in Egypt*, which first appeared in 1639-40, where all three protagonists are seen together. Rembrandt, however, often took liberties with biblical texts to enhance the emotional poignancy of the scene. The story of the family of Joseph was one of Rembrandt's favorite biblical subjects. He graphically portrayed Joseph fleeing Potiphar's wife's attempted seduction in an etching in 1634. The scene of accusation occurs twice: in the Washington painting

and in one in Berlin, also dated 1655. The compositions of these paintings are virtually identical, but the moods are different. In the Berlin version Joseph appears outwardly agitated rather than restrained: his eyes glance upwards and one hand is raised. These paintings, however, create very different impressions and are not mere repetitions. Now that the Washington painting has been cleaned, the vibrancy of its colors and the rich handling of paint can be fully appreciated.

Although the reasons that the two versions exist are not known, the subject must have had personal associations for Rembrandt. Titus served as the model for Joseph. Rembrandt may have been drawn to the subject because, at this time, he was also beset by accusations from a woman scorned, Geertje Dircx. In 1649 she sued Rembrandt for breach of promise, a suit that was followed by years of litigation. The theme of false accusation also arises in Mantegna's drawing *Calumny of Appelles* which Rembrandt owned and copied at about this time. The costume and angular stance of Potiphar are reminiscent of a number of studies after Indian miniatures that Rembrandt made in the mid-1650's.

(Arthur K. Wheelock)

Lessing J. Rosenwald, a retired businessman and one-time Chairman of the Board of Directors of Sears, Roebuck and Co., brought together one of the country's choicest collections of Master prints and drawings in a long life of devotion to art. The gift of this collection, with one stroke, created a prints and drawings department for the National Gallery that made it equal to those in New York, Philadelphia, Boston and Chicago.

Rosenwald purchased more than 85 of the prints engraved after Bruegel's designs by Cornelis Cort, Frans Huys, and others. Among them are a series of 12 Alpine landscapes and many complex allegorical compositions. The earliest Bruegel purchase was from the 1928 Boerner sale, the most recent from the Los Angeles collectors, Josephine and Jacob Zeitlin in 1964, the year Rosenwald executed his gift

to the National Gallery of Art.

In 1959 Mr. Rosenwald bought, from the New York dealer William H. Schab where many of the fine graphics in the Rosenwald collection originated, *The Festival of Saint George*, c. 1559. Village festivals such as this one were the subjects of several of Bruegel's most appealing paintings as well as his designs for prints. This particular scene is generally considered to be one of his finest. The carnival site teems with events to be enjoyed as one's eye moves about the frolicking peasants—from a woman on a swing inside the hut at the far left, to the wheeled winged-dragon creature spouting smoke near the center, to the dog tugging at the girl's skirt slightly below, and the tiny birds, perched at the upper right, observing the action. Like many of Bruegel's subjects, *The Festival of Saint George* was published by Hieronymous Cock.

Falconet's sculpture is an elegant but restrained expression of the age of Rococo. Parisian by birth and close to the Court of Versailles, Falconet gained admission to the Salon at an early age. He excelled in exquisitely carved allegories that captured the spirit and catered to the taste of his time. A professor at the Academy since 1761, he was called to Petrograd in 1766 by Catharine II of Russia, to design and execute an equestrian monument of Peter the Great. This, his best known sculpture, recaptured the grandeur of the Baroque and has been compared with the work of Bernini. Upon his return to Paris, after 15 years, he discovered that tastes had changed under the new king. This caused him to give up sculpture and devote the last ten years of his life to writing treatises on art.

Venus, the goddess of love and beauty, is seen riding through her oceanic habitat in a shell propelled by dolphins; she is seated in an attitude of relaxed amusement at the attentions paid her by two young putti. The skillful handling of such details as *Venus's* modishly curled coiffure and embroidered drapery reflects fashion rather than mythology. Indicative of the sculptor's mastery of the marble is the group's pyramidal composition, freely penetrated by open spaces. The theme of Venus seated on a shell pulled by dolphins, with doves and putti, was popular in France during the latter part of the reign of Louis XV.

The portrait character of *Venus's* face led, as early as 1841 when this sculpture was first recorded, to her identification as Madame de Pompadour, mistress of Louis XV from 1745 to 1764. The object's earliest known attribution was to Edme Bouchardon, and its more recent attribution to Falconet is not generally accepted. It is notable that Falconet portrayed Madame de Pompadour in another allegorical guise, as Friendship, in a biscuit de Sèvres group of which an example can be found at the Wadsworth Atheneum. The mischievous putto kissing the right hand of the National Gallery's *Venus* recalls both Falconet's impishly smiling *Amour menaçant* at the Louvre, made for Madame de Pompadour, and the child kneeling to kiss the right hand of the heroine in Falconet's celebrated *Pygmalion and Galatea* at the Hermitage.

Madame de Pompadour as the Venus of the Doves is one of 46 sculptures the National Gallery received from the Kress Foundation in the postwar era. Samuel H. Kress, a one-time schoolteacher who became an immensely successful chain store owner, fell in love with Italian art and amassed it more systematically than anyone before or since. With the death of Andrew Mellon in 1937, the distinction of being the world's premier private art collector befell the aging Samuel H. Kress. Two years later he decided to make the National Gallery the main repository of his art. In consultation with the Gallery's curators, the Kress Foundation kept adding examples of European as well as Italian art to the nation's collections—even after the benefactor's death and into the 1950s.

37

90

127

110

Writing about his friend in the year of this "combine painting" was completed, John Cage claimed that there was no more subject in a combine than there is in a page from a newspaper: "Each thing that is there is a subject. It is a situation involving multiplicity." Multiple forms? Multiple meanings? There are forms of relative constancy in the history of art with meanings changing from one culture to the next: the image of a handsome youth becomes Apollo to the Greeks, Buddha to the Gandhara Indians, Christ to the sculptor of the Ile de France. Conversely, there has been a constancy of meaning throughout a succession of forms: the pagan Priapus degenerates into a tail-sprouting, horned and hoofed (d)evil in Byzantine manuscripts, to ultimately transmogrify into a Bruegelian toad. Transformations entangle the one-to-one relationship between the sign and what it signifies. Contemporary art, in which history's long train of forms and images piles up accordion-fashion, has become an exercise in unscrambling the sign from the signified.

Rauschenberg, with maddening impartiality, presses into endless intellectual picture frames objects and ideas as well as their equivalents and analogues, all relevant to him and all meaningful to us as we share one and the same finite world. He moves from object to idea (clock-face → wheel → motion → skate → accident → paint spill → art) and from idea to object (before noon → afternoon → time running → time running out → timelessness → creation → picture); from idea to idea (timing → motion → speed → chance → risk → suspense → gesture) and from object to object (hands → spokes → planks → dropcloth → tin can → pigment → painting). Just as we visually uncombine this combine, can we literally dissect its title to some avail? *Reservoir* is made up of: *re*, international prefix meaning *again*; *serve*, as in being available; and *voir*, French for seeing and speaking the truth when combined into *voir dire*. *Reservoir*, a font of art information, truly serves a visual purpose, again and again.

Reservoir entered the National Museum of American Art in 1969 as a gift from S.C. Johnson & Son, a national cleaning products company. Mr. and Mrs. H. F. Johnson, earlier in that decade, had commissioned the dealer Lee Nordness to assemble a representative collection of contemporary American paintings. Furthering a reputation for art patronage established with its headquarters, the famous Johnson's Wax Building designed by Frank Lloyd Wright, the Wisconsin corporation toured these paintings internationally, then gave them to the nation.

Three years after having seen her work in the Salon of 1874, Edgar Degas visited the young artist's studio and invited her to join his group of Impressionists and take part in its shows. "I accepted with delight," Mary Cassatt later explained. "At last I could work in complete independence, without bothering about the eventual judgment of a jury." The daughter of a wealthy Pittsburgh banker, Mary Cassatt, at age 33, was in the right place at the right time. She was self-taught in museums, she had traveled extensively, and she was self-critical to a fault. Degas may have been her mentor and frequent companion, but she preferred Pissarro as a teacher: "...he could have taught stones how to draw correctly." It has been said, somewhat uncharitably, that Mary Cassatt's contribution to painting was modest, her influence negligible, but her effect on American taste profound. Not only was there the rumor of her lending money to Durand-Ruel when this famous art dealer was on the verge of ruin in 1884, but she induced family and friends, among them the Havemeyers, the Stillmans and the Whittemores, to buy pictures. At tea parties, Cassatt showed and tried to sell canvases Pissarro left in her care.

The Caress was painted just after the turn of the century when all lessons of Impressionism had been absorbed and the artist had settled on the woman-and-child theme as her personal subject, treating it with a tenderness that is foreign to the Impressionist mode. The seated woman holds a baby on her lap and a child by her side. The viewer cannot help but notice the mother's lack of involvement and what seems to be a deliberate decision, on the artist's part, to avoid the pyramidal composition that is the rule for this type of grouping. Instead, she brings the three heads to the same height and presses their bodies into the same plane—an unusual solution. The brushwork shows none of the constraint that characterizes the composition, and its loose, bravura style prompts comparison with that of Sargent.

William T. Evans was among this country's first collectors of American art. The 800 paintings he bought between the early 1880s and 1913 made him the largest collector of American art up to World War I. He sought out local artists in their studios, he made friends and enemies, he sold at auction when it suited him or when business reverses forced him to do so, and he belonged to every club and organization that promoted the mutual acquaintance of artists and connoisseurs. A resident of New York, not given to travel abroad, Evans may well have seen Mary Cassatt's *The Caress* in 1910 when it was exhibited at the Lotos, a club to which he belonged. Six years prior to that it had been entered in the Art Institute of Chicago's Annual Exhibition where it had been awarded a $500 trophy on principle, which the artist refused. Durand-Ruel remained owner of the picture until 1909, sold it to an American, bought it back, and then, in 1910, sold it again, this time to William T. Evans. William H. Truettner, in an article on this patron of the National Museum of American Art, speculates that Evans, who never included Sargent and Whistler in his collection, might have disapproved of their preference for living in Europe. If that were so, then Cassatt suffered a similar reprobation; within a year's time William T. Evans rid himself of this painting by giving it to the Smithsonian Institution, where the Evans Collection constitutes a major holding.

Childhood fascination with native Americans shaped the destiny of George Catlin. Raised in a rural region of Pennsylvania rich with Indian relics and lore, he developed a curiosity about Indian customs and a deep affection for the people. Although trained as a lawyer, he soon acknowledged that his real talent was for drawing and painting. His success as a portrait painter earned his recognition and acceptance into the Pennsylvania Academy in 1824, and to the National Academy of Fine Arts in 1826.

Catlin could have chosen a comfortable career as a portrait painter of the wealthy, but rather sought to fulfill his dream, to visit, paint and collect artifacts from as many of the Indian groups west of the Mississippi as he could contact. To accomplish his goal, he lived and died a poor man, suffering much hardship and personal loss. Yet through his sacrifice, he has left invaluable documentation of the final days of many of our indigenous people and their great cultures.

In 1830, Catlin went to St. Louis, the gateway to the West. He met with General William Clark, co-adventurer of the Lewis and Clark expedition. With Clark's approval and assistance, Catlin learned much about the people and made many contacts before his journey began. On March 26, 1832, he embarked on the steamboat *Yellow Stone*, to ascend the Missouri River, not to return to St. Louis until the Fall of 1835. He contacted such tribes as the Mandan, Choctaw, Pawnee, Sioux and Comanche.

Letters and Notes on the Manners, Customs and Conditions of North American Indian, a two volume journal, was compiled during the travels. Catlin told of the encounter with a Comanche war party. He described and painted the leader, Little Spaniard:

"A gallant little fellow...represented to us as one of the leading warriors of the tribe... He is half Spanish, and being half-breed, for whom they generally have the most contemptuous feelings, he had been all of his life thrown into the front of battle and danger; at which post he has signalized himself, and commanded the highest admiration and respect of the tribe for his daring and adventurous career..."

Catlin assembled the most comprehensive record of major tribes of the American West and planned for the collection to be purchased by the United States government. He exhibited his Indian Gallery in New York, Washington, Baltimore, Boston and Philadelphia, but the government would not purchase the collection. Discouraged, he took the collection to London and Paris, where the exhibitions were tremendously successful, but a financial disaster. Many of the works were distributed among his creditors, one of whom was Joseph Harrison, Jr., of the Harrison Boiler Works, at that time the largest locomotive building concern in the world. He paid off the principal debts against the Indian Gallery and shipped it to Philadelphia.

In 1879, Harrison's heirs gave the Catlin Indian Gallery collection to the Smithsonian Institution. Over 400 paintings were placed in the collection of the U. S. National Museum, a branch of the largest institution, and first exhibited in 1883. They were later assigned to the National Museum of Natural History and then to the National Collection of Fine Arts. When the National Collection of Fine Arts acquired its own building, the Catlin Indian Gallery, which included *Little Spaniard, a Warrior*, was housed there.

(Dorothy Downs)

The Phillips Collection

155

163

The Phillips Collection, in essence a finite private hoard made accessible to the public, would stagnate if it were not for incidental, non-family gifts, such as the Katherine S. Dreier Bequest, and for a carefully calibrated acquisitions program. Laughlin Phillips maintains Duncan Phillips' public-spirited tradition and like his father, makes strong commitments to individual artists with whose work the collection continues to be enriched. Frank Stella is one such artist. His contribution to American art in the second half of this century bears comparison, in vanguard terms, with Arthur Dove's fifty years before. *Pilicia II*, defiantly modernist and expansively American but unmistakably in debt to the Cubist and Constructivist traditions, is often seen hanging, at the Phillips Collection, near the Braques for which this pioneering institution has justly become renowned.

During the spring, summer and fall of 1970, Frank Stella worked on 40 drawings which formed the basis for 40 large scale works, executed in three versions each, with some exceptions, and given the titles of 18th century wooden synagogues destroyed in Poland and Russia during 1939-45. The whole series, a distinct chapter in the artist's prolific oeuvre, had been completed by 1974. In the first version the medium is paint and collage on canvas. In the second version, indicated, as in the first and third, by a Roman numeral behind the title, the medium is paint (acrylic) and collage (felt and board) on wood. The effect is one of low relief, parallel to the picture plane. In the third version the medium is paint and collage on honeycombed cardboard affixed to an interlocking system of tilted planes. *Pilicia II* is the second version of No. 36 in the series and was executed in 1973. It was acquired in 1974 from a 1973 exhibition at the Phillips Collection entitled, *Frank Stella, Recent Work*.

Frank Stella's "Polish Village" series had a breakaway connection to his own 1965-66 irregular polygons, sometimes referred to as his "New Hampshire" series. These new images were irrefutably inspired by a wealth of new information, just then transpiring to New York, about Malevich's architectural drawings, Tatlin's and Rodchenko's reliefs and Liubov Popova's architectonic paintings. Philip Leider has correctly pointed out that the convergence of Stella's work after 1970 with that of the Russian Constructivists, was less a matter of simple influence than one of the artist's moral identification with that heroic, history-reforming introduction of abstract principles in all the arts. Although Stella sees a parallel between the Eastern Synagogues' elaborate carpentry and the interlocking structure that is so prominent a motif in his 1970-74 constructions, the ultimate appropriateness of the titles in the "Polish Village" series is that, to the artist, the trail of blackened synagogues commemorated from Bogoria to Rzochow maps out the "Munich-Moscow axis" of Russian Constructivism, thus lending to the series a heretofore uncontemplated political dimension.

In a 1930 account of his life, Kurt Schwitters reminisced about the birth of MERZ, the Hannover variant on Dada with which, from 1918 on, he became identified: "Then suddenly that glorious revolution was upon us...things really started happening...I had to shout my jubilation out to the world...penury forced me to seize whatever I could find...One can even shout out through refuse, and that is what I did, nailing and gluing it together. This I called MERZ—a prayer about the victorious end of the war, victorious as once again peace had prevailed. Everything had broken down in any case and new things had to be made out of the fragments..."

Although it is customary to explain that Schwitters arrived at the MERZ designation of his work by removing KOM and -UND PRIVATBANK from a printed announcement and pasting it in the center of a picture exhibited in his Berlin gallery, the 1930 reminiscence would have us perceive MERZ (short for merci) as a sigh that, mercifully, the war had ended. Yet others have hinted at the word's close resemblance to the French *merde*, a term appropriate to the debris from which Schwitters fashioned his pictures.

Equating *Kommerz* with *Mercury*, the god of trade and the messenger of the gods, it was but one swift step for Schwitters to raid his mail and to press into formal service what hit his fancy and suited his taste. In a centripetal arrangement, the wrapper of a package addressed to the artist, a Dada announcement mailed from France, a receipt for payment and a variety of newspaper fragments both in German and in French, alternate with public transportation tickets, three over-sized letters from a poster, a candy paper, envelopes and snippets of a patterned fabric. Opaque, monochromatic paint gives these variegated ingredients a homogenious appearance.

For his composition, Schwitters is indebted to some of the artists with whom he exhibited his work at the Galerie Der Sturm from 1919 on. A word collage of that year in the Morton G. Neumann collection in Chicago significantly singles out, among others, Kandinsky, Chagall, Campendonck, Klee, Carrà and Severini. Futurism, its Russian variant Cubo-Futurism, and its German Expressionist interpretation at the hands of Feininger and Marc, all funneled through Herwarth Walden's Berlin gallery, provided Schwitters' early pictures with their force lines and their dynamic interplay of circular and triangular shapes. A comparison of *Radiating World* with *Das Grosse Ichbild (Merz 9B)* of 1919, and *Merzbild 31* of 1920, which must have immediately preceded it, produces compelling similarities and corroborates their eclectic Futurist source.

The Société Anonyme, Inc., or Museum of Modern Art, was founded by Katherine S. Dreier, assisted by Marcel Duchamp and Man Ray, in the year Schwitters painted his *Radiating World*. "Acting as a leaven in the art world of America by being always ahead or abreast of the times," as its first annual report has put it, the Société Anonyme exhibited that winter a number of Schwitters collages. Later in the decade, Dreier and Duchamp traveled to Hannover and, in 1929, Miss Dreier, at Schwitters' invitation, gave a lecture at "Die Abstrakten Hannover." The record is incomplete on the date of *Radiating World's* acquisition by Miss Dreier but we do know that it was included in both *Cubism and Abstract Art* and *Fantastic Art, Dada, Surrealism* at The Museum of Modern Art in 1936. Duncan Phillips was offered the Dreier bequest in 1952 and chose from among the pictures formerly in Miss Dreier's personal collection Schwitter's *Radiating World* and 15 additional ones by Braque, Mondrian, Klee and Archipenko, among others.

Arthur Garfield Dove, Cornell-educated son of an upstate New York brick manufacturer, quite happily applied himself to magazine illustration until, in 1908, he pulled up stakes and sailed for France. In Paris he saw the Fauves, and on the Côte d'Azur he painted in an Impressionistic style. After one year he returned to New York where he looked up Stieglitz who invited the artist to join "291." Settled in Westport, Connecticut, Dove created, in 1911, a series of six paintings, *Abstractions No. 1* to 6, all based on landscape motifs. Closely paralleling Kandinsky's and the Fauve treatment of nature, they have gone into history as the first non-objective art sprung from native soil. In a letter to the collector Arthur Jerome Eddy, Dove elucidated his working method: starting with a simple motif, but gradually moving away from its objective appearance, he began to "think subjectively" and to "remember certain sensations *purely through their form and color*, that is, by certain shapes, planes, light, or character lines determined by the meeting of such planes."

Dove's paintings strike a balance between the Symbolist modes of turn-of-the-century art and the chromatic experiments of his contemporaries, the Synchromists. He mistrusted the analytical methods of Cubism, for he preferred a more intuitive attitude toward life and creation. A mood of poetic reverence toward nature characterizes his mature style. Dove's art is now rooted in the earth, monitoring its rhythms and pulsations, then turned to the sky, resonant with color and light. Related to Dove in aspirations and accomplishments is Georgia O'Keeffe, another member of the "291" gallery, who still continues in that pantheistic and peculiarly American vein.

Duncan Phillips fell under the spell of Dove's work when first seeing it at Stieglitz's. Dove became the only painter whom Phillips supported with a modest but regular stipend. *Golden Storm* was his first acquisition in 1925, the year Dove painted it. Thanks to their correspondence, one of this century's more interesting artist-patron relationships has been recorded for posterity. On March 13, 1926, Duncan Phillips voiced his pleasure with the newly acquired *Golden Storm* but, at the same time, expressed his concern that the metallic golds and bronzes might not prove permanent. Could the artist protect his picture with something other than varnish which would ruin it?

Phillips begged Dove not to be as careless as that "spiritual ancestor" of his, Albert Pinkham Ryder, whose magical surfaces with their cracks and fissures troubled him very much. He then balanced that advice by praising Dove for having captured in his *Golden Storm* the "rhythm of the universe" and "a divine activity." Five years later, Dove retorted with an offer to either restore the darkened picture or to exchange it for one that would not give the collector problems. Duncan Phillips described its condition in detail but admitted to liking it so much that he would not give it up even if it had deteriorated—he would simply have to buy more works in the future to replace it. There are 48 paintings by Dove in the Phillips Collection to attest to this resolution.

Sterling and Francine Clark Art Institute

If anything confirms the high regard in which those caring for the Clark legacy are holding the work of Pierre Auguste Renoir, it is the reproduction, on the cover of the Sterling and Francine Clark Art Institute's *Twenty-five Year Report*, of *A Girl with a Fan* in this exhibition. Reportedly, Renoir was the founder's favorite painter. Robert Sterling Clark bought his first picture by this artist in 1916 when he lived in the French capital. There were 36 more to follow, making the Clark Art Institute a major repository of Renoir's work along with the Barnes Foundation in Merion, Pennsylvania. Most of the Clark Renoirs, depicting women alone at various activities, date from the 1870s and 1880s. Three were painted in the 1890s, none in the 20th century, although the artist lived until 1919. Apparently, Mr. Clark preferred Renoir's pictures of the Impressionist period. In recent years, as a result of David S. Brooke's concern for the collection's conservation, these Renoirs have been brought back to their original coloristic splendor.

From Naples where he had been attracted by the Bay, Mount Vesuvius and the local museum, Renoir wrote to a friend in November 1881: "I feel a little lost when away from Montmartre...I am longing for my familiar surroundings and think that even the ugliest Parisian girl is preferable to the most beautiful Italian." No wonder. At age 40, Renoir had fallen in love with a Parisian girl, Aline Charigot, who was far from ugly and as good a reason as any to come back. At Easter, that same year, he had stood up his friend Théodore Duret who wanted to take Renoir along on a trip across the Channel. We owe the painter thanks for that decision, for in the course of the summer he put down upon canvas his impressions of a boating party having lunch at the Restaurant Fournaise on the small isle of Chatou. The result was, of course, *Le Déjeuner des Canotiers*, one of Renoir's all time great pictures, in the Phillips Collection. The film director Jean Renoir, in a 1962 book on his father, and John Rewald, the Berenson of Impressionism, may not agree on the correct identification of all of the participants in that party, but there seems to be consensus on the identity of the young woman cuddling a dog while peering across the table. She is Aline Charigot, the woman Renoir would marry in 1890. When we compare this young Parisian's physiognomy, dress and hat in the Phillips Collection *Boating Party* with the features of whoever posed, presumably that same year, for *A Girl with a Fan* then we cannot help being struck by a resemblance which may well make the Clark picture a portrait of Renoir's new-found love. While of no particular bearing on its quality, it does lend piquancy to a painting otherwise distinguished by a flattened perspective in the Japanese manner (the fan underscores this) and by a wealth of flowers pressed into a continuous color-saturated composition with the sitter's coiffed head and painted fan.

The undisputed genius of Dutch art, Rembrandt van Rijn, is represented in this exhibition with two religious subjects, one taken from the Old, the other taken from the New Testament, both dating from the mid-1650s, a period when external troubles (the threat of bankruptcy) and inner uncertainties precipitated a crisis in the artist's life. Both are accusatory, with more apology than passion, Potiphar's wife of Joseph's lack of attentiveness, Christ of his disciples' failing watchfulness. In such forgiving insight into human nature and its essential frailty, Rembrandt's compassionate character stands eloquently revealed.

Matisse once remarked that, however anachronistic, Rembrandt's biblical scenes preserve the gravity and the humility of the scriptures better than those virtual documentaries by 19th century artists who went to live in the Holy Land. When Albrecht Dürer, Rembrandt's chief graphic rival in Europe, imagined the *Agony in the Garden*, he cast the high drama of betrayal in a rhetorical and visionary form. He, too, missed what Rembrandt's lay Christian spirit almost effortlessly accomplished. Instead of impressing the viewer with an erudite imitation of Palestine, instead of turning Gethsemane into a Walpurgis Night of the soul, Rembrandt's *Christ Finding the Apostles Asleep* is a Dutch Reformed account, pure and simple, of God's inimitable ways with men.

The Clark drawing in brown ink and wash places the three sleeping figures in front of a verdant mountain landscape with a distant tower vertically extending the erect and pleading figure of Christ. The setting is Italianate as are most of Rembrandt's painted landscapes. No darkness is lurking nor is there any evidence of soldiers at the gate. Clearly, the artist eschewed the scene's dramatic stock-in-trade. He was consistent throughout in the four known variants on this theme, each representing a successive moment of increased response, but none pandering to feelings of outrage.

Robert Sterling Clark collected prints and drawings as well as paintings and the decorative arts. The Rembrandt drawing purchase, from Colnaghi in 1913, came in the second year of his involvement with art and presaged the formation of what now ranks as one of the most distinguished and most scholarly recorded drawing collections in the United States.

Robert Sterling Clark collected silver by the 18th century English master Paul de Lamerie with the same vigor and dedication he showed in his pursuit of paintings by that other favorite of his, Pierre-Auguste Renoir. Clark's interest in de Lamerie developed relatively late in his collecting career. Fourteen items by this silversmith can be documented as having been acquired in the 1930s. The *Cup and Cover* of 1742 was purchased by the Institute's founder in London in 1931. Characteristic of the high rococo and exuberantly carved, this two-handled cup is easily the most spectacular piece by de Lamerie in the Clark collection. Eclipsed only by the wine cistern formerly in the household of the Duke of Sutherland and now in the Minneapolis Art Institute, this particular cup and cover exists in several versions, at The Metropolitan Museum of Art and in the Gilbert Collections on loan to the Los Angeles County Museum of Art.

As the focal point of this decorative
riot, the infant Bacchus sits amid
vineyards, engaged in the production of
wine; on one side he squeezes grapes into a
vat, on the reverse he operates a wine
press. Both versions of the fleshy infant are
framed within an irregularly shaped
cartouche, defined by scrolling tendrils.
Within these cartouches de Lamerie
depicted grape arbors and scenes suggestive
of the Mediterranean. Harmonious with
the Bacchic theme, two human masks,
possibly Dionysus or a satyr, peer down at
the child. A flurry of grapes, blossoms and
grape leaves surround the cartouche,
underscoring the cup's vegetal opulence.

The wine-making motif is continued in
the handles which have been transformed
into woody grape vines around which
leaves and tendrils wind. No naturalistic
detail is overlooked; on the arch of the
handle two snails emerge from their shells.
Another animal motif is that of two
inebriated lions struggling to stay afloat, on
the cup's foot, in a sea of swirling scrolls,
shells and grapes. This fluid quality is also
noticeable in the decoration of the lid.
Designed as a double dome, the cover
inverts the bulging outlines of the cup.
Entwined among the flowers, shells and
scrolls are two exulting infants who appear
to be tritons, one hoisting a shell horn, the
other sounding his trumpet. A finial
heaped with grapes among which a small
lizard spies his prey, completes the
vinification theme.

51

63

223

Worcester Art Museum

29

The Worcester Art Museum portrait of *Mrs. Perez Morton* was painted in 1802, approximately seven years after Stuart had established himself in Philadelphia, then the gayest and most cosmopolitan of American cities. Ostensibly called back from Europe to paint George Washington, he became the favorite of a pseudo aristocracy of wealthy Federalists who wanted Stuart to memorialize them for posterity. The sitter of this portrait, the former Sarah Wentworth Apthorp, of Braintree (now Quincy), Massachusetts, married Perez Morton, a prominent lawyer, in 1781. She was a poetess and a woman renowned for her grace, intelligence and charm. Referred to as the "American Sappho," Mrs. Morton published a variety of poetry and prose, including *Quâbi, or The Virtues of Nature* (1797); *Beacon Hill* (1791) and *My Mind and its Thoughts* (1823).

This picture exemplifies Stuart's approach to portraiture. It has been frequently said that he was a "face painter." In Mrs. Morton's likeness, he concentrated on bringing the head to life, while subordinating the body and the clouds in the background. Clearly capturing the wit for which she was known, he tinged it with irony and sadness. Her brown eyes gaze directly at the spectator as she arranges her mantilla. Radiography has revealed that the artist originally intended to place the sitter's crossed hands in her lap but painted out his preliminary drawing when he decided to put her in the more spontaneous pose of adjusting her toilette. In fairness to the artist's intentions, it should be pointed out that however much we may like its improvisational tone, Stuart thought of *Mrs. Perez Morton* as unfinished. He painted her three times that year; the Worcester sketch was found in Stuart's studio after his death in 1828.

Stuart's daughter, Jane, sold the unfinished sketch of *Mrs. Perez Morton* to Ernest Tuckerman of Newport in 1862. At his death, it passed to Joseph Tuckerman who bequeathed the portrait to the honorable Stephen Salisbury of Worcester, who in turn donated it to the Worcester Art Museum, requesting that it be labeled as a gift of the grandchildren of Joseph Tuckerman. The portrait of *Mrs. Perez Morton* was received less than a year after Salisbury and 50 prominent citizens had helped the institution into being. Not only had he donated the land and a substantial sum of money, this founding patron of the Worcester Art Museum, upon his death in 1905, enriched the collection with the pictures he had gathered and secured its continuation with a generous endowment.

Martin Schongauer's *Christ on the Cross with the Virgin and St. John* is one of a small number of important 14th and early 16th century German prints purchased in the early 1930s under the directorship of Francis Henry Taylor. By 1934, the Worcester Art Museum had acquired nearly 10,000 prints through gift and purchase. Seeing the need to build up a more balanced collection and with the intent of pointing the way for the Trustees to consider only outstanding prints, Taylor chose to present them with this fine example of the work of one of the first painters to produce a significant body of engraved works.

During his lifetime and thereafter, Schongauer's prints enjoyed wide circulation all over Europe and, because of their exquisite beauty and simplicity, they were often copied by painters and sculptors alike. His prints are considered to have been the greatest influence on the work of Albrecht Dürer, who became Germany's subsequent master of engraving. The crucifixion was often treated by Schongauer; six different versions of this same subject exist. Identical in their essentials, slight variations are proof of the artist's continued search for an ideal solution in presenting this theme. His composition derives from two basic sources—the traditional German devotional picture and the paintings he had seen on his travels to the Netherlands. That his work owes profound debt to Netherlandish painting, particularly to that of Roger van der Weyden, can be seen in the treatment of the fluttering draperies and the realistic landscape.

(Ann W. Heymann)

29 *Martin Schongauer,* Christ on the Cross with the Virgin and St. John

91 *Jean Honoré Fragonard,* The Return of the Drove, *1765-70*

65 *Chinese,* Recumbent Water-Buffalo, *Ming Dynasty, Norton Gallery, p. 226*

Jean Honré Fragonard's popularity during his lifetime as a painter and engraver was remarkable and due in part to his willingness to follow the fashions of his day. A wide range of subject matter was addressed by this painter of landscapes, portraits, decorative and historical pictures as well as the erotica which gained him a reputation for wanting "to shine in the boudoir." Coming from a family of Provence merchants, he possessed a commercial sensibility and connections with art dealers which made it unnecessary for him to rely on official support, although he did receive commissions from King Louis XV and Mme. Du Barry.

Fragonard began his studies at about age 20 as a pupil of Chardin. He was soon accepted into the studio of Boucher, the King's Painter, who encouraged him to compete for the Prix de Rome, which he immediately won. Four years of study in Rome, where he was encouraged to sketch the surrounding countryside, completed his studies, and he returned to Paris as a privileged artist awarded membership in the French Academy and a studio at the Louvre. Soon after settling in the studio, he began a series of pastorals in the mode of Ruysdaël, an artist whose work he had studied along with Rembrandt's. About 100 such paintings, including *The Return of the Drove*, were completed before he abandoned the subject. This painting, now in the Worcester Museum, shows the fine hand that was to become famous for its fluent brushwork, design and exquisite color.

The Return of the Drove is part of the Theodore T. and Mary G. Ellis collection given to the Museum in 1940. Mr. Ellis, a Worcester newspaper publisher and inventor, amassed his collection between 1917 and 1933. Particularly strong in French and Italian painting, it was the single largest addition to European art in the Museum at the time. A generous Ellis Acquisition Fund allows the Museum to add to its holdings as well as to maintain its present collection.

(Ann W. Heymann)

91

65

225

Norton Gallery and School of Art

In March 1891, the Symbolist poet Octave Mirbeau yielded to requests from Pissarro and Mallarmé that he write an article in the Figaro in support of the reputation of Paul Gauguin and to promote the auction of 30 of his canvases put up for sale at the Hôtel Drouot. The sale was to enable Gauguin to escape to Tahiti. The article was reprinted as introduction to the catalogue. Records are vague as to whether *Christ in Gethsemane* entered Mirbeau's collection as the result of a successful bid or as a return of the favor, but it is fitting that a pictorial highlight of the Symbolist movement should start its distinguished journey to Palm Beach on the walls of one of that movement's first proponents. The men of letters at the Café Voltaire knew Gauguin as a frequent visitor and active participant in their discussions; they respected him as the painter most committed to their point of view.

Gauguin painted this unique picture in Le Pouldu, a remote village in Brittany where the simple faith of the peasants and the road shrines expressing that faith may have inspired the artist to deal with a religious subject. Yet, no sooner have we looked beyond the title and the setting it suggests, than we become aware that Christ, with his massive head, aquiline nose and flaming red hair and beard, betrays every last feature of the artist himself. In Gauguin's mind, creative activity was linked closely with suffering and death. *Agony in the Garden* (as *Christ in Gethsemane* came to be called) illustrates the theme of the artist's self-sacrifice for creative goals, grafted onto the traditional Romantic image of the persecuted artist who identified with Christ in his passion.

In the years prior to his departure for the hoped-for paradise, Gauguin had shifted away from Pissarro's Impressionist style, had broken with Vincent van Gogh (their quarrel need not be retold) and had fallen under the spell of Emile Bernard and his friends in Pont-Aven. The primitivism he had experienced in Martinique began to show, as well as the Symbolist contention that feeling and emotion can be supported, in a picture, by color, shape and line. The Norton picture's brooding spirituality anticipates the pagan deities of Tahiti.

Acquired in 1971, just prior to a rise in Jackson Pollock's international reputation that put his work out of reach of all but investment cartels and foreign governments, *Night Mist* splendidly rewards the Gallery's foresight. Stylistically, it ranks as "transitional" and represents, in the progressive development of this artist's oeuvre, the waning of primordial figuration and atavistic subjects and the ascendancy of an "allover" method of painting. "Psychic automatism" is the term used for this pictorial analogue to stream of consciousness writing. Pollock was still a few years away from achieving pure gestural abstraction.

Abstract Expressionism was in its formative years. Surrealism held sway but Cubism had not been forgotten. To structurally articulate his often large format paintings, Pollock resorted to the analytic Cubist grid still in general use. It was crowded, then overlaid and eventually obliterated. As for content, his vocabulary included shapes that were gleaned from Picasso, Miró and Masson as well as from the Altamira cave and Navajo sand painters. Opinions vary (William S. Rubin has exhaustively dealt with this) as to the Jungian vs. Freudian "screen" through which signals from the inner world and from the world around him were received and reflected by the artist. Strongly interested in symbolism, he sought analysis, and its effect on his work is a matter of record. He had little contact with the Surrealists in exile whose work he knew mostly in reproduction. Withdrawn and not particularly fond of the European example, he was inclined to keep his own counsel.

Admittedly, there are harsh and awkward passages in *Night Mist* as Pollock struggled with the conflicting demands of content and style. The raw power of its cacaphonous imagery is unmistakable. Far from living up to that Modernist dictate of flatness, the black space is dense and threateningly real. While the night is made palpable in *Night Mist*, a vivid reminder of his former mythic subjects' chthonic origins, the mist heralds the gossamer threads of silver enamel soon to descend upon Pollock's canvases as frost upon a window pane.

For the significance of its collections, the Norton Gallery and School of Art is equaled only by the John and Mable Ringling Museum in all of Florida. Typically, they both result from the resolve of civic minded collectors to share their resources with the people of this state and to provide for their care and expansion so as to benefit future generations. The Gallery was founded in 1940 by Ralph Hubbard and Elizabeth Calhoun Norton with the gift of their private collection. Through purchases made with funds provided in trust by the founders, with contributions from various donors and through gifts from art collectors, the Gallery can now boast a first rate representation of 19th and early 20th century French painting and sculpture, American art from 1900 to the present and a small but distinguished collection of Chinese art.

The Chinese collection breaks down in five major areas: archaic bronzes, archaic jades, Buddhist sculpture, late jade carvings and ceramics. The *Recumbent Water-Buffalo* of the mid-Ming period, recently featured in a *Director's Choice* exhibition, was selected for its strong compact form, striking naturalism and elegant carving. The color is a lustrous sage-green and the surface shows graying mottlings. There are some half dozen similar figures posed in the same manner and having roughly the same proportions in collections here and abroad.

It is recorded that the Ming Emperor Yung Lo acquired a jade figure of this type early in his reign (1403-1414) and brought it to Peking where it was displayed in his newly built palace in the Forbidden City. Lo's prized possession served as a model for copyists and imitators but, itself, remained part of the imperial collections until the time of the Boxer uprisings in 1900 when the palaces were looted. Although the *Recumbent Water-Buffalo* that came into the possession of Oscar Raphael and can now be found in the British Museum, is traditionally thought of as the emperor's original treasure, there is no proof positive so the Norton Water-Buffalo has as good a chance as any of being that one time denizen of the Forbidden City.

(Adapted from Horace H. F. Jayne)

201 Frank Stella, Pilicia II, 1973
The Phillips Collection, Washington, D.C.
197 Robert Rauschenberg, Reservoir, 1961
*National Museum of American Art, Smithsonian
Institution*

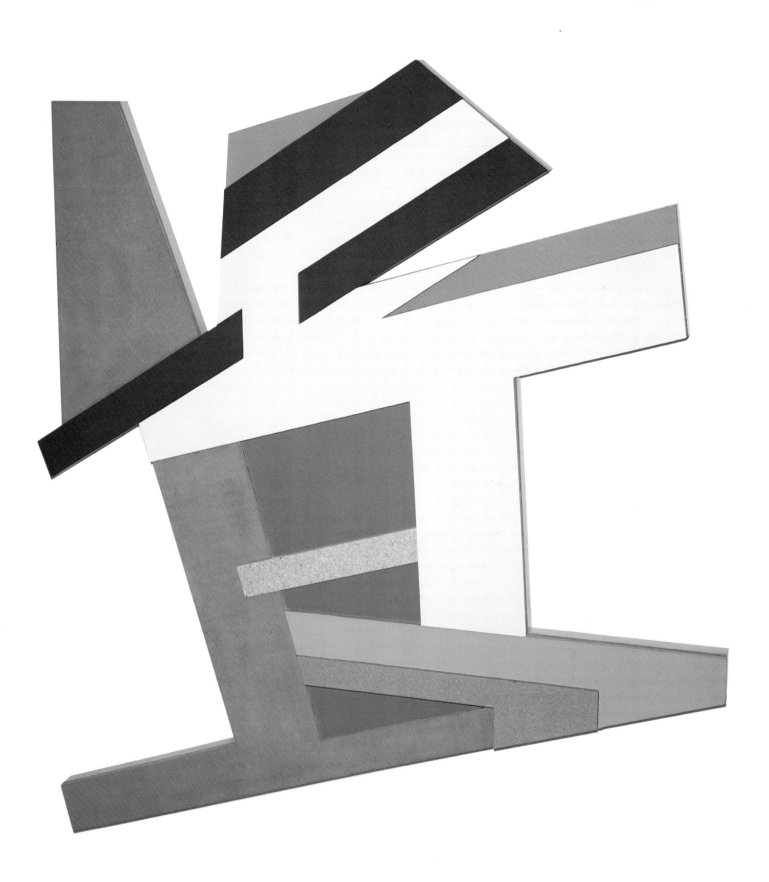

231

List of Works in the Exhibition

The sequence followed in this listing corresponds to the layout of the exhibition thus becoming a visitors' guide.

1 Egyptian, possibly 18th Dynasty (1570-1314 B.C.)
Feline
Bronze with rock crystal, 12 in. [30.5 cm] long
Cincinnati Art Museum
Gift of Mr. and Mrs. John J. Emery, 1972
Ill. p. 71

2 Egyptian, 26th Dynasty (663-332 B.C.)
Head of a King
Granite with traces of red pigment, 9 7/8 in.
[25 cm] high
The Walters Art Gallery, Baltimore, Maryland
Ill. p. 45

3 Persian, Achaemenian (5th century B.C.)
Bowl with repoussé decoration
Silver, 11 3/8 in. [29 cm] diameter
The Metropolitan Museum of Art, New York
Gift of the Kevorkian Foundation, 1955
Exhibitions:
Profil du Metropolitan Museum of Art de New York: de Ramsès à Picasso, Musée des Beaux-Arts, Bordeaux, France, 1981
Ancient Persia: The Art of an Empire, University Art Museum, The University of Texas at Austin, 1978; also
The Walters Art Gallery, Baltimore
Ill. p. 144

4 Cypriot
Head of a Votary and *Head of a Female*, 470-450 B.C.
Limestone, votary, 14 1/8 in. [35.9 cm] high
female, 11 7/16 in. [29 cm] high
The Metropolitan Museum of Art, New York
Cesnola Collection of Antiquities from Cyprus;
Purchased by subscription, 1874-76
Ill. p. 145

5 Roman
Zeus Ammon, c. 120-150
Marble, 12 3/16 in. [31 cm] high
Museum of Fine Arts, Boston
Gift of Edward Perry Warren by exchange, 1959
Provenance:
Sir Robert Mond
Lord Nathan, Churt House, Rotherfield,
Crowborough, Sussex
Exhibitions:
Aspects of Ancient Greece, Allentown Art Museum, Pennsylvania, 1979
The Ruins of Rome, The University Museum, University of Pennsylvania, Philadelphia, 1964;
also Massachusetts Institute of Technology, Cambridge, 1965
Ill. p. 56

6 Chinese, Shang Dynasty (c. 1750-1100 B.C.)
Kuang-ting (3-legged vessel), Anyang period, 1300-1100 B.C.
Bronze, 13 in. [33 cm] long
Lowe Art Museum, The University of Miami, Coral Gables, Florida
Gift of Stephen Junkunc III, 1958
Provenance:
Stephen Junkunc III, Chicago
C. T. Loo, New York
Exhibitions:
An Exhibition of Ancient Chinese Ritual Bronzes, The Detroit Institute of Arts, 1940
Ill. p. 77

7 Chinese, Shang Dynasty (c. 1750-1100 B.C.) or Western Chou (1100-770 B.C.)
Ts'un in the Shape of an Owl
Bronze, 12 1/2 in. [31.7 cm] high
The Minneapolis Institute of Arts
Bequest of Alfred F. Pillsbury, 1950
Provenance:
Alfred F. Pillsbury
Ill. p. 116

8 Chinese, Eastern Chou Dynasty (771-265 B.C.)
Pi disc, Spring and Autumn Period, 771-476 B.C.
Jade, 9 5/8 in. [24.5 cm] diameter
Seattle Art Museum
Eugene Fuller Memorial Collection, 1939
Exhibitions:
Chinese Jades throughout the Ages, Arts Council of Great Britian and Oriental Ceramic Society, Victoria and Albert Museum, London, 1975
Gift to a City, Portland Art Museum, Oregon, 1965
Art of Ancient East, Fine Arts Pavilion, Seattle World's Fair, 1962; also
The University Museum, University of Pennsylvania, Philadelphia
The Cleveland Museum of Art (as *Chinese Jade*), 1962-63
Early Chinese Jade, Museum of Art, University of Michigan, Ann Arbor, 1953
Ill. p. 213

9 Chinese, Northern Wei Dynasty (386-535)
Head of a Bodhisattva, early 6th century
Painted sandstone, 22 in. [56 cm] high
The Dayton Art Institute
Gift of the Honorable Jefferson Patterson, 1959
Provenance:
Temple cave at Yun-Kang, Shansi Province
Ill. p. 60

10 Chinese, T'ang Dynasty (618-906)
Equestrian Figure, 7th-8th century
Glazed earthenware, 15 1/2 in. [39.4 cm] high
The Nelson-Atkins Museum of Art, Kansas City
Nelson Fund, 1949
Ill. p. 119

11 Indian, Central India or Rajasthan
Ganga, 9th century
Red sandstone, 25 x 23 x 8 3/4 in.
[63.5 x 58.4 x 22.2 cm]
Los Angeles County Museum of Art
From the Nasli and Alice Heeramaneck Collection
Museum Associates Purchase, 1969
Exhibitions:
The Arts of India and Nepal: The Nasli and Alice Heeramaneck Collection, Museum of Fine Arts, Boston, 1967; also
Phoenix Art Museum, 1972
Ill. p. 120

12 Nepalese
Standing Figure of Vishnu, 10th century
Gilt bronze, 9 11/16 in. [24.6 cm] high
The Brooklyn Museum
Gift of Frederic B. Pratt, 1929
Exhibitions:
The Art of Nepal, The Asia Society, New York, 1964
Ill. p. 49

13 Japanese, Heian period (12th century)
Guardian Deity
Gilt bronze, 7 11/16 in. [19.5 cm] high
Museum of Fine Arts, Boston
Gift of Ellen H. Gleason, 1947
Ill. p. 56

14 Chinese, Southern Sung Dynasty (1127-1279)
Three Chün-ware Cups
Glazed stoneware, 2 cups,
3 7/16 in. [8.7 cm] diameter
1 cup, 3 3/8 in. [8.5 cm] diameter
Fogg Art Museum, Harvard University, Cambridge, Massachusetts
Gift of Ernest B. Dane, Class of 1892, and Helen P. Dane, 1942
Provenance:
Ernest Blaney Dane and Helen Pratt Dane
Ill. p. 53

15 Attributed to Lo-ch'uang (Chinese, 13th century, late Sung Dynasty)
Han-Shan Reading a Scroll
Ink on paper, 23 3/8 x 11 3/8 in.
[59.3 x 28.9 cm]
University Art Museum, University of California, Berkeley
Museum purchase, 1970
Provenance:
S. Yabumoto Ltd., Tokyo, Japan
Ill, p. 46

16 Pre-Columbian Mexico, Olmec (13th-6th century, B.C.)
Figure of Shaman in Transformation Pose, c. 800 B.C.
Stone with traces of red pigment, 7 1/8 in.
[18 cm] high
The Art Museum, Princeton University
Gift of Mrs. Gerard B. Lambert, 1976
Ill. p. 187

17 Pre-Columbian Mexico, Maya (late Classic Period, 750-950)
Hacha in the form of a Human Head
Stone, 12 in. [30.5 cm] high
The Art Institute of Chicago
Ada Turnbull Hertle Fund, 1970
Ill. p. 68

18 Pre-Columbian Peru, Lambayeque Valley, Chimu
Cup with Frog Motif, 900-1100
Gold, 5 5/8 in. [14.3 cm] high
Dallas Museum of Art
The Nora and John Wise Collection, gift of Mr. and Mrs. Jake L. Hamon, the Eugene McDermott family,
Mr. and Mrs. Algur H. Meadows and the Meadows Foundation, and
Mr. and Mrs. John D. Murchison, 1976
Ill. p. 65

19 German, Hildesheim (12th century)
Follower of Eilbertus
Arm Reliquary (from Guelph Treasure), c. 1175
Silver gilt and enamel, 20 in. [50.8 cm] high
The Cleveland Museum of Art
Purchased by the John Huntington Art and Polytechnic Trust, 1930

Provenance:
Ducal House of Brunswick-Lüneburg,
Germany
Treasury, Cathedral of St. Blasius,
Brunswick, Germany
Exhibitions:
Die Zeit der Staufer, Wurttembergisches
Landesmuseum, Stuttgart, Germany, 1977
Ill. p. 72

20 French, Limoges (first half of 13th century)
The Crucifixion: plaque for a book cover
Champlevé enamel on gilt copper,
12 13/16 x 8 1/4 in. [32.5 x 21 cm]
The Pierpont Morgan Library, New York
Provenance:
J. Pierpont Morgan, 1910
Seligman, Paris, 1908
Octave Homberg
Exhibitions:
The Year 1200, Metropolitan Museum of Art,
New York, 1970
Ill. p. 154

21 French, Limoges (late 12th century)
Crucifix, 1190-1200
Champlevé enamel on copper,
14 13/16 x 9 7/8 in. [37.5 x 25 cm]
The Walters Art Gallery, Baltimore
Exhibitions:
The Year 1200, The Metropolitan Museum of Art,
New York, 1970
Ill. p. 35

22 French, Limoges (13th century)
Châsse: Scenes of St. Stephen, 1220-30
Champlevé enamel on gilt copper,
4 x 4 1/8 x 2 7/8 in.
[10.1 x 10.5 x 7.3 cm]
Memorial Art Gallery of the University of
Rochester, New York
R. T. Miller Fund, 1949
Provenance:
Parke-Bernet Galleries, New York
Joseph Brummer, New York, 1949
Otto H. Kahn, New York
Exhibitions:
The Crusades, University Art Gallery, State
University of New York at Binghamton, 1980
Medieval Art in Upstate New York, Everson
Museum of Art of Syracuse and Onondaga
County, New York, 1974
Ill. p. 191

23 Italian, possibly Padua (14th century)
*Single leaf from an Antiphonary depicting
the Last Judgment within an initial "A"*, c. 1300
Tempera and gold leaf on vellum,
21 5/8 x 14 3/8 in. [55 x 36.5 cm]
The Pierpont Morgan Library, New York
Provenance:
J. Pierpont Morgan, 1907
L. S. Olschki, Florence
Exhibitions:
Medieval and Renaissance Music Manuscripts,
Toledo Museum of Art, 1953
Ill. p. 154

24 Hungarian, (14th century)
*Single leaf from a life of Christ and
the Saints: St. Bartholomew*, c. 1340

Tempera with gold leaf on vellum,
8 1/2 x 6 1/2 in. [21.5 x 16.5 cm]
The Pierpont Morgan Library, New York
Purchase, 1955
Provenance:
Christopher Norris of Polesden Lacey, Bookham,
England, 1936
Sotheby's, London, 1909
Angelo Saluzzo, 1630
Giovanni Battista Saluzzo (1579-1642), Genoa
Ill. p. 134

25 French, Atelier of the Diptychs of
the Passion (mid-14th century)
Diptych: The Nativity and the Crucifixion
Ivory, 4 7/8 x 3 3/8 in. [12.4 x 8.5 cm]
The Metropolitan Museum of Art, New York
Rogers Fund, 1911
Exhibitions:
Medieval Images, The Katonah Gallery, Katonah,
New York, 1979
Treasures from the Metropolitan, Indianapolis
Museum of Art, 1971
Ill. p. 147

26 French, 15th century
Book of Hours: page depicting the Entombment,
c. 1450
Tempera with gold on vellum, 19th century
velvet binding, 6 1/4 x 4 3/8 in. [16 x 11 cm]
The Walters Art Gallery, Baltimore, Maryland
Provenance:
L. S. Olschki, Florence
Thorpe, 1833
P. & A. Hanrott, London
Ill. p. 44

27 **FRA ANGELICO** (Guido di Pietro) (Italian,
c.1400-1455)
The Temptation of St. Anthony the Abbot, c. 1430
Tempera on panel, 7 1/4 x 11 1/16 in.
[18.4 x 28 cm]
The Museum of Fine Arts, Houston
Edith A. and Percy S. Straus Collection, 1944
Provenance:
Percy S. Straus, 1930
K. W. Bachstitz, The Hague
A. S. Drey, Munich
Count Ingenheim of Schloss Reisewitz, Silesia
William IV of Prussia
Exhibitions:
*Mostra delle opere di Fra Angelico nel V
Centenario della morte (1455-1955)*,
Palazzo Apostolico Vaticano, Rome, 1955; also
Museo di San Marco dell' Angelico, Florence,
1955
Ill. p. 100

28 **LIPPI**, Filippino (Italian, Florentine, 1457-1504)
The Lamentation of Christ, c. 1485
Brown ink heightened with white,
7 1/8 x 10 3/8 in. [18 x 26.3 cm]
Allen Memorial Art Museum, Oberlin College,
Ohio
R. T. Miller, Jr. Fund, 1954
Provenance:
Mrs. Langton Douglas, 1953
P. & D. Colnaghi, London
C. R. Rudolf, London, 1936
Henry Oppenheimer, London, 1917
Earl of Pembroke, Salisbury

Exhibitions:
The Italian Renaissance, Vassar College Art
Gallery, Poughkeepsie, New York, 1968
An American University Collection, London
County Council, Kenwood, 1962
Master Drawings of the Italian Renaissance, The
Detroit Institute of Arts, 1960
Great Master Drawings of Seven Centuries, M.
Knoedler & Co., New York, 1959
Ill. p. 175

29 **SCHONGAUER**, Martin
(German,c.1435-1491)
Christ on the Cross with the Virgin and St. John
Engraving, 11 1/2 x 7 5/8 in. [29.2 x 19.4 cm]
Worcester Art Museum
Museum purchase, 1934
Provenance:
Fürstlich Hohenzollernsches Museum,
Sigmaringen, Germany
Ill. p. 224

30 **RAPHAEL** (Raffaello Santi) (Italian, Urbino,
1483-1520)
Emilia Pia da Montefeltre, 1502-1504
Oil and probably some tempera on wood,
16 3/4 x 11 1/4 in. [42.5 x 28.5 cm]
The Baltimore Museum of Art
The Jacob Epstein Collection, 1951
Provenance:
Jacob Epstein, 1925
Kleinberger Galleries, New York, 1925
Coray-Stoop Collection, Erlenbach, Switzerland
Vienna art market, early 1920s
Fondaco dei Tedeschi, Venice
Inventory of the Medici, Florence
Storerooms of Urbino
Exhibitions:
Raphael and America, National Gallery of Art,
Washington, D.C., 1983
Ill. p. 42

31 **COSTA**, Lorenzo (Italian, Bologna,
c.1460-1535)
Portrait of a Lady, c. 1506
Oil on canvas, transferred from panel,
17 5/8 x 13 5/8 in. [44.7 x 34.6 cm]
The Currier Gallery of Art, Manchester,
New Hampshire
Currier Funds, 1947
Provenance:
Nicholas M. Acquavella, New York, 1945
Jules S. Bache, New York, 1927
Kleinberger Galleries, New York, 1927
Mumm von Schwarzenstein, Frankfurt am Main,
1873
Private collection, Milan
Ill. p. 123

32 Italian, Caffagiolo (16th century)
Plate: David with the Head of Goliath, c. 1510-20
Majolica, 13 1/2 in. [34.3 cm] diameter
The Metropolitan Museum of Art, New York
Robert Lehman Collection, 1975
Provenance:
Robert Lehman, New York
Hearst Collection
Ill. p. 146

33 DÜRER, Albrecht (German, 1471-1528)
Design for Mural Decoration (for Nuremberg
Town Hall), 1521
Brown ink with watercolor on cut and mounted
paper, 10 1/16 x 13 3/4 in. [25.5 x 35 cm]
The Pierpont Morgan Library, New York
Provenance:
J. Pierpont Morgan
Charles Fairfax Murray, 1902
Sir John Charles Robinson
Private Collector
Sir Peter Lely
Ill. p. 133

34 ISENBRANT, Adriaen (active 1510-1551)
*Diptych: Madonna and Child with a
Hillensberger Donor*, 1513
Oil on wood panel, 12 1/2 x 8 3/8 in.
[31.2 x 21.3 cm]
Lowe Art Museum, The University of Miami,
Coral Gables, Florida
Samuel H. Kress Collection, 1961
Provenance:
National Gallery, Washington, D.C., 1939
Samuel H. Kress, New York, 1927
A. Contini Bonacossi, Rome, after 1923
Ernst Augustus, Duke of Brunswick and Lüneburg
King George V of Hannover, Schloss
Herrenhausen, after 1831-1878
Bernard Hausmann, Hannover, before 1827
Ill. p. 77

35 Italian, Milan (16th century)
*Casket, with coat of arms of Pier Luigi Farnese,
First Duke of Parma and Piacenza*, 1545-47
Wood overlaid with iron damascened in gold
and silver, 5 7/8 x 13 7/8 x 8 7/8 in.
[15 x 35.2 x 22.5 cm]
The Metropolitan Museum of Art, New York
Purchase, Morris Loeb Gift, 1956
Provenance:
Trivulzio, Milan
Ill. p. 147

36 LOTTO, Lorenzo (Italian, Venice, 1480-1556)
*Portrait of a Dominican Friar as
St. Peter Martyr*, c. 1549
Oil on canvas, 34 13/16 x 26 3/4 in.
[88.5 x 68 cm]
Fogg Art Museum, Harvard University,
Cambridge, Massachusetts
Gift of Edward W. Forbes in memory of
Alice F. Cary, 1964
Provenance:
Edward Waldo Forbes, 1906
C. Fairfax Murray, London
Exhibitions:
The Italian Heritage (Benefit for the Committee
to Rescue Italian Art), Wildenstein & Co.,
New York, 1967
Ill. p. 37

37 After Pieter Bruegel (Flemish, c. 1528-1569)
The Festival of Saint George, c. 1559
Etching and engraving, 13 3/16 x 20 11/16 in.
[23.4 x 52.4 cm]
National Gallery of Art, Washington, D.C.
Rosenwald Collection, 1964
Provenance:
Lessing J. Rosenwald, 1959
William H. Schab, New York

Exhibitions:
Lessing J. Rosenwald: Tribute to a Collector,
National Gallery of Art, Washington, D.C., 1982
*Prints by Peter Bruegel from the National Gallery of
Art, Rosenwald Collection*, Rutgers University Art
Gallery, New Brunswick, New Jersey, 1973-74
Ill. p. 217

38 VISCHER, Georg (German, 1528-1592)
Fertility
Bronze, 23 1/4 in. [59 cm] high
Museum of Art, Rhode Island School of Design,
Providence
Museum Appropriation and Friends Fund, 1920
Exhibitions:
The Italian Heritage, Wildenstein & Co.,
New York, 1967
Renaissance Bronzes in American Collections,
Smith College Museum of Art, Northampton,
Massachusetts, 1964
Master Bronzes, The Buffalo Fine Arts Academy,
Albright Art Gallery, Buffalo, New York, 1937
An Exhibition of European Art 1450-1500,
The Brooklyn Museum, New York, 1936
Ill. p. 189

39 After Giovanni da Bologna (Italian, 1524-1608)
Mercury, after 1600
Bronze, 22 3/4 in. [57.8 cm] high
Los Angeles County Museum of Art
Gift of Mitchell Samuels, 1951
Provenance:
Vincent Astor
Astor family collection
Jacques Seligmann
Sir Thomas Gibson Carmichael, England
Exhibitions:
The Figure in Bronze: An Italian Classical Heritage,
Museum of Fine Arts of St. Petersburg, Florida,
1981; also
J.B. Speed Art Museum, Louisville, Kentucky
Ill. p. 121

40 GHEYN II, Jacques de (Dutch, 1565-1629)
Mountain Landscape, 1590-1600
Brown ink with black chalk,
11 1/2 x 15 3/8 in. [29.2 x 39 cm]
The Pierpont Morgan Library, New York
Purchased as the gift of the Fellows, 1967
Provenance:
R. M. Light & Co., Boston, 1967
James Murray Usher, London
Mrs. Murray Baillie, Ilston Grange,
near Leicester
Exhibitions:
*Il Paesaggio nel disegno del cinquecento
europeo*, Académie de France à Rome,
Villa Medici, Rome, 1972-73
Ill. p. 155

41 VANNI, Francesco (Italian, c. 1563-1610)
Madonna with Infant Jesus and St. John
Red chalk, 7 x 5 1/4 in. [17.7 x 13.4 cm]
Bowdoin College Museum of Art,
Brunswick, Maine
Bequest of the Honorable James Bowdoin III,
1811
Provenance:
James Bowdoin III, Boston, Massachusetts

Exhibitions:
*The Draughtsman's Eye: Late Italian Renaissance
Schools and Styles*, The Cleveland Museum of Art,
1979
Ill. p. 51

42 DUPRÉ, Guillaume (French, c. 1576-1643)
*Pair of medals: Francesco de'Medici and
Maria Magdalena of Austria*, 1613
Bronze, hollow cast, 3 11/16 in.
[9.3 cm] diameter, each
Bowdoin College Museum of Art, Brunswick,
Maine
Molinari Collection, 1966
Exhibitions:
*Medals and Plaquettes from the Molinari Collection
at Bowdoin College*, Bowdoin College Museum of
Art, 1976; also
Carpenter Galleries, Dartmouth College
Ill. p. 50

43 SUSINI, Antonio (Italian, Florentine,
died 1624)
Lion Attacking a Horse
Bronze, 12 in. [30.5 cm] long
The Detroit Institute of Arts
City of Detroit purchase, 1925
Provenance:
Julius Goldschmidt
Ill. p. 92

44 GUERCINO (Giovanni Francesco Barbieri)
(Italian, 1591-1666)
Boy in a Large Hat from *Album of Caricatures*,
c.1630-1650
Brown ink with iron gall wash, 6 1/2 x 4 3/4 in.
[16.5 x 12.1 cm]
The Art Museum, Princeton University
Dan Fellows Platt Collection, 1948
Provenance:
Dan Fellows Platt, 1928
Savile Gallery, London
Clara J. Pearce
W. E. Price
Lt. Col. John Palmer, 1881
Sir Joshua Reynolds
Ill. p. 187

45 CASTIGLIONE, Giovanni Benedetto (Italian,
1610-1665)
A Pagan Sacrifice, c. 1645-50
Oil on paper, 22 5/8 x 16 3/4 in. [57.6 x 42.5 cm]
The Art Institute of Chicago
Gift of Clarence Buckingham, 1968
Provenance:
Charles Slatkin Galleries, New York, 1967
Lord Kenneth Clark of Saltwood
E. Parsons, London, 1928
Sir W. Drake
Ill. p. 68

46 HONTHORST, Gerrit van (Dutch, 1590-1656)
The Flea Hunt, 1621
Oil on canvas, 52 1/4 x 78 1/2 in.
[133 x 199.5 cm]
The Dayton Art Institute
Museum purchase with funds provided in part by
the Art Ball, 1980

Provenance:
H. Shickman Gallery, New York
Xavier de Salas, London
A. Cirera, 1950
Howard Spensley, London
Ill. p. 81

47 **BRUGGHEN,** Hendrick ter (Dutch, 1588-1629)
Old Man Writing by Candlelight, c. 1627
Oil on canvas, 25 5/8 x 20 3/4 in.
[65.8 x 52.7 cm]
Smith College Museum of Art,
Northampton, Massachusetts
Gift of Adeline F. Wing ('98) and Caroline R.
Wing ('96), 1957
Provenance:
G. Cramer, The Hague
J. Oomkens, Huizen
Mej. E. L. A. C. ter Brugghen, Baarn, 1926
J. R. Baron van Keppel, Apeldoorn
Exhibitions:
Hendrick Terbrugghen in America, The Dayton
Art Institute, 1965; also
The Baltimore Museum of Art
Let There Be Light, Wadsworth Atheneum,
Hartford, 1964
The Young Rembrandt and His Times,
John Herron Museum of Art, Indianapolis, 1958
Ill. p. 158

48 **GOYEN,** Jan van (Dutch, 1596-1656)
The Thunderstorm, 1641
Oil on canvas, 54 1/4 x 72 1/8 in.
[137.8 x 183.2 cm]
The Fine Arts Museums of San Francisco
Purchased by the City and County of
San Francisco, 1948
Provenance:
Baroness Mathilda Louisa Thyssen-Bornemisza,
Lenox, Massachusetts, 1948
Baron Heinrich Thyssen-Bornemisza, Schloss
Rohoncz, Hungary, 1929
Baron d'Erlanger, Paris, 1901
Arthur Kay, Glasgow, 1889
P. IJver, Amsterdam, 1771
Gerrit Braamcamp, Amsterdam
Exhibitions:
The Young Rembrandt and His Times,
John Herron Museum of Art, Indianapolis, 1958;
also *The Fine Arts Gallery*, San Diego, 1958
Ill. p. 197

49 **HALS,** Frans (Dutch, 1581/95? - 1666)
Joseph Coymans, 1644
Oil on canvas, 33 x 27 1/2 in. [84 x 70 cm]
Wadsworth Atheneum, Hartford
The Ella Gallup Sumner and
Mary Catlin Sumner Collection, 1958
Provenance:
Louis Kaplan, New York, 1945
Mrs. Isabel van Wie Willys, New York
John North Willys, Toledo and New York
Maurice Kann, Paris
Sir James Carnegie, Bart., 9th Earl of Southesk,
London, 1850
Exhibitions:
*Frans Hals: Exhibition on the Occasion of the
Centenary of the Municipal Museum of Haarlem,
1862-1962*, Frans Hals Museum, Haarlem, 1962
Ill. p. 104

50 **HEEM,** Jan Davidsz de (Dutch, 1606-1684)
Still Life, c. 1645
Oil on canvas, 17 3/4 x 24 1/16 in.
[45.1 x 61.1 cm]
Allen Memorial Art Museum, Oberlin College,
Ohio
Mrs. F. F. Prentiss Fund, 1954
Provenance:
Eugene L. Garbáty, Berlin and New York
Dr. Leyendecker, Berlin
Hermitage, Leningrad
Exhibitions:
Treasures from the Allen Memorial Art Museum,
The Minneapolis Institute of Arts, 1966
An American University Collection, London
County Council, Kenwood, 1962
Ill. p. 165

51 **REMBRANDT** Harmensz van Rijn (Dutch,
1606-1669)
Christ Finding the Apostles Asleep, c. 1654
Brown ink, 7 3/16 x 11 in. [18.3 x 27.9 cm]
Sterling and Francine Clark Art Institute,
Williamstown, Massachusetts
Provenance:
Robert Sterling Clark, 1913
Colnaghi, London
J. P. Heseltine, London
R. P. Roupell, London
Exhibitions:
*Seventeenth-Century Dutch Drawings from
American Collections*, organized by International
Exhibitions Foundation, Washington, D.C.,1977,
to National Gallery of Art, Washington, D.C.
The Denver Art Museum
Kimbell Art Museum, Fort Worth
Rembrandt After 300 Years, The Art Institute
of Chicago, 1969; also
The Minneapolis Insitute of Arts, 1969
The Detroit Institute of Arts, 1970
Treasures from the Clark Art Institute, Wildenstein
& Co., New York, 1967
Ill. p. 223

52 **REMBRANDT** Harmensz van Rijn (Dutch,
1606-1669)
Joseph Accused by Potiphar's Wife, 1665
Oil on canvas, 41 5/8 x 38 1/2 in.
[105.7 x 97.8 cm]
National Gallery of Art, Washington, D.C.
Andrew W. Mellon Collection, 1937
Provenance:
M. Knoedler & Co., New York
Empress Catherine II, for the Hermitage, 1763
J. E. Gotzkowsky, Berlin, 1760
G. Hoet, The Hague
Exhibitions:
*Gods, Saints & Heroes: Dutch Painting
in the Age of Rembrandt*, National Gallery
of Art, Washington, D.C., 1980; also
The Detroit Institute of Arts
Rijksmuseum Amsterdam
Rembrandt in the National Gallery of Art,
National Gallery of Art, Washington, D.C., 1969
Ill. p. 232

53 **MAN,** Cornelis de (Dutch, 1621-1706)
Interior of Oude Kerk, Delft, c. 1660
Oil on canvas, 41 x 48 1/4 in. [104 x 122 cm]
Columbus Museum of Art, Ohio
Museum purchase, Howald Fund II, 1981

Provenance:
Richard J. Collins, New York
Ill. p. 75

54 **STEEN,** Jan (Dutch, c. 1626-1679)
Moses Striking the Rock, c. 1660-61
Oil on canvas, 37 3/8 x 38 3/4 in.
[94.9 x 98.4 cm]
John G. Johnson Collection
Philadelphia Museum of Art
Provenance:
John G. Johnson, 1893
Baron Konigswarter, Vienna, 1892
A. Hulot, Paris, 1868
Prince Demidoff, Galleria San Donato, Florence
C. J. Nieuwenhuys, 1837
Count F. de Robiano, Brussels, 1826
Roothaan, Amsterdam, 1818
P. N. Quarles van Ufford, Amsterdam
A. Delfos, 1781
J. Tak, Zoeterwoude, 1745
Zeger Tierens, The Hague
Exhibitions:
Old Masters and the Bible, The Israel Museum,
Jerusalem, 1965
Seven Centuries of Painting, The California
Palace of the Legion of Honor and The
M. H. de Young Memorial Museum,
San Francisco, 1939-40
Ill. p. 173

55 **HOBBEMA,** Meindert (Dutch, 1638-1709)
Wooded Landscape with Watermill
Oil on canvas, 40 1/4 x 53 in. [102.2 x 134.6 cm]
The Minneapolis Institute of Arts
The William Hood Dunwoody Fund, 1941
Provenance:
M. Knoedler & Co., 1941
Baron Gustave de Rothschild, Paris, 1835
Baroness de Rothschild, Baron Alphonse de
Rothschild, Paris
M. Zachary, 1828
Charles Offley, Esq.
Crawford, 1806
Exhibitions:
*Paintings and Sculpture from the Minneapolis
Institute of Arts*, M. Knoedler & Co., New York,
1957; also
The Society of the Four Arts, Palm Beach,
Florida, 1957
Old Masters, from Midwestern Museums,
Dayton Art Institute, 1948
A Thousand Years of Landscape East and West,
Museum of Fine Arts, Boston, 1945
Great Dutch Masters, Duveen Galleries,
New York, 1942.
Ill. p. 114

56 **HONDECOETER,** Melchior de (Dutch
1636-1695)
Poultry in a Landscape
Oil on canvas, 36 3/4 x 44 7/8 in.
[93.7 x 113.3 cm]
The Toledo Museum of Art
Gift of Edward Drummond Libbey, 1949
Provenance:
H. Van der Ploeg, Amsterdam
Exhibitions:
*Dutch Exhibition Commemorating 300th
Anniversary of Landing of the Dutch*, Wilmington
Society of Fine Arts, Delaware, 1951
Ill. p. 215

57 RUBENS, Peter Paul (Flemish, 1577-1640)
Portrait of the Archduke Ferdinand, 1635
Oil on canvas, 45 3/4 x 37 in. [116.2 x 94 cm]
The John and Mable Ringling Museum of Art,
Sarasota, Florida
Museum purchase, 1948
Provenance:
J. Pierpont Morgan, 1898
The Honorable Greville Richard Vernon
Robert Vernon, First Baron Lyveden
The Earl of Upper Ossory
Sir Joshua Reynolds, 1771
Exhibitions:
*Masterworks from the John and Mable Ringling
Museum of Art*, Wildenstein & Co., New York,
1981; also
Tampa Museum, Florida, 1981
P.P. Rubens, Koninklijk Museum voor Schone
Kunsten, Antwerp, 1977
*From El Greco to Pollock: Early and Late Works
by European and American Artists*, Baltimore
Museum of Art, 1968
Arts of Man, Dallas Museum of Fine Arts, 1962
The Pierpont Morgan Treasures, Wadsworth
Atheneum, Hartford, 1960
Rubens, Wildenstein & Co., New York, 1951
Ill. p. 195

58 TENIERS, David (The Younger) (Flemish,
1610-1690)
Tavern Scene, 1680
Oil on canvas, 17 1/4 x 23 1/2 in.
[43.8 x 59.7 cm]
Memorial Art Gallery of the University of
Rochester, New York
Buswell-Hochstetter Bequest, 1955
Provenance:
Ralph Hochstetter, Buffalo, New York, 1941
Mrs. Henry Buswell (Bertha Hochstetter Buswell)
Lord Huntingfield, England
Exhibitions:
*European Paintings from the Rochester Memorial
Art Gallery*, Munson-Williams-Proctor Institute,
Utica, New York, 1967
Ill. p. 196

59 VELAZQUEZ, Diego de Silva y (Spanish,
1599-1660)
Philip IV, King of Spain, c. 1655
Oil on canvas, 22 1/4 x 19 3/4 in.
[56.3 x 50.2 cm]
Cincinnati Art Museum
Bequest of Mary M. Emery, 1927
Provenance:
Mary M. Emery, Cincinnati, 1925
C. Romer-Williams, London
Marshal Soult(?), Duke of Dalmatia, 1809-1812(?)
Exhibitions:
Baroque Art, The Denver Art Museum, 1971
El Greco to Goya, John Herron Museum of
Art, Indianapolis, 1963; also
Museum of Art, Rhode Island School of
Design, Providence
Soldiers and Saints in Old Spain and New,
Joslyn Art Museum, Omaha, 1962
Masterpieces of Spanish Paintings, Columbus
Gallery of Fine Arts, Ohio, 1954
Opening Exhibition, Birmingham Museum of
Art, Alabama, 1951
Forty-Three Portraits, Wadsworth Atheneum,
Hartford, 1937

Spanish Paintings from El Greco to Goya,
The Metropolitan Museum of Art, New York,
1928
Ill. p. 59

60 LORRAIN, Claude, (Gellée) (French,
1600-1682)
The Rest on the Flight into Egypt, c.1634
Oil on canvas, 29 1/2 x 36 in.
[74.9 x 90.5 cm]
Joslyn Art Museum, Omaha
Museum purchase, 1957
Provenance:
Koetser Gallery, London, 1956
Sir H. W. Duff-Gordon, 1911
Sir Herbert Edmund Lewis, 1883
Reverend Sir Gilbert Lewis
Exhibitions:
*France in the Golden Age: Seventeenth-Century
French Paintings in American Collections*,
Galeries Nationales d'Exposition du Grand
Palais, Paris, 1982; also
The Metropolitan Museum of Art, New York
The Art Institute of Chicago
Ill. p. 177

61 POUSSIN, Nicolas (French, 1594-1665)
The Holy Family with the Infant St. John, 1655
Oil on canvas, 76 x 50 1/2 in. [193 x 128.3 cm]
The John and Mable Ringling Museum of Art,
Sarasota, Florida
Provenance:
John Ringling, 1929
Earl of Yarborough
Sir Richard Worsley, 1751-1808
Collection Pointel
Exhibitions:
Nicolas Poussin, Musée National du Louvre,
Palais du Louvre, Paris, 1960
Ill. p. 210

62 MILLET, Jean-François, called Francisque
(Flemish, 1642-1679)
Landscape with Mountains and a Plume of Smoke,
after 1660
Oil on copper panel, 13 7/8 x 17 7/8 in.
[34.2 x 45.5 cm]
University Art Museum, University of California,
Berkeley
Museum purchase, 1968
Provenance:
F. Kleinberger, New York
Ill. p. 47

63 LAMERIE, Paul de (British, 1688-1751)
Cup and Cover, 1742
Silver, 15 1/2 in. [39.3 cm] high
Sterling and Francine Clark Art Institute,
Williamstown, Massachusetts
Provenance:
Robert Sterling Clark, 1931
Crichton & Co., New York
Exhibitions:
Treasures from the Clark Art Institute,
Wildenstein & Co., New York, 1967
Ill. p. 223

64 French, 18th century
Parade Helmet (Burgonet) and *Shield (Medusa)*,
c.1760
Bronze, silvered and gilded,
helmet, 15 in. [38 cm] high
shield, 23 1/8 x 15 1/4 in. [58.7 x 38.7 cm]
The Metropolitan Museum of Art, New York
Rogers Fund, 1904
Provenance:
Collection Maurice de Tallyrand-Périgord,
Duc de Dino, Paris
Collection Joyeau, sold in Paris, 1849
Anonymous collection, sold in Paris, 1845
Exhibitions:
*Profil du Metropolitan Museum of Art de New York:
De Ramsès à Picasso*, Musée des Beaux-Arts,
Bordeaux, 1981
Medieval and Renaissance Arms and Armor,
Los Angeles County Museum of Art, 1952; also
1953-54
California Palace of the Legion of Honor,
San Francisco
Department of Fine Arts, Carnegie Institute
Ill. p. 132, 146

65 Chinese, mid-Ming Dynasty (1368-1644)
Recumbent Water-Buffalo, 16th-17th century
Jade, 11 3/8 in. [28.9 cm] long
Norton Gallery and School of Art,
West Palm Beach, Florida, 1942
Ill. p. 225

66 Tibetan (17th century)
Tanka: Guru Drag-po-che and Retinue
Tempera and gold on cotton, 31 x 25 in.
[78.7 x 63.5 cm]
The Newark Museum
Crane Collection, 1911
Provenance:
Dr. Albert L. Shelton, Tibet
Ill. p. 129

67 ROSHU, Fukaye (Japanese, 1699-1757,
Edo Period)
Utsunoyama: The Pass through the Mountains
Six-fold screen, color and gold on paper,
53 3/8 x 107 in. [135.6 x 271.7 cm]
The Cleveland Museum of Art
Museum purchase, John L. Severance Fund, 1954
Provenance:
Howard C. Hollis, Cleveland
T. Hara, Yokohama
Exhibitions:
Japanese Decorative Style, The Cleveland Museum
of Art, 1961
*Masterpieces of Asian Art in American
Collections*, Asia House, New York, 1960
Ill. p. 62-3

68 SMIBERT, John (American, 1688-1751)
Portrait of James Bowdoin II, 1736
Oil on canvas, 34 7/8 x 26 7/8 in.
[88.6 x 68.3 cm]
Bowdoin College Museum of Art, Brunswick,
Maine, 1826
Provenance:
Sarah Bowdoin Dearborn, widow of
James Bowdoin III
Bowdoin family collection

Exhibitions:
Masterworks by Artists of New England, The Currier Gallery of Art, Manchester, New Hampshire, 1982
The Painter and the New World, Musée des Beaux-Arts de Montreal, Canada, 1967
Ill. p. 36

69 **WEST,** Benjamin (American, 1738-1820)
Portrait of Stephen Carmick, 1756
Oil on canvas, 47 1/8 x 37 1/8 in.
[119.7 x 94.3 cm]
The Santa Barbara Museum of Art
The Preston Morton Collection of American Art, 1960
Provenance:
Hirschl & Adler, 1960
Louis G. Carmick, 1934
Louis Carmick, 1876
The Carmick family
Exhibitions:
First Flowers of Our Wilderness, University of Arizona Museum of Art, Tucson, 1976; also
Santa Barbara Museum of Art
Wichita State Museum, Kansas
Georgia Museum of Art, Athens
Vignettes of American Art and Life,
Honolulu Academy of Arts, Hawaii, 1976
Ill. p. 202

70 **COPLEY,** John Singleton (American, 1738-1815)
Portrait of Colonel George Watson, 1768
Oil on canvas, 50 x 40 in. [127 x 101.6 cm]
New Orleans Museum of Art
Museum purchase, 1977 Art Acquisition Fund Drive and Women's Volunteer Committee Funds
Provenance:
Steven Straw Company
Henderson Inches, Brookline, Massachusetts
Martin Brimmer, 1892
Sarah Watson Brimmer, Roxbury
George Watson
Ill. p. 161

71 Attributed to Eliphalet Chapin (American, 1741-1807)
Connecticut Chippendale Dressing Table, c. 1780
Cherry, 32 5/8 x 34 7/8 x 19 3/4 in.
[82.8 x 88.6 x 50.2 cm]
Yale University Art Gallery, New Haven, Connecticut
The Mabel Brady Garvan Collection, 1930
Provenance:
Francis P. Garvan
Exhibitions:
Connecticut Furniture, Wadsworth Atheneum, Hartford, 1967
Ill. p. 140

72 **BURT,** Benjamin (American 1729-1805)
Two Beakers, 1797
Silver, 3 1/2 in. [8.9 cm] high
Hood Museum of Art, Dartmouth College, Hanover, New Hampshire
Given anonymously, 1966
Provenance:
Private collection, Massachusetts
Daughters of John Bray
Major John Bray, Massachusetts
Ill. p. 99

73 **REVERE II,** Paul (American, 1735-1818)
Water Pitcher, 1804
Silver, 6 1/4 in. [15.9 cm] high
Hood Museum of Art, Dartmouth College, Hanover, New Hampshire
Given anonymously, 1966
Provenance:
Private collection, Massachusetts
Daughters of John Bray
Major John Bray, Massachusetts, 1804
Ill. p. 99

74 **STUART,** Gilbert (American, 1755-1828)
Mrs. Perez Morton, c. 1802
Oil on canvas, 29 1/8 x 24 1/8 in. [74 x 61.3 cm]
Worcester Art Museum
Gift of the Grandchildren of Joseph Tuckerman, 1899
Provenance:
Stephen Salisbury III
Ernest Tuckerman, Newport, 1862
Jane Stuart
Mrs. Gilbert Stuart
Exhibitions:
American Art from the Collection of the Worcester Art Museum, Amon Carter Museum, Fort Worth, 1979
Kaleidoscope of American Painting, Nelson-Atkins Museum of Art, Kansas City, 1978
19th Century America, The Metropolitan Museum of Art, New York, 1970
Gilbert Stuart, Portraitist of the Young Republic 1755-1828, National Gallery of Art, Washington, D.C., 1967; also
Museum of Art, Rhode Island School of Design, Providence
Art in the United States: 1670-1966, Whitney Museum of American Art, 1966
Retrospective Exhibition of Portraits by Gilbert Stuart, John Herron Museum of Art, Indianapolis, 1942
A Century of Progress Exhibition of Paintings and Sculpture, The Art Institute of Chicago, 1933
Loan Collection of Portraits and Pictures of Fair Women, Copley Hall, Boston, 1902
Ill. p. 230

75 **ZAPATA,** Marcos and Cipriano Gutierrez y Toledo (Cuzco, Peru, 18th century)
Adoration of the Magi, c. 1750
Oil on canvas overlaid with gold, 74 x 49 5/8 in.
[188 x 126 cm]
The Denver Art Museum
Frank Barrows Freyer Memorial Collection, 1969
Provenance:
Mr. and Mrs. Frank Barrows Freyer, 1923
Ill. p. 83

76 **GOYA,** Francisco Jose de (Spanish, 1746-1828)
Gossiping Women, c. 1787-91
Oil on canvas, 23 3/16 x 57 1/4 in.
[58.9 x 145.4 cm]
Wadsworth Atheneum, Hartford
The Ella Gallup Sumner and Mary Catlin Sumner Collection, 1929
Provenance:
Durlacher Bros., New York
Vicomte de Mendecourt, Paris
Marquesa de Bermejillo del Rey, Madrid

Exhibitions:
Goya and his Time, Owen Fine Arts Center, Southern Methodist University, Dallas, 1982-83
Goya, Mauritshuis, The Hague, 1970; also Orangerie des Tuileries, Paris
75 Masterworks: an Exhibition of Paintings in Honor of the Seventy-Fifth Anniversary of The Portland Art Association, 1892-1967, The Portland Art Museum, Oregon, 1967-68
A. Everett Austin, Jr.: A Director's Taste and Achievement, The John and Mable Ringling Museum of Art, Sarasota, 1958
Masterpieces from Wadsworth Atheneum, Hartford, M. Knoedler & Co., New York, 1958
Paintings by Goya from American Collections, The Metropolitan Museum of Art, New York, 1955
Man and His Years, The Baltimore Museum of Art, 1954
Francisco Goya, Virginia Museum of Fine Arts, Richmond, 1953
Spanish Paintings of the XVI to XX Centuries, Lyman Allyn Museum, New London, Connecticut, 1948
Spanish Painting, The Toledo Museum of Art, 1941
The Art of Francisco Goya, Art Institute of Chicago, 1941
Masterpieces of Art, New York World's Fair, 1939
Francisco Goya—His Paintings, Drawings and Prints, The Metropolitan Museum of Art, New York, 1936
Ill. p. 105

77 **REYNOLDS,** Sir Joshua (British, 1723-1792)
Miss Esther Jacobs, 1761
Oil on canvas, 36 x 28 3/4 in. [91.4 x 73 cm]
The Toledo Museum of Art
Gift of Mrs. Samuel A. Peck, 1953
Provenance:
Mrs. Samuel A. Peck, New York
Mrs. H. P. Whitney, New York
W. C. Whitney, New York
Charles John Wertheimer, London, 1884
Marquess of Hertford, 1796
Ill. p. 214

78 **STUBBS,** George (British, 1724-1806)
Rufus, c. 1762-65
Oil on canvas, 25 1/2 x 30 1/2 in.
[64.8 x 77.5 cm]
Indianapolis Museum of Art
Gift of Mr. and Mrs. Eli Lilly, 1947
Exhibitions:
Romantic Art in Britian, 1760-1860, The Detroit Institute of Arts, 1968
Ill. p. 103

79 **GAINSBOROUGH,** Thomas (British, 1727-1788)
Returning from Market, c. 1771-72
Oil on canvas, 40 x 50 in. [101.6 x 127 cm]
Cincinnati Art Museum
Gift of Mary Hanna, 1946
Provenance:
Mary Hanna, before 1931
William, First Earl of Dudley, 1875
Rev. John Lucy, Warwick

Exhibitions:
Masterpieces, a Memorial Exhibition for Adele R. Levy, Wildenstein & Co., New York 1961
Exhibition of British Painting, Birmingham Museum of Art, Alabama, 1957
Ill. p. 71

80 **PIRANESI,** Giovanni Battista (Italian, 1720-1778)
Gondola, 1744-45
Brown ink wash, with black chalk, 11 5/8 x 26 7/8 in. [29.6 x 68.3 cm]
The Pierpont Morgan Library, New York
Bequest of Junius S. Morgan and gift of Henry S. Morgan, 1966
Provenance:
Junius S. Morgan and Henry S. Morgan, New York
Mrs. J. P. Morgan, New York
Exhibitions:
Piranesi, Hayward Gallery, London, 1978
Ill. p. 155

81 **TIEPOLO,** Giovanni Battista (Italian, Venice, 1692-1770)
Girl with a Lute (Pandorina), c. 1753-57
Oil on canvas, 36 1/4 x 29 1/2 in. [92.1 x 75 cm]
The Detroit Institute of Arts
Gift of Mr. and Mrs. Henry Ford II, 1957
Provenance:
Private collection, New York
Duc de Dino, Paris
Ill. p. 90

82 **GUARDI,** Francesco (Italian, Venice, 1712-1793)
Venice: The Grand Canal above the Rialto
Oil on canvas, 21 x 33 3/4 in. [53.3 x 85.7 cm]
The Metropolitan Museum of Art, New York
Purchase, 1871
Provenance:
Count Cornet, Brussels
The Earls of Shaftesbury, St. Giles' House, Wimborne, Dorset, England
Exhibitions:
Masterpieces of Painting in the Metropolitan Museum of Art, Museum of Fine Arts, Boston, 1970
Mostra dei Guardi, Palazzo Grassi, Venice, 1965
Ill. p. 149

83 **JOUVENET,** Jean (French, 1644-1717)
Adoration of the Magi
Oil on canvas, 51 1/4 x 38 1/4 in. [130.1 x 97.2 cm]
The Detroit Institute of Arts
Founders Society purchase, Robert H. Tannahill Foundation Fund, 1978
Provenance:
Georg Schaefer, Schweinfurt, Germany
J. R. Ollerenshaw, 1910
Ill. p. 93

84 **WATTEAU,** Antoine (French, 1684-1721)
La Danse Champêtre, c. 1706-10
Oil on canvas, 19 1/2 x 23 5/8 in. [59.6 x 60 cm]
Indianapolis Museum of Art
Gift of Mrs. Herman C. Krannert, 1974

Provenance:
Mr. and Mrs. Herman C. Krannert, Indianapolis
J. K. Lily, Indianapolis
Max Safron Galleries, New York
Wildenstein & Co., New York
Private collection, France
Ill. p. 103

85 Chinese, Ch'ing Dynasty (1644-1911)
Champion Vase, first half 18th century
Cloisonné enamel on gilt bronze, 9 3/8 in. [23.8 cm] high
The Phoenix Art Museum
The Clague Collection
Museum purchase and gift of Robert H. Clague, 1982
Exhibitions:
Chinese Cloisonné: The Clague Collection, The Phoenix Art Museum, 1982-83; also
Art Museum of South Texas, Corpus Christie
Brooks Memorial Art Gallery, Memphis
Fine Arts Museum of South Mobile, Alabama
Columbus Museum of Art, Ohio
Ill. p. 182

86 Indian, Mughal (1550-1750)
A Princess and her Attendant, 18th century
Opaque watercolor on paper, 12 1/4 x 8 in. [31 x 20.3 cm]
Museum of Art, Rhode Island School of Design, Providence
Museum Appropriation, 1917
Ill. p. 188

87 **NATOIRE,** Charles-Joseph (French, 1700-1777)
The Toilette of Psyche, 1745
Oil on canvas, 78 x 66 1/2 in. [198 x 169 cm]
New Orleans Museum of Art
Bequest of Judge Charles F. Claiborne, 1940
Provenance:
Randolph Newman, New Orleans, 1897
James Robb, New Orleans, 1845
Jerome Bonaparte, 1842
Joseph Bonaparte, 1808
Spanish Nobleman in Madrid, 1790
Louis XV
Exhibitions:
Fragonard & His Friends: Changing Ideals in Eighteenth Century Art, Museum of Fine Arts, St. Petersburg, Florida, 1982-83; also
Arkansas Art Center, Little Rock, 1983
Ill. p. 107

88 **BOUCHER,** François (French, 1703-1770)
Arion on the Dolphin, 1748
Oil on canvas, 33 7/8 x 53 3/8 in. [86 x 135.5 cm]
The Art Museum, Princeton University
The Fowler McCormick, Class of 1921, Fund, 1980
Provenance:
Eugene Victor Thaw, New York
Jacques-Onesyme Bergeret, Paris, 1764
French Royal Collection, 1749
Ill. p. 163

89 German, Meissen Porcelain Factory
America, c. 1745
Porcelain on gilt bronze base, 14 in. [35.5 cm] high
Wadsworth Atheneum, Hartford
Gift of J. P. Morgan, 1917

Provenance:
J. P. Morgan, New York
Exhibitions:
The European Vision of America, The Cleveland Museum of Art, 1976; also
National Gallery of Art, Washington, D.C.
Galeries Nationales d'Exposition du Grand Palais, Paris, 1976-77
Ill. p. 85

90 **FALCONET,** Étienne-Maurice (French, 1716-1791)
Madame de Pompadour as the Venus of the Doves
Marble, 29 1/2 x 28 x 18 in. [75 x 71.1 x 45.7 cm]
National Gallery of Art, Washington, D.C.
Samuel H. Kress Collection, 1952
Provenance:
Wildenstein & Co., New York
Duc de Cambacères, Paris
M. de Périgny
Ill. p. 217

91 **FRAGONARD,** Jean-Honoré (French, 1732-1806)
The Return of the Drove, 1765-70
Oil on canvas, 25 1/4 x 31 1/2 in. [64.1 x 80 cm]
Worcester Art Museum
Theodore T. and Mary G. Ellis Collection, 1940
Provenance:
Mary G. Ellis, Worcester
Theodore T. Ellis
Marquis d'Harcourt, 1925
Marquise d'Harcourt, 1921
Féral, 1880
H. Walferdin
Exhibitions:
Three Masters of Landscape: Fragonard, Robert, and Boucher, Virginia Museum of Fine Arts, Richmond, 1981
Fragonard, The National Museum of Western Art, Tokyo, 1980; also
The Kyoto Municipal Museum
Age of Elegance: The Rococo and its Effect, The Baltimore Museum of Art, 1959
French Eighteenth Century Painters, The Minneapolis Institute of Arts, 1954; also
Wildenstein & Co., New York
Six Centuries of Landscape, The Montreal Museum of Fine Arts, 1952
Ill. p. 225

92 French, 19th century, unknown painter
Portrait of a Young Woman Called Mademoiselle Charlotte du Val d'Ognes, c. 1800
Oil on canvas, 63 1/2 x 50 5/8 in. [161.3 x 128.6 cm]
The Metropolitan Museum of Art, New York
Bequest of Isaac D. Fletcher, 1917
Mr. and Mrs. Isaac D. Fletcher Collection
Provenance:
Mr. and Mrs. Isaac D. Fletcher, New York
Baron Maurice de Rothschild, Paris, before 1914
The families of Val d'Ognes and Hardouin de Grosville
Exhibitions:
100 Paintings from the Metropolitan Museum, The Hermitage, Leningrad, 1975; also
The Pushkin Museum, Moscow
Diamond Jubilee Exhibition: Masterpieces of Painting, Philadelphia Museum of Art, 1950-51
Ill. p. 131

93 DELACROIX, Eugène (French, 1798-1863)
Combat between the Giaour and the Pasha, 1826
Oil on canvas, 23 1/2 x 28 7/8 in.
[59.6 x 73.4 cm]
The Art Institute of Chicago
Gift of Mrs. Bertha Palmer Thorne,
Mrs. Rose Movius Palmer,
Mr. and Mrs. Arthur M. Wood and
Mr. and Mrs. Gordon Palmer, 1962-65
Provenance:
Mr. and Mrs. Gordon Palmer,
Mr. and Mrs. Arthur M. Wood,
Mrs. Bertha Palmer Thorne,
Mrs. Rose Movius Palmer, 1956
Pauline Kohlsaat Potter, 1943
Potter Palmer II, 1918
Berthe Honore Palmer, 1902
Potter Palmer I, 1892
Charles Mahler, 1848
Alexandre Dumas, père, 1827
Ill. p. 66

94 INGRES, Jean-Auguste-Dominique (French,
1780-1867)
Study for the Portrait of Mme d'Haussonville,
c. 1843
Pencil, 9 3/16 x 7 3/4 in. [23.3 x 19.6 cm]
Fogg Art Museum, Harvard University,
Cambridge, Massachusetts
Bequest of Meta and Paul J. Sachs, 1965
Provenance:
Paul J. Sachs, 1927
Wildenstein & Co., New York, 1920
Alfred Beurdeley
Exhibitions:
*Harry D. M. Grier Memorial Loan Exhibition;
Paintings and Drawings Related to Works in
the Frick Collection*, The Frick Collection,
New York, 1972
*Ingres et son Temps, Exposition organisée
pour le centenaire de la mort d'Ingres*,
Musée Ingres, Montauban, 1967
Ill. p. 53

95 CHASSERIAU, Théodore (French, 1819-1856)
Roman Battle Scene, after 1845
Charcoal, conté crayon, red and white chalk,
wash, 19 1/2 x 24 in. [49.5 x 61 cm]
The Nelson-Atkins Museum of Art, Kansas City
Nelson Fund, 1959
Exhibitions:
French Masters, Rococo to Romanticism, University
of California at Los Angeles Art Galleries, 1961
Ill. p. 119

96 BONVIN, François (French, 1817-1887)
La Femme de l'Artiste Lisant, 1861
Charcoal and conté crayon, 9 1/2 x 11 13/16 in.
[49.5 x 30 cm]
The Detroit Institute of Arts
Founders Society purchase, Henry Ford II Fund,
1979
Provenance:
Mr. and Mrs. Germain Seligman
Vitale Bloch
Ill. p. 92

97 BRETON, Jules (French, 1827-1906)
The Vintage at Château Lagrange, 1864
Oil on canvas, 36 1/4 x 88 5/8 in.
[92.1 x 225.1 cm]
Joslyn Art Museum, Omaha
Gift of the Friends of Art Collection, 1932
Provenance:
Friends of Art, Omaha, 1916
M. Knoedler & Co., New York, 1912
Acosta Nichols, 1888
Comte Duchâtel, Château Lagrange, Medoc,
Bordeaux
Ill. p. 166

98 MOREAU, Gustave (French, 1826-1898)
*Young Thracian Maiden Carrying the Head of
Orpheus*, c. 1865
Oil on canvas, 39 1/2 x 25 3/8 in.
[100.4 x 64.5 cm]
Washington University Gallery of Art, St. Louis
University purchase, Parsons Fund, 1965
Provenance:
Jacques Seligmann & Co., New York
Benouville Family, 1906
M. Panckoucke
Exhibitions:
*The Earthly Chimera: The Fear of Woman in
19th-Century Art*, David and Alfred Smart
Gallery of the University of Chicago, 1981
The Work of Gustave Moreau, Los Angeles County
Museum of Art, 1974
Ill. p. 192

99 COURBET, Gustave (French, 1819-1877)
The Greyhounds of the Comte de Choiseul, 1866
Oil on canvas, 35 x 45 3/4 in. [88.9 x 116.2 cm]
The Saint Louis Art Museum
Gift of Mrs. Mark C. Steinberg, 1953
Provenance:
Mrs. Mark C. Steinberg
Mlle Juliette Courbet, Paris, c. 1915
Exhibitions:
Gustave Courbet, 1819-1877, Musée National
du Louvre, Palais du Louvre, Paris, 1977-78; also
Royal Academy of Arts, London
*Französische Malerei des 19. Jahrhunderts;
von David bis Cézanne*, Haus der Kunst, Munich,
1964-65
Gustave Courbet 1891-1877, Philadelphia
Museum of Art, 1959-60; also
Museum of Fine Arts, Boston, 1960
*Masterpieces Recalled: A Loan Exhibition
of 19th and 20th Century French Paintings*,
Paul Rosenberg & Co., New York, 1957
*De David à Toulouse-Lautrec; chefs d'oeuvres
des collections Américaines*, Musée de l'Orangerie,
Paris, 1955
*Great French Paintings, An Exhibition in Memory
of Chauncey McCormick*, The Art Institute of
Chicago, 1955
Courbet alla XXVII Biennale di Venezia, Italy, 1954
Ill. p. 181

100 DEGAS, Edgar (French, 1834-1917)
La Savoisienne, 1873
Oil on canvas, 24 x 18 in. [61 x 45.7 cm]
Museum of Art, Rhode Island School of Design,
Providence
Museum appropriation, 1923
Provenance:
Durand-Ruel, New York, 1923

Exhibitions:
Edgar Degas: The Reluctant Impressionist,
Museum of Fine Arts, Boston, 1974
Masterpieces of Art, Seattle World's Fair, 1962
Edgar Degas, Los Angeles County Museum
of Art, 1958
*A Loan Exhibition of Degas for the Benefit of the
New York Infirmary*, Wildenstein & Co., New
York, 1949
Works by Degas, Cleveland Museum of Art, 1947
Edgar Degas, Smith College Museum of Art,
Northampton, Massachusetts, 1933
Ill. p. 167

101 RODIN, Auguste (French, 1840-1917)
President Sarmiento, 1894-96
Bronze, 43 in. [109.2 cm] high
Foundry mark: Alexis Rudier, Paris
Rodin Museum, Philadelphia
Bequest to the City of Philadelphia
by Jules E. Mastbaum, 1929
Ill. p. 172

102 African, Nigeria, Benin
Hornblower, early 17th century
Brass, 23 7/16 in. [59.5 cm] high
The Brooklyn Museum
Gift of Mr. and Mrs. Alastair Bradley Martin,
1955
Provenance:
Mr. and Mrs. Alastair Bradley Martin, 1950
Sotheby's, London
John Hunt, Ireland
Sidney Burney
Collected in Benin, c. 1897
Ill. p. 38

103 Oceanic, Polynesia, Hawaii
Temple Figure, 18th century
Wood, 31 5/8 in. [80.4 cm] high
New Orleans Museum of Art
Bequest of Victor K. Kiam, 1977
Provenance:
Victor K. Kiam, New York, 1967
J. J. Klejman, New York, 1967
Richard Hall Clarke family, 1806
John Rowe, Bristol, 1806
James Parkinson, London, 1786
Sir Ashton Lever, 1779
Captain James Cook, 1778
Exhibitions:
Art of the Pacific Islands, National
Gallery of Art, Washington, D.C., 1980
Artificial Curiosities, Bernice Pauahi
Bishop Museum, Honolulu, Hawaii, 1978
Ill. p. 160

104 Oceanic, Polynesia, Maori, New Zealand
(Central North Island)
*Ancestor Figure, Gable for a Chief's House
(tekoteko)*, first half 19th century
Wood, 19 1/4 in. [48.9 cm] high
The Fine Arts Museums of San Francisco
de Young Art Trust, 1971
Provenance:
Avery Brundage
Ill. p. 206

105 American, Empire Period
Coverlet, "Bird of Paradise" design, Portsmouth,
Ohio, c. 1845
Wool and linen, 87 x 72 in. [221 x 182.9 cm]
Dayton Art Institute
Bequest of the Estate of Blanche Adamson, 1968
Provenance:
Misses Blanche and Cora Adamson and
Mrs. Zoa Adamson Aulabaugh, Dayton, Ohio
Ill. p. 80

106 American Indian, Navajo
Classic Serape (The Spiegelberg Serape), c. 1840-60
Woven wool, 84 x 54 in. [212.2 x 137.2 cm]
Lowe Art Museum, The University of Miami,
Coral Gables, Florida
Gift of Alfred I. Barton, 1956
Provenance:
Alfred I. Barton
Fred Harvey Co., George Sealy collection
Spiegelberg family, Santa Fe
Ill. p. 77

107 American Indian, Northwest Coast
Tsimshian, Nisqa
Mask: young girl with braids, late 19th-
early 20th century
Painted wood, hair, 12 1/8 x 8 1/8 in.
[30.7 x 20.6 cm]
Portland Art Museum, Oregon
Helen Thurston Ayer Fund, 1946
Provenance:
Julius Carlebach, New York
Museum of the American Indian, Heye
Foundation
Exhibitions:
Sacred Circles, 2000 Years of American Indian Art,
Arts Council of Great Britian, London, 1976;
also
Nelson Gallery of Art and Atkins Museum of
Fine Arts, Kansas City, 1977
Ill. p. 185

108 American Indian, Cherokee
Bandolier Bag, before 1900
English wool trade cloth with beads, ribbon,
31 in. [78.8 cm] long
The Denver Art Museum
Museum purchase, 1971
Provenance:
Guy Wood, Tallahassee
Ill. p. 95

109 HICKS, Edward (American, 1780-1849)
Peaceable Kingdom, c. 1830-35
Oil on canvas, 17 1/2 x 23 1/2 in.
[44.4 x 59.7 cm]
The Museum of Fine Arts, Houston
The Bayou Bend Collection,
Gift of Miss Ima Hogg, 1954
Provenance:
Collection of Ima Hogg and William C. Hogg
Hirschl & Adler, New York
Mrs. Henrietta C. Collins
Amos Campbell, Pennsylvania
Ill. p. 100

110 CATLIN, George (American, 1794-1872)
Little Spaniard, a Warrior, 1834
Oil on canvas, 29 x 24 in. [73.7 x 61 cm]
National Museum of American Art,
Smithsonian Institution
Gift of Mrs. Joseph Harrison, Jr., 1965
Provenance:
Joseph Harrison, Jr.
Catlin Indian Gallery
Ill. p. 218

111 COLE, Thomas (American, 1801-1848)
The Pic-Nic, 1846
Oil on canvas, 47 7/8 x 71 7/8 in.
[121.6 x 182.6 cm]
The Brooklyn Museum
A. Augustus Healy Fund B, 1967
Provenance:
Family of James Brown until 1967
James Brown, commissioned from the artist, 1845
Exhibitions:
*Masterpieces of American Painting from
The Brooklyn Museum*, The Saint Louis Art
Museum, 1976
Retrospective of a Gallery: Twenty Years, Hirschl
and Adler, New York, 1973
Retrospective: Thomas Cole, Memorial Art
Gallery of the University of Rochester,
New York, 1969; also
Munson-Williams-Procter Institute, Utica,
Albany Institute of History and Art
Whitney Museum of American Art, New York
Ill. p. 49

112 WHISTLER, James Abbott McNeill (American,
1834-1903)
Coast of Brittany: Alone with the Tide, 1861
Oil on canvas, 34 5/16 x 45 9/16 in.
[87.2 x 115.7 cm]
Wadsworth Atheneum, Hartford
In memory of William Arnold Healy, given by
his daughter Susie Healy Camp, 1925
Provenance:
Ross Winans, Baltimore
George Whistler
Exhibitions:
Americans in Brittany and Normandy, 1860-1910,
Pennsylvania Academy of the Fine Arts,
Philadelphia, 1982; also
Amon Carter Museum, Fort Worth
Phoenix Art Museum
National Museum of American Art, Washington,
D.C., 1983
Whistler in New England Collections, Museum of
Fine Arts, Boston, 1978
*From Realism to Symbolism: Whistler and His
World*, Wildenstein & Co., New York, 1971
James McNeill Whistler, Nationalgalerie, Berlin,
1969
James McNeill Whistler, The Art Institute of
Chicago, 1968; also
Munson-Williams-Procter Institute, Utica, 1968
Christie's Bi-Centenary Exhibition 1766-1966,
Christie, Manson and Woods, London, 1967;
Whistler, The Arts Council of Great Britian,
London, 1960; also
M. Knoedler & Co., New York, 1960
American Classics of the Nineteenth Century,
The Currier Gallery of Art, Manchester, New
Hampshire, 1958

Hundert Jahre Amerikanische Malerei, organized by
The American Federation of Arts for the United
States Information Agency, 1953-54, to
Städelsches Kunstinstitut und Städtische Galerie,
Frankfurt
Bayerische Staatsgemäldesammlungen, Munich
Hamburger Kunsthalle
Schloss Charlottenburg, Berlin
Kunstsammlungen der Stadt, Düsseldorf
Galleria Nazionale d'Arte Moderna, Rome
Palazzetto Reale, Milan
Whitney Museum of American Art, New York
Ill. p. 105

113 EAKINS, Thomas (American, 1844-1916)
*William Rush Carving His Allegorical Figure of
the Schuylkill River*, 1876-77
Oil on canvas mounted on masonite,
20 1/8 x 26 1/8 in. [51.1 x 66.4 cm]
Philadelphia Museum of Art
Gift of Mrs. Thomas Eakins and
Miss Mary Adeline Williams, 1929
Provenance:
The artist, Philadelphia
Exhibitions:
American Art and the Quest for Unity, The
Detroit Institute of Arts, 1983
Thomas Eakins: Artist of Philadelphia, Philadelphia
Museum of Art, 1982; also
Museum of Fine Arts, Boston
Thomas Eakins Retrospective Exhibition, Whitney
Museum of American Art, 1970
100th Anniversary, Corcoran Gallery of Art,
Washington, D.C., 1969
American Vision, Wildenstein & Co., New York,
1957
Famous American Paintings, Dallas Museum of
Fine Arts, 1948
American Paintings, Tate Gallery, London, 1946
Eakins Centennial Exhibition, M. Knoedler & Co.,
New York, 1944
Century of Progress, Art Institute of Chicago,
1934
Ill. p. 170

114 HEADE, Martin Johnson (American,
1819-1904)
Orchids and Spray Orchids with Hummingbirds,
1880s
Oil on canvas, 20 x 12 in. [58.8 x 30.5 cm]
Museum of Fine Arts, Boston
Gift of Maxim Karolik for the Karolik Collection
of American Paintings, 1815-65, 1947
Provenance:
Maxim Karolik, 1946
Robert G. Ingersoll, Dobbs Ferry, New York
Exhibitions:
An American Flower Show, Heritage Plantation,
Sandwich, Massachusetts, 1980
Martin Johnson Heade, University of Maryland
Art Gallery, College Park, 1969
Ill. p. 57

115 ELMER, Edwin Romanzo (American,
1850-1923)
Mourning Picture, 1890
Oil on canvas, 28 x 36 in. [71 x 91.5 cm]
Smith College Museum of Art, Northampton,
Massachusetts
Museum purchase, 1953

Provenance:
Maud Vallona Elmer, Greenfield, Massachusetts
Estate of the artist's wife, Ashfield
The artist
Exhibitions:
Art of the Naives-Themes and Affinities,
Haus der Kunst, Munich, 1975; also
Kunsthaus Zürich
American Self-Portraits, 1670-1973, National
Portrait Gallery, Washington, D.C., 1974
*The Hand and the Spirit: Religious Art in America
1770-1900*, Dallas Museum of Fine Arts, 1973;
also Indianapolis Museum of Art
Art of the United States, Whitney Museum of
American Art, New York, 1966
De Lusthof der Naiven, Museum Boymans-van
Beuningen, Rotterdam, 1964; also
Musée National d'Art Moderne, Paris
American Art, Brussels World's Fair, 1958
American Primitive Art, The Museum of Fine
Arts, Houston, 1956
Hundert Jahre Amerikanische Malerei, organized
by The American Federation of Arts for the
United States Information Agency, 1953-54, to
Städelsches Kunstinstitut und Städtische
Galerie, Frankfurt
Bayerische Staatsgemäldesammlungen, Munich
Hamburger Kunsthalle
Schloss Charlottenburg, Berlin
Kunstsammlungen der Stadt, Düsseldorf
Galleria Nazionale d'Arte Moderna, Rome
Palazzetto Reale, Milan
Whitney Museum of American Art, New York
Ill. p. 135

116 **MORAN,** Thomas (American, 1837-1926)
Grand Canyon of the Yellowstone, 1893
Oil on canvas, 20 x 16 in. [50.8 x 40.6 cm]
The Fine Arts Museums of San Francisco
Gift of Mr. and Mrs. John D. Rockefeller, 3rd,
1979
Exhibitions:
*The West as Art: Changing Perceptions of
Western Art in California Collections*, Palm Springs
Desert Museum, California, 1982
Thomas Moran: A Search for the Scenic, The Guild
Hall Museum, East Hampton, New York, 1980-81
*American Art: An Exhibition from the Collection of
Mr. and Mrs. John D. Rockefeller 3rd*, The Fine
Arts Museums of San Francisco, 1976
Ill. p. 207

117 **HOMER,** Winslow (American, 1836-1910)
The Wreck, 1896
Oil on canvas, 30 x 48 in. [76.1 x 122 cm]
Museum of Art, Carnegie Institute, Pittsburgh
Museum purchase, 1896
Exhibitions:
Winslow Homer Exhibition, Whitney Museum
of American Art, New York, 1973; also
Los Angeles County Museum of Art
The Art Institute of Chicago
Art of the United States: 1670-1966,
Whitney Museum of American Art, 1966
Winslow Homer at Prout's Neck, Bowdoin
College Museum of Art, Brunswick, Maine, 1966
Four Centuries of American Masterpieces, Better
Living Center, New York World's Fair, 1964
Golden Gate International Exposition, M. H. de
Young Memorial Museum, San Francisco, 1940
Two Hundred Years of American Painting,
The Baltimore Museum of Art, 1938

Texas Centennial Exhibition, Dallas Museum of
Fine Arts, 1936
Panama-Pacific Exposition, San Francisco, 1915
First Annual Exhibition, Carnegie Institute,
Pittsburgh, 1896
Ill. p. 179

118 **PISSARRO,** Camille (French, 1831-1903)
The Red House, 1873
Oil on canvas, 23 3/8 x 28 7/8 in.
[59.3 x 73.3 cm]
Portland Art Museum, Oregon
Bequest of Winslow B. Ayer, 1935
Provenance:
Durand-Ruel, Paris, 1919
Exhibitions:
Impressionism, Pomona College Art Department,
Claremont, California, 1966
Ill. p. 168

119 **MONET,** Claude (French, 1840-1926)
Meadow at Giverny in Autumn, late 1880
Oil on canvas, 36 1/4 x 32 1/8 in.
[92 x 81.5 cm]
Museum of Fine Arts, Boston
Juliana Cheney Edwards Collection; Bequest
of Hannah Marcy Edwards in memory of her
mother, 1939
Provenance:
Grace M. Edwards, Boston, 1931
Hannah Marcy Edwards, Boston, 1916
Prince de Wagram, Paris
Exhibitions:
*Corot to Braque: French Paintings from the
Museum of Fine Arts, Boston*, The High Museum
of Art, Atlanta, 1979; also
Seibu Museum, Tokyo
Nagoya City Museum, Japan
National Museum of Modern Art, Kyoto
The Denver Art Museum, 1980
Claude Monet, Wildenstein & Co., New York,
1945
Ill. p. 40

120 **RENOIR,** Pierre Auguste (French, 1841-1919)
A Girl with a Fan, c. 1881
Oil on canvas, 25 5/8 x 21 1/4 in. [65 x 54 cm]
Sterling and Francine Clark Art Institute,
Williamstown, Massachusetts
Provenance:
Robert Sterling Clark, 1939
Durand-Ruel, New York
Prince de Wagram
M. Rosenberg
Durand-Ruel, Paris
Legarde sale, 1903
Jean Laroche, Paris
Exhibitions:
The Crisis of Impressionism, The University
of Michigan Museum of Art, Ann Arbor, 1980
Treasures from the Clark Art Institute,
Wildenstein & Co., New York, 1967
Ill. p. 231

121 **CÉZANNE,** Paul (French, 1839-1906)
Madame Cézanne in Blue, c. 1885-87
Oil on canvas, 29 3/16 x 24 in.
[74.1 x 60.9 cm]
The Museum of Fine Arts, Houston
Robert Lee Blaffer Memorial Collection;
Gift of Sarah Campbell Blaffer, 1947

Provenance:
Étienne Bignou, Paris
W. Halvorsen, Oslo, Norway
Ambroise Vollard, Paris
Exhibitions:
Cézanne, Musée St. Georges, Liège, Belgium,
1982; also
Musée Granet, Aix-en-Provence, France
*La Peinture Française dans les Collections
Américaines*, Musée des Beaux Arts, Bordeaux,
1966
*Important European Paintings from Texas
Private Collections*, Marlborough-Gerson Gallery,
New York, 1964
Art from Ingres to Pollock, University Art
Museum, University of California, Berkeley, 1960
Art in the Twentieth Century, San Francisco
Museum of Art, 1955
Cézanne: Paintings, Watercolors, Drawings, The
Art Institute of Chicago; also
The Metropolitan Museum of Art, New York,
1952
Ill. p. 87

122 Oceanic, Melanesia, Papua New Guinea,
East Sepik Province, Sawos people
Ancestral Figure, 19th century
Painted wood, fiber, 72 in. [183 cm] high
The Metropolitan Museum of Art, New York
The Michael C. Rockefeller Memorial
Collection, Bequest of Nelson A. Rockefeller,
1979
Provenance:
Nelson A. Rockefeller, 1959
Exhibitions:
Primitive Art Masterworks, American Federation
of Arts New York, tour 1975-77
Sculpture from the Pacific Islands, The
Metropolitan Museum of Art, New York, 1974
Ill. p. 148

123 **GAUGUIN,** Paul (French, 1848-1903)
Agony in the Garden, 1889
Oil on canvas, 28 1/2 x 36 in. [72.4 x 91.4 cm]
Norton Gallery and School of Art, West Palm
Beach, Florida, 1946
Provenance:
E. and A. Silberman Galleries, New York, 1941
Sir Michael Sadler, London
Ambroise Vollard, Paris, 1903
Octave Mirbeau, 1891
The artist
Exhibitions:
Vincent van Gogh and the Birth of Cloisonism,
Art Gallery of Ontario, Toronto, 1981; also
Rijksmuseum Vincent van Gogh, Amsterdam,
1981
Masterpieces of Art, Seattle World's Fair, 1962
Renoir to Picasso, The Joe and Emily Lowe Art
Gallery of the University of Miami, Coral
Gables, Florida, 1963
Art Nouveau, Museum of Art, Carnegie Institute,
Pittsburgh, 1960
Gauguin: Paintings, Drawings, Prints, Sculpture,
The Art Institute of Chicago, 1959; also
The Metropolitan Museum of Art, New York,
1959
Art Unites Nations, E. and A. Silberman
Galleries, New York, 1957
Paul Gauguin, Society of the Four Arts,
Palm Beach, 1956

Painting, School of France, Atlanta Art
Association Galleries, 1955; also
Birmingham Museum of Art, Alabama, 1955
The Two Sides of the Medal, The Detroit Institute
of Arts, 1954
*Paul Gauguin: His Place in the Meeting of East
and West*, The Museum of Fine Arts, Houston,
1954
Ill. p. 227

124 **GOGH,** Vincent van (Dutch, 1853-1890)
Mademoiselle Ravoux, 1890
Oil on canvas, 19 3/4 x 19 3/4 in.
[50.2 x 50.2 cm]
The Cleveland Museum of Art
Bequest of Leonard C. Hanna, Jr., 1958
Provenance:
Leonard C. Hanna, Jr., Cleveland, 1939
Mrs. Cornelius J. Sullivan
Katherine S. Dreier, New York
Bernheim-Jeune & Cie, Paris
Exhibitions:
Leonard C. Hanna, Jr., Memorial Exhibition, The
Cleveland Museum of Art, 1958
Ill. p. 73

125 **LUCE,** Maximilien (French, 1858-1941)
La Rue Mouffetard, c. 1889
Oil on canvas, 31 5/8 x 25 1/4 in.
[80.4 x 64 cm]
Indianapolis Museum of Art
The Holliday Collection, 1979
Provenance:
W. J. Holliday, 1969
Hammer Galleries, New York, 1966
Private Collection, France
Ill. p. 84

126 **MUNCH,** Edvard (Norwegian, 1863-1944)
The Kiss (Der Küss), 1897-1902
Color woodcut, 18 3/8 x 18 1/4 in.
[46.7 x 46.3 cm]
The Minneapolis Institute of Arts
The Herschel V. Jones Fund, by exchange, 1979
Reference:
Gustav Schiefler, *Verzeichnis des Graphischen
Werks Edvard Munchs bis 1906*, Berlin, Bruno
Cassirer, 1907, #102
Ill. p. 117

127 **CASSATT,** Mary (American, 1844-1926)
The Caress, 1902
Oil on canvas, 32 7/8 x 27 3/8 in.
[83.4 x 69.5 cm]
National Museum of American Art, Smithsonian
Institution
Gift of William T. Evans, 1911
Provenance:
William T. Evans, 1910
Durand-Ruel, 1909
Miss Anne Thompson, 1909
Durand-Ruel
Exhibitions:
The Art of Mary Cassatt (1844-1926), Isetan
Museum, Tokyo, 1981; also
Otani Memorial Art Museum, Nishinomiya
American National Exhibition in Moscow, through
United States Information Agency, 1959
*25th Biennial Exhibition of Contemporary American
Oil Painting*, Corcoran Gallery of Art,
Washington, D.C., 1957

Expatriates, Whistler, Cassatt, Sargent,
Munson-Williams-Proctor Institute, Utica, New
York, 1953
Half a Century of American Art, The Art Institute
of Chicago, 1940
Inaugural Exhibition, The Mint Museum of Art,
Charlotte, North Carolina, 1936
Ill. p. 218

128 **SARGENT,** John Singer (American, 1856-1925)
In Switzerland, 1908
Watercolor, 9 7/16 x 12 5/8 in. [24 x 32 cm]
The Brooklyn Museum
Purchase by Special Subscription, 1909
Provenance:
The artist
Exhibitions:
Five American Masters of Watercolor, Terra
Museum of American Art, Evanston, Illinois,
1981
Ten American Masters of Watercolor, The Katonah
Gallery, Katonah, New York, 1978
*Masterpieces of American Painting from the
Brooklyn Museum*, Davis and Long Company,
New York, 1976; also
The Saint Louis Art Museum
Ten Americans, Masters of Watercolor,
Andrew Crispo Gallery, New York, 1974
Eight American Masters of Watercolor, Los
Angeles County Museum of Art, 1968; also
M. H. de Young Memorial Museum,
San Francisco
Seattle Art Museum
The Private World of John Singer Sargent,
Corcoran Gallery of Art, Washington, D.C.,
1964; also
The Cleveland Museum of Art
Worcester Art Museum
Munson-Williams-Proctor Institute, Utica
*Exhibition of Water Colors: Homer, Sargent, and
Marin*, Colorado Springs Fine Arts Center, 1947
Ill. p. 49

129 **BONNARD,** Pierre (French, 1867-1947)
Fête sur l'Eau (Regatta), 1913
Oil on canvas, 28 3/4 x 39 1/2 in.
[73 x 100.3 cm]
Museum of Art, Carnegie Institute, Pittsburgh
Presented through the generosity of
Mrs. Alan M. Scaife, 1963
Provenance:
Estate of Pierre Bonnard, 1947
Exhibitions:
The Inquiring Eye of Pierre Bonnard,
Wildenstein & Co., New York, 1981
A French Way of Seeing, The High Museum of
Art, Atlanta, 1974
12 Years of Collecting, Wildenstein & Co.,
New York, 1973
Pierre Bonnard, Royal Academy of Arts, London,
1966
Bonnard and His Environment, The Museum of
Modern Art, New York, 1964; also
The Art Institute of Chicago, 1965
The Los Angeles County Museum of Art, 1965
Ill. p. 169

130 **ATGET,** Eugène (French, 1857-1927)
Corsets, Boulevard de Strasbourg, c. 1905
Albumen print, 8 3/4 x 6 7/8 in.
[22.2 x 17.5 cm]
The Art Institute of Chicago
Julien Levy Collection, 1975
Provenance:
Julien Levy, Bridgewater, Connecticut
Ill. p. 69

131 **ROUSSEAU,** Henri, (French, 1844-1910)
The Muse of the Poet Guillaume Apollinaire,
c. 1909
Oil on canvas, 24 3/4 x 15 1/4 in.
[62.8 x 38.7 cm]
The Phoenix Art Museum
Gift of Mr. and Mrs. Henry R. Luce, 1962
Exhibitions:
Die Kunst der Naiven-Themen und Beziehungen,
Kunsthaus Zürich, 1975
Inner Circle, Milwaukee Art Center, 1966
*Paintings and Sculpture from the Phoenix
Art Museum Collection*, El Paso Museum of Art,
1965
Art since 1889, University of New Mexico Art
Gallery, Albuquerque, 1964
Henri Rousseau, Wildenstein & Co., New York,
1963
Ill. p. 183

132 **MATISSE,** Henri (French, 1869-1954)
La Fille aux Yeux Verts (Girl with Green Eyes), 1908
Oil on canvas, 26 x 20 in. [66 x 50.8 cm]
San Francisco Museum of Modern Art
Bequest of Harriet Lane Levy, 1950
Provenance:
Purchased by Michael Stein for
Miss Harriet Lane Levy, 1908
Galerie Bernheim-Jeune, Paris
Exhibitions:
Matisse, The National Museum of Modern Art,
Tokyo, Japan, 1981; also
The National Museum of Modern Art, Kyoto
The "Wild Beasts": Fauvism and its Affinities,
The Museum of Modern Art, New York, 1976;
also
San Francisco Museum of Art, 1976
Modern Masters: Manet to Matisse, organized by
International Council of The Museum of Modern
Art, New York, 1975, to
Art Gallery of New South Wales, Sydney,
Australia
National Gallery of Victoria, Melbourne,
Australia
Gauguin and the Decorative Style, The Solomon R.
Guggenheim Museum, New York, 1966
Henri Matisse, Retrospective 1966, The UCLA Art
Council and the University of California at Los
Angeles Art Galleries, 1966; also
The Art Institute of Chicago
The Museum of Fine Arts, Boston
Rétrospective Henri-Matisse, Musée National d'Art
Moderne, Paris, 1956
Les Fauves, Arts Club of Chicago, 1956
Inaugural Exhibition, Fort Worth Art Center, 1954
Henri Matisse, Portland Art Museum, Oregon,
1952

Henri Matisse, The Museum of Modern Art, New York, 1951; also
The Cleveland Museum of Art, 1952
The Art Institute of Chicago
San Francisco Museum of Art
The Los Angeles Municipal Art Department
10th Anniversary Exhibition: French Painting of the 19th and 20th Centuries, Santa Barbara Museum of Art, 1951
Ill. p. 198

133 KANDINSKY, Vasily (Russian, 1866-1944)
Group in Crinolines, 1909
Oil on canvas, 37 1/2 x 59 1/8 in.
[95.2 x 150.2 cm]
The Solomon R. Guggenheim Museum, New York, 1945
Provenance:
Karl Nierendorf, New York, 1942
Willem Beffie, Amsterdam and Brussels, 1913
The artist
Exhibitions:
Kandinsky in Munich: 1896-1914, The Solomon R. Guggenheim Museum, New York, 1982
Kandinsky at the Guggenheim Museum, The Solomon R. Guggenheim Museum, New York, 1972; also
Los Angeles County Museum of Art
Walker Art Center, Minneapolis
Vasily Kandinsky, 1866-1944: A Retrospective Exhibition, The Solomon R. Guggenheim Museum, New York, 1963; also
Musée National d'Art Moderne, Paris
Gemeentemuseum, The Hague
Kunsthalle Basel
45 Oeuvres de Kandinsky Provenant du Solomon R. Guggenheim Museum, New York, Palais des Beaux-Arts, Brussels, 1957; also
Musée National d'Art Moderne, Paris
Tate Gallery, London
Musée des Beaux-Arts, Lyon
Kunstnerns Hus, Oslo
Galleria Nazionale d'Arte Moderna, Rome
Wassily Kandinsky Memorial Exhibition, The Arts Club of Chicago, 1945
In Memory of Wassily Kandinsky, The Museum of Non-Objective Painting, New York, 1945
Ill. p. 143

134 HARTLEY, Marsden (American, 1877-1943)
The Iron Cross, 1915
Oil on canvas, 47 1/4 x 47 1/4 in. [120 x 120 cm]
Washington University Gallery of Art, St. Louis
University purchase, Bixby Fund, 1952
Provenance:
Paul Rosenberg & Co.
Exhibitions:
American Masters of Twentieth-Century Art, Oklahoma Art Center, Oklahoma City, 1982
Marsden Hartley, Whitney Museum of American Art, New York, 1980-81
Marsden Hartley, Painter/Poet, University of Texas, Austin, 1968-69
Stieglitz and His Circle, The Museum of Modern Art, New York, 1962-63
College and Community Around Art, Allen Memorial Art Gallery, Oberlin College, 1953
Ill. p. 199

135 African, Gabon, Mahongwe-Kota Culture (19th century)
Bwete (Guardian Figure)
Wood, brass, iron, 21 in. [53.4 cm] high
Seattle Art Museum
Katherine White Collection, 1981
Provenance:
Katherine White, 1964
Judith Small
Charles Ratton, Paris, 1937
Dr. Hans Himmelheber
Ill. p. 213

136 PICASSO, Pablo (Spanish, 1881-1973)
Guitar on a Table, 1912
Oil, sand, charcoal on canvas,
20 1/8 x 24 1/4 in. [51.1 x 61.6 cm]
Hood Museum of Art, Dartmouth College, Hanover, New Hampshire
Gift of Nelson A. Rockefeller, class of 1930, 1975
Provenance:
Nelson A. Rockefeller
Gertrude Stein
Exhibitions:
Four Americans in Paris, The Museum of Modern Art, New York, 1970
Ill. p. 86

137 BRAQUE, Georges (French, 1882-1963)
Playing Card and Pipe (Carte et Pipe l'Echo de Paris), 1913-14
Oil on canvas, 16 x 13 in. [40.6 x 33 cm]
Memorial Art Gallery of the University of Rochester, New York
Marion Stratton Gould Fund, 1954
Provenance:
Perls Galleries, New York
Stanley Barbee, Los Angeles
Perls Galleries, New York
Alsatian private collection
Galerie Kahnweiler, Paris
Exhibitions:
Kubismus—Annäherung an einen Stil, Kunsthalle Köln, West Germany, 1982
Inaugural Exhibition, Arizona State College Art Gallery, Flagstaff, 1966
Braque: An American Tribute, Saidenberg Gallery, New York, 1964
Picasso-Braque-Gris: Cubism to 1918, Perls Galleries, New York, 1954
Ill. p. 191

138 GLEIZES, Albert (French, 1881-1953)
Paysage (Landscape), 1913
Oil on canvas, 36 3/8 x 28 5/8 in.
[92.4 x 72.7 cm]
Columbus Museum of Art, Ohio
Gift of Ferdinand Howald, 1927
Provenance:
Ferdinand Howald, 1927
John Quinn, New York, 1916
Exhibitions:
The Noble Buyer: John Quinn, Patron of the Avant-Garde, Hirshhorn Museum and Sculpture Garden, 1978
Ferdinand Howald/Avant-Garde Collector, Wildenstein & Co., London, 1973; also
National Gallery of Ireland, Dublin
National Museum of Wales, Cardiff
Ferdinand Howald/Avant-Garde Collector, The Society of the Four Arts, Palm Beach, Florida, 1975

The Cubist Epoch, Los Angeles County Museum of Art, 1971; also
The Metropolitan Museum of Art, New York
The Ferdinand Howald Collection, Wildenstein & Co., New York, 1970
Painters of the Section d'Or, Albright-Knox Art Gallery, Buffalo, New York, 1967
Albert Gleizes 1881-1953: A Retrospective Exhibition,
The Solomon R. Guggenheim Museum, New York, 1964-65; also
San Francisco Museum of Art
City Art Museum of St. Louis
Krannert Art Museum, University of Illinois, Champaign
Columbus Gallery of Fine Arts, Ohio, 1965
National Gallery of Canada, Ottawa
Albright-Knox Art Gallery
Arts Club of Chicago
Ill. p. 61

139 GRIS, Juan (Spanish, 1887-1927)
Glasses and Newspaper, May 1914
Gouache, conté crayon and chalk on paper and canvas, 24 x 15 in. [61 x 38 cm]
Smith College Museum of Art, Northampton, Massachusetts
Gift of Joseph Brummer, 1921
Provenance:
Joseph Brummer, New York
Galerie Kahnweiler, Paris
Exhibitions:
Art for Study: The Modern Tradition, Mead Art Museum, Amherst College, 1968
Cubist Works, The Wellesley College Art Museum, 1967
The Heroic Years: Paris 1908-1914, The Museum of Fine Arts, Houston, 1965
1914, The Baltimore Museum of Art, 1964
Juan Gris, The Museum of Modern Art, New York, 1958; also
The Minneapolis Institute of Arts
The San Francisco Museum of Art
The Los Angeles County Museum of Art
Forty-four Major Works from the Smith College Collection, Institute of Contemporary Art, Boston, 1954
Paintings and Drawings from the Smith College Collection, M. Knoedler & Co., New York, 1953
Pictures for a Picture of Gertrude Stein as a Collector and Writer on Art and Artists, Yale University Art Gallery, New Haven, 1951; also
The Baltimore Museum of Art
Collage, The Museum of Modern Art, New York, 1948
A Retrospective Exhibition of the Work of Juan Gris, Cincinnati Art Museum, 1948
Four Spaniards: Dali, Gris, Miro and Picasso, The Institute of Modern Art, Boston, 1946
Juan Gris, 1887-1927, Buchholz Gallery, New York, 1944
Retrospective Loan Exhibition: Juan Gris (1887-1927), Jacques Seligmann & Co., New York, 1938
Post-War European Painting, Vassar College Art Gallery, Poughkeepsie, 1934
Ill. p. 158

140 **ARCHIPENKO,** Alexander (American, born Russia, 1887-1964)
La Lutte, 1914, cast 1966
Bronze, 7/8, 23 1/2 in. [59.7 cm] high
Milwaukee Art Museum
Purchase, Virginia Booth Vogel Acquisition Fund, 1983
Provenance:
Zabriskie Gallery, New York
Estate of the artist
Exhibitions:
Archipenko: the Parisian Years, 1908-1921, The Museum of Modern Art, New York, 1970
Archipenko, International Visionary, traveling exhibition to Europe organized by the Smithsonian Institution, 1969-70
Archipenko Memorial Exhibition, University of California at Los Angeles Art Galleries, and U.S. tour, 1967-69
Ill. p. 124

141 **LIPCHITZ,** Jacques (American, born Lithuania, 1891-1973)
Spanish Servant Girl, 1915
Bronze, 3/7, 34 5/8 in. [88.2 cm] high
Portland Art Museum, Oregon
The Evan H. Roberts Memorial Sculpture Fund, 1977
Provenance:
Marlborough Gallery, New York
Exhibitions:
Jacques Lipchitz (1891-1973): Sculptures and Drawings from the Cubist Epoch, Marlborough Gallery, New York, 1977
Jacques Lipchitz Skulpturen and Zeichnungen 1911-1969, Nationalgalerie, Berlin, 1970
Ill. p. 184

142 **FEININGER,** Lyonel (American, 1871-1956)
Church of the Minorites (II), 1926
Oil on canvas, 43 1/8 x 37 3/8 in. [109.6 x 95 cm]
Walker Art Center, Minneapolis
Gift of the T. B. Walker Foundation, Gilbert M. Walker Fund, 1943
Provenance:
Buchholz Gallery, New York
Museum am Anger, Erfurt, Germany, 1926
Exhibitions:
Lyonel Feininger, Marlborough-Gerson Gallery, New York, 1969
Lyonel Feininger 1871-1956: A Memorial Exhibition, Pasadena Art Museum, 1966; also
Milwaukee Art Center
The Baltimore Museum of Art
Lyonel Feininger Memorial Exhibition, The Cleveland Museum of Art, 1959; also 1959-61
The San Francisco Museum of Art
The Minneapolis Institute of Arts
Albright-Knox Art Gallery, Buffalo
Museum of Fine Arts, Boston
Arts Council Gallery, London
Kunsthalle, Hamburg
Museum Folkwang, Essen
Staatliche Kunsthalle Baden-Baden
Famous Paintings and Famous Painters, Dallas Museum of Fine Arts, 1958
European Masters of Our Time, Museum of Fine Arts, Boston, 1957
The Work of Lyonel Feininger, The Print Club of Cleveland and The Cleveland Museum of Art, 1951

19th and 20th Century European and American Paintings, Des Moines Art Center, 1948
Feininger, The Museum of Modern Art, New York, 1944
Ill. p. 127

143 **BELLOWS,** George (American, 1882-1925)
Polo at Lakewood, 1910
Oil on canvas, 45 1/4 x 63 1/2 in. [115 x 161.3 cm]
Columbus Museum of Art, Ohio
Columbus Art Association purchase, 1911
Provenance:
The artist
Exhibitions:
George Wesley Bellows/Paintings, Drawings, Prints, Columbus Museum of Art, 1979; also
Virginia Museum of Fine Arts, Richmond
Des Moines Art Center
Worcester Art Museum
The Growing Spectrum of American Art, Joslyn Art Museum, Omaha, 1975
XIX, An Exhibition Honoring the XIX Olympiad, The Phoenix Art Museum, 1968
The World of Art in 1910, The Isaac Delgado Museum of Art, New Orleans, 1960
George Bellows/A Retrospective Exhibition, National Gallery of Art, 1957
George Bellows: Paintings, Drawings and Prints, The Art Institute of Chicago, 1946
Survey of American Painting, Carnegie Institute, Department of Fine Arts, Pittsburgh, 1940
The Twentieth Anniversary Exhibition, The Cleveland Museum of Art, 1936
Memorial Exhibition of the Work of George Bellows, The Metropolitan Museum of Art, New York, 1925
Ill. p. 75

144 **HENRI,** Robert (American, 1865-1929)
Ballet Girl in White, 1909
Oil on canvas, 77 1/8 x 37 1/4 in. [195.9 x 94.6 cm]
Des Moines Art Center
Gift of the Des Moines Association of Fine Arts, 1945
Provenance:
Des Moines Association of Fine Arts, 1927
The artist
Exhibitions:
Pioneers: Early 20th Century Art from Midwestern Museums, Grand Rapids Art Museum, Michigan, 1981
Paintings, Drawings, Sculptures, Prints from Twenty-three Iowa Collections, Art Department, University of Iowa, Iowa City, 1961
Robert Henri Memorial Exhibition, The Metropolitan Museum of Art, New York, 1931
Ill. p. 96

145 African, Zaire, Chokwe
Chair with head on back and figures on rungs
Wood and hide, 22 1/2 x 10 1/4 x 17 in. [57.1 x 26 x 43.2 cm]
Dallas Museum of Art
The Clark and Frances Stillman Collection of Congo Sculpture, gift of Eugene and Margaret McDermott, 1969
Provenance:
Clark and Frances Stillman
Blondiau collection, Brussels
Ill. p. 79

146 **CARRÀ,** Carlo D. (Italian, 1881-1966)
The Swimmers (Nuotatrici), 1910
Oil on canvas, 41 1/2 x 62 in. [105.5 x 157.5 cm]
Museum of Art, Carnegie Institute, Pittsburgh
Gift of G. David Thompson, 1955
Provenance:
Rose Fried Gallery, New York, 1955
Private collection, Japan
Exhibitions:
Futurism and the International Avant-Garde, Philadelphia Museum of Art, 1981
The Beauty of Sports: The Olympics—Ancient and Modern, Munson-Williams-Proctor Institute, Utica, 1980
Futurismus, 1909-1917, Städtische Kunsthalle Düsseldorf, 1974
Quattro Maestri del Futurismo, XXXIV Biennale di Venezia, 1968
Twentieth Century Italian Art, The Baltimore Museum of Art, 1966
Futurism, The Museum of Modern Art, New York, 1961; also
The Detroit Institute of Arts
The Los Angeles County Museum of Art, 1962
Ill. p. 179

147 **BALLA,** Giacomo (Italian, 1871-1958)
Dynamism of a Dog on a Leash (Leash in Motion), 1912
Oil on canvas, 35 3/8 x 43 1/4 in. [89.9 x 109.9 cm]
Albright-Knox Art Gallery, Buffalo, New York
Bequest of A. Conger Goodyear to George F. Goodyear, life interest, and Albright-Knox Art Gallery, 1964
Provenance:
Purchased from the artist by A. C. Goodyear, New York, 1938
Galerie Der Sturm, Berlin
Exhibitions:
Futurism and the International Avant-Garde, Philadelphia Museum of Art, 1980-81
L'Oeuvre de Marcel Duchamp, Musée National d'Art Moderne, Centre National d'Art et de Culture Georges Pompidou, Paris, 1977
For earlier exhibitions, see
Futurism and the International Avant-Garde, Philadelphia Museum of Art, 1980, p. 22-23
Ill. p. 55

148 **CHIRICO,** Giorgio de (Italian, 1888-1978)
The Duo, 1915
Oil on canvas, 32 1/4 x 23 1/4 in. [81.9 x 59 cm]
The Museum of Modern Art, New York
James Thrall Soby Bequest, 1979
Provenance:
James Thrall Soby
Pierre Matisse Gallery, New York, 1935
Paul Eluard
Exhibitions:
Giorgio de Chirico, The Museum of Modern Art, New York, 1982; also
Tate Gallery, London
Haus der Kunst, Munich, 1983

Musée National d'Art Moderne, Centre National d'Art et de Culture Georges Pompidou, Paris
Four Modern Masters, international traveling exhibition of The Museum of Modern Art, New York, to:
Museu de Arte de São Paulo/Assis Chateaubriand, São Paulo, Brazil, 1981
Museo Nacional de Bellas Artes, Buenos Aires, Argentina, 1981
Museo de Bellas Artes, Caracas, Venezuela, 1981
Glenbow Museum, Calgary, Alberta, Canada, 1981-82
Ill. p. 136

149 LÉGER, Fernand (French, 1881-1955)
Composition, 1923-1927
Oil on canvas, 51 1/2 x 38 1/4 in.
[130.8 x 97.1 cm]
Philadelphia Museum of Art
A. E. Gallatin Collection, 1952
Provenance:
Albert Eugene Gallatin, New York, 1935
Galerie L'Effort Moderne, Paris, 1927
Exhibitions:
Fernand Léger, Albright-Knox Art Gallery, Buffalo, New York, 1982; also
The Montreal Museum of Fine Arts
Dallas Museum of Fine Arts
Fernand Léger, The Art Gallery of South Australia, Adelaide, under the auspices of the International Council of the Museum of Modern Art, New York, 1976
Philadelphia in New York, The Museum of Modern Art, New York, 1972-73
Paintings from the Arensberg and Gallatin Collections of the Philadelphia Museum of Art, The Solomon R. Guggenheim Museum, New York, 1962
Fernand Léger, The Museum of Modern Art, New York, 1935
Ill. p. 173

150 CHAGALL, Marc (Russian, born 1887)
Peasant Life (La Vie Paysanne), 1925
Oil on canvas, 39 3/8 x 31 1/2 in. [100 x 80 cm]
Albright-Knox Art Gallery, Buffalo, New York
Room of Contemporary Art Fund, 1941
Provenance:
Pierre Matisse Gallery, New York
Exhibitions:
Marc Chagall Retrospective, Moderna Museet, Stockholm, 1982; also
Louisiana Museum, Humlebaek, Denmark, 1983
For earlier exhibitions, see
Contemporary Art, 1942-72 Collection of the Albright-Knox Art Gallery, New York, Praeger, 1973, p. 338
Ill. p. 41

151 BRANCUSI, Constantin (Rumanian, 1876-1957)
View of the Studio: Endless Column, Bird in Space, c. 1922
Gelatin silver print, 9 15/16 x 7 7/8 in. [25.2 x 20 cm]
The Museum of Fine Arts, Houston
Museum purchase with funds provided by Mrs. Lucille Bowden Johnson in honor of Frances G. and Alexander K. McLanahan, 1982
Provenance:
Prakapas Gallery, New York
Ill. p. 101

152 BRANCUSI, Constantin (Rumanian, 1876-1957)
Mlle Pogany II, 1925
Polished bronze, 17 in. [43.2 cm] high
Yale University Art Gallery, New Haven
The Katherine Ordway Collection, 1980
Provenance:
Katherine Ordway, c. 1925
Ill. p. 141

153 JENSEN, George (Danish, 1866-1935)
Compote, design introduced 1918
Silver, 8 in. [20.3 cm] high
The Newark Museum
Gift of Louis Bamberger, 1922
Ill. p. 128

154 LALIQUE, René (French, 1860-1945)
Tourbillon Vase, c. 1925
Pressed and acid polished glass, 7 7/8 in. [20 cm] high
The Toledo Museum of Art
Gift of Florence Scott Libbey, 1979
Ill. p. 234

155 SCHWITTERS, Kurt (German, 1887-1948)
Radiating World (Merzbild 31 B-Strahlende Welt), 1920
Oil and paper collage on composition board, 37 1/2 x 26 3/4 in. [95.3 x 68 cm]
The Phillips Collection, Washington, D.C.
Katherine S. Dreier Bequest, 1953
Provenance:
Katherine S. Dreier, Connecticut
Exhibitions:
The Dada Spirit 1915-1925, Museo de Arte Contemporaneo de Caracas, 1981
The Spirit of Surrealism, The Cleveland Museum of Art, 1979
Tendencies of the Twenties, Staatliche Museen, Preussischer Kulturbesitz, Berlin, 1977
Kurt Schwitters and Related Developments, La Jolla Museum of Contemporary Art, 1973
In Memory of Katherine S. Dreier 1877-1952, Yale University Art Gallery, New Haven, 1953
Paintings from New York Private Collections, The Museum of Modern Art, New York, 1946
Fantastic Art, Dada, Surrealism, and *Cubism and Abstract Art*, The Museum of Modern Art, New York, 1936
Ill. p. 220

156 MONDRIAN, Piet (Dutch, 1872-1944)
Fox Trot B, 1929
Oil on canvas, 17 3/8 x 17 3/8 in. [44 x 44 cm]
Yale University Art Gallery, New Haven
Gift of Collection Société Anonyme, 1941
Exhibitions:
Brancusi and Mondrian, Sidney Janis Gallery, New York, 1982
De Stijl 1917-1931, Walker Art Center, Minneapolis, 1982; also
Hirshhorn Museum and Sculpture Garden, Washington, D.C.
Piet Mondrian 1872-1944 Centennial Exhibition, The Solomon R. Guggenheim Museum, New York, 1971; also
Kunstmuseum Bern, Switzerland
Piet Mondrian, Nationalgalerie, Berlin, 1968
Fifty Years of Modern Art, The Cleveland Museum of Art, 1966

The Classic Tradition in 20th Century Art, The Walker Art Center, Minneapolis, 1953
Piet Mondrian Retrospective Exhibition, The Museum of Modern Art, 1945
Ill. p. 138

157 KLEE, Paul (Swiss, 1879-1940)
New Harmony (Neue Harmonie), 1936
Oil on canvas, 36 7/8 x 26 1/8 in. [93.6 x 66.3 cm]
The Solomon R. Guggenheim Museum, New York
By exchange, 1971
Provenance:
Galerie Beyeler, Basel, 1971
Heinz Berggruen, Paris, 1971
Benjamin Baldwin, New York, 1949
Nierendorf Gallery, New York, 1939
D. H. Kahnweiler, Paris, 1937
Exhibitions:
Paintings, drawings and prints by Paul Klee, The Museum of Modern Art, New York, 1950
Exhibition of 20th Century (banned) German Art, City Art Museum of Saint Louis, 1939; also
Smith College Museum of Art, Northampton, Massachusetts
William Rockhill Nelson Gallery of Art, Kansas City
San Francisco Museum of Art, 1940
Exhibition of Twentieth Century German Art, New Burlington Galleries, London, 1938
Tentoonstelling Abstracte Kunst, Stedelijk Museum, Amsterdam, 1938
Paul Klee: oeuvres récentes, Galerie Simon, Paris, 1938
Ill. p. 113

158 PICASSO, Pablo (Spanish, 1881-1973)
Dog and Cock, 1921
Oil on canvas, 61 x 30 1/4 in. [155 x 76.8 cm]
Yale University Art Gallery, New Haven
Gift of Stephen C. Clark, B.A. 1903, 1958
Provenance:
Stephen C. Clark, New York, 1949
The Museum of Modern Art, New York, 1942
Galerie Paul Rosenberg, Paris, 1939
Jerome Stoneborough, Paris
Galerie Paul Rosenberg, Paris, 1921
Exhibitions:
Picasso Retrospective, The Museum of Modern Art, New York, 1980
Picasso, an American Tribute, the Twenties, Paul Rosenberg & Co., New York, 1962
Ill. p. 140

159 MATISSE, Henri (French, 1869-1954)
Seated Nude (Grand Nu Assis), 1923-25
Bronze, 4/10, 31 x 32 x 14 in. [78.7 x 81.3 x 35.6 cm]
The Currier Gallery of Art, Manchester, New Hampshire
Currier Funds, 1964
Provenance:
Mr. and Mrs. Theodor Ahrenberg, Stockholm
Ill. p. 123

160 KIRCHNER, Ernst Ludwig (German, 1880-1938)
Street Scene (Strassenszene), 1926-27
Oil on canvas, 47 1/4 x 39 in. [120 x 99 cm]
Milwaukee Art Museum
Gift of Mrs. Harry Lynde Bradley, 1977

Provenance:
Estate of the artist
Exhibitions:
Meisterwerke des deutschen Expressionismus,
Kunsthalle, Bremen, Germany, 1960; also
Kunstverein, Hannover
Gemeentemuseum, The Hague
Wallraf-Richartz Museum, Cologne
Kunsthaus, Zürich, 1961
Ill. p. 108

161 **STIEGLITZ,** Alfred (American, 1864-1946)
Georgia O'Keeffe, 1918
Silver print, 8 x 10 in. [20.3 x 25.4 cm]
The Metropolitan Museum of Art, New York
Gift of David A. Schulte, 1928
Ill. p. 148

162 **O'KEEFFE,** Georgia (American, born 1887)
White Flowers on Red Earth, No. 1, 1943
Oil on canvas, 26 x 30 1/4 in. [66 x 76.8 cm]
The Newark Museum
Museum purchase, John J. O'Neill Bequest Fund,
1946
Provenance:
An American Place, New York
Exhibitions:
Painting in the United States, Carnegie Institute,
Department of Fine Arts, Pittsburgh, 1944
Ill. p. 110

163 **DOVE,** Arthur G. (American, 1880-1946)
Golden Storm, 1925
Metallic paint on wood, 18 1/2 x 20 1/2 in.
[47 x 52 cm]
The Phillips Collection, Washington, D.C., 1926
Provenance:
The artist
Exhibitions:
Arthur Dove and Duncan Phillips: Artist and Patron,
The Phillips Collection, 1981-82; also
The High Museum of Art, Atlanta
William Rockhill Nelson Gallery and Atkins
Museum of Fine Arts, Kansas City
The Museum of Fine Arts, Houston
Columbus Museum of Art
The Seattle Art Museum
Milwaukee Art Museum
Arthur Dove, San Francisco Museum of Art,
1975; also
Albright-Knox Art Gallery, Buffalo
The St. Louis Art Museum
The Art Institute of Chicago
Des Moines Art Center
Whitney Museum of American Art, New York,
1975-76
Roots of Abstract Art in America 1910-1930,
National Collection of Fine Arts, Washington,
D.C., 1966
Amerika Schildert, Stedelijk Museum, Amsterdam,
1950
*Dove Retrospective Exhibition—Paintings:
1908-1946*, The Downtown Gallery, New York,
1947
Exhibition II: Arthur G. Dove, The Intimate
Gallery, New York, 1926
Ill. p. 220

164 **MALEVICH,** Kazimir (Russian, 1878-1935)
Congress of Committees on Rural Poverty (front
and back covers), 1918
Color lithograph, edition 10 or 12
front: 11 1/2 x 11 1/2 in. [29 x 29 cm]
back: 7 7/8 x 7 7/8 in. [20.1 x 20.1 cm]
Dallas Museum of Art
Purchased through The Art Museum League
Fund in honor of Mr. and Mrs. James H. Clark,
1978
Ill. p. 79

165 **PEVSNER,** Antoine (Russian, 1886-1962)
Bas Relief en Creux, 1926-27
Brass and bronze, 23 3/4 x 24 5/8 x 12 1/4 in.
[60.3 x 62.5 x 31.1 cm]
Washington University Gallery of Art, St. Louis
University purchase, McMillan Fund, 1946
Provenance:
Art of This Century Gallery, New York, 1942
Exhibitions:
Paris-New York, Musée National d'Art Moderne,
Centre National d'Art et de Culture Georges
Pompidou, Paris, 1977
20th-Century Sculpture, The Museum of Modern
Art, New York, 1952-53
Naum Gabo - Antoine Pevsner, The Museum of
Modern Art, New York, 1948
Origins of Modern Sculpture, City Art Museum of
St. Louis, 1946
Ill. p. 193

166 **WINGQUIST,** Sven (Swedish, 1879-1953)
Self-Aligning Ball Bearing, 1929
Chrome-plated steel, 8 1/2 in. [21.5 cm]
Manufactured by SKF Industries, U.S.A.
Collection, The Museum of Modern Art, New
York, Gift of the manufacturer
Note: The exhibited piece is a small (3 15/16 in.
[10 cm] diameter) version of the one owned by
The Museum of Modern Art
Ill. p. 150

167 **WESTON,** Edward (American, 1886-1958)
Pepper No. 30, 1930
Gelatin silver print, 9 1/2 x 7 9/16 in.
[24.2 x 19.2 cm]
San Francisco Museum of Modern Art
Gift of Mrs. Drew Chidester
©1981 Arizona Board of Regents,
Center for Creative Photography
Ill. p. 204

168 **RODCHENKO,** Alexander (Russian,
1891-1956)
Chauffeur, 1933
Gelatin silver print, 11 1/4 x 16 in.
[28.6 x 40.6 cm]
The Museum of Modern Art, New York
Mr. and Mrs. John Spencer Fund, 1970
Provenance:
Mrs. Caio Garrubba, New York
Ill. p. 152

169 **EVANS,** Walker (American, 1903-1975)
*Graveyard, Houses and Steel Mill, Bethlehem,
Pennsylvania*, 1935
Gelatin silver print, 7 1/2 x 9 1/2 in.
[19 x 24 cm]
The Minneapolis Institute of Arts
Gift of D. Thomas Bergen, 1975

Provenance:
Lunn Gallery, Washington, D.C.
Ill. p. 117

170 **LAUGHLIN,** Clarence John (American, born
1905)
Darkness in Daylight (Belle Grove Plantation), 1953
Gelatin silver print, 10 11/16 x 13 1/2 in.
[27.2 x 34.2 cm]
New Orleans Museum of Art
Museum purchase, 1973
©1953 by Clarence John Laughlin and
The Historic New Orleans Collection
Provenance:
Witkin Gallery, New York
Ill. p. 160

171 **SMITH,** W. Eugene (American, 1918-1978)
Smoky City, 1955-56
Gelatin silver print, 23 3/4 x 19 7/8 in.
[60.5 x 50.6 cm]
Museum of Art, Carnegie Institute, Pittsburgh
Museum purchase: Gift of Vira I. Heinz Fund
of the Pittsburgh Foundation, 1982
Provenance:
Carnegie Library of Pittsburgh
Ill. p. 178

172 **DAVIS,** Stuart (American, 1894-1964)
Place Pasdeloup, 1928
Oil on canvas, 36 1/4 x 28 3/4 in. [92.1 x 73 cm]
Whitney Museum of American Art, New York
Gift of Gertrude Vanderbilt Whitney, 1931
Provenance:
Juliana Force, New York
Exhibitions:
Stuart Davis Memorial Exhibition, National
Collection of Fine Arts, Smithsonian Institution,
Washington, D.C., 1965; also
The Art Institute of Chicago
Whitney Museum of American Art, New York
University of California at Los Angeles Art
Galleries
European Tour organized by United States
Information Agency, Washington, D.C., 1966,
to:
American Embassy Gallery, London
Musée National d'Art Moderne, Paris
Amerika Haus Gallery, West Berlin
Stedelijk Museum, Amsterdam
Vintage Moderns, State University of Iowa,
Iowa City, 1962
1959 Fine Arts Festival, Coe College,
Cedar Rapids, Iowa
Brussels Universal and International Exhibition,
Brussels, 1958
Stuart Davis, Walker Art Center, Minneapolis,
1957; also
Des Moines Art Center
San Francisco Museum of Art
Whitney Museum of American Art, New York
*American Painting: Second Quarter of the 20th
Century*, The Jacksonville Art Museum, Florida,
1956-57
Paris: Many Happy Returns, Museum of Art,
Rhode Island School of Design, Providence, 1951
Amerika Schildert, Stedelijk Museum, Amsterdam,
1950
From the Armory to the Present, The Society of the
Four Arts, Palm Beach, 1950
Themes and Variations in Painting and Sculpture,
The Baltimore Museum of Art, 1948

Stuart Davis, The Museum of Modern Art, New York, 1945
XVII Biennale di Venezia, United States Pavilion, 1934
American Exhibition, The Museum of Modern Art, New York, 1932-33
Ill. p. 157

173 **SHEELER,** Charles (American, 1883-1965)
Western Industrial, 1955
Oil on canvas, 22 7/8 x 29 in. [58 x 73.5 cm]
The Art Institute of Chicago
Gift of Mr. and Mrs. Leigh B. Block, 1977
Provenance:
The Downtown Gallery, New York
Exhibitions:
Charles Sheeler, National Collection of Fine Arts, Smithsonian Institution, Washington, D.C., 1968
Ill. p. 69

174 **HOPPER,** Edward (American, 1882-1967)
Seven A.M., 1948
Oil on canvas, 30 x 40 in. [76.2 x 101.6 cm]
Whitney Museum of American Art, New York
Purchase and exchange, 1950
Provenance:
Frank R. M. Rehn Gallery, New York
The artist
Exhibitions:
Edward Hopper: The Art and the Artist, Whitney Museum of American Art, New York, 1980-81; also
Hayward Gallery, London
Stedelijk Museum, Amsterdam
Städtische Kunsthalle, Düsseldorf
The Art Institute of Chicago
San Francisco Museum of Modern Art
Revised version as:
The World of Edward Hopper, 1982, to
The Art Gallery of South Australia, Adelaide
National Gallery of Victoria, Melbourne
Queensland Art Gallery, Brisbane
The Art Gallery of New South Wales, Sydney
The American Scene and New Forms of Modernism, 1935-1954, The Katonah Gallery, Katonah, New York, 1976
Edward Hopper, Newport Harbor Art Museum, Newport Beach, California, 1972; also
Pasadena Art Museum, California
São Paulo 9, Rose Art Museum, Brandeis University, Waltham, Massachusetts, 1968
Edward Hopper, Whitney Museum of American Art, New York, 1964; also
The Art Institute of Chicago
The Detroit Institute of Arts
City Art Museum of St. Louis
Living American Artists to Israel, organized by the American Federation of Arts, 1959, to
Helena Rubinstein Pavilion, Tel Aviv
Bezalel National Museum, Jerusalem
Museum of Modern Art, Haifa
American Realism in the 20th Century, La Napoule Art Foundation, Alpes-Maritimes, France, 1958
200 Years of American Art, Vancouver Art Gallery, Canada, 1955
XXVI Biennale di Venezia, American Pavilion, 1952
Revolution and Tradition, The Brooklyn Museum, New York, 1951

Edward Hopper Retrospective Exhibition, Whitney Museum of American Art, New York, 1950; also
Museum of Fine Arts, Boston
The Detroit Institute of Arts
Ill. p. 137

175 **KUHN,** Walt (American, 1880-1949)
Lancer, 1939
Oil on canvas, 45 1/2 x 26 1/4 in. [115.6 x 66.7 cm]
The Currier Gallery of Art, Manchester, New Hampshire
Currier Funds, 1958
Provenance:
Maynard Walker Gallery, New York
Exhibitions:
Walt Kuhn Retrospective Exhibition, Amon Carter Museum, Fort Worth, 1978; also toured
Walt Kuhn Retrospective, University Art Gallery, The University of Arizona, Tucson, 1966
Fifty Years of Modern Art, The Cleveland Museum of Art, 1966
Walt Kuhn Memorial Exhibition, Cincinnati Art Museum, 1960
Ill. p. 109

176 **GIACOMETTI,** Alberto (Swiss, 1901-1966)
Man Pointing, 1947
Bronze, 5/6, 69 3/4 in. [177 cm] high
Des Moines Art Center
Coffin Fine Arts Fund, 1976
Provenance:
Mrs. Michela Suzanne Weintraub, New York
Pierre Matisse Gallery, New York
Ill. p. 97

177 **MIRÓ,** Joan (Spanish, born 1893)
Portrait of Mistress Mills in 1750, 1929
Oil on canvas, 46 x 35 1/4 in. [116.7 x 89.6 cm]
The Museum of Modern Art, New York
James Thrall Soby Bequest, 1979
Provenance:
James Thrall Soby
Exhibitions:
90th Birthday Exhibition, Fundacion Joan Miró, Barcelona, 1983
Miró in America, Museum of Fine Arts, Houston, 1982
Four Modern Masters, international traveling exhibition of The Museum of Modern Art, New York, to
Museu de Arte de São Paulo/Assis Chateaubriand, São Paulo, Brazil, 1981
Museo Nacional de Bellas Artes, Buenos Aires, Argentina, 1981
Museo de Bellas Artes, Caracas, Venezuela, 1982
Glenbow Museum, Calgary, Alberta, Canada, 1981-82
Ill. p. 151

178 **PICASSO,** Pablo (Spanish, 1881-1973)
Minotauromachy, 1935
Etching, 19 1/2 x 27 7/16 in. [49.6 x 69.6 cm]
The Museum of Modern Art, New York
Purchase Fund, 1947
Reference:
Georges Bloch, *Catalogue de l'Oeuvre gravée et lithographié, 1904-1967*, Berne, 1968, #288
Ill. p. 152

179 **RIVERA,** Diego (Mexican, 1886-1957)
The Flower Carrier (The Flower Vendor), 1935
Oil and tempera on masonite, 48 x 47 3/4 in. [122 x 121.3 cm]
San Francisco Museum of Modern Art
Albert M. Bender Collection
Gift of Albert M. Bender in memory of Caroline Walter, 1935
Exhibitions:
Art of Latin America since Independence, Yale University Art Gallery, 1966; also
University Art Museum, University of Texas at Austin
San Francisco Museum of Art
La Jolla Museum of Art, California
Isaac Delgado Museum of Art, New Orleans
Modern Mexican Painters, The Institute of Modern Art, Boston, 1941; also
Phillips Memorial Art Gallery, Washington, D.C.
The Cleveland Museum of Art
Portland Art Museum, Oregon, 1942
San Francisco Museum of Art
Santa Barbara Museum of Art
Ill. p. 205

180 **CALDER,** Alexander (American, 1898-1976)
Cage within a Cage, c. 1939
Metal, wood, string, 37 1/2 x 58 3/4 x 21 in. [95.2 x 149.2 x 53.3 cm]
Whitney Museum of American Art, New York
Gift of the Howard and Jean Lipman Foundation, 1975
Provenance:
Perls Galleries, New York
The artist
Exhibitions:
Calder's Universe, Whitney Museum of American Art, New York, 1976-77; also
The High Museum of Art, Atlanta
Walker Art Center, Minneapolis
Dallas Museum of Fine Arts
Calder's Universe (second version, 1978-79), to
San Jose Museum of Art, California
Portland Art Museum, Oregon
The Phoenix Art Museum
Joslyn Art Museum, Omaha
Loch Haven Art Center, Orlando, Florida
Hirshhorn Museum and Sculpture Garden, Washington, D.C.
The Currier Gallery of Art, Manchester, New Hampshire
Calder's Universe (third version, 1979-80), to
The Seibu Museum of Art, Tokyo
Kitakyushu City Museum of Art
The Prefectural Museum of Modern Art, Hyogo, Kobe
Yokohama City Gallery
Ill. p. 157

181 **ERNST,** Max (German, 1891-1976)
An Anxious Friend, 1944, cast 1957
Bronze, 5/9, 26 3/8 in. [67 cm] high
The Solomon R. Guggenheim Museum, New York
Gift of Dominique and John de Menil, 1959
Provenance:
Alexandre Iolas Gallery, New York, 1957

Exhibitions:
Surrealists, organized by Serge Sabarsky Gallery
and Charles Byron, 1983, to
Isetan Museum, Tokyo
Hiroshima Castle Museum
Yokohama Museum
Prefectural Museum, Yamanashi
Asahikawa Museum
Osaka Municipal Museum of Fine Arts
Forty Modern Masters: An Anniversary Show,
The Solomon R. Guggenheim Museum, 1978
Selected Sculpture and Works on Paper, The
Solomon R. Guggenheim Museum, 1969
Twentieth Century Sculpture, Philbrook Art
Center, Tulsa, Oklahoma, 1962
Inaugural Selection, The Solomon R. Guggenheim
Museum, 1960
Max Ernst, Alexandre Iolas Gallery, New York,
1957
Ill. p. 143

182 **MOORE,** Henry (British, born 1898)
Three Figures in a Setting, 1942
Ink and wax crayon on grey prepared paper,
17 3/4 x 16 3/4 in. [45.1 x 42.5 cm]
Santa Barbara Museum of Art
Gift of Wright S. Ludington, 1945
Provenance:
Buchholz Gallery, New York
Exhibitions:
European and American Sculpture of the 40's,
University Art Gallery, University of California,
Santa Barbara, 1973
Drawings and Sculpture by Henry Moore, Arkansas
Art Center, Little Rock, 1965
Henry Moore, University of Arizona Museum of
Art, Tucson, 1965
Henry Moore, Art Center, La Jolla, California,
1963; also
Los Angeles Municipal Art Gallery
Ill. p. 209

183 **DALI,** Salvador (Spanish, born 1904)
Honey is Sweeter than Blood, 1941
Oil on canvas, 20 1/8 x 24 in. [51 x 61 cm]
The Santa Barbara Museum of Art
Gift of Mr. and Mrs. Warren Tremaine, 1949
Provenance:
Dalzell Hatfield Galleries, Los Angeles, 1945
The artist
Exhibitions:
Salvador Dali Retrospective, Isetan Museum,
Tokyo, 1982; also
Daimaru Museum, Osaka
Kitakyushu City Museum of Art
Hokkaido County Museum, Sapporo
*Modern Masters of Spanish Painting: Legacy of Spain
XXth Century*, The Fine Arts Gallery of San
Diego, 1969
The Film and Modern Art, Los Angeles Municipal
Art Gallery, 1969
Seventy-Five Masterworks, Portland Art Museum,
Oregon, 1968
Salvador Dali, Los Angeles Municipal Art Gallery,
1964
Figure: Past and Present, Long Beach Museum of
Art, California, 1961
Spanish Masters, The Fine Arts Gallery of
San Diego, 1960; also
University of California at Los Angeles Art
Galleries, 1960

After Surrealism, San Francisco Museum of Art,
1959
Ill. p. 209

184 **MAGRITTE,** René (Belgian, 1898-1967)
The Liberator, 1947
Oil on canvas, 39 x 31 in. [99 x 78.7 cm]
Los Angeles County Museum of Art
Gift of William Copley, 1952
Provenance:
Copley Gallery, Beverly Hills
Exhibitions:
René Magritte, Musée National d'Art Moderne,
Centre National d'Art et de Culture Georges
Pompidou, Paris, 1979
European Art: The Postwar Decade, 1945-1955,
Des Moines Art Center, 1978
Paintings by René Magritte, The Taft Museum,
Cincinnati, 1977
*Peintres de l'imaginaire, symbolistes et surréalistes
belges*, Galeries Nationales d'Exposition du Grand
Palais, Paris, 1972
René Magritte, The Museum of Modern Art,
New York, 1966; also
Rose Art Museum, Brandeis University,
Waltham, Massachusetts
The Art Institute of Chicago
Pasadena Art Museum
University Art Museum, University of California,
Berkeley
After Surrealism, The San Francisco Museum of
Art, 1959
Ill. p. 111

185 **HYPPOLITE,** Hector (Haitian, 1894-1948)
The Adoration of Love, c. 1946-48
Oil on cardboard, 29 1/2 x 23 1/2 in.
[74.9 x 59.7 cm]
Milwaukee Art Museum
Gift of Mr. and Mrs. Richard B. Flagg, 1978
Exhibitions:
Haitian Art, The Brooklyn Museum,
1978-79; also
Milwaukee Art Museum
Nationalgalerie, Berlin
New Orleans Museum of Art
Ill. p. 125

186 **ALBRIGHT,** Ivan (American, 1897-1983)
The Wild Bunch (Hole in the Wall Gang), 1950-51
Oil on canvas, 30 1/2 x 42 in. [77.5 x 106.7 cm]
The Phoenix Art Museum
Gift of Mrs. Thomas E. Hogg, 1967
Provenance:
Kennedy Galleries, New York
Exhibitions:
Ivan Albright: a retrospective exhibition, The Art
Institute of Chicago, 1964; also
The Whitney Museum of American Art,
New York, 1965
Ill. p. 164

187 **GORKY,** Arshile (American, born Russia,
1904-1948)
The Liver is the Cock's Comb, 1944
Oil on canvas, 73 1/4 x 98 in. [186 x 249 cm]
Albright-Knox Art Gallery, Buffalo, New York
Gift of Seymour H. Knox, 1956
Provenance:
Sidney Janis Gallery, New York
Mrs. Jean Lamson Hebbeln

Exhibitions:
Arshile Gorky—A Retrospective, The Solomon R.
Guggenheim Museum, New York, 1981; also
Dallas Museum of Fine Arts
Los Angeles County Museum of Art, 1981-82
For earlier exhibitions, see
*Contemporary Art, 1942-72 Collection of the
Albright-Knox Art Gallery*, New York, Praeger,
1973, p. 415
Ill. p. 55

188 **POLLOCK,** Jackson (American, 1912-1956)
Night Mist, 1944-45
Oil on canvas, 36 x 74 in. [91.4 x 188 cm]
Norton Gallery and School of Art, West Palm
Beach, Florida, 1971
Provenance:
S. I. Newhouse, Jr.
Harry Anderson, California
Estate of the artist
Exhibitions:
Jackson Pollock, Musée National d'Art Moderne,
Centre National d'Art et de Culture Georges
Pompidou, Paris, 1982
Abstract Expressionism: The Formative Years,
Herbert F. Johnson Museum of Art, Cornell
University, Ithaca, New York, 1978; also
Seibu Museum of Art, Tokyo
Whitney Museum of American Art, New York
Ill. p. 233

189 **NEWMAN,** Barnett (American, 1905-1970)
Onement IV, 1949
Oil and casein on canvas, 33 x 38 in.
[83.8 x 96.5 cm]
Allen Memorial Art Museum, Oberlin College,
Ohio
National Endowment for the Arts
Museum Purchase Plan and gift of anonymous
donor, 1969
Provenance:
The artist
Ill. p. 175

190 **STILL,** Clyfford (American, 1904-1980)
Untitled (Ph-174), 1960
Oil on canvas, 113 1/8 x 155 7/8 in.
[287.3 x 396 cm]
San Francisco Museum of Modern Art
Gift of Mr. and Mrs. Harry W. Anderson, 1974
Provenance:
Marlborough Gallery, New York
Exhibitions:
America, Galerie Beyeler, Basel, Switzerland,
1971
Clyfford Still, Marlborough-Gerson Gallery,
New York, 1969
Ill. p. 201

191 **ROTHKO,** Mark (American, born Russia,
1903-1970)
Untitled #11 - 1963
Oil on canvas, 75 1/2 x 69 1/4 in.
[191.7 x 175.9 cm]
The Nelson-Atkins Museum of Art, Kansas City
Gift of the Friends of Art, 1964
Provenance:
The artist
Ill. p. 89

192 **TOBEY,** Mark (American, 1890-1976)
Parnassus, 1963
Oil on canvas, 82 1/8 x 47 3/8 in.
[208.6 x 128.3 cm]
Seattle Art Museum
Virginia Wright Fund, 1974
Provenance:
Willard Gallery, New York
Exhibitions:
Mark Tobey 1930-1967, Miami-Dade Community
College, Florida, 1975-76
American Art: Third Quarter Century, Seattle
Art Museum, 1973
Expo '70, Osaka, Japan, 1970
Tobey's 80, Seattle Art Museum, 1970-71
Mark Tobey Retrospective, Dallas Museum of
Fine Arts, 1968
*The Poetry of Vision: An International Exhibition of
Modern Painting and Ancient Celtic Art*, Royal
Dublin Society, National Museum of Ireland,
Dublin, 1967
Mark Tobey, Stedelijk Museum, Amsterdam,
1966; also
Kestner-Gesellschaft, Hannover
Kunsthalle Bern,
Städtische Kunsthalle, Düsseldorf
Ill. p. 200

193 **DUBUFFET,** Jean (French, born 1901)
Topographie au Nid de Pierres, 1958
Oil and collage on canvas, 38 1/2 x 60 in.
[97.8 x 152.4 cm]
Hood Museum of Art, Dartmouth College,
Hanover, New Hampshire
Gift of Joachim Jean Aberbach (by exchange),
1975
Provenance:
Joachim Jean Aberbach
Ill. p. 99

194 **LOUIS,** Morris (American, 1912-1962)
Untitled #189, 1959
Acrylic on canvas, 98 x 132 in.
[248.9 x 335.3 cm]
Des Moines Art Center
Gift of Gardner Cowles, by exchange, 1972
Provenance:
Lawrence Rubin Gallery, New York
William S. Rubin, New York
Galerie Lawrence, Paris
Exhibitions:
Morris Louis: The Veil Cycle, Walker Art Center,
Minneapolis, 1977-78; also
The Denver Art Museum
Fort Worth Art Museum
Everson Museum of Art, Syracuse, New York
The Baltimore Museum of Art
25 Years of American Painting 1948-1973,
Des Moines Art Center, 1973
Ill. p. 88

195 **HOFMANN,** Hans (American, born Germany,
1880-1966)
Goliath, 1960
Oil on canvas, 84 1/8 x 60 in. [213.6 x 152.4 cm]
University Art Museum, University of California,
Berkeley
Gift of the artist, 1966

Exhibitions:
*Hans Hofmann 1880-1966: An introduction to his
paintings*, The Edmonton Art Gallery, Alberta,
Canada, 1982
American Painting, 1930-1980, Haus der Kunst,
Munich (organized by the Whitney Museum of
American Art), 1981-82
hans hoffman: A Retrospective Exhibition,
Hirshhorn Museum and Sculpture Garden with
The Museum of Fine Arts, Houston, 1976-77
*Hans Hofmann Paintings: A Selection from the
University of California Collection*, La Jolla
Museum of Art, 1968
Hans Hofmann: 21 Hofmanns from Berkeley,
Honolulu Academy of Arts, 1968
Masterpieces from University Collections,
University of Kentucky Art Museum, Lexington,
1967
*Hans Hofmann: 21 Paintings from the Collection of
the University of California, Berkeley*, Stanford
University Museum and Art Gallery, California,
1966
Ill. p. 39

196 **SMITH,** David (American, 1906-1965)
Cubi IX, 1961
Stainless steel, 106 1/4 in. [270 cm] high
Walker Art Center, Minneapolis
Gift of the T.B. Walker Foundation
Provenance:
Marlborough-Gerson Gallery, New York
Exhibitions:
David Smith: Seven Major Themes, National
Gallery of Art, Washington, D.C., 1983
*The Great Decade of American Abstraction:
Modernist Art 1960-1970*, The Museum of Fine
Arts, Houston, 1974
Ill. p. 112

197 **RAUSCHENBERG,** Robert (American, born
1925)
Reservoir, 1961
Combine painting: oil, pencil, fabric, wood,
metal on canvas with 2 electric clocks, rubber
tread wheel and spoked wheel rim,
85 1/2 x 62 1/2 x 14 3/4 in.
[217.2 x 158.8 x 37.5 cm]
National Museum of American Art, Smithsonian
Institution
Gift of S.C. Johnson and Son, Inc., 1969
Exhibitions:
*Paintings in the United States from Public Collections
in Washington, D.C.*, by the International
Communications Agency, U.S. Department of
State, to Galerias del Palacio De Bellas Artes,
Mexico City, 1980
Art: USA, 102 works by living American artists,
acquired and circulated prior to their donation to
the National Museum of American Art by S.C.
Johnson & Son, Racine, Wisconsin, to 19
institutions in America and 24 abroad, 1963-67
Ill. p. 229

198 **DINE,** Jim (American, born 1935)
Colour of the Month of August (Painting Pleasures),
1969
Acrylic on canvas with collage, 86 x 99 in.
[218.4 x 251.5 cm]
The Denver Art Museum, Colorado
National Endowment for the Arts Foundation
Fund, Hilton Hotel Corporation, Albert A. List
Foundation, Alliance for Contemporary Art and
anonymous donors, 1979
Provenance:
Pace Gallery, New York
Exhibitions:
Jim Dine Retrospective, Whitney Museum of
American Art, New York, 1970
Ill. p. 95

199 **SEGAL,** George (American, born 1924)
Times Square at Night, 1970
Light, plaster, wood, plastic, electrical parts,
108 x 96 x 96 in. [274.3 x 243.8 x 243.8 cm]
Joslyn Art Museum, Omaha, Nebraska
Museum purchase, 1972
Provenance:
Sidney Janis Gallery, New York
The artist
Exhibitions:
George Segal, The Seibu Museum of Art, Tokyo,
1982-83; also
The Museum of Modern Art, Seibu Takanawa,
Karuizawa
The Museum of Modern Art, Toyama
The National Museum of Art, Osaka
George Segal: Sculpture, Walker Art Center,
Minneapolis, 1979; also
San Francisco Museum of Modern Art, 1979
Whitney Museum of American Art, New York
George Segal: Environments, Institute of
Contemporary Art, University of Pennsylvania,
Philadelphia, 1976; also
The Baltimore Museum of Art, 1976
George Segal, Ausstellung der Kunsthalle
Tübingen, West Germany, 1972; also
Städtische Galerie im Lenbachhaus, Munich,
1973
Ill. p. 176

200 **MOTHERWELL,** Robert (American,
born 1915)
Untitled, 1971
Acrylic on canvas, 108 x 144 in.
[274.3 x 365.8 cm]
Walker Art Center, Minneapolis
Gift of the T.B. Walker Foundation, 1972
Provenance:
The artist
Exhibitions:
Robert Motherwell Paintings, Lawrence Rubin
Gallery, New York, 1972
Ill. p. 127

201 **STELLA,** Frank (American, born 1936)
Pilicia II, 1973
Acrylic, felt and other media on wood,
pressed board, wallboard and cardboard,
110 x 98 in. [279.4 x 249 cm]
The Phillips Collection, Washington, D.C., 1973
Provenance:
Knoedler Contemporary Art, New York
Ill. p. 228

202 **CHAMBERLAIN,** John (American, born 1927)
Added Pleasure, 1975-82
Painted and chromium plated steel,
111 x 53 x 36 in. [281.9 x 134.6 x 91.5 cm]
The John and Mable Ringling Museum of Art,
Sarasota, Florida
Museum purchase, 1983
Provenance:
The artist
Exhibitions:
John Chamberlain Reliefs 1960-1982, The John
and Mable Ringling Museum of Art, Sarasota,
1983
Ill. p. 211

203 **HANSON,** Duane (American, born 1925)
Football Player, 1981
Polyester resin, oil paint, 43 1/4 in.
[109.9 cm] high
Lowe Art Museum, The University of Miami,
Coral Gables, Florida
Museum purchase through public subscription,
1982
Provenance:
The artist
Ill. p. 64

Index of Artists in the Exhibition

Index of Lending Institutions